In the Peanut Gallery with
Mystery Science Theater 3000

In the Peanut Gallery with *Mystery Science Theater 3000*

Essays on Film, Fandom, Technology, and the Culture of Riffing

Edited by ROBERT G. WEINER
and SHELLEY E. BARBA

*Forewords by Kevin Murphy
and Robert Moses Peaslee*

Afterword by Mary Jo Pehl

McFarland & Company, Inc., Publishers
Jefferson, North Carolina, and London

ALSO OF INTEREST

Marvel Graphic Novels and Related Publications: An Annotated Guide...,
by Robert G. Weiner (McFarland, 2008)

Graphic Novels and Comics in Libraries and Archives: Essays...,
edited by Robert G. Weiner (McFarland, 2010)

Captain America and the Struggle of the Superhero:
Critical Essays, edited by Robert G. Weiner (McFarland, 2009)

LIBRARY OF CONGRESS CATALOGUING-IN-PUBLICATION DATA

In the peanut gallery with Mystery Science Theater 3000 :
essasys on film, fandom, technology and the culture of riffing /
edited by Robert G. Weiner and Shelley E. Barba ; forewords by
Kevin Murphy and Robert Moses Peaslee ; afterword by Mary Jo Pehl.
p.   cm.
Includes bibliographical references and index.

ISBN 978-0-7864-4532-5
softcover : 50# alkaline paper ∞

1. Mystery science theater 3000.   2. Motion pictures—Review.
I. Weiner, Robert G., 1966–   II. Barba, Shelley E., 1982–
PN1992.77.M9716   2011   791.45'72—dc22   2011000212

BRITISH LIBRARY CATALOGUING DATA ARE AVAILABLE

On the cover: Joel Hodgson with the robots Crow and Tom Servo
from *Mystery Science Theater 3000* (Comedy Central/Photofest)

Manufactured in the United States of America

McFarland & Company, Inc., Publishers
Box 611, Jefferson, North Carolina 28640
www.mcfarlandpub.com

To Mary Jo Pehl, Kevin Murphy, J. Elvis Weinstein,
Joel Hodgson, Frank Conniff, Trace Beaulieu,
Paul Chaplin, Bridgett Jones Nelson, Jim Mallon,
Bill Corbett, and Michael J. Nelson —
YOU are true masters of comedy.

———————————————

And to ALL MSTies, this book is for you.

Table of Contents

Acknowledgments

Together, the editors would like to thank Kevin Murphy, Mary Jo Pehl, Dr. Robert Moses Peaslee and director Rick Sloane for their contributions to this project, as well as Joel Hodgson and Trace Beaulieu (thanks for the OK to publish the interview).

Individually, the editors wish to thank the following:

From Shelley E. Barba, thank you to my parents for allowing me to watch such a strange show as a child. Thanks to my *MST3K* friends who made me feel cool for knowing about the show: Joe Hall, Derek Moreland, John McCormick, Kenny Ketner, Liz Barnhill, John Perrin, Matt Philips, Kat Lukens and Mathias Bestevenn. Thank you to my colleagues who keep me writing: Joy Perrin, Kimberly Vardeman, Cynthia Henry, Laura Heinz and Rob Weiner. And a special thank you to Ian Barba for his support and keeping the cats occupied while I worked on this book.

From Robert G. Weiner, special thanks and dedication to my mother, Marilyn May Weiner, to my father, Dr. Leonard Weiner, and to Larry and Vicki Weiner.

Thanks for the memories of all the Yahoo's and cuddles from Zowie and Remy. I miss you. And thanks to all my furry friends who bring joy to my life but especially to Poncho and Sunshine and my new little buddy Eddie, who warm my heart.

Thanks to Sara, TAG, JLF (for saving all those *Home Theater* columns) and John O., and special thanks to Kraig and Sara Willis for circulating the tapes.

Thanks also to Chris Cornell and the folks at the *Satellite News* for posting our CFP to begin with. Thanks to the organizers of the SWTXPCA: Phil, Ken, Sally, Lynnea.

Thanks again to Shelley B., Kevin M., John C., and Thomas N. for their help with my *Blood Hook* piece.

Thanks to the dean of the Texas Tech Library, Dr. Donald Dyal, and all the associate deans. Thanks to all the staff of the TTU libraries and SWC for their support. Thanks to the staff of Document Delivery — you are my lifeblood.

Thanks to my colleagues in the IS department — Laura for always good advice, Dr. Jon, Innocent, Arlene, Cynthia, Carrye, Jake, Minerva, Brian, Sheila, Esmeralda, Sandy, Donnell, and Tom. Special thanks to Kimberly V. and Jack B. for your editorial help.

A special thank you to Samuel Dyal for going to lunch with me, and always being on the look-out for interesting info. Thanks to Mikel Coale, and Jon Harp for tracking down stuff. A big thank you to Chris Medvetz for everything.

Thanks to Ronald DeGroot for being so cool to us at the Cinematic Titanic gigs.

Thanks also to Ian Barba, Jim Brewer, Marina Oliver, Jack Ryder, Jason Blood, Ed Veal, KD, SA, LG, ZT, KJ, Mark Key, and Justin McDonald; Dr. Sam Dragga, Dr. Alison Whitney, Dr. Erin Collopy, Dr. Scott Baugh, and Dr. Jim Bush, Andrew Howard and Tom Blackburn (for always being willing to watch an episode or two), Susan Hidgalo, Hank McCoy, Bobby Drake, Lynn Whitfield, Greggery Peccary and Freedonia P.

Thanks to all my friends, ex-girlfriends/wife and anyone who has indulged me by watching my favorite short, "What to do on a Date," and my favorite episode, *Final Justice*.

Hats off to Crow, Tom Servo, Gypsy, Cambot, Magic Voice, Nanites, Professor Bobo, TV's Frank, Joel Robinson, Dr. Clayton Forrester, Dr. Larry Erhardt, Gizmonic Institute, Pearl Forrester, the Info-Club Poobahs, Prop Masters, Torgo, Ortega, Pitch, Mike Nelson, Dropo, Observer (Brain Guy), and all those who love weenie roasts.

Foreword:
Riffing and You (and Riffing)

by Kevin Murphy

Apparently since I've spent the better part of two decades as one of the few professional riffers out there, Mr. Weiner (or is it Doctor Weiner?) — Rob asked me to write a few words about riffing for this august study. I'll now attempt to undermine his intellectual work with a lot of hooey.

So, where did this all begin, this riffing? This looking at things and saying things about them to the amusement of others? Perhaps the first Neanderthal to look at the fluid, delicate image of a bison on a cave wall in what would eventually become Altimera, and then whisper to his cohort "That dog looks pregnant" was the first riffer. If his cohort laughed, then indeed yes. The earliest famous example I like to cite is Act V of Shakespeare's *A Midsummer Night's Dream*, in which the brave and bemused players finally get to present their setting of *Pyramus and Thisbe*, before the noble and rowdy audience, who riff from start to finish. I'll assume that Shakespeare was simply relating what actually happened during the more tedious or really dumb parts of his plays.

The first real, honest-to-god riff I ever saw, and remembered as such, was Mel Brooks' animated short called "The Critic." On the screen, we see the kind of abstract pop-art animation we kids were subjected to in art class and on the non-funny Sunday morning "educational" shows. Over the droning soundtrack of a nondescript jazzy baroque ditty comes an old man's loud, croaking voice, "Vat da Hell is dis?" And he doesn't stop, even at the urging of his fellow viewers (of course a violation of riffing etiquette). See, all he's doing is saying what everybody's thinking.

By the way, "The Critic" won the 1964 Academy Award for Best Animated Short.

Now you can argue with me all day about the Sanctity of the Artist and His work, about the audience's role in the experience, which is — what, to sit there, shut up and take it? What if the Artist and His Work roundly suck? I mean, just plain awful? What then? Why are we compelled just to sit there, shut up and just take it? Sure we could leave, but then we just feel like chumps. We don't hesitate to bellow at a sporting event (except tennis and golf, maybe cricket, which could all use a few thousand vuvuzelas), and every decent stand-up comic knows that you either stay one step ahead of your heckler, or you die in flames. What makes movies so special other than the fact that you paid upwards of ten bucks to see what's essentially animation with half-human-half-digi actors chasing each

1

other in digi-cars or fighting digi-robots or sucking face with digi-vampires? I mean what the Hell, half the people there don't care and the other half are tweeting.

We haven't always just sat there and taken it, nor do we now. In one year of Cannes, I went to three screenings where people felt perfectly justified to holler at the screen. And at La Scala, there has been a centuries-old tradition of booing bad singers off the stage, encouraging their exit with the softer vegetables from your pantry.

But this wasn't riffing. No, see, Shakespeare, in Act V, he was riffing. He was using the act of talking back to enhance, to heighten, to punctuate. The play is a forum for the act, and the audience, the real audience, out there in the dark, is not invited to join in, save in approval by applause or disapproval by produce. He was letting the Pros do it. And this is a good thing—Shakespeare was smart enough to write a delightfully bad staging of a bad play, and through riffing made a bad play tolerable, fun, actually kind and even noble.

And so, without expectations nearly as lofty as those I've noted above, we riff. In live venues, in commentary tracks, on DVDs and downloads, we riff the good, more often the bad, most often the awful. We riff to entertain, we riff to laugh. We riff because to do otherwise is madness. The great and very funny writer George Saunders once said that good humor is always a surprise. Its cuts through the data that streams endlessly through our endlessly preoccupied minds. The joke unlooked for is the one that makes us laugh the hardest. And hopefully, it's a bit smart. Riffing has to be smart to work, though the jokes don't necessarily have to be, so consider it an enjoyable lesson in semiotics, a close reading of a cinematic text with fart jokes added.

Riffing's the bug up the skirt, it's Margaret Dumont's puffery and Groucho's asides, it's your cousin photo-bombing your Aunt Mary's wedding by flashing her tits behind Grandma while she has her picture taken with the groom. It's subversive, surprising, often reviled, and it's something we all like to do. And I get to do it for a living.

Besides maybe Anthony Bourdain, I have the best job I know.

Kevin Murphy is one of the co-creators of *MST3K* and was the voice of the robot Tom Servo on the show for nine seasons.

Foreword

by Robert Moses Peaslee

Watching *Mystery Science Theater 3000 (MST3K)* for the first time feels like an initiation into something profoundly outside the mainstream. It confronts the newcomer as at once an impermeable inside joke and an immediately obvious conceit one wishes they had thought themselves to produce. It celebrates film even as it champions its deconstruction.

I first came to *MST3K* in my high school years, introduced to the show by the same friend who had prepped me in nerdy cynicism with healthy doses of Berkeley Breathed's political comic *Bloom County* and the late-night radio madness of Dr. Demento. Such precursors fostered a critical habit: they presented "old" manifestations of mainstream popular culture (the comic strip and the radio variety show) while simultaneously breaking down their respective forms and inserting a discomfited awareness of power structures into traditionally escapist media. They made us feel like adults because we "got it" and our parents didn't.

MST3K, then, was a revelation. Here was a group of people thinking like we were, doing many of the same things we were doing when watching bad television or commenting on slavish pop culture consumption. The show put a premium on seemingly spontaneous humor, quick thinking, and insider knowledge. It was a weekly paean to intertextuality. It made being a geek, for two hours at least, feel really good.

Although my fandom for the show never flowered to the point of tape-sharing, message boards, or other modes of "textual poaching" (Jenkins, 1992), I nonetheless remained appreciative of those moments when an otherwise unremarkable session of channel-surfing would alight me serendipitously upon the deck of the Satellite of Love. Like any truly valuable cultural product, *MST3K* not only entertained, it educated. Best Brains' efforts brought back into view those odd bits of cinema pushed into eddies by the relentless mainstream. It made a budding film geek understand just how little he really knew about film at all.

My life since those early days has thus been an ongoing effort to always dig deeper into the potential of all forms of cinema, especially those forms most people found to be "bad," if they were aware of them at all. The journey, in this regard, continues; I suspect I am not alone.

Several commentators herein suggest that *MST3K*, in both form and fan context, is best seen as an early precursor of what we have come to call "Web 2.0." The show, they suggest, offered opportunities for networked communication between audience members that had the potential to impact content in the same way that the show's trademark riffing remade the movies under "examination." This paratextual activity created a sense of active ownership among fans fiercely protective of the show (some of whom, it seems clear, have found their way into academia and crafted pieces for this volume).

MST3K certainly whet the consumer appetite for more than just consumption, and its more or less simultaneous development alongside electronic communication technologies allowed the show to develop the following that would subsequently defend it over and over again. But Hodgson, Murphy, Beaulieau, et al. left a legacy perhaps even more profound. It's hard to imagine the amazing growth of the San Diego Comic Con and its attendant influence upon Hollywood television and film production without the infiltration into the halls of power of hundreds of MSTies harboring ideas about "quality" genre production. The taste community that consistently imposed itself upon the suits at places like Comedy Central and the Sci-Fi (or SyFy) network was one that moved well beyond traditional (and passive) fan activities like letter writing and respectful adoration. Such a "target market" clearly presaged similar communities who would go on to accept Peter Jackson's invitation to comment on his upcoming production of the *Lord of the Rings* trilogy, who would badger George Lucas to lighten up his totalitarian grip upon his *Star Wars* material, and who would allow *Lost*, perhaps the most obfuscating text in television history, to see realized its full potential. In short, perhaps *MST3K* moved Hollywood toward an understanding that audiences appreciative of deep, rather than broad, storytelling devices could be profitable if managed correctly.

Moreover, the many denizens of the movie blogosphere certainly owe much to *MST3K* for making an encyclopedic knowledge of exploitation film not only cool but profitable. While Thomas Doherty of the *Chronicle of Higher Education* recently found cause to proclaim the "death of film criticism" in the era of *Ain't It Cool* and *Rotten Tomatoes*, one might rather say that film criticism has been democratized and that all those film nerds out there with giant libraries — but no pedigree — are suddenly empowered to deploy that knowledge in the public domain (typos and all). Certainly, Joel/Mike, Crow and Tom Servo are to be credited in part for fostering this audaciousness. This professionalization of taste online, which is really a mirror of the riffing that made *MST3K* what it was, has had an impact upon Hollywood content. Just as both the "official" *MST3K* commentary tracks and those submitted by fans through the show's website changed the texts they engaged in real time, the increasing power of the fanboy (and, lest we forget the power of *Twilight*, fangirl), especially in the context of digital communication and social networking technologies, has changed the landscape of mainstream American cinema. When J.J. Abrams sends Leonard Nimoy to the Alamo Drafthouse in Austin, TX — home of head geek Harry Knowles and Fantastic Fest, the largest genre film festival in the U.S. — with a mandate to drop a surprise world premiere of *Star Trek* on those in attendance (and expecting a *Wrath of Khan* screening), the center of the cinematic universe has been knocked off its axis. This is no longer your father's film industry. While blockbuster films were perhaps at one time made to appeal to the widest possible audience while making some cursory attempt to mollify the hardcore, we see now a landscape in which major films are produced for the "true fans" of the genre or source material (*LOTR*, *The Dark Knight*, *Watchmen*, *Iron Man*, *Kick-Ass*) and if the masses follow the core audience into the theater (which they often do not), even better. This is a remarkable — if perhaps fleeting — development in an industry so traditionally focused on the bottom line, and it owes much to the kind of critical viewership and commentary encouraged by the Best Brains formula.

Finally, as evidenced by the *MST3K* team's battles over copyright and distribution, the show was an important force in bringing into focus the problems and opportunities posed by a remix culture. As Brett Gaylor has argued in his excellent, if polemic, film *Rip! A Remix Manifesto* (2009), "culture always builds on the past" and "the past will always try to control the future." An attack on the corporate tyranny inherent in current U.S. copyright law, Gaylor's film makes a convincing case that authorial right is always susceptible to the maxim that there is nothing new under the sun and that the criminalization of remixing music, video and other forms of culture is fundamentally about institutional rather than individual interests. Profiling such remix luminaries as the Mouse Liberation Front (which co-opted the Mickey Mouse image in a variety of amusing ways), sample guru Girl Talk, and open source crusader Lawrence Lessig, Gaylor shows how remixing is tantamount to creation, especially in the digital age. The Best Brains team would be an easy inclusion here in their pioneering amalgamation of Grateful Dead–esque tape sharing, postmodern meta-funk syncopation, and openness toward audience co-production. They were a networked, co-creative remix enterprise before there was a truly viable digital culture in any widespread sense.

The book you are about to read is a labor of love for all concerned. This will be clear enough in your engagement with the individual chapters, but more opaque, perhaps, in its manifestation as a totality. That this overdue work exists at all, however, is due to the tenacity of Rob Weiner and Shelley Barba, scholars whose connection with this material is one of respect, commitment, candor, and critique. Their editing of this volume is a profound service to the study of alternative cinema, fandom, intertexuality, new media, relationships between consumption and production, political economy, and perhaps a dozen other fields. It is an excellent example of the fecundity that can result from asking a diverse group of scholars from a multitude of disciplines to comment upon an intriguing and under-examined topic. It also happens to be, upon its publication, the definitive work on *MST3K* as a cultural phenomenon.

Is it too much to suggest that a little cable-access television show changed the way we watch movies? Perhaps. But I'm going to say it anyway. You are invited to heckle.

REFERENCES

Doherty, Thomas. "The Death of Film Criticism." *Chronicle of Higher Education.* (February 28, 2010). Accessed 6/15/2010. http://chronicle.com/article/The-Death-of-Film-Criticism/64352/.
Gaylor, Brett (dir). *Rip a Remix Manifesto.* New York, N.Y. : Disinformation, 2009. DVD.
Jenkins, Henry. *Textual Poachers: Television Fans and Participatory Culture.* New York: Routledge, 1992.

Robert Moses Peaslee is a professor of electronic media and communications in the College of Mass Communications at Texas Tech University, Lubbock.

Introduction

by Robert G. Weiner and Shelley E. Barba

It's like watching a movie with your funniest friends!
> — Michael J. Nelson/RiffTrax promotional blurbs

If you allow, a movie experience will be a meditation of sorts.... If you just let down your defenses a little and let it play.... Share the laughs and the gasps, let those emotions out a little, and you can become part of the story.... During hard times people go to the movies, to sit together and feel better for a while. If movies could do nothing else for us this would be enough.... It requires an audience to complete the art form. A public audience, a group of people sharing the experience. This is what the filmmakers intend....
> — Kevin Murphy/*A Year at the Movies* (202, 251,303)

Generally speaking doing new things is dangerous. The first person to explore new territory is most likely the first to die. But if the human race did not constantly adapt to new situations it would be extinct. So society produces crazies. I don't know how. We do dangerous things that most people think are crazy. That is how society makes progress (62).
> — J. G. Eccarius

The above quote from J.G. Eccarius' 1992 transgressive novel, *Last Days of Christ the Vampire*, could have been about the beginnings of *Mystery Science Theater 3000* (*MST3K*)— that little puppet show which was nominated eight times for the CableAce award, twice for the Emmy, and which won the Peabody. When Joel Hodgson first met with director and producer Jim Mallon to discuss his idea for a show in which puppets make funny comments during bad movies, Mallon could have thought Hodgson was nuts, but instead he was attracted to the idea and decided to give it a try. The "petri dish" for *MST3K* was a "scrappy little independent UHF TV Station, KTMA" in Minneapolis (Mallon 2008; 1996: xxx). There, Mallon, Hodgson, and others like Kevin Murphy, Josh Weinstein, and Trace Beaulieu played a central role in creating the show in 1988 and made television and cultural history. Other contributors to the *MST3K* folklore include Michael J. Nelson, Mary Jo Pehl, Bridgett Jones Nelson, Paul Chaplin, Frank Conniff, and Bill Corbett, who joined the show throughout its ten year history on mainstream cable.

The concept of puppets in space reacting to cheap movies certainly seemed a crazy idea, but like other quirky comedies *Seinfeld* and *Monty Python's Flying Circus*, there was something about *MST3K* that took hold. The show was first up picked up by the fledgling Comedy Channel/Central and then by the Sci Fi Channel, and Universal/Gramercy released a major theatrical feature film *MST3K The Movie* in 1996. Like *Monty Python*, and *Seinfeld*, *MST3K*'s humor was offbeat, but also like those shows, it was very intelligent and thoughtful. While the early shows were a little rough, gradually the riffs got better and better, and Michael J. Nelson, whom Kevin Murphy has called "perhaps the funniest person alive" (2002: 275), was brought in as head writer. Ultimately, despite a very vocal and large fan base, the show became too much for mainstream cable and was cancelled after seven seasons on Comedy Central, then later after three seasons on the Sci Fi Network. Still, one has to wonder how a show like *MST3K* with its quirky premise ever got off of the ground. The truth is, in the words of *Time* film critic Richard Corliss, "*Mystery Science Theater 3000* is just about the smartest, funniest show TV has produced" (1995: 27). That the show has gone on to a degree of mainstream critical acceptance is evidenced by *Time Magazine*'s 2007 list regarding it as one of the "100 Best Shows of All Time" (Poniewozik). *TV Guide* also in 2007 put it in the "Top Cult Shows Ever," coming in at 13 out of 30 (*TV Guide News*).

Writing Comedy

Comedy is arguably the hardest type of material to write and be consistently good. Today, most comedy on television and in movie theaters has no class; it is crude, vulgar,

The Titans of Comedy: Cinematic Titanic Dallas 2008. Standing, left to right: Frank Conniff, Mary Jo Pehl, Trace Beaulieu, J. Elvis Weinstein, Joel Hodgson, with Rob Weiner in front. Photograph by Joe Ferrer, courtesy of Rob Weiner.

and frankly just not funny. *MST3K* has a classiness that has never been surpassed. The jokes or riffs come from all aspects of popular culture including music, film, politics, and literature; it is all over the landscape. Not everyone watching can get all the jokes, but there are enough that even if one only gets half of the jokes, it is an extremely funny and rewarding experience. The writers of *MST3K* and now *RiffTrax* and *Cinematic Titanic* (Figure 1) make riffing look easy and seamless, which is the mark of good comedy writing.

However, a great deal of hard work and thought goes into writing the riffs. One only has to hear the marginal quality of some of the fan *iRiffs* to know how hard the writers work to produce a quality product. Granted, not every riff is a winner, but if the writers get it right 60–70 percent of the time and they usually do better than this. The riffs are still funnier than most of the comedy being produced today. The name of the show's production company, Best Brains, says it all. The writers of *MST3K*, *RiffTrax*, and *Cinematic Titanic* belong in the same company as Comedy's royalty like the Marx Brothers, Spike Jones, Laurel and Hardy, Will Rogers, Buster Keaton, Harold Lloyd, Bill Cosby, etc.

MST3K Fan Films

If imitation is indeed the greatest form of flattery, *MST3K* has been the recipient of flattery from its earliest days on. Fan Films started to pop up as early as 1992 with Ryan Johnson's take on *Star Trek V*. Other fan tributes include *Mystery Fandom Theater 3000*, Garage Productions riffing of *Battle of the Worlds* (1995), Jason Soto's *B-Movie Central 5000*, and *Mystery Spatula Theater 11*, among numerous others. There is also a webpage devoted to fan films and live fan performances: *The Mystery Science Theater 3000 Fanvid and Live-performance Database*. Folks like Josh Way and the Incognito Cinema Warriors XP have released their own riffing DVDS through their own websites as well as through RiffTrax.com. Some of the above fan-videos have their own followings. The rise in attempts by Fan Films to imitate *MST3K's* comic genius brings *iRiffs to over 400 entries*. According to *RiffTrax.com,* "An iRiff is a home-made audio commentary that you can upload to the RiffTrax Store and sell to our thousands of daily visitors." In 1997 Best Brains reached out to fans and officially sanctioned a live electronic fan riffing of Roger Corman's *The Day the World Ended* (1955). While none of the cast or writers were involved, the fan riffing was "based on the live, participatory *MST3K—The Home Game*." According to the website, *Daddy O's Drive in* Dirt, "prior to the premiere of episode *801,-REVENGE OF THE CREATURE*, the Sci-Fi Channel aired *The Day World Ended* during which on-line MSTies could make funny comments, which appeared at the bottom of the TV screen." The fan culture around the show has a fascinating history unto itself.

The Editors' Personal *MST3K* Journeys

ROB'S "SINBAD UNPLUGGED"

In 1992, I was a graduate student in American history, and I remember getting together with some of my classmates from our Historical Methods class in one of their apartments after leaving a bar. One of them started talking about this new show on cable in which silhouetted figures were making fun of old movies and how cool it was. Somehow that comment stuck with me, but it was not until 1993 that I actually watched the show. It was at musician Jason Joseph's house where the *Magic Voyage of Sinbad* was playing, and the phrase "Sinbad unplugged" has stuck in my mind for 17+ years now (Murphy 1993, Episode 505). Periodically, on the weekends I went over to watch the show with others. The show haunted my psyche; it was like a popular culture history lesson. Later, when I was living in Denton, Texas, working on my Master of Library Science, my classmates Kraig and Sarah Willis would give me tapes of *MST3K* to watch on those long school nights. From watching the tapes, I was introduced to the dos and don'ts of dating, the evil one Pitch, *Swamp Diamonds*, Martians and Santa Claus, the Colossal Man, and all of those peculiar invention exchanges. I can say with all sincerity that *MST3K* got me through graduate school. I would go over to the Willis household and watch the show with others (which is always fun and the way the show should be watched). We watched "Wanna play some football?" (from the riffing of *Laserblast*) when it first aired (Beaulieu 1996, Episode 706) and went to the theater to see *Mystery Science Theater 3000: The Movie* which remains to this day one of my best movie/theater going experiences.

The first discussion I had with the woman who became my wife was about *Mystery Science Theater*. Although the marriage collapsed, my love for the show just grew and grew. In 2002, I tried to put together a *MST3K* area for the Southwest Popular Culture Association. I sent out a call for papers and a print flyer.

Previously, I had been successful in organizing a number of areas for SWPCA including Popular Music and Silent Film, and in 1998 I founded the Grateful Dead area. I thought academic MSTies (the name for fans of the show) would come in droves. I could not have been more wrong. Only one person from the fan group, *MSTies Anonymous*, came. He drove over ten hours straight from Colorado to Albuquerque, New Mexico, to give a twenty minute presentation and then drove back. He gave a great presentation and the session was well attended, but no one else responded to the Call for Papers who could actually come to the conference. So perhaps an academic panel on the show was well before its time. Given the interest in the show today, it might be time for someone to revisit the idea or even put together a whole conference or fan convention on the show. Since that time, I've gone to several *Cinematic Titanic* live shows, attended the theater events for *RiffTrax,* and hatched the idea for the book (or digital device) you hold in your hands.

SHELLEY'S KITTEN WITH A WHIP

Reading others' experiences with *MST3K*, it is hard not to feel like I did something wrong, that I broke a fan-rule by discovering the show by pure chance. On a Saturday afternoon while my mother was out and my father napped, I got to control the remote to find something to watch. This was quite a task for a tween in the days when Disney was a premium channel, and as I was clicking closer to Nickelodeon, I found a movie with Ann-Margret. I recognized her from *Newsies* and *Viva Las Vegas*, so I stopped. It was an "old" movie, but Nick-at-Nite had shown me the delight in programs like *The Dick Van Dyke Show* and *My Three Sons*. However, this was delight unlike anything Mary Tyler Moore had been in. The silhouettes of two cute robots and a sweet-looking man making jokes made this old movie new, and they had me under their spell.

For the next five years of my life, *MST3K* was something I had just on my own. My classmates, cousins, and parents did not like the show, the few who knew of it. So, I would watch the episodes alone and laugh at the jokes I understood. Even though I did not get many jokes an episode, I got enough to know the show was good. Here were people and robots who could make a terrible situation — being stuck in space — fun. They could also make awful movies have value to those who would have ignored them otherwise. As I did not have anything like the Internet to tell me any different, I felt like I was their lone West Texas fan.

It was not until my junior year in high school that I fell into a group of friends who watched and loved *MST3K* as much as I. In fact, knowing about Tom Servo and Crow T. Robot served as enough "nerd cred" to become a fast friend and accepted into the group. In the following eleven years, I have repeatedly forged strong friendships with others MSTies through college, graduate school and various jobs, including my friendship with Rob.

While it seems that other people fondly remember the people who first shared a tape or told them about this neat little show on Comedy Central, I remember the people I bonded with simply because we both know that "eggs are complicated" and should "cost like $100 a piece" (Murphy 1996, Episode 702). Others who knew, like I did, that there is something of value in every artistic expression even if it seems horrible. A show that can demonstrate such a valuable life lesson certainly deserves its own scholarly dissection, and I am glad I could be a part of it.

It Has Never Been Better for Fans of *MST3K*

Twenty years after the little puppet show aired and ten years after its cancellation, *MST3K* is more popular than ever. Riffing has become its own cultural phenomenon. One can find hundreds of websites related to the show, tape and DVD traders abound, and nearly all of the episodes (including some of the KTMA shows which hopefully will see official release someday) are preserved at the *Digital Archive Project* in varying degrees of quality. Many of the shows have official release on DVD through Rhino and recently in beautiful DVD box sets by Shout Factory.

In the interim, Joel Hodgson, Josh Weinstein and Trace Beaulieu worked on *Freaks and Geeks*, and Mike Nelson, Bill Corbett, and Kevin Murphy did the *Film Crew* (releasing four DVDs). Frank Conniff did standup, and worked as producer of *The Drew Carey Show* and *Sabrina the Teenage Witch*. Mike Nelson created RiffTrax to provide commentaries, usually with Kevin Murphy and Bill Corbett, for Hollywood blockbusters that you can download. They also have released an assortment of DVDS, including a return to riffing those lovely mental hygiene shorts. Joel Hodgson, Mary Jo Pehl, J. Elvis Weinstein, Trace Beaulieu, and Frank Conniff, have reformed as Cinematic Titanic and have released DVDs riffing some old-time flicks, bringing back the spirit of the original show.

What is even more exciting is that both RiffTrax and Cinematic Titanic have been doing live gigs. News about the former cast members is at your fingertips through the Internet. The official fan page, *Satellite News* (www.MST3KINFO.com), always has good current information. The Robots, voiced in part by Paul Chaplin, were even brought back officially for a brief moment in new flash animation shorts at www.mst3k.com. One can still find clips from the KTMA shows, swag you can buy, and other tidbits of fun there. At the time of this writing, MSTies have the best of *all* possible worlds: official releases of the original show, DVDs from the former cast members, and live gigs. Being a *MST3K* fan has never been more exiting or fun, and the list of MSTies keeps growing as new folks discover the wonders of the show.

Nothing Is Sacred: Just Relax, Frank Zappa, and American Sarcasm

MST3K is firmly planted in the concept of classic American liberalism (not partisan politics). In the same satiric vein as Will Rogers and the Firesign Theatre is the idea that we are free to pursue life and freedom, and that nothing is sacred. The show lampoons everything from politics, music, literature, and media figures, and it reminds us to "chill." Nelson has even lampooned his own work (Nelson, 2000: 286–288); people should have fun and "just relax." Although programs like *South Park* and the *Boondocks* have much more violent and crude humor, those shows too remind us that anything and anyone is fair game and not to take ourselves so seriously.

MST3K, like Frank Zappa, tells us anything is game to be parodied. But like Zappa's compositions, there is a lot of hard work and thought that goes into creating the shows. Zappa always complained that folks never understood there were notes and work behind his humor music. The Zappa and *MST3K* connection goes even further as members of the cast are known fans of Zappa. The data filled fan site *Ward-E* has a complete list of all the "Frank Zappa References in MST3K" by Michael Slusher (2002).

American political sarcasm has a history as long as the nation itself. Sequential art and cartoons have been used to convey ideas since the 1740s (Lordan, 2006). During the credits of many of the *MST3K* shows the cast gave thanks to the authors of the First Amendment and to the teachers of America, once again showing a fondness for the American principles of personal liberty.

The writers and cast of the show also have taken some of our sacred films and ripped them. RiffTrax has riffed good movies like *Lord of the Rings*, *Halloween*, *The Dark Knight*, *Casino Royale* and even classics like *Casablanca*. Again, the point is to have fun and not take anything too seriously.

MST3K Literature and the Academy

As academic librarians, we are keenly aware of the need to document, preserve, and study humanities' collective memory. This book is part of that process; it was created to enlarge the body of literature out there for scholars and fans to use. However, we are aware that many fine writings on this topic already exist. For example, the principle members of the show have produced a number of literary works:

- Michael J. Nelson continues to write for *Home Theater* magazine. He has written books and hilarious commentary for a number of Pop Art books including *Goth-Icky: A Macabre Menagerie of Morbid Monstrosities* and *Love Sick: A Smoldering Look at Love, Lust, and Marriage* (2005). His other works include his book of movie/popular commentary, *Mike Nelson's Movie Megacheese* (Nelson 2000), the novel *Death Rat* (2003),and the foreword for Glen Kay and Michael Rose's *Disaster Movies* (2006).
- Trace Beaulieu wrote and published his quirky comic *Here Come the Big People* (1997).
- Bill Corbett continued to write and produce his own plays, some of which he has published including *Hate Mail* (2004) and *The Big Slam* (1999). He apparently has several unpublished scripts in university archives.
- Mary Jo Pehl has kept busy by writing comedic pieces for the likes of *Life's a Stitch: The*

Best of Contemporary Women's Humor (edited by Anne Safran Dalin, 2002). She had a piece in *Scott Bateman's Sketchbook of Secrets and Shame* (2006) and contributed to the series *Funny Ladies* which is on DVD and available as a book audio download through audible.com. Mary Jo also released an excellent e-book, *Snapshots*, through iTunes, and is working on a comic, *Jailbait*, which is forthcoming from Bluewater productions. She and Bill Corbett both contributed to *The Playrights' Center: Monologues for Women* (2005).

These are just a few of the projects that the cast members have written or are working on. We realize there are literarily hundreds of websites, interviews, articles, podcasts, and fan information out there on the Internet, but we hope that this little discussion has helped put things in perspective in terms of the literature by the cast members.

We should not forget the book that no MSTie should be without, *The Mystery Science Theater 3000 Amazing Colossal Episode Guide*, written by the writers and cast members. The book was released in 1996 and goes through Season 6, with a little about the feature film. The cast continued to write episode guides online for Season's 8–10 and their thoughts on Season 7 (available at *www.Mst3kinfo.com*). This volume is long out of print and is in need for a new published edition. Even well known MSTies like Joe Barlow (2000) and E. Mitchell (2009) have published film-related books.

Although the academic literature on *MST3K* is sparse, that does not mean it is non-existent. As early as 1993, the show was being talked about in such publications as *Bright Lights Film Journal* (Macor 1993) and *Spectator: The University of Southern California Journal of Film & Television* (Griffin 1993). *Time* film critic Richard Corliss talked about his love of the show in a 1995 issue of *Film Comment*. In 2007, the *Journal of Film & Video* published an article looking at "Media Consciousness, and the Postmodern Allegory of the Captive Audience" of *MST3K*. The show's bots, Crow T. Robot and Tom Servo, made a cameo appearance in a 1996 article from *Mechanical Engineering*, which argued that the use of the robots and the show's premise offered the "perfect, postmodern moment" (Porush, 57). There have also been a number of articles in various academic books like *The Essential Cult TV Reader* (2010) and Jessica Royer's article related to gender in 2000's *Fantasy Girls*. *MST3K* also has cropped up in the occasional thesis or dissertation (Macor 2000; Schroder 2003). However, considering that there are not as many academic writings on the show as say on *Star Trek, The X-Files* or *Buffy the Vampire Slayer*, we hope that this volume can help fill some of the gap.

When we first put out the Call for Papers and contributors for this volume, some fans were worried that we were taking the show too seriously, or that we were exploiting the show for our own ends. Nothing could be further from the truth. We realize that it is "just a show" and that we "should just relax," but nothing makes a scholar or fan happier than a lively discussion. We hope *Mystery Science Theater 3000: Essays on History, Technology, Film, Fandom, and the Culture of Riffing*, is a beginning of that discussion.

REFERENCES

Barlow, Joe. *100 Nights in the Dark : A Collection of Contemporary Film Reviews and Essays*. San Jose, CA: Writers Club Press, 2000.
Bateman, Scott ed., *Scott Bateman's Sketchbook of Secrets and Shame*. Middletown, NJ: Word Riot Press, 2006.
Beaulieu, Trace (director), Kevin Murphy (writer), Michael J. Nelson (writer) et al. Episode 706, *Laserblast*. Shout Factor, 2008.
Beaulieu, Trace, Jimmy Palmiotti, Amanda Conner. *Here Come the Big People*. Ottawa, IL: Event Comics, 1997.

Corbett, Bill. *The Big Slam*. New York : Dramatists Play Service, 1999.

_____. "Excerpt from *Hungry Ghosts*." In Kristen Gandrow, Polly K. Carl, eds., *The Playrights' Center Monologues for Women*. Portsmouth, NH: Heinemann, 2005.

Corbett, Bill, and Kira Obolensky. *Hate Mail: A Comedy*. New York: Playscripts, 2004.

Corliss, Richard. "Play *MST* for Me." *Film Comment*. 31: 4 (July/August 1995): 26–35.

Eccarius, J.G. *The Last Days of Christ the Vampire*. San Francisco: III Publishing, 1992.

Griffin, Sean. 1993. "Play MST-y for Me: The Discursive Excess of Mystery Science Theater 3000." *Spectator: The University of Southern California Journal of Film & Television*. 14: 1 (Fall 1993): 66–77.

"H01— THE DAY THE WORLD ENDED." *Daddy O's Drive-In Dirt*. Accessed 6/16/2010 http://www.mst3k info.com/daddyo/di_H01.html.

Holtzclaw, Robert. "*Mystery Science Theater 3000*." In David Lavery, ed., *The Essential Cut TV Reader*. Lexington: University of Press of Kentucky, 2010.

King, John. "*Mystery Science Theater 3000*, Media Consciousness, and the Postmodern Allegory of the Captive Audience." *Journal of Film & Video*. 59: 4 (Winter 2007): 37–53.

Lordan, Edward J. *Politics, Ink: How America's Cartoonists Skewer Politicians from King George III to George Dubya*. Lanham, MD: Rowman & Littlefield, 2006.

Macor, Alison Grace. "The Visible Audience: Participation, Community and Media Fandom." Ph.D. dissertation, University of Texas at Austin, 2000.

Macor, Alison. "Camp on Cable." *Bright Lights Film Journal*. 11 (Fall 1993): 41–44.

Mallon, Jim. "KTMA: The Birthplace of MST3K (Part One)." *MST3K.com*. 2008. Accessed 6/16/2010 http://www.mst3k.com/memoirs.html.

Mallon, Jim, Trace Beaulieu, Kevin Murphy et al. "Early Mythology: The KTMA Years and the Road to Network Television." In *Mystery Science Theater 3000: Amazing Colossal Episode Guide*. New York: Bantam Books, 1996.

Mitchell, E. *The Amazing, Incredible, Shrinking, Colossal, Bikini-Crazed CREATURE FROM THE PUBLIC DOMAIN*. Denver: Outskirts Press, 2009.

Murphy, Kevin. *A Year at the Movies: One Man's Filmgoing Odyssey*. New York: HarperCollins, 2002.

Murphy, Kevin (director), Michael J. Nelson (writer), Joel Hogdson (writer) et al. Episode 505, *The Magic Voyage of Sinbad*, 1993.

Murphy, Kevin (director), Michael J. Nelson (writer), Mary Jo Pehl (writer) et al. Episode 702, *The Brute Man*, 1996.

The *Mystery Science Theater 3000 Fanvid and Live-performance Database* 2009. Accessed 6/16/2010 http://bindingpolymer.com/mst3kfanvids/legacy/index.html.

Mystery Science Theater 3000. Digital Archive Project. 2010. Accessed 6/16/2010 http://dapcentral.org/modules.php?op=modload&name=MasterList2&file=index&show=1.

Nelson, Michael J. *Death Rat*. New York: HarperEntertainment, 2003.

_____. "Foreword." In Glenn Kay and Michael Rose, *Disaster Movies*. Chicago: Chicago Review Press, 2006.

_____. *Mike Nelson's Movie Megacheese*. New York: HarperCollins, 2000.

Nelson, Michael J., and Charles S. Anderson Design Company. *Goth-Icky: A Macabre Menagerie of Morbid Monstrosities*. New York: Harry N. Abrams, 2005.

_____. *Love Sick: A Smoldering Look at Love, Lust, and Marriage*. New York: Harry N. Abrams, 2005.

Pehl, Mary Jo. *Funny Ladies*, Episode 3. Port Washington, NY : Koch Vision DVD, 2003/2004. (Download available at: http://www.audible.com/adbl/site/entry/offers/partnerPromotions.jsp?BV_UseBVCookie=Yes&productID=PF_TVDC_000009.

_____. "Mono" in Anne Safran Dalin ed., *Life's a Stitch: The Best of Contemporary Woman's Humor*. New York: Random House, 2002.

_____. "Phyllis" in Kristen Gandrow, Polly K. Carl eds., *The Playrights' Center Monologues for Women*. Portsmouth, NH: Heinemann, 2005.

_____. *Snapshots*. Itunes, 2008. Available: http://www.apple.com/itunes/affiliates/download/?id=305569 382.

Poniewozik, James. "The 100 Best TV Shows of All-TIME." *Time Magazine*, 2007. Accessed 7/26/2010. http://www.time.com/time/specials/2007/completelist/0,29569,1651341,00.html.

Porush, David, quoted in Michael Valenti. "A Robot Is Born." *Mechanical Engineering*. 118: 6 (June 1996): 50–57.

RiffTrax.com "What is an iRiff?" www.rifftrax.com 2010. Accessed 6/16/2010 http://www.rifftrax.com/iriffs/cat.

Royer, Jessica A. "What Happened on Earth? *Mystery Science Theater 3000* as a reflection of Gender Roles and Attitudes Towards Woman." In Elyce Rae Helford, ed., *Fantasy Girls: Gender in the New Universe of Science Fiction and Fantasy Television*. Lanham, MD: Rowman & Littlefield, 2000.

Shroder, Till. "Did You Get That?— Referentiality and Cultural Knowledge in PULP FICTION AND MYSTERY SCIENCE THEATER 3000." MA thesis submitted to the Department of Philosophy and Humanities, Free University of Berlin, 2003.

Slusher, Michael." List: Frank Zappa References in MST3K." *Ward-E.* 2002. Accessed 6/17/2010 http://www.mst3kinfo.com/ward_e/listzap.html.

TV Guide News. "TV Guide Names the Top Cult Shows Ever." *TV Guide.com* (June 26th, 2007). Accessed 7/26/2010. http://www.tvguide.com/news/top-cult-shows-40239.aspx.

PART ONE

Directors

1

There's Been an Accident at the Studio: How We Made Hobgoblins!

by Rick Sloane

You think the series is done, you think you've had it, and then a movie like *Hobgoblins* shows up and injects new life into the show. Or a new death, depending on how you look at it.
— Michael J. Nelson

It's been over twenty years since I made the first *Hobgoblins*, a no-budget film that was one of many puppet movies to follow *Gremlins*. *Ghoulies* appeared first, *Critters* came next, then all at once, *Hobgoblins*, *Munchies* and *Troll*. The titles and box art were so interchangeable that few people could have distinguished them from each other.

Hobgoblins was released on video in early 1988 and it sold very well, particularly in the foreign markets and I even considered making a sequel two years later. The film, however, faded into oblivion until a decade later, when it was resurrected by the writers of *Mystery Science Theater 3000*. It became one of their all-time highest rated episodes and gave the movie cult status. Now, there isn't a day that goes by when I don't get at least a couple of emails from fans on Facebook, telling me how much they love the film. Who would have figured?

I've heard stories of many filmmakers who were angered by the *MST3K* treatment of their movies. One director was even rumored to have sent them death threats. This amazes me, what did they think *MST3K* was going to do to their movie on that show, congratulate them for good filmmaking?

I'll always remember the first time I saw the *MST3K* version of *Hobgoblins*. This was long after USA Network had aired all six of my *Vice Academy* movies, so I was very familiar with having my movies interrupted with mocking commentary. The *MST3K* writers pulled no punches; nothing was off limits. I laughed throughout the entire airing of *Hobgoblins*; they had greatly improved my film, and it would never be the same without their riffing.

My laughter ended abruptly when they dragged out a mannequin of me and did a fake interview over the end credits. (I won't quote any of the q&a, everyone already knows it word for word.) I was so mortified, but realized that as the film's director, I had it coming. I never took it personally. If *Rocky Horror* creator Richard O'Brien went to a midnight screening of his film, I doubt he'd be yelling back at the audience to stop making fun of

18

his movie. It's like being a host on *Saturday Night Live*. You know there will be jokes at your expense, but it's an honor to be part of it.

I've since exchanged emails with many of the *MST3K* cast members, and even met Mary Jo Pehl when she came to Los Angeles. She said she felt awkward at first about the *MST3K* riffing treatment of my film. I was happy for the fame the show brought me. MJ even said I was possibly the only filmmaker who appreciated what they did to their movie.

"Boy, that sure is a bad movie, won't you?"

Best Brains originally contacted me to see if I had any films that were suited for *Mystery Science Theater 3000*. I've never figured out how it became public knowledge (an urban myth), but numerous people have posted online that I personally submitted *Hobgoblins* to the show. They made it sound like it was a bad thing, but unlike many other filmmakers, at least I got paid for the humiliation. But I do want to clarify that it was through USA Network, who owned the Sci-Fi Channel, that Best Brains had contacted me first.

The Visitants was the first film I suggested to them. It's a far superior movie to *Hobgoblins*, it's my homage to bad 1950s alien invader movies, *Plan 9 from Outer Space* in particular. The characters were dressed outlandishly, the colors were bright and garish, the dialogue was corny and mockable, and I felt it had all the elements of a true cult film. *MST3K* passed on *The Visitants*, saying it was too intentionally campy and not bad enough. I guess it wasn't meant to be. They asked again what else I had available, and I submitted *Hobgoblins* to them. The rest is history.

Hobgoblins director Rick Sloane with one of the film's namesake creatures and the DVD box set from *MST3K*, which revitalized the movie. Mark Berry / Hot Cherry © Mark Berry/Bizzare Archive. Courtesy of Mark Berry and Rick Sloane.

The entire style of *Hobgoblins* was heavily influenced by my love for really bad movies which I developed in my teens. I was in high school when the book, *The Fifty Worst Films of All Time* (Medved 1979) came out. I instantly became obsessed with the cult status of some of the films; their fame was due completely to how bad they were considered by viewers. I think the term, "so bad, it's good," may have even originated from this book. The Nuart, a Los Angeles revival house movie theater, began running double bills of some of the movies from the book. I remember going to a screening of *Robot Monster* and *Santa Claus Conquers the Martians*. I knew immediately that these were the kind of movies I wanted to make, cheap, over the top, laughable and cheesy.

Few people believe that anyone would set out to make an intentionally bad movie, but this was the same year *Attack of the Killer Tomatoes* was made. I now had a mission: to make my own bad movie. I began production on *Hobgoblins* in 1987, at the peak of the huge direct-to-video market, when you could easily get a distribution deal just based on a good title and a two sentence synopsis.

I was twenty-five years old at the time, early in my career when my budgets were ridiculously minuscule. *Hobgoblins* got in the can for around $15,000, which is incredibly cheap considering it was shot on 35mm film. I did it by filming all the night exteriors without permits, the owners of the parking lot that doubled for the movie studio never found out that we used their property in the film. Same for the city overlook that became Reputation Road, and the exterior of the house where Daphne fights one of the puppets on the lawn. We never paid for any of these locations.

Even riskier penny-pinching was that I shot the entire movie on outdated rolls of films, since they could be bought for only pennies a foot. You can't tell we used outdated film stock in the daylight scenes, but in some of the night exteriors, the color is a little muddy in places, which was the least of the film's problems.

It's a no-brainer to see where we saved the most money: the puppet fabrication. I had never done a puppet movie before, so I had no idea what it would cost to have one custom-created. I went to Kenneth J. Hall, who had worked on *Ghoulies*, to get a price quote. I can't remember how much he originally asked to make them, but I told him I only had $1,500 to spend on all four puppets. He hesitated and said he would have to cut a few corners, such as only one would have a moveable mouth. It sounded good to me at the time.

It wasn't until the night before filming that he delivered the final puppets. I was very pleased with the way they looked; I wanted them to be a cross between the cute Gremlins at the beginning of the film, and the evil ones who create all the havoc at the end. I asked Ken how to operate them, to make their arms move and make their eyes blink. He paused for a moment, then told me because of their low cost, that they couldn't do any of those things. I knew we were in trouble. But hey, if Ed Wood could make the Bela Lugosi octopus fight in *Bride of the Monster* work, so could I. Having a puppet operator on set might have helped, but we couldn't afford one. Instead I let one of the production assistants, a woman who had just gotten out of a mental hospital, operate them. That's one of the reasons you see them shaking around in a Thorazine induced haze through most of the movie.

Film production began the following day. The scenes at Kevin and Amy's sparsely decorated house were shot first. The house belonged to a friend of one of the lead actors and was free, so beggars can't be choosers. The first day included the infamous garden tool fight scene. This is one of the few times I am going to pass blame to someone else for one of the film's worst scenes. The foreign distributor insisted on a scene of Nick in army combat. I

"Let's get the hell out of here before anyone sees this movie." From left: Kelley Palmer, Steven Boggs, Paige Sullivan and Tom Bartlett. Photograph by Rick Sloane, courtesy of Rick Sloane.

certainly had no money to rent an army base and fill it with dozens of extras, or choreograph an elaborate fight sequence. I came up with a compromise—Nick teaches Kevin man-to-man combat by challenging him to a rake fight. This is still one of the few scenes that truly makes me cringe whenever I think about it. The fight originally ran for less than a minute, Kevin is knocked down once, and it ends. The distributor wanted me to stretch the scene, so I went back and used every single take from every camera angle. Kevin gets knocked down three times before Nick is finally victorious. It's the most painful three and a half minutes you'll ever see. It's the exact same moves repeated over and over, most not usable, each time Kevin hits the ground. The scene took forever to edit; there are almost one hundred cuts in three minutes. The film's composer, Alan Dermarderosian, had the idea to add the Casio hit sounds whenever the tools struck each other. Just in case the scene wasn't bad enough already.

It gets even worse; I was trying to imitate a fight scene from a bigger budget film. I've never admitted this before in interviews, but watch the finale of *Streets of Fire*. It's one of my favorite films; Michael Pare and Willem Dafoe have a five minute pick-axe duel to the death for almost five minutes. It's incredibly well staged and expertly edited, and is probably one of the best fight scenes done in any movie. Go and get a DVD of that film and watch the pick-axe fight while you think of the garden tool fight in *Hobgoblins*. You will be on the floor laughing when you see the two side by side.

"Can you catch a venereal disease from watching a movie?"

What about the trashy women that populate *Hobgoblins*? In less than a year after making *Hobgoblins*, I would make my most successful film, *Vice Academy*, which focused entirely on a world where all the women dressed and acted like sluts. I would have that

Rick Sloan recalls that Daphne (Kelley Palmer) was rolling on the lawn with a hobgoblin puppet at 5 A.M. while all the neighbors yelled at us to "shut up!" Courtesy Rick Sloane.

sleazy style perfected by then, it had completely developed as a major part of *Hobgoblins*. The *MST3K* writers quickly picked up on this joke, they even devoted an entire sketch to my portrayal of women.

Daphne is the most obvious of the film's tramps, dressed in her garish spandex valley girl outfits, which were already out of style by five years when we made the movie. She's the most brazen, oversexed and outspoken of all the characters. It's tricky to count exactly how many times Daphne has sex with Nick in the film; at least twice in the bouncing van, and once more while Kevin leaves to save Kyle from being pushed off a cliff in his car.

Then there's Amy, the plain repressed girl who fantasizes about being a stripper dressed in full rock video slut attire, at the seediest of all places, Club Scum. Amy has some of the raunchiest dialogue in the film, though *MST3K* wisely excised it for television. When Road-rash offers her a ride on his motorcycle, she taunts Kevin with, "Riding a motorcycle is like sitting on the world's largest vibrator."

Trashy phone sex operator Fantazia rivals them both with her skin-tight gold spandex pants, ratted hair and foul mouth. Some of her dialogue was so disgusting that *MST3K* left an entire scene on the cutting room floor. "I'm going to see a movie today, it's only rated PG, I want you to show up and make it rated 'X.' Sneak in the rear door and when the lights go down, drop your pants and show me a full moon. Pull me down and roll me on those sticky floors. Lick that artificial butter flavor off my body."

And we can't forget Pixie, the beehived harlot barmaid, who turns tricks on the side between go-go dances.

So where exactly does *Hobgoblins* go wrong? Deciphering the cause is like picking through the shrapnel after a tragic plane crash. Even I'm not sure where to begin. The actors take a good deal of flack for the film's sheer awfulness, but they all said their dialogue the way I had written it. I wanted the five kids to have a Scooby-Doo quality, driving around in their van and defeating the creatures, and I use the term "creatures" loosely.

Kevin was supposed to be a goody-two shoes kind of guy, wimpy, whiny and constantly henpecked by his frigid girlfriend. He tries to keep a straight face no matter how ridiculous the situation. Watch how seriously he listens to McCreedy's flashback exposition of the Hobgoblins' ridiculous origin.

Amy was a badly written copy of Sandy from *Grease*, the nice girl who finds happiness only after she reforms into a slut. Fortunately, when she decides to become a stripper, she manages to choose a club where all she has to remove are her gloves. While probably a virgin who has never gone to second base with her boyfriend Kevin, she is ready to go all the way with the rough and tumble bouncer at Club Scum.

Daphne was a low-rent Madonna, with the same bad attitude and even a more garish taste in fashion. She was ripe for the picking when it came to choosing the character who would be the first to battle a Hobgoblin. Thinking she hears her boyfriend's van, she's ambushed outside by a Hobgoblin with a clown horn. She struggles impatiently on the front lawn until one of the puppets tackles her to the ground, in a mind numbing struggle where it's clear the puppet is completely lifeless and she's doing all of its movements.

Nick was a poor man's Rambo, overly macho, but much dumber. He haplessly throws himself onto a live grenade, and escapes with only a few minor injuries in one of the film's hardest to believe moments. Though we never see it, you know he has a bumper sticker on the van that reads, "If the van's a rocking, don't come knocking." When you watch him in that infamous garden tool fight, you know here's a man who knows how to handle a hoe.

And poor Kyle, dressed in hot pink shorts that the actor himself brought from home. Caught up in a world of sexual addiction where he resorts to using his best friend's telephone to make calls to 976 sex lines. When he finally meets Fantazia, the girl of his demented dreams, he's more interested in watching her tease her hair then to make any kind of move on her. Just as well; girls who try to push you over a cliff in your car aren't the kind you want to bring home to meet your mother.

The award for the worst acting possibly belongs to old man McCreedy. An ancient security guard at an abandoned movie studio, he manages to keep the fact that he's harboring fugitives from another planet in one of their film vaults a secret. Rather than simply locking the vault door shut, he just warns dimwitted assistant guards to stay away from it, only to watch them die needlessly throughout the movie. The actor playing McCreedy was decades younger than the character, the make-up artist aged him twenty years to look decrepit. Unfortunately, he choose an exaggerated limp when he walked, which made him look like a missing link. Of all the characters, McCreedy has the most dialogue which makes the audience howl in disbelief. I've always noticed the similarities of McCreedy to Torgo in *Manos: Hands of Fate*, another truly horrific film which I first saw recently.

I actually approached John Carradine to play McCreedy. His agent agreed, but he wanted too much money. I think it was for the best; he deserves to be remembered for his Academy Award–winning role in *The Grapes of Wrath*, and not for appearing in one of the worst films of all time.

Throw in a few other oddball characters, like Pixie, a '60s throw-back go-go dancer, whose beehive is so tall that it took two wigs and six hours of teasing to create it; the MC of Club Scum, a Pee Wee Herman–esque man in an ill-fitting red sequined jacket and heavy pancake make-up; Nick, an army sergeant who goes out in public in full uniform with a traveling stash of grenades and weapons; and Roadrash, a degenerate bouncer whose job is to keep out clientele who look too classy to be at Club Scum.

"Can we make it a point next time, that films need to be made by filmmakers?"

Herein lies much of the charm of *Hobgoblins*, and a good chunk of its cult appeal! In all its bizarreness, the characters are all instantly memorable. None of them are believable or particularly likable, but you could easily imagine which one you'd dress up as on Halloween. Their dialogue was so hokey that it effortlessly lends itself to parody. A better script and normal costumes and this film would have been forgotten as quickly as all the other *Gremlins* knock-offs.

What are some of the other worst moments in the film *MST3K* mocked, besides the interview the show faked with me? Not sure if there's enough space to include them all. Besides the embarrassing garden tool fight, there are just too many to name.

My most cringe-worthy moment is during McCreedy's flashback of the creatures arriving from outer space. I sent a crew member to a local prop house to search for a 1950s-style flying saucer. I don't know what it was that he brought back, but it looked like a buoy you'd see floating in the ocean. It was the last shot of the film and the sun was starting to rise, so we had to shoot it quickly. A fishing line flips open the cheap plastic lid, and the puppets sit there, almost motionless, since there was no way to manipulate them in the space capsule. It was painful for me to watch as we filmed it, and even with music and sound effects, it's still the worst looking shot in the movie.

There are those two blatant stock shots I lifted from other movies to save money. I certainly couldn't afford to actually roll a car off a cliff and have it burst into flames, or have the entire second story of a building explode. And since I didn't hire a fire marshal, it would have truly been dangerous as hell to attempt.

I always thought I did a good job of matching Kyle's car when it heads over the cliff, (even the car wants out of the movie). Fans thought otherwise, and spotted the switch instantly. When the film was first released, everyone asked me if the car was a miniature. I hadn't thought of that, but I could have saved a great deal of money by simply igniting a Matchbox car as it rolled down a small hill.

The building exploding in the film's finale is a somewhat better effort. I was fortunate to find the stock shot before we filmed the scene, so at least the actors are looking in the right direction. I even grabbed a shot of Kevin and McCreedy running past a similar brick building before the explosion, so at least it was a more convincing match.

By far the most dangerous scene we shot was when the stuntman, doubling as Nick, gets lit on fire. Again, no permit or fire marshal, and since we did it in one take, we accidentally ignited the ceiling of the club. The crew hosed down the stuntman with fire extinguishers, then quickly aimed them up at the ceiling before the fire got out of hand.

I'm not sure which puppet sequence is the worst. There's their lifeless first appearance riding the go-cart, halfway through the movie, looking like some fancy plush dolls. They originally appeared in the first five minutes when they kill Dennis, the first security guard, but the puppets looked so cheap that I wisely never used the shot. You don't get to see how bad the puppets look until much later in the film.

I think the worst fight sequence is when Daphne, Kyle and Amy dance spastically to a ditty of an '80s tune, later titled, "It's the '80s do a lot of coke and vote for Ronald Reagan," by the *MST3K* writers. The puppets "attack" them on the couch, which easily lent the film to one of its best riffs, "Someone is rubbing puppets on us."

And wimpy Kevin, trying to be brave at work when an '80s moussed hair thug appears on the studio lot and threatens McCreedy. After boldly firing a gun into the air to scare him away, Kevin mutters, "I wish Amy could have been here to see this." (What, fire a pop gun and whine another line?)

And poor Fontanelles! I had wanted a band to appear at Club Scum, primarily to fill some screen time. A friend recommended them and I thought they'd be perfect. *MST3K* had a blast parodying their song "Kiss Kicker" with an endless array of other titles like Fish Picker, Pig Liquor, Swiss Knickers. More than any of the actors, the band was truly horrified by the jokes made during their number. They never got a record deal, and fans are always asking me where to find their recordings.

The ten-minute ending squeezes in more bad moments than any other ten-minute sequence. In less than two minutes, McCreedy blows up the film vault with the puppets inside, which he could have done in the beginning and saved us all from an hour and a half of misery. Nick returns, barely injured from the grenade explosion, and hops in the van with Daphne for another round of bouncing sex. You think it can't get any worse? Kyle manages to squeeze in one more line asking McCreedy to use the telephone so he can make another sex line call. Before you get a chance to groan at it all, another Fontanelles song bursts onscreen for the end credits, much like "The Time Warp" reprise from *Rocky Horror*, only you don't want to get up and dance this time.

"This scene makes me feel like clubbing ... the director."

I've always had an expression I call the curse of *Hobgoblins*. Out of the cast, the majority would never make a second film. For some odd reason, a number of the first-time actors who appeared in smaller roles in *Hobgoblins* would go on to fame in other projects.

Everyone who has seen *Pulp Fiction* recognizes Duane Whitaker as Maynard, the degenerate pawn shop owner. The character is very similar to Roadrash, the bouncer at Club Scum. I recently asked Duane if Quentin Tarantino had seen *Hobgoblins* when he cast him, and Duane politely told me that he hadn't. Of all the cast, Duane seems to have the most uneasiness whenever asked about the film.*

Daran Norris went on to become a major cartoon voice actor, playing multiple roles in *Fairly Odd Parents*, voicing one of the puppets in *Team America* and numerous other shows. He has no regrets whatsoever about appearing in *Hobgoblins*. He's incredibly nice whenever asked about playing the MC of Club Scum in the film.

Tamara (Bakke) Clatterbuck works non-stop on soap operas, most notably *The Young and the Restless* and *The Guiding Light*. She's very much sought after for guest roles in television, and amazingly she began her career as the spandex-clad Fantazia.

I would go on to greater success with the sexy comedy *Vice Academy* series, made less than a year after Hobgoblins. It aired on late-night cable for seven years and had five successful sequels. The following year I made *Marked for Murder*, a serious crime drama with

*Editor's note: Dwane Whitaker is from our hometown of Lubbock, Texas.

Rick Sloane and the cast of *Hobgoblins* reunite at a 2010 autograph show: from left to right Kelley Palmer (Daphne), Rick Sloane (director), Steven Boggs (Kyle) and Tom Bartlett (Kevin). Photograph by DJ Schroeder, courtesy of Rick Sloane.

Wings Hauser and Martin Sheen. This one earned good reviews; even Leonard Maltin gave it two and a half stars. The film even played theatrically overseas!

There's a strange legacy that *Mystery Science Theater 3000* has given *Hobgoblins*. Because of them, the film has developed a faithful cult following. *MST3K* was responsible for viewers voting it as one of the worst films ever made on the Internet Movie Database and also on Wikipedia. When they first aired *Hobgoblins* on *MST3K*, it got so many votes that it climbed to the top of the IMDB worst film's list, stopping at number two, only behind *Gigli*. It's slipped since then, the rating varies from month to month, it typically teeters around being the 25th worst film ever made.

Even in foreign countries where they don't speak English and *MST3K* has never aired, the dubbed versions of the movie have been cited as the worst film ever made. Go on *YouTube* and you can find several of the foreign versions. The one from Spain is the funniest, the dubbing actors really captured the voices of the original cast, and someone even took the time to select their favorite worst moments from the film.

"I'm going back in time to kick Rick Sloane in the shins..."

I almost forgot I wrote a sequel to *Hobgoblins* back in the late '80s. With all the attention the film had recently received, I decided go back and shoot it twenty years later. *Hobgoblins 2* was a tricky undertaking in filmmaking. Bad films are generally not known for spawning sequels (though there was a *Return of the Killer Tomatoes* and *Killer Tomatoes Eat France*). I remained faithful to the original 1989 script, I wanted the film to look like

The *Hobgoblins* cast, at the end of the shoot. From left, Jeffrey Culver (McCreedy), who was going to reprise his role in *Hobgoblins 2* but had to bow out because of health problems; Steven Boggs (Kyle), who now manages high-end hotels; Kelley Palmer (Daphne), who went on to run a talent agency and remains in the business; Tom Bartlett (Kevin), who works behind the camera as a lead man in an art department; Paige Sullivan (Amy), who retired from acting to become a mom; and Billy Frank (Nick), who is a feature film producer. Courtesy Rick Sloane.

it was made twenty years ago and never released. McCreedy has been committed to a mental hospital for blowing up the studio and blaming it on the Hobgoblins. The puppets return and go after Kevin and his friends all over again.

I had to recast the leads, since in the script, they were all still the same age. I sought out look-alike actors and dressed them in the same wardrobe as if it were still the '80s. Best of all, the original puppets had aged remarkably well, so I was able to use them again, this time with better puppet operators.

While I don't think I was fully able to recapture the charm of the original film, the sequel definitely has its moments. McCreedy has another long and laughable warning tale for Kevin about what the Hobgoblins are capable of, and it's just as bad as the first film. Fantazia now does internet sex and attacks Kyle by reaching out through the computer screen. Instead of riding a go-cart, one of the puppets climbs aboard a riding lawn mower and tries to run down Nick; plus an ending where everyone stands around as they watch a stock shot of another burning building. I hope the former cast of *MST3K* will consider riffing *Hobgoblins 2*. It won't be the same without their commentary.

It's unlikely that I'll revisit *Hobgoblins* for a third time, but there is a script for one more installment. In the script, McCreedy dies twenty years later, and all the original actors reunite at his funeral. In his video will, McCreedy gives them all one final warning to never wish for anything because it might come true. Kevin later makes the horrible mistake of wishing McCreedy hadn't died, only to make him rise from the dead. And we all know bad things come in threes.

I've since learned to laugh at all the bad reviews I've received because of *Hobgoblins*. Some of them are actually really clever. My personal favorites: "Rick Sloane should marry Stephenie Meyer, then they could just torture each other with their HORRIBLE stories." "If complete lack of talent was a crime, writer-director Rick Sloane would be serving a life sentence."

Though I've only read it online, one of the *MST3K* writers credits *Hobgoblins* as shooting straight to the top of the list of the worst films they've ever done. I've always felt like I had a co-dependent relationship with *MST3K*. They embarrassed me with their jokes, and I'm sure it was painful for them to have to watch my film repeatedly to write all their material. But together, I gave them one of their most popular episodes and they brought second fame to my otherwise forgotten film. We may not be a healthy combination, but for some reason, it's worked out really well for both of us.

"Hobgoblins, Hobgoblins, what are you going to do with those Hobgoblins?" Now try reading that a second time without singing along to it. Now there's a legacy I'm proud of!

REFERENCES

Medved, Harry. *The Fifty Worst Films of All Time*. London: Angus and Robertson, 1979.

2

"Remember: Only *you*
can prevent Roger Corman":
The King of the Bs Under Siege

by Cynthia J. Miller

Known as the "King of the Bs," "The Drive-In Deity," and "the Pope of Pop Cinema," Roger Corman has left his imprint, fingerprints, smudges, and splatters on the culture of American popular film, and *Mystery Science Theater 3000* has returned the favor. At 84 years old, Corman has produced, directed, or acted in over 300 films, and more than 50 made-for-television movies. Thirty-two of those films were made in the 1950s, with titles that promised tales of the scary and the scandalous, ranging from *Not of This Earth* (1957), and *Attack of the Giant Leeches* (1959), to *Sorority Girl* (1957), and *Teenage Doll* (1957). Ten of those have been logged into the annals of *MST3K*'s seasons of sarcasm — seven directed by Corman and three crediting him as executive producer.

Corman's output, it would seem, brings out the best (or is it the worst?) in the caustic companions of *MST3K*. Chants of "Cor-man! Cor-man" make it clear that this isn't just (funny) business — it's personal.

While Corman is perhaps most widely known for his later work — such as his cinematic renditions of the tales of Edgar Allan Poe, brought to life by an eerie Vincent Price, or the murderous bellows of a giant plant demanding "FEE-EED ME" — it was his early work in the '50s that truly earned him the title of "King of the B's," as well as earning him the slings and arrows of Joel/Mike, Crow, and Tom Servo. But why? What is it about poor Roger and his films that make both of them such enjoyable targets?

When Corman began producing and directing these early motion pictures in 1954, he ushered in a new generation of exploitation films to grindhouse theaters and drive-ins across America, as major studios were phasing out the Bs. Corman mined the depths of Poverty Row to rework old themes — menacing creatures, interplanetary threats, and of course, girls gone bad. All was not well with the decade known for drive-ins, credit cards, and TV dinners.... Sorority girls, the undead, and blood-lusting aliens all had their place in Corman's universe of things no longer under the control of either nature or culture. Were these films merely exploitation flicks made on-the-cheap, or observations of value systems and normative behaviors simply too tongue-in-cheek to gain notice?

As we explore the love-hate relationship between Corman's work and *MST3K*, we wonder if, perhaps, our hosts *have* noticed, and if the director's attempts at social commentary on the cheap have left him vulnerable to the barbs and taunts of their riffing because the inherent contradictions in his ethics are just too good to pass up — the veneer of exploitation appears just a bit too thin. If the promise of cheap women and cheaper monsters is only designed to lure audiences to a thinly-veiled lecture on social ills, we might wonder if Corman's got it coming. After all, at first, and maybe second, glance, it would appear that the man who authored *How I Made a Hundred Movies in Hollywood and Never Lost a Dime* (1998) had priorities that lay elsewhere. Corman, however, explains it this way:

> If you look at all of my films, you'll see I work on two levels — the text and the subtext. The text, or surface of the film, is generally an exploitation subject that can be advertised and sold to the public. Beneath the surface I'm saying something that is important to me; my feelings about the world or my political convictions. Or both. Somewhere there is a vision of hope, a statement that things have been or will be better [McGee, 1988: xii].

Clearly, for Corman, as well as for our riffing friends at *MST3K*, it *is* all about him; or as our robot friends would say: "To be like the Cor-man; to live like the Cor-man."

"Cormanvision"

MST3K's love-hate relationship with Corman's work reaches back to 1955 to unearth both *The Day the World Ended* and *Swamp Women* (released on television as *Swamp Diamonds*), although the films did not air

The monster from *It Conquered the World* (1956).

until episodes H01 and 503, respectively. They are preceded, in the *MST3K* anthology, by *It Conquered the World* (episode 311 [1956]), *Teenage Caveman* (episode 315 [1958]), and *Viking Women and the Sea Serpent* (episode 317 [1957]). The show's Corman collection is rounded out with *Gunslinger* (episode 511 [1956]) and *The Undead* (episode 806 [1957]). The King of the Bs also presided over three other *MST3K* offerings, as executive producer: *Attack of the Giant Leeches* (episode 406 [1959]), *High School Big Shot* (episode 618 [1959]), and *Night of the Blood Beast* (episode 701 [1958]). (The former cast of *MST3K* still mines Corman for material as Cinematic Titanic riffed *The Wasp Woman* and RiffTrax *Little Shop of Horrors*). Throughout each of these screenings, as with all *MST3K* features, the riffs are abundant, and brimming over with pop culture references and commentaries that create an ongoing mash-up

Promotional poster for *It Conquered the World* (1956).

of television, film, commodities, and social norms. No cultural icon is safe; no tradition or taboo is sacred, from Scientology to Spam. Innuendo, critique, and self-congratulatory barbs abound, as Joel, Crow, and Tom Servo fill in the intellectual "dead spots" in films purported to be the worst "cheesy movies" found by Joel's bosses at Gizmonic Institute for their humorously sadistic experiments on his brain. Characters are lampooned, plots are shredded, and production techniques derided in a steady stream of sarcastic one-upmanship.

With Corman's films, however, the riffs' additional focus on the filmmaker construct

Corman smells like teen spirit with *Teen Age Caveman* (1958).

Promotional poster for *Swamp Women* (1955).

a type of commentary seldom found in other *MST3K* screenings. Films like *Teenage Caveman* are not only riffed as individual works, they also become part of a meta-riff, if you will — a commentary on Corman's oeuvre, as well as his vision — creating an intertextuality among the films, as they simultaneously reference and mock each other *and* the filmmaker who brought them into being.

This strategy is particularly effective for linking the backgrounds, narratives, and special effects of Corman films outside the *MST3K* anthology with those already included, thus extending the reach of the show's critique across Corman's work. During a languid sweep of the bayou landscape in *Swamp Diamonds* (aka *Swamp Women*), for example, Joel and the robots riff on a typical low-budget filmmaking strategy:

> Ahem ... Hey ...
> Rog? ...
> Hey, Roger's getting footage for another movie!
> Uh ... Rog? Over here buddy ... Rog?
> Roger!! [Mallon 1993, Episode 503].

Similarly, in *It Conquered the World*, as an alien craft swoops across the screen, Joel muses "Look at that crappy special effect.... How do they get away with that?" to which Tom replies, "Roger Corman" (Mallon 1991, Episode 311). Throughout the Corman episodes of *MST3K*, the responsibility for bad special effects, camera work, and directorial vision are horizontally linked from film-to-film, as well as vertically linked and brought to rest squarely on Corman's shoulders.

These textual links among Corman's films require a different type of watching from other episodes of the show. They not only require that audience members possess the appropriate knowledge of American visual media and popular culture to "decode" the *MST3K's* humor, they also require audiences to function as an interpretive community at a level specific to Corman's early work and reputation if they are to make the most of the riffing. The caustic commentary still retains humor for those unfamiliar with the director's early career, but for audience members aware of the details of Corman's low-budget history — the cheesy monsters, repurposed footage, hasty production, and gratuitous use of the female form — the riffs provide an intricate web of observations that not only offer additional humor, but affirm the viewers' status as "insiders" in Corman's B-movie universe, as well. And for "those in the know," there simply is so much fodder for critique.... "Oh, Roger Corman, this is going to go down hard, guys" (Mallon 1993, Episode 503).

Celluloid Maverick

Part of what makes Corman such a riff-magnet is his status as an icon of cinematic sludge. However, the title "King of the Bs" was never one Corman sought, nor one he has accepted, at least overtly, with anything beyond gracious tolerance. When a *New York Times Magazine* article on him elaborated on all the B pictures he had made, Corman stopped reading, and never finished the piece, asserting that "the only thing worse than being pigeon-holed is being wrongly pigeon-holed" (Corman, 1998: 36). He objected to the use of the term "B movie" to describe his film projects, as they were never intended to be paired with big-budget, star-driven "A features," as in the days of the old studio system, but rather, were meant to stand alone in all their schlock and glory. He simply called them "exploitation films" in those early days — films that were "ripped from the headlines" — a phrase he liked to use, which was lifted directly from the promotional materials of 1930s exploiters like Ben Judell (Corman, 1998: 58). And in many respects, Corman's films certainly were exploitation — they exploited hot topics of the day, the distributors like American Releasing Corporation that bargained them into theaters, the cast and crew who worked on them, the gullibility of motion picture audiences and their wallets.

The 1950s were highly successful for Corman in that respect — he saturated the market with pictures costing well under $100,000, often by asking his cast and crew to endure their share of the hardships of low-budget filmmaking, for instance, camping out in an abandoned hotel with running water but no electricity in the middle of bayou country during the shooting of the 1955 film *Swamp Women* (known to *MST3K* audiences as *Swamp Diamonds*) or shooting in the desert with non-union workers, as was the case with *Beast with 1,000,000 Eyes* (1955) made for $23,000 (Naha, 1982: 14). Corman's first independent film, *The Monster from the Ocean Floor* (1954), was filmed in six days, for $11,000, and the "monster squid" of the title was actually a puppet filmed through a cloudy fish tank (Merritt, 2000: 124; Corman, 1998: 20). The mantra of Corman's filmmaking was "when you make a movie for nearly nothing, it's easy to turn a profit," and his first seventeen films were very profitable. He churned out visually entertaining movies that drew his target audience — young people between 12 and 25 — to drive-ins and hardtop cinemas in record numbers. The keys to success were a sensational title, a shocking trailer, and a freakish lobby poster. In 1956, when the one-two punch of a blizzard and a newspaper strike threatened to cancel the opening of Corman's first double-bill: *The Day the World Ended* (1955) and *The Phantom from 10,000 Leagues* (1955), his independent distributing company, American Releasing, staged a "horror caravan": characters dressed in monster suits paraded through the streets. Young people filled the theater, and the promotional stunt was a success (McGee, 1988: 11).

Low-budgets with a profit, market saturation, and sensationalist tactics, combined with a quirky, demanding persona and enough filmmaking bravado to earn him the descriptor "maverick" launched Roger Corman on a prolific career that has spanned over 50 years. He has mentored industry figures like Martin Scorsese, Jack Nicholson, Francis Ford Coppola, and Peter Bogdanovich, and garnered numerous honors and awards — including a Bram Stoker, an Independent Spirit Award, Filmmaker of the Year from American Cinema Editors, a Lifetime Achievement award from the Casting Society of America, and most recently, Lifetime Achievement Awards from both the Producers Guild and Video Software Distributors Association. But no matter how often his feet may have trod the stairs to an award podium, *MST3K* hauls him back to his roots — the low end of the cinematic gene pool — like kids from the old neighborhood who never let him forget from whence he came. Any claim to later achievement is forfeit when the riffing starts. As credits proudly proclaim "Directed by Roger Corman," they're met with inevitable sarcasm: "Oh, this is *really* encouraging!" (Mallon 1991, Episode 311).

Exploiting the Exploiter

In keeping with his ascent up the cinematic food chain in later years, Corman followed industry trends in referring to his work as "genre" or "high concept" films, but he remained content to frame his early work as "exploitation." But the unforgiving taunts of *MST3K*'s riffing never let audiences, or Corman, forget that his work falls short, even there.

Exploitation became a distinct category of films during the 1920s, when they were relegated to grindhouses and low end theaters. Sometimes called "blues," these were "adults only" flicks — with titles like *She Devil Island* (1936) and *Dance Hall Dames* (1933). Exploitation films lured audiences to dabble in the forbidden — to "watch on the wild side" — as they violated taboos of the industry and polite society alike. The exploitation category became more fluid over time, expanding to include standard 1950s drive-in movie fare aimed at teenagers out for a night of cheap thrills in Dad's Chevy. This created a mainstream niche for countless low-budget tales, but as Corman's *MST3K* critics are quick to riff, the director's cheesy effects ("The family that glows together stars in a Corman film together"), scantily clad women ("Okay, this is *definitely* a Corman flick now!"), and awkward narrative devices ("That was a stupid, pointless death, but doubtless Corman has others up his sleeve") are really burlesques of exploitation's cinematic tropes, rather than advancing or perfecting the genre's themes and archetypes — indulging in self-conscious excesses that turn even the most disturbing devices into ready fodder for the show's lampooning — exploitation gone awry (1997, *MST3K*— The Home Game).

This becomes particularly apparent as we consider Eric Schaefer's outline of the five unifying elements of classic exploitation films, in the classic *Bold! Daring! Shocking! True! A History of Exploitation Films, 1919–1959* (1999). First, and foremost, the films focused on the forbidden — sex and sex hygiene, prostitution, drugs, nudity, burlesque, and anything else considered to be off limits. The offending activity was also the life-force of the film, not merely an unmentionable side note. By reveling in the illicit, the producers and distributors of these films thumbed their noses at both the industry's cautionary standards and the Production Code Administration, seizing on the space created by their prohibitions to create a unique niche for themselves.

The second unifying element of the genre was that these films were made on the cheap, by independent producers. With meager budgets, the filmmakers abandoned most production values and industry conventions, instead allowing the forbidden spectacle to carry set, technique, and dialogue. Exploitation films were also, in line with Schaefer's third point, independently distributed. The circulation of these low-budget forays into the forbidden tended to be on a road show or states' rights basis, rather than carried out by the major companies that distributed more wholesome industry fare. Linked to this is the fourth unifying element: that the films were exhibited in theaters not associated with the majors. Typically, these shows played in grindhouses or were relegated to run-down theaters bordering on skid row, away from "decent folk." Exploiters relied on sensational promotion tactics to draw attention to their films to counter the shoddy production values and lack of familiar star power.

One final thing that, as Schaefer notes, most of the classic exploitation films had in common is that, unlike mainstream films, there were never many prints of any given movie in circulation. Also unlike mainstream films, though, exploitation films could be in circulation for decades — long after the slick production techniques of high budget studio films had passed from notice, tawdry spectacle lived on.

If, in fact, these criteria can be viewed as "standards," then Corman's 1950 Bs certainly filled several. His early work set new lows in production standards — films were often shot in as few as ten days, sets were used two and three times, and cast members were sometimes required to make their own costumes, like the actors hired to play the lead creatures in the 1959 thriller, *Attack of the Giant Leeches*, who made their costumes out of raincoats. Corman once commented that "We don't have the time or money to be good, so we stick to action"

(Gray, 2004: 62). Made on a shoestring, and sensationalized to the hilt, films like *Beast with 1,000,000 Eyes*, *Not of This Earth*, and *Attack of the Crab Monsters* clearly promised shock and gore — and according to their promotional images, audiences could count on a terrorized, scantily clad young woman or two thrown in for good measure. However, the films' sensationalist come-ons were just that, and seldom was a lewd or outrageous moment to be had. In fact, studio executives were outraged to find that the first print of *Beast with 1,000,000 Eyes* didn't even have a monster. Shot from the science fiction script of "The Unseen" by Tom Filer, about a being from space that takes control of the birds and animals around a desert ranch, the film was marketed to exhibitioners as *Beast with 1,000,000 Eyes* in one of the most unabashed acts of exploitation advertising in Corman's career. Corman was forced to find someone to make a monster fast and cheap, which led him to art editor, Paul Blaisdell. For the cost of materials and $200, he built a little hand puppet and a miniature spaceship which were quickly photographed and inserted into the movie. While *MST3K* didn't include this bit of classic Corman in its offerings, an episode of "*MST3K*— The Home Game," demonstrated audiences' insider knowledge of the film and its key role in the director's portfolio when, during a revealing scene from *The Day the World Ended* (1955), an audience member quipped "How to build a monster for ten dollars!" (1997, *MST3K*— The Home Game).

Riffing the '50s

So, if we think of "fast, cheap, and out of control" as shorthand for Shaefer's criteria for classic exploitation, Corman's 1950s B movies excelled at the first two, but fell woefully short of the last. Due, in part, to his earlier-stated desire to underscore exploitation with a moral or ethical subtext, Corman's Bs were, in fact, *highly* controlled. They lacked the risk — the sex, drugs, and shocking truth — to which renowned exploiter David Friedman referred when he advised that exploitation films could focus on anything, "as long as it was in bad taste." Not only did they fall short of the forbidden, they didn't even come close, making Corman a stationary target for riffs mocking his failure to incite in his audiences any emotional reaction beyond disappointment. What they gave audiences in exchange, however, was a self-conscious over-the-top treatment of the exploitation genre, in the service of social commentary on "things gone bad" — a hint of the consequences of excess, loss of control, and violations of the "natural" social order of life in the '50s.

Yet, it is precisely these shortcomings that are the stuff of which good riffing is made: Corman's utter lack of production ethics in his early Bs created cultural parody, while his aspirations to earnest social commentary in his exploitation films parodied the genre, as well. Under those circumstances, riffing Corman is only natural. Digging a bit deeper, however, what *MST3K*'s abusive love affair with Corman and his films suggests is the possibility that those two shortcomings, taken together, create a whole that is more than the sum of its parts. Perhaps, Corman's films are, in fact, "good to think" (and riff) because they offer contemporary audiences a vision of America in the 1950s in all its inherent contradiction and self-parody as it came to terms with the era's rapid social change. Like a fun-house mirror, where each shift awkwardly exaggerates another feature, perhaps Corman's films elicit riffs — and laughs — because of the discomfort their only partial warping of perspective creates. At their core, the characters are real. In what they represent, the monsters are real. The costumes, well, they're all Corman.

"Hey! Death looks like dry ice!"

"This is kinda like the *Night of the Living Dead*—without the Living Dead!"

"Did anyone's career survive this film?"

"Roger! Oh, Roger!"

"Wait—Corman is God?" [1997, *MST3K*—The Home Game: *The Day the World Ended*].

REFERENCES

Corman, Roger. *How I Made a Hundred Movies in Hollywood and Never Lost a Dime.* New York: Da Capo Press, 1998.

Gray, Beverly. *Blood-sucking Vampires, Flesh-eating Cockroaches, and Driller Killers: Roger Corman: An Unauthorized Life.* New York: Thunder's Mouth Press, 2004.

Mallon, Jim (director), Michael Nelson (writer), Trace Beaulieu (writer) et al., Episode 311 *It Conquered the World* 1991.

Mallon, Jim (director), Michael Nelson (writer), Trace Beaulieu (writer) et al., Episode 503 *Swamp Diamonds* 1993.

McGee, Mark Thomas. *Roger Corman: The Best of the Cheap Acts.* Jefferson, NC: McFarland & Company, Inc., Publishers, 1988.

Merritt, Greg. *Celluloid Mavericks: A History of American Independent Film.* New York: Thunder's Mouth Press, 2000.

"*MST3K*—The Home Game," *The Day the World Ended* no credits, 1997.

Naha, Ed. *The Films of Roger Corman: Brilliance on a Budget.* New York: Arco Publishing, 1982.

Schaefer, Eric. *Bold! Daring! Shocking! True! A History of Exploitation Films, 1919-1959.* Durham, NC: Duke University Press, 1999.

PART TWO

Specific Films

3

Communists and Cosmonauts
in *Mystery Science Theater 3000*:
De-Camping East Germany's
First Spaceship on Venus/Silent Star

by Sebastian Heiduschke

On December 29, 1990, the Comedy Channel aired *First Spaceship on Venus* as Episode 11 in Season 2 of the weekly comedy show *Mystery Science Theater 3000* (*MST3K*).[1] The film was the first of only four German productions on the show and remained the only East German film that space janitor Joel Robinson and his robotic sidekicks, Tom Servo and Crow T. Robot, riffed during their time on the Satellite of Love (SOL).[2] During a total of eleven seasons, the weekly series used B-movie fare, mostly cheap sci-fi flicks from the 1960s and 1970s, as topics for their snarky comments. This East German film, I argue, only qualified as heckling material because the *MST3K* episode used the dubbed and heavily edited 79-minute U.S. version released under the title *First Spaceship on Venus* instead of the original, 94-minute East German-Polish co-production *Der schweigende Stern* (*Silent Star*) by acclaimed East German director Kurt Maetzig. Cold War editing practices altered *Silent Star,* the expensive and cinematically outstanding science-fiction film from 1960, to regular B-movie fare, making it prime heckling fodder for the three silhouetted viewers on the SOL.[3] Hence, poking fun at a film that in its original version would have been "too good to be Camp" (Sontag, 1967: 278) became possible, since the U.S. edit *First Spaceship* exhibited the features that Susan Sontag describes as necessary for camp.

Sontag's essay "Notes on 'Camp'" appeared in 1964; it explains the fascination with and appreciation of kitsch. She anticipates Theodor Adorno's idea of a "dialectic of the ugly" (Adorno, 1997: 47) insofar as she illustrates how camp attempts to capture the spirit of euphuistic objects through an evaluation of their potential cult value. Essentially, *MST3K* replicates this appreciation in its methodology of "riffing" the original film, that is, in slanting the things that may be seen as "camp" in the films from the 1960s and 1970s. In other words, camp mocks the ostensibly outdated items of a past pop culture, and *MST3K* is a prime practitioner of this style of cultural critique. The success of the show illustrates that receptive audiences cherished the format of *MST3K* and shared the required humor to endure the weekly torture of bad sci-fi films with the crew on SOL.

Aesthetically, the basic premise of *MST3K* dictated a very specific type of film. A mad scientist, Dr. Forrester, who seeks to find the perfect weapon for world domination uses a series of B movies with the hope of driving the world's population insane. He abducts dry-witted janitor Joel Robinson as a guinea-pig for his brainwashing scheme, who, to preserve his sanity, builds a number of robots to keep him company during the screenings on the SOL — and to exchange sarcastic comments. According to *The Mystery Science Theater 3000 Amazing Colossal Episode Guide*, the gross of the films screened consisted of "several truly awful, a few horrifying, and a small handful that can serve as the maw of Hell itself" (Beaulieu, 1996: vii). *Silent Star*, however, the film serving as mold for *First Spaceship*, was exactly the opposite of a B movie. In 1960, East Germany's state-owned studio DEFA (*Deutsche Film-Aktiengesellschaft*) and Poland's Zespol Filmowy "pulled out all production stops for its first science-fiction effort, delivering a quality product in 70mm 'Totalvision' format, four-track sound, and satiny Agfacolor…. When it premiered, … [*Silent Star*] had become the most expensive DEFA film ever made" (Soldovieri, 1998: 385). According to official accounts, it attracted a sizeable 200,000 East German spectators in the first thirteen weeks following its release (Soldovieri 1998).

The edited version *First Spaceship* distributed by Crown International changed the original film's political message of a socialist, peaceful world by changing and eliminating essential dialogue. Even more, the abbreviated version made the cinematography of *Silent Star*— its stunning display of color, extravagant sets, and profligate special effects — appear as gaudy elements of a Hollywood B sci-fi flick. For example, funky spacesuits made the space travelers look like Ewoks; silly props transformed household goods into futuristic gizmos; special effects, such as a semi-intelligent magmatic substance, appeared to be washing back and forth on the landing squad's feet; dialogue rivaled James Kirk's exchanges with Leonard "Bones" McCoy; and arachnid alien robots were now interstellar messengers. These supplied ample riffing opportunity for remarks by Joel and the robots. *Silent Star*, a film "too good to be Camp" because it was neither bad art nor kitsch, but "merit[ed] the most serious admiration and study" (Sontag, 1967: 278) had become *First Spaceship*, a paradigm for *MST3K*; these paradigmatic films, as John King called them, were "almost empirically bad in their inception, by any standards one could choose: writing, acting, editing, directing, lighting" (King, 2007: 46).

Based on Polish science-fiction author Stanislaw Lem's first published novel, *Astronauci*, from 1951, *Silent Star* tells the story of an audacious enterprise undertaken by an international team of renowned specialists to solve the secret message of a spool-like object discovered in the Gobi desert.[4] It is set in 1970, when a team, led by the Soviet commander Arsenew and joined by astronauts Talua from Africa, Chen Yu from China, Robert Brinkmann from Germany, Sikarna from India, the female doctor Sumiko Ogimura from Japan, and Saltyk from Poland, embarks on the international spacecraft *Kosmokrator* to the planet Venus, the origin of the mysterious object. There, they learn the fate of the Venusians, who perished when a massive weapon designed to attack Earth malfunctioned and triggered a nuclear chain reaction that devastated the planet's surface and wiped out the entire civilization. Three astronauts sacrifice their lives during the expedition to allow the remaining crew to return safely to Earth to warn about the dangers of nuclear war. Film scholar Sonja Fritzsche notes that East German director Kurt Maetzig "intended the adventure film to be a statement for peace in the nuclear-armed world of the Cold War" (Fritzsche, 2006a: 374). By making changes to the dialogue, the English soundtrack of *First Spaceship* creates a different interpretation of world peace by re-nationalizing the leader of the expedition as a Frenchman,

Durant, and by converting the (East) German daredevil pilot from Robert Brinkmann to Raimund Brinkman, thus adding a second American — a hero who would sacrifice his life — to the story.

Silent Star sought to imitate the East German literary genre *technischer Zukunftsroman* (hard science fiction novel) with the goal to craft "equivalent, ideologically appropriate" films promoting socialism (Fritzsche, 2006a: 365). The film went through four years of ideological development in East Germany and Poland until both studios and their political watchdogs came to a consensus. A piece of socialist sanctioned art, it belonged to the "pantheon of high culture," as it manifested a message of communist "truth, beauty, and seriousness" (Sontag, 1967: 286). When Crown International released *First Spaceship*, it had stripped *Silent Star* of its political subtext. This, too, suited the parameters *MST3K* required for films to be included, since it looked for those that "emphasiz[ed] texture, sensuous surface, and style at the expense of content" (Sontag, 1967: 278).

Yet why is it so important to scrutinize the differences between *Silent* Star and *First Spaceship* if both versions are sci-fi films from the 1960s? After all, as Jessica Royer suggests, it "is nearly impossible to separate the film shown on an episode of *MST3K* from the heckling that accompanies it. [...] The television audience thus receives the film in a new form and in a new context" (Royer, 2000: 116). Furthermore, had an *MST3K* episode shown the original film, was the response by the riffers likely to have been similar? Some intertextual considerations may help explain that knowledge about the film shown on *MST3K* would have done more than merely offered "insight into the cultural era from which the films come" (Royer, 2000: 117).

The *MST3K* narrative sequences that divide the episode and the riffs of the films in the show reveal that Joel and the robots are confined to a reading of the film through their cultural filter of a U.S. Cold War perspective. For instance, relabeling the East German Brinkmann into the American Brinkman — "the first man on the moon," according to the narrative voiceover in *First Spaceship*— exposes an ironic twist. Only five years before *Silent Star*, director Kurt Maetzig had completed a two-part biopic about East German Communist leader Ernst Thälmann with Günther Simon playing the lead role. The actor who starred as Brinkmann also appeared in more than sixty political DEFA films and epitomized one of East German cinema's cinematic communist martyrs who sacrificed himself for the greater good of the people. His heroic death on Venus thus echoes the Thälmann myth that East German audiences would have understood. *Silent Star* constantly replays familiar political concepts of communism clad in space outfits. Consequently, the edits and changes to *Silent Star* result in a film that no longer reconciles cinematic sci-fi with the literary style of socialist realism (Fritzsche 2006b). *First Spaceship*, in comparison, appears "disengaged, depoliticized — or at least apolitical" and introduces "an attitude which is neutral with respect to content" that can be treated as camp "in terms of the degree of artifice, of stylization" (Sontag, 1964: 277).

The major editing that transformed *Silent Star* into *First Spaceship* takes place in the two sequences addressing the release of the atomic bomb on Hiroshima (Ciesla, 2002: 135–136). This alteration deletes the moral undertone of both sequences and of the entire plot because it changes the Japanese doctor Sumiko from a victim of nuclear Holocaust into a campy female figure resisting an emotional engagement with Brinkmann. In the original version, two sequences right before the lift-off of the *Kosmokrator* show how Sumiko reminds the assembled audience of the cruel 1945 event that ended World War II in the Pacific but had lasting effects on the population and expresses her confidence in the international space mission as an event that will forge the peace-loving (socialist) nations together. Later, Sumiko adds a personal note when she confides to Brinkmann that the radiation following Hiroshima left her unable to have healthy children. These combined six minutes of *Silent Star* shrink to fifty-six seconds of a personal conversation between Brinkmann and Sumiko that obliterates the political and moral victimization of Sumiko in favor of a brief if emotional dialogue about how there is no place for love on a spaceship. The loss of the tragic context gives way to "a victory of 'style' over 'content,' 'aesthetics' over 'morality,' of irony over tragedy" (Sontag, 1964: 287) when Crow T. Robot comments upon Sumiko's pledge, "we must not speak about that [love] ever" with, "let's talk about your pancreas" against the background of Brinkmann's heartbeat displayed on a medical monitor overhead.

Serious issues such as the reconfiguration of race and the addition of an at least subliminal layer of racial segregation in *First Spaceship* are defused in the *MST3K* version by way of disguising the potentially problematic scenes. Joel and the robots point the viewers' attention away from the action onto the background, riffing that instead of the potentially sticky sequences. For instance, the editing and dubbing practices used to create *First Spaceship* distort the friendly camaraderie between the African Talua and the Soviet Arsenew in *Silent Star*: radical cuts shorten an extended scene of sixty-one seconds to barely thirty-four seconds, reducing a dialogue among equals to Arsenew ordering the black African to "recheck the radar, Talua," to which Talua replies, "right away, Professor" (Mallon 1990, Episode 211). Burghard Ciesla explains this change from equal blacks and whites into a subordinate black and a dominant white with U.S. segregation politics that were still prevalent in the 1960s (Ciesla, 2002: 132–133). Tom Servo distracts the 1990s audience when he comments on a technician in the background, who "is wearing a T-shirt — it says 'T.'" Here, *MST3K* reaches the pinnacle of camp: "to dethrone the serious" while proposing "a comic vision of the world" (Sontag, 1964: 288).

The radical removal of the quarter hour that made *Silent Star* into *First Spaceship* influenced patterns of gender representation, as well. Whereas the female Japanese doctor Sumiko Ogimura plays an equal role next to her male space travelers in *Silent Star*, in *First Spaceship*, her role is reduced to a supporting figure taking care of the household duties on the spaceship, such as providing the male astronauts with food and tending to their injuries. A total of more than seven minutes of Sumiko's dialogue was edited out from *Silent Star* (Ciesla, 2002: 135–136), putting her in line with the other female supporting roles. Now, she appears in *First Spaceship* in a traditionally female profession, similar to the news commentator for the TV station "Intervision" and the radio operator at the moon base Luna 3 (reminiscent of the telephone operators in the time before automated dialing was introduced). Before the cuts, those dialogues showed her as an independent, strong-willed, and emancipated person. For example, when *Kosmokrator* passes the location where Sumiko's husband suffered a deadly accident while working on the moon base Luna III, the Chinese linguist describes Sumiko as a role model for China's women because of her independence and willpower. *Silent Star* thus represented East German cinema's approach to "equal" representation of women in film. Based on Lenin's ideological premises, "women's equality was constitutionally guaranteed" (Berghahn, 2005: 175), and already in the 1950s, forty percent of East Germany's workers were female (Kolinsky 1993). Typically, screen heroines also worked to contribute to communist success, and "gender relationships are portrayed as devoid of sensuality but full of socialist consciousness-raising discourse" (Berghahn, 2005: 178). Read in this context, Sumiko occupies a position as screen heroine in *Silent Star*, whereas *First Spaceship* relegates her to "the roles society considered appropriate for women during the 1950s and '60s and the gendered typing of the characters women play in these movies" (Royer, 2000: 117), inviting a stereotypical reading of the women in *First Spaceship* for the three hecklers of *MST3K*. Even though Sumiko's original role in *Silent Star* is by no means limited to the traditional submissive gender roles of the 1950s female, *First Spaceship* presents itself as testimonial of 1950s misogynistic stereotyping.

In the eyes of Jessica Royer, misogyny is precisely what makes *First Spaceship* appeal to the all-male audience on SOL as women in *MST3K* are "ridiculed for assertiveness as well as passivity [...], immediately reduced to sexual objects" (Royer, 2000: 123). Feminist film theorist Laura Mulvey explains this strategy of producing cinematic gender stereotypes as "language of the dominant patriarchal order" (Mulvey, 1999: 835) that duplicates the role of women as object of the male gaze. "The woman displayed has functioned on two levels," Mulvey writes, "as erotic object for the characters within the screen story, and as erotic object for the spectator within the auditorium" (Mulvey, 1999: 838). Picked up by *MST3K*, Joel and the robots occupy the space of the male spectator, and in their "pre-reading" of the films for audiences through the process of riffing, they appear to display signs of the male gaze that reduces women to erotic objects. Indicative of this sexist behavior in *First Spaceship* are comments by the two robots of "horny — heini — homey — heenee" and "hrrrr" (Mallon 1990, Episode 211) accompanying the on-screen event of Sumiko undressing to undergo an artificially-induced sleep period in preparation for the launch. These utterances replicate sounds men produce when they objectify the female body through gazing; still, they appear comical coming from the mouths of the two robots who — despite being gender coded though the mimicking of an objectifying male gaze — are only parroting stereotypical male behavior. However, the scene in question is void of an erotic subtext in *Silent Star*: we only see Sumiko's nude back for the fraction of a second when she disrobes to get underneath the white sheets, wearing white underwear that completely cover her buttocks. The alterations allow the robots to misread Sumiko as stereotypical woman "in quotation marks" (Sontag, 1967: 280) and appreciate her in a campy fashion as "sexless" body (Sontag, 1967: 279).

It is interesting that Cold War politics paved the way for an East German film to be included as part of a pop-cultural tradition on American TV. Without the severe editing that removed fifteen minutes from the film to retell the story of an international peace mission to Venus as an American space adventure, only three West German films had found their way onto the screen of the SOL. Unbeknownst to American audiences, the supposedly low-budget production served to them under the title *First Spaceship on Venus* topped the production budgets of two studios as *Silent Star*, was directed by a proliferate, famous director, included some of the biggest stars of Eastern European cinema, and aimed to combine both a socialist-didactic approach with first-class entertainment genre cinema. The question remains if *Silent Star* would have provided a similar riffing experience for *MST3K*. When the New York–based distributor First Run Features, according to their own website, "acquired a reputation for its controversial catalog of daring independent fiction and non-fiction films" — also acquired the U.S. distribution rights to *Silent Star* in 2005 along with two other DEFA films, they called them "provocative, hugely influential and highly entertaining, [...] mind-bending stories of space exploration, alien races and utopian dreams (or nightmares)" (First Run Features 2005). North American film encyclopedias acknowledged the extraordinary quality of the films as "critically acclaimed serious space film with good special effects" and the "first influential post-war space opera from Eastern Europe" (DEFA Film Library 2005). On the other hand, some critics reviewing the box set of DEFA's sci-fi flicks displayed a lack of historical awareness and limited their viewing to a hermeneutic reading of their visual experience. They described DEFA's sci-fi as "chintzy, freaky, [...] exceedingly nerdy [...] and absolutely tripped out" (First Run Features 2005), descriptors often used for camp films. In 1990, *MST3K* would have snubbed *Silent Star* because of its clear commitment to communist ideals, whereas in 2005, fifteen years after the collapse of the Soviet Union and the end of the Cold War, it and similar films from the Cold War period have now shifted into camp.

NOTES

1. In this essay I follow the practice to count the 1988/89 episodes aired on KTMA-TV as Season 0.
2. The three other German productions or co-productions were *The Castle of Fu Manchu* (Mallon 1992, Episode 323), *Secret Agent Super Dragon* (Beaulieu 1993, Episode 504), and *Hamlet* (Murphy 1999, Episode 1009).
3. See, for instance, Warren 1982.
4. I was unable to locate the bibliographic information for the 1951 Polish edition.

REFERENCES

Adorno, Theodor. *Aesthetic Theory.* in Gretel Adorno and Rolf Tiedemann eds., Robert Hullot-Kentor trans. Minneapolis: U of Minnesota P, 1997.
Beaulieu, Trace (director), Michael Nelson (writer), Paul Chaplin (writer) et al., Episode 504 *Secret Agent Super Dragon* 1993.
Beaulieu, Trace. *The Mystery Science Theater 3000 Amazing Colossal Episode Guide.* New York: Bantam, 1996.
Berghahn, Daniela. *Hollywood Behind the Wall: The Cinema of East Germany.* Manchester: Manchester UP, 2005.
Ciesla, Burghard. "Droht der Menschheit Vernichtung? *Der schweigende Stern — First Spaceship on Venus*: Ein Vergleich." Ralf Schenk, and Erika Richter, eds. *Apropos Film: 2002.* Berlin: Bertz, 2002: 121–136.
DEFA Film Library. "The Silent Star." *DEFA Film Library* 2005. Accessed 4/2/2010. http://www.defafilmlibrary.com/product_info.php?manufacturers_id=30&products_id=68&osCsid=93e37a2e7863e5ceb951b447aa6b189d.
First Run Features. *DEFA Sci-Fi Collection* 2005. Accessed 4/2/2010. http://firstrunfeatures.com/defascifiboxsetdvd.html.
Fritzsche, Sonja. "East Germany's *Werkstatt Zukunft*: Futurology and the Science Fiction Films of *defa-futurum*." *German Studies Review.* 29: 2 (May 2006a): 367–385.
Fritzsche, Sonja. *Science Fiction Literature in East Germany.* New York: Peter Lang, 2006b.
King, John. "*Mystery Science Theater 3000*, Media Consciousness, and the Postmodern Allegory of the Captive Audience." *Journal of Film & Video.* 59: 4 (2007): 37–53.
Kolinsky, Eva. *Women in Contemporary Germany: Life, Work and Politics.* 2nd ed. Oxford: Berg, 1993.
Lem, Stanislaw. *Astronauci.* Warsaw: Czytelnik, 1953.
Maetzig, Kurt (director), Günther Simon, Yoko Tani, et al. *Der schweigende Stern.* DEFA, 1960.
Mallon, Jim (director), Trace Beaulieu (writer), Michael Nelson (writer), et al. Episode 211 *First Spaceship on Venus* 1990.
Mallon, Jim (director), Michael Nelson (writer), Paul Chaplin (writer), et al. Episode 323 *The Castle of Fu Manchu* 1992.
Mulvey, Laura. "Visual Pleasure and Narrative Cinema." In Leo Braudy, and Marshall Cohen, eds. *Film Theory and Criticism: Introductory Readings.* New York: Oxford UP, 1999: 833–844.
Murphy, Kevin (director), Murphy, Kevin (writer), Bridget Jones (writer) et al., Episode 1009 *Hamlet* 1999.
Royer, Jessica. "What's Happening on Earth? *Mystery Science Theater 3000* as Reflection of Gender Roles and Attitudes Toward Women." In Elyce Helford, ed. *Fantasy Girls: Gender in the New Universe of Science Fiction and Fantasy Television.* Lanham: Rowman, 2000: 115–133.
Soldovieri, Stefan. "Socialists in Outer Space: East German Film's Venusian Adventure." *Film History.* 10 (1998): 382–398.
Sontag, Susan. "Notes on 'Camp.'" *Against Interpretation and Other Essays.* New York: Farrar, 1967. 275–292.
Warren, Bill, with research associate Bill Thomas. *Keep Watching the Skies! American Science Fiction Movies of the Fifties.* Volumes I and II. Jefferson, NC: McFarland & Company, Inc., Publishers, 1982, 1986.

4

The Semiotics of Spaceflight on the Satellite of Love

by Matthew H. Hersch

Of the public intellectuals the *New York Times* canvassed in July 1969 to provide their opinion of the first landing by humans on the surface of the Moon, the words of historian Lewis Mumford were neither the most dismissive nor the most provocative. Those belonged to Pablo Picasso ("It means nothing to me. I have no opinion about it, and I don't care") (Picasso 1969: 6). Mumford's criticism, though, was worse: he found the landing not irrelevant but dangerous. *Apollo 11*'s dramatic rocket flight was "a symbolic act of war," "deliberately planned as a means of swiftly perfecting the equipment for total examination," and cloaked in scientific aspirations that "shrivel under rational examination and candid moral appraisal."

To Mumford, the apparatus of spaceflight served no purpose but to harm humanity. Gripped by a collective insanity, though, Americans were cheering the Moon landing like a "national sporting event whose excitement is augmented by the fact that, as in speed racing, it provides the ever-present possibility of a spectacularly violent death" (Mumford 1969: 6).

Years later, a janitor in the kind of technoindustrial laboratory-factory Mumford would have criticized found himself a victim of the militarism, technophilia, and dubious science of spaceflight. Before he could realize what was happening to him, Joel Robinson (Joel Hodgson) was blasted into Earth orbit by the evil Dr. Clayton Forrester (Trace Beaulieu) and Dr. Laurence Erhardt (Josh Weinstein), first in a fit of vindictiveness, and later, to determine the psychological effects of watching bad movies in space. Twenty years after humankind's first voyage to the Moon, the basic-cable cult series *Mystery Science Theater 3000* presented audiences with the most bleak portrayal of spaceflight ever to appear on television. Imprisoned on a gigantic spacecraft, amused only by the robot friends he builds to assuage his loneliness, Joel laments his victimization and mocks the science fiction films inflicted upon him, in which all of the excesses of his own culture are laid bare. In dissecting these films, Joel and friends (a talented team of writer/performers) poke fun not only at bad acting and shoddy camera work, but the hypermasculinity, nationalism, and technological utopianism that created his spacecraft and motivated Cold War space exploration.

Inside the Satellite of Love

Low-wage corporate drones unwittingly shot into orbit by the Gizmonic Institute, series host Robinson and his successor, Mike Nelson (Michael J. Nelson), are not the typical stowaways of the "reluctant" astronaut genre. Trapped on the Satellite of Love (a vehicle named in tribute to the Lou Reed ballad) and forced to watch bad movies, Joel and Mike are Warholian social critics who use their mastery of American popular culture to identify the absurdities of big-budget space exploration. Inspired by the countercultural space cinema of the 1970s — movies that featured lonely, frazzled astronauts longing for home — *MST3K* is a satire within a satire. The men's experience in space is itself a riff on American science fiction cinema, which they spend their time critiquing. Two tragedies intended by their directors to be sober representations of plausible space missions, *Rocketship X-M* and *Space Travelers* explicitly address criticisms of space exploration, including its loneliness and inherent dangers.

While criticism of the Space Race was unrelenting during the Cold War in the nation's editorial pages and science journals, American television audiences were largely spared the worst of it. Popular media of the 1960s (often encouraged by the National Aeronautics and Space Administration) emphasized the heroism of the astronauts and the "aura of competence" surrounding their activities (McCurdy 1997: 84). Stock astronaut-types in *The Twilight Zone* and *I Dream of Jeannie* provided audiences with imperturbably masculine (if romantically aloof) go-getters who could be relied upon to face down the danger of spaceflight and worry themselves little with the reasons for such adventures (Sobchack 1990: 108). By the 1970s, more nuanced evocations of spaceflight had begun to slowly displace the heroic narratives of popular culture in the previous decade.

Filmmakers of the late 1960s and early 1970s increasingly dared to recast the astronaut, once the epitome of squareness, as progressive, dissenting voices in societies losing their connection to the organic. *Silent Running* (1972) placed a traditional literary character in an interplanetary setting, with disturbing results. In *Silent Running*, futuristic space botanist Freeman Lowell (Bruce Dern), obviously modeled on American naturalist Henry David Thoreau, wanders through deep space tending a garden, accompanied only by his own paranoia and a cadre of helpful robots (Trumbull 1972). *Silent Running* would prove a significant influence upon Hodgson, especially in the creation of his own off-beat on-screen persona and *MST3K*'s friendly automatons. "I think the most direct link is to the Douglas Trumble film *Silent Running*, which had a huge influence on me as a kid," Hodgson recalled in one interview. "I think Bruce Dern did a great job, and it's such great subject matter — a hippie in space. I knew I was backward engineering ideas from that film and as time went on..." ("20 Questions Only Joel Hodgson Can Answer about *MST3K*" 1999).

Technology run amok is the running theme throughout the series, as Joel finds himself tortured remotely by the mad scientists of "Deep 13": a vault-like sublevel of the Gizmonic Institute strewn with apparatus and other laboratory detritus. In the 1953 adaptation of H. G. Wells' *War of the Worlds*, Dr. Clayton Forrester was a benevolent scientist who labors to save humanity from invading Martians. Beaulieu's Forrester, though, is an Einstein-haired misanthrope more interested in controlling the world than saving it. The *MST3K* audience learns relatively little about the Gizmonic Institute during the show: overhead shots of the institute appearing briefly during *MST3K*'s credits suggest a cross between a Ford Motor Company's River Rouge Plant and a space-age amusement park.

Details about the design and construction of the SOL are also tantalizingly spare, but its bone-like appearance — two large compartments separated by imposing corridors — suggests the interplanetary vehicle *Discovery* of *2001: A Space Odyssey* or *Silent Running*'s space freighter *Valley Forge*. According to Beaulieu (who crafted the SOL model), a commercial mining starship depicted in the 1979 film *Aliens* was a major inspiration for the ship ("20 Questions for Trace Beaulieu" 1999). As with many cinematic space vessels of the 1970s, cabin interiors also evoke the austere palate of a World War II warship. (*Silent Running*, in fact, was actually filmed on the decommissioned USS *Valley Forge*, an Essex-class aircraft carrier.) Even with its dingy 1970s aesthetic, the thousand-foot vessel is an impressive bit of industrial design. Like naval vessels, the ship contains numerous compartments serving different functions: at one end of the vessel, the crew bides its time in between films, which appear without warning in a theater that Joel, Mike and friends must enter through a long, imposing corridor to complete their duties.

Chipper despite his predicament, Joel remains respectful and childlike, addressing Dr. Forrester as "sir" and submitting to his to experimental objectives. Even in captivity, Joel is creative and resilient. In his free time, he creates a number of inventions (of dubious utility) out of spare parts, inexplicably exchanging knowledge of their workings with his captors in Deep 13. Joel also appears to have made significant modifications to the ship's original equipment, including the construction of a variety of robot "friends": Cambot, Gypsy, Tom Servo, and Crow T. Robot. Joel's powers, though, are not infinite: his robots are cobbled together from spare or cannibalized parts (gumball machines, bowling pins), and they require frequent maintenance. Gypsy's intellectual abilities are especially degraded, as she must utilize her cognitive faculties to run the SOL's "higher functions."

The aesthetic of the *MST3K* is barely above that of the films it skewers. Many of the films Joel and company much watch were developed as low-budget B movies: lesser movies in two-film matinees crafted with hastily-written scripts, semiprofessional actors, and rudimentary recycled effects, often padded with stock footage. While certain of the movies seem to have been labors of love by eclectic (if unskilled) directors, others are shameless exploitation films intended to vaguely resemble popular contemporary motion pictures about bikers, beatniks, and space monsters. Among this collection of misfires, though, are a small number of movies with solid pedigrees, decent casts, and respectable production values. Two American films about space exploration, *Rocketship X-M* (1950) and *Space Travelers* (1969), are significant entries in the *MST3K* canon despite being respectable artistic products. Ironically, both films are inadvertent cautionary tales about spaceflight: celebrating its technology while demonstrating its tremendous human cost.

Episode 201: *Rocketship X-M*

The years immediately following the end of World War II saw a brief window of enthusiasm for the possibilities of interplanetary rocket travel, encouraged by German military rocketry experiments during the War and cultivated by émigrés like Willy Ley and Wernher von Braun in the years that followed (Neufeld 2007: 252–59). Stand-outs among these films were many with impressive screenwriting talent, technical accuracy, and surprising effects shots. *Rocketship X-M*, though, was not one of them. Written and filmed to premiere prior to the release of 1950's *Destination Moon* (an impressive achievement that brought together the talents of producer George Pàl, science fiction author Robert Heinlein, and space fantasy artist Chester Bonestall), *Rocketship X-M* was a shameless effort by budget filmmaker Robert Lippert to cash in on anticipation surrounding the former film (Warren 2009: 223). With a set design inspired by a 1949 spaceship spread in *Life* magazine, *Rocketship X-M* was neither the worst movie *MST3K* would skewer nor the most brain-dead. Miraculously shot in 18 days on a budget of $94,000 (one-fifth the budget of *Destination Moon*), *Rocketship X-M* nonetheless emerged as a respectable science fiction thriller with a substantial lead actor (Lloyd Bridges) and grossed over $1 million at the box office ("Love in a Spaceship at Criterion," 1950: 23).

Lewis Mumford's fear that all space technology was in effect military technology receives powerful support from *Rocketship X-M*, which recycled surplus aircraft equipment for sets, German V-2 rocket footage for special effects, and U.S. military clothing for costumes. Presaging a generation of similar films (and America's own astronaut selection eight years later), *Rocketship X-M*'s writer/director Kurt Neumann placed the crew under the stewardship of Air Force pilot Floyd Graham (Bridges), who embraces what would become the American astronaut archetype of the 1960s: a virile military man unafraid and unbowed even under circumstances of great stress. The film's narrative of spaceflight is also complicated by warnings of the dangers of nuclear war; uncredited scriptwriting support by blacklisted author Dalton Trumbo likely elevated the film's message, which both encourages space exploration and warns of the potential misuse of rocket technology for nuclear war, an idea only in its infancy in 1950 (Warren 2009: 708–11).

Originally airing on September 22, 1990, Joel and the Bots' assault on *Rocketship X-M* was a milestone for the series, introducing the performer lineup that would carry *MST3K* until Hodgson's departure from the show in 1993 (Mallon 1990, Episode 201). Also making its first appearance in the episode was "Rocket Number Nine," an external camera on the SOL named for a composition by experimental jazz artist Herman Poole Blount, better known as Sun Ra. The composition, from Sun Ra's 1972 album *Space Is the Place*, is one of the more famous of the musician's afrofuturist works, which conceptualized spaceflight in unabashed utopian terms. As to be expected, though, Joel and the Bots mercilessly mock the ambiguous and conflicting themes of *Rocketship X-M*'s voyage, especially the weird mix of belligerence and altruism espoused by its crew. The crew's mission is less about exploration than domination of the heavens: the ship's inventor hopes that "an unassailable base could be established on the Moon to control world peace," or as Joel describes: "our kind of world peace." The mission is announced amid great secrecy to journalists who are barred from reporting the event, and the rocket launches at night. "Tonight we will launch the first manned spaceship" the mission's leader announces, prompting Joel to retort, "then we love."

Throughout the film, the tropes of American spaceflight receive a thorough thrashing, including frequent riffs on Bridge's insipid, libidinous astronaut Graham and the ship's navigator, who they address as "Dirk Square Jaw" in honor of his blankness and chiseled features. The American space program's unseemly association with wartime Nazi rocketry also earns a vigorous mocking. NASA, during the 1950s and 1970s, drew heavily upon the experience of German émigré engineers like von Braun, despite their association with Adolf Hitler's despised wartime V-2 rocketry program. The film's use of stock footage of V-2 launches and the sight of a character who vaguely resembles von Braun observing the rocket's liftoff in a blockhouse gives rise to repeated gags about von Braun and American spaceflight's German origins.

At once pro- and anti-militarist, the screenplay is a hodge-podge of contradictions. Threatened with legal action if they depicted a flight to the Moon, Lippert was forced to order a last minute change to the screenplay, concocting a propulsion problem aboard the rocket that sends the astronauts accidentally to Mars, where they discover a civilization that has destroyed itself in a nuclear war (Warren 2009: 709). This plot twist injects some much-needed action into the script, as well as opportunities for various characters to decry the militarism that seems to have destroyed the Martian society. After radiation-scarred Martians kill several members of the crew, Graham, the badly injured navigator, and chemist Dr. Lisa van Horn (Osa Massen) return from their journey with their fuel supply so exhausted that they are unable to slow their descent. By this point in the film, Graham and van Horn have begun a tepid romance; the scene depicting their plunge to Earth is intended to be mournful but inspiring, as the heroic astronauts embrace and radio important engineering information to ground control before they perish. Humankind, the audience is informed by another character, will continue the exploration of space, an ostensibly rousing speech later duplicated in *Space Travelers*. For Joel and the Bots, though, the twin themes of space travel are not exploration and love, but claustrophobia and annihilation.

Watching the three remaining crewmembers of Rocketship X-M plummet to their deaths at the end of their ill-fated flight is, ultimately, too much for crew of the SOL, who leave the theater during the movie's closing credits in utter disgust and dismay at their own predicament. Earlier in the episode, Joel had attempted unsuccessfully to convince Deep 13 trainee "TV's Frank" to release them from orbital imprisonment, only to be foiled by Dr. Forrester. Reflecting on the anticlimactic dénouement of the film they had just finished watching, Crow (Beaulieu) is crestfallen, and Joel contemplates the only movie that, under the circumstances, would have made them feel worse:

> CROW: Boy, nothing more depressing than being locked in a capsule watching a movie about people dying in a capsule.
> JOEL: Yeah, why don't you just show us *Marooned*?
> FORRESTER: We couldn't get it.

Slipping out of character in Episode 201, Dr. Forrester reveals an essential quandary of the producers of *MST3K*: that the show can only air films that are in the public domain or, given the production team's tiny budget, inexpensive to license. Ironically, two years later, *MST3K* would acquire a print of *Marooned* intended for cable distribution, which, at least temporarily, had fallen out of copyright, enabling the show's writers to deconstruct the film as they had originally intended.

Episode 402: *Space Travelers (Marooned)*

By 1969, film of space travelers was commonplace on television, as NASA's real astronauts (and their Soviet counterparts) racked up a series of successful Earth orbital and lunar missions, culminating in the *Apollo* landings of 1969–72. Among the most technically accurate (and, as turns out, influential) space films of the 1960s was Jim Sturges's *Marooned*, which arrived in theaters in November 1969, days before the flight of *Apollo 12*. The film was a Columbia Pictures adaptation of a 1964 novel by Martin Caidin about a Soviet cosmonaut who helps to rescue an American astronaut stranded in orbit when his retrorocket misfires (Caidin 1964). Updated to incorporate space technology of the late–1960s period, the film version of *Marooned* placed a three-man crew in an *Apollo* spacecraft stricken with the failure of its main engine. Complicating the crisis for the men of *Ironman 1* is their fatigue and mental collapse: having just completed a long-duration stay at an orbiting space station, they are unfit for complex duty. Despite the near-hopelessness of the crew's predicament, NASA hastily organizes a rescue mission that receives unexpected assistance from a Soviet spacecraft already in orbit.

Unlike *MST3K* detritus like *Manos: The Hands of Fate*, the film *Marooned* was critically respected for its cinematic achievements, especially its visual effects, for which it won an Academy Award, with additional nominations for cinematography and sound. "This ambitious, conscientious Columbia movie is admirably intelligent all the way," Howard Thompson wrote for the *New York Times*, praising the film for its brilliant direction and "scientific savvy" (Thompson 1969: 65). The film featured a high-power cast of Hollywood notables (including Gregory Peck as a NASA manager and Gene Hackman as unhinged astronaut named Buzz Lloyd) cast as what appear to be thinly fictionalized versions of real NASA personnel. Authentic set design and plot details included a visit by the crew to the future Skylab Orbital Workshop, then in its design stages. *Marooned* also played a direct role in convincing American and Soviet authorities to conduct a joint orbital mission with NASA, which actually flew as the 1975 *Apollo-Soyuz* Test Project. Insider appeal and special effects, though, could not compensate for the film's overacting, plodding narrative, and extended suffocation sequences. Thompson wondered about its "antiseptic" feel and odd lack of real thrills.

Space Travelers, a poorly-edited version of the film, provided *MST3K's* writers with a rare opportunity and a formidable challenge: to skewer an Oscar winner far better made than any film they had previously encountered. In the episode, which originally aired on June 6, 1992, *MST3K's* writers rose to the challenge with a series of thoughtful riffs and host segments directed less at the filmmakers' lack of technical skills (for they were quite sufficient) than on the American space agenda of the 1960s, which the film recapitulates while inadvertently criticizing (Mallon 1992). Utterly unfazed by the absurdity of three astronauts marooned in space mocking a film about three astronauts marooned in space, Joel and the Bots substitute biting social commentary for the usual wisecracks about wayward stage hands and amateur thespians. Their remarks encompass a wide array of commentary on the space program in general, especially on the stereotypical pilots and government hacks who parade across the screen, barking orders and dishing trite declarations. In this effort, *Space Travelers* is a soft target: its script reduced language to unemotional technological particulars, celebrating men among the crew who respond to the stress of their travails without the slightest bit of sentimentality (Sobchack 1987: 152–53). These jokes begin immediately, with a turgid launch sequence that works, Crow declares, sarcastically, because it creates characters — anonymous, helmeted astronauts; rows of identical engineers — that the audience really cares about.

Another running gag by Crow evokes the emphasis within military technologies on systems of command and control. Like the air defense computers Paul Edwards describes in the *Closed World*, the computer-controlled instrumentation of the Mission Control Center in Houston, Texas, and *Ironman I's Apollo* Command Module contain a bewildering assortment of switches intended to provide crewmembers with a synthetic view of their environment and the illusion of control over it (Edwards 1996). The jokes reach a crescendo in a host segment in which Crow, exploiting Beaulieu's excellent Peck impression, recreates Peck's performance in the film while Joel and Tom Servo pretend to float alongside him in a cardboard spacecraft. In Crow's imagination, the cockpit instrumentation not only controls vital ship systems but allows the astronauts influence over their prestige and legacy:

CROW: "'Hold' on your 'power' and 'glory' switches."
JOEL: "Roger on that 'hold' on glory, sir."

The capsule can even control dreaded (and, in *Space Travelers*, unseen) hippies, with switches for "SDS dissident controls," a reference to the radical Students for a Democratic Society, which dissolved amid chaotic infighting months before *Marooned*'s release in theaters.

The irony of course, is that feelings of power provided by the Command Module's switches and dials is illusory: *Space Travelers*, like *Rocketship X-M*, is an unintentional story of technological failure, as machines intended to operate quietly and reliably in the background nonetheless fail catastrophically. Like Joel and Frank's invented exchanges, they appear to work only on paper, and garner respect as long as they are not turned on (a common criticism lobbed at the military technology of the Cold War). Science fiction films of the 1950s and 1960s often treated spaceships (all of which were manufactured with nonexistent technology) as thoroughly routine and domesticated spaces, so as not to detract from the human dramas occurring within them (Sobchack 1987: 73). *Rocketship X-M*'s craft, though, is a prototype Moon rocket launched without any real data on fuel performance, and it sputters to a halt halfway through its journey. And *Space Travelers'* *Ironman 1*'s *Apollo* spacecraft is literally a death trap.

Little in the way of narrative occurs in *Space Travelers*: the badly mutilated edit eliminates several important scenes and a subplot involving a Russian spacecraft that may be able to help the stranded Americans if it can change its orbit (which appears, at first impossible). Instead, Joel and Bots groan through several excruciating scenes of an overacting Hackman suffocating in a space capsule, punctuated by cutaways to board meetings by NASA managers that generally end in solemn nodding by Peck (to Crow's delight). Ultimately, though, NASA's chief astronaut prevails upon his superiors to launch a successful rescue mission, which receives unexpected help from the Soviet craft and its lone cosmonaut. Joel and the Bots, who are already familiar with *Marooned*, understand the final, seemingly nonsensical plot twists that resolve the crisis.

Short of air awaiting rescue, the crew of *Ironman 1* realize they must sacrifice one life to save the rest, a burden eventually assumed by the spacecraft's commander, played by Richard Crenna. The scene prompts Joel to contemplate his own mortality and the likelihood that, like the space crew in the film, he and the Bots might one day need to sacrifice one of their number to preserve the rest. Instead of cultivating his melancholy, the Bots splash cold water on Joel's with a dispiriting observation. Only Joel needs air to breathe, and only Joel faces danger in space. Joel is the only non-machine on the SOL, the only one who does not "belong" there, and the only liability in the event of trouble. Robots, are, instead, perfectly suited to the harsh environment of the cosmos. It is Joel who is out of place in space, and the Bots have lost no sleep over his fate.

The observation begs the obvious question: why has NASA subjected the very human crew of *Ironman 1* to such tortures? Violent death — murder, explosion, asphyxiation —figure prominently in both *Rocketship X-M* and *Space Travelers*, with neither film providing, at least to the *MST3K* writers' satisfaction, a suitable justification for the astronauts' sacrifices. Toward the end of the *Space Travelers*, with the astronauts' situation looking increasingly bleak, Peck provides a short speech to reporters repeating the familiar rationales of discovery and sacrifice unchanged since *Rocketship X-M*: an exorable human need to explore. In one host segment, Joel and friends offer another common rationalization for spaceflight: the numerous supposed "spin-off technologies" that the space program has supposedly incubated. The gang then rattle off a nonsensical series of examples of consumer products having no conceivable connection to NASA (including "spats" and the "Swedish steam cooker"). Ultimately, Joel mockingly concludes, "the Space Race has contributed so much to our life that we really couldn't even understand it all. All we know is that it's friendly and good for us and we need it really, really a lot" (Mallon 1992). For Mumford, Joel's conclusion is exactly the kind of cognitive dissonance that kept America's space program alive.

Conclusion

By the early 1990s, America's human spaceflight program had transformed from a "crash" project aimed at exploration of the Moon and planets, to a permanent infrastructure offering increasingly routine (though occasionally deadly) visits to Earth orbit. Like NASA, Joel is in limbo on the Satellite of Love, exploring space for reasons more egomaniacal than practical. Why should humans travel in space? Ultimately, neither *Rocketship X-M* nor *Space Travelers* provides a convincing answer, and after watching these films, Joel and friends are left even more despondent about their predicament. Yet despite their despair, all of the space travelers depicted in these *MST3K* episodes carry on with their work: inventing, exploring, and reporting their findings: especially Joel, who would appear to have little reason to communicate so faithfully with Deep 13. While critical of the visions of space travel depicted in the movies they watch, the crew of the Satellite of Love do not evince the kind of indignant dismissal of the space program found among Mumford or many other commentators of the 1960s. What they mock are spaceflight's associations with the worst excess of American culture: bad science, xenophobia, militarism, exaggerated gender norms. In their loving and encyclopedic knowledge of space fiction, *MST3K*'s writers reveal themselves to be, not rather harsh critics, but disappointed admirers. Spaceflight, they had been told, would usher in utopia. Instead, it produced madness in those who supported it and death for many of the brave few who attempted it. Ultimately, there is little logic to their continued efforts: rather, Dr. Forrester and Joel build machines to explore space for reasons that are not entirely rational — a lonely outcast's desire to create a world of his own.

REFERENCES

MST3K Episodes
Mallon, Jim (director), Kevin Murphy (writer), Joel Hodgson (writer), et al. Episode 201 *Rocketship X-M* 1990.
Mallon, Jim (director), Kevin Murphy (writer), Joel Hodgson (writer), et al. Episode 402 *Space Travelers* 1992.

Films
Haskin, Byron (director), H.G. Wells, Barré Lyndon. *The War of the Worlds*. Paramount Pictures, 1953.
Kubrick, Stanley (director), Stanley Kubrick, Arthur C. Clarke, et al. *2001: A Space Odyssey*. Metro-Goldwyn-Mayer, 1968.
Scott, Ridley (director), Dan O'Bannon, Ronald Shusett, et al. *Alien*. Twentieth Century–Fox Productions, 1979.
Sturges, John (director), *Marooned*. Columbia Pictures Corporation, 1969.
Trumbull, Douglas (director), Deric Washburn, Michael Cimino, et al. *Silent Running*. Universal Pictures, 1972.

Published Sources
Caidin, Martin. *Marooned*. New York: Dutton, 1964.
Edwards, Paul N. *The Closed World: Computers and the Politics of Discourse in Cold War America*. Cambridge: MIT Press, 1996.
"Love in a Spaceship at Criterion." *New York Times*, May 27, 1950: 23.
McCurdy, Howard E. *Space and the American Imagination*. Washington, D.C.: Smithsonian Institution Press, 1997.

Mumford, Lewis. "No: 'a Symbolic Act of War....'" *New York Times*, July 21, 1969: 6.

Neufeld, Michael J. *Von Braun: Dreamer of Space, Engineer of War.* New York: A.A. Knopf, 2007.

Picasso, Pablo. "Pablo Picasso." *New York Times*, July 21, 1969: 6.

Sobchack, Vivian Carol. *Screening Space: The American Science Fiction Film.* New York: Ungar, 1987.

_____. "The Virginity of Astronauts: Sex and the Science Fiction Film." In Annette Kuhn, ed. *Alien Zone: Cultural Theory and Contemporary Science Fiction Cinema.* New York: Verso, 1990, 108.

Thompson, Howard. "'Marooned,' Space Film, Opens the New Ziegfeld: Story Built on Perils of Planetary Trips." *New York Times*, December 19, 1969: 65.

"20 Questions Only Joel Hodgson Can Answer about *MST3K.*" *Satellite News* January, 1999. Accessed 4/1/2010. http://www.*MST3K*info.com/satnews/brains/20q.html.

"20 Questions for Trace Beaulieu." *Satellite News* Winter 1999. Accessed 4/1/2010. http://www.*MST3K*info.com/satnews/brains/20q.html.

Warren, Bill, with research associate Bill Thomas. *Keep Watching the Skies! American Science Fiction Movies of the Fifties; the 21st Century Edition.* Jefferson, NC: McFarland & Company, Inc., Publishers, 2009.

5

Resurrecting the Dead: Revival of Forgotten Films through Appropriation

by Cheryl Hicks

Despite protestations by its creators that it was merely a cow town puppet show, for ten seasons *Mystery Science Theater 3000* provided audiences with a shining example of the postmodern aesthetic in action. Literary critic Terry Eagleton provided a definition describing what qualifies as postmodern, stating, "There is, perhaps, a degree of consensus that the typical post-modernist artifact is playful, self-ironizing.... Its stance towards cultural tradition is one of irreverent pastiche and its contrived depthlessness undermines all metaphysical solemnities, sometimes by a brutal aesthetics of squalor and shock" (Harvey 1990: 7–9). By this standard, *Mystery Science Theater 3000* well fits the definition of the postmodern. With the showing of grade-Z films providing the "squalor and shock," *MST3K* would playfully satirize both the low budget films they presented as well as popular culture as a whole. The heart of the show centers on one of the favorite tools of postmodern artists, appropriation. In order to create the show, *MST3K* would appropriate low budget films, films that otherwise may have never found an audience.

In the terms of visual arts, appropriation occurs when an artist recontextualizes part or all of a previously created work in order to produce a new artwork. The appropriated object, although having been placed within a new viewing context, still remains accessible to the spectator in its original form. By presenting the work in a different light to the audience, the artist is able to bring new life to the appropriated object (Tate 2010). An example of this can be found in the works of video artist Dara Biranbaum. Biranbaum would re-edit films and television series in order to bring the subtext in the original to the forefront, such as in her work *Technology/Transformation: Wonder Woman,* in which she re-edited clips from the 1970's Television show *Wonder Woman* (Ferrer 2004). Appropriation art often contains elements of satire and parody. For example, Marcel Duchamp in his work *L.H.O.O.Q* satirized traditional attitudes toward fine art and artists by drawing a moustache on a cheap reproduction of the *Mona Lisa*. Similar to Marcel Duchamp drawing a moustache on the *Mona Lisa*, the staff at Best Brains used parody to bring new energy into the B movies they appropriated.

There are several different methods for recontextualizing an appropriated object. Artists such as Duchamp recontextualized appropriated objects by placing them in a gallery setting. Biranbaum recontexualized appropriated television shows through the use of editing. For

MST3K, creating a new viewing context for the films they appropriated would be accomplished through the use of riffing. In each episode of *MST3K*, the castaways on the Satellite of Love would comment constantly on the film unfolding in front of them. Riffing is a term created by the staff at Best Brains, Inc. to describe the process of creating a running satirical commentary concurrent with the presentation of a film. Because of the density and frequency of the riffs, the topics covered in the riffs would include a very broad range, including comments on the film's action (or inaction as the case may be), cultural references both common and obscure, and simple scatological humor. The use of these riffs would create a completely different context for the audience to view the film, thus drastically changing the viewing experience from viewing the film by itself.

Many of the films appropriated by *MST3K* are of the lowest caliber, poorly made even by B movie standards. These films failed to find an initial audience due to their inability to follow the rudimentary rules of filmmaking. However, by riffing on the faults of a particular film, *MST3K* was able to create a context where the film's flaws, once cause to avoid viewing these films, were now being gleefully celebrated. The riffing would help to bring out the campiness of otherwise dull movies. Susan Sontag noted in her essay "Notes on Camp," "Camp is a vision of the world in terms of style — but a particular style. It is the love of the exaggerated, the 'off,' of things-being-what-they-are-not" (Sontag 1961: 279). The films featured on *MST3K* are most certainly "off," attempting to mirror Hollywood product but failing, due to limitations in budget and limitations in talent. The new frame for viewing these films created by *MST3K*'s riffing highlights the fact that, despite the filmmaker's best attempts, these films do not behave in a way that is in keeping with audience expectations of what a film should look like, thus the riffing plays up the camp factor. The use of riffing transforms the films from excruciating to enjoyable. As noted by Sherri Linden in an article written upon the show's 20th anniversary, "With their silhouettes in the lower right-hand corner of the screen and their pop-culture mash-up of Groucho Marxian wordplay, literate backtalk, and goofy sound effects, sci-fi clunkers became communal comedy treasures" (Linden 2008). Indeed, by using riffing to provide a new viewing context for it's audience, *MST3K* help transform films that had previously been considered unwatchable into films that were a joy to watch.

Having a film appropriated for use on *MST3K* would prove to be beneficial to the status of these low-grade films. The use of these movies by the show brought new attention to these films, many of which had been widely unseen for many years and for the most part had been long forgotten by the public. Because of *MST3K*, these films have experienced a second life and a broader audience than they received upon their initial releases. The effect that *MST3K*'s appropriation and recontextualization had on sparking renewed interest in obscure movies can be readily seen by examining four films in particular. These films are Hal P. Warren's *Manos: The Hands of Fate* and a trio of films by Coleman Francis consisting of *The Beast of Yucca Flats, The Skydivers,* and *Red Zone Cuba*. Looking at the history of these films prior to their use on *MST3K* and the response to them after appearing on the show demonstrates how being featured on the show could help revive interest and create a new fan base for films that had previously been languishing in obscurity.

The genesis for *Manos: The Hands of Fate* occurred when El Paso fertilizer salesman Hal P. Warren met Academy Award–winning screenwriter and producer Stirling Silliphant while Silliphant was in Texas scouting possible locations for an upcoming project. Conversations with Silliphant in a local coffee shop led Warren, who was a member of the El Paso amateur theater, to wager that he could make and distribute a horror film on his own using only a minimal budget. Using the notes written on napkins while in the coffee shop, Warren drafted the script for a film he tentatively named *The Lodge of Sins* (Ross 2005).The story created by Warren focuses on a family consisting of husband Michael, wife Margaret, daughter Debbie, and a poodle named Peppy as they set off on their first family vacation. En route to their destination, the family becomes lost in the desert. They end up at a decrepit lodge where they encounter a caretaker/satyr named Torgo. The hopelessly lost Michael entreats Torgo to let the family stay the night at the lodge. Torgo agrees, despite the fact that his "Master would not approve." The Master is a supernatural leader of a cult devoted to the god Manos. The arrival of the family causes much discord between the Master, his wives, and Torgo. Eventually, Torgo and the Master's first wife are sacrificed, Margaret and Debbie are procured as new brides for the Master, and Michael replaces Torgo as the one who "takes care of the place while the Master is away."

Warren began recruiting a cast and crew to help in committing his vision to celluloid with a script and a $19,000 budget. Warren included fellow actors from the El Paso Theater to play the main roles in the film, while the parts of the Master's wives were to be played by models from a local agency called Mannequin Manor. The skeleton shooting crew was comprised mostly of college students. In lieu of payment for working on the film, Warren promised to give each participant a percentage of the back-end profits (Brandt 2002).

The limitations of shooting a movie with little money and an amateur cast and crew are quite evident in *Manos*. The film was shot using a camera that was only able to shoot 30 seconds of film at a time before having to be reloaded. As a result of this, the film was edited in a manner where a scene will cut or fade out only to end up back in the same scene that immediately preceded it. The camera was also incapable of recording sync sound, thus resulting in the need to overdub the dialogue between characters. The dubbing that was done in post-production was performed only by six people, thus resulting in ridiculous vocal performances as the actors attempted to disguise this fact, such as the high-pitched whine used for the couple's daughter or the bizarre vocal inflections used for the character Torgo. Most of the scenes are underlit, severely limiting the movement of the cast to a radius of a few feet. This causes many laughable moments, such as when the couple's search for their missing daughter goes no further than the front porch. It appears from watching *Manos* that little footage was left on the cutting room floor. In one scene, the clapboard can be clearly seen being pulled out of the frame. The film contains a seemingly endless series of shots of driving footage. The majority of these scenes contain no dialogue whatsoever. Some of these driving scenes were supposed to serve as background for an opening credits sequence with titles superimposed over the footage, but the pointless scenes were allowed to remain in the final cut of the film after the plan to add the titles was either scrapped or completely forgotten by Warren. The camera is allowed to linger on the actor's faces both long before and after they have delivered their lines. This causes any viewer of the film to share in the obvious awkwardness felt by cast as the actor's eyes dart around, waiting for their cues (Brandt 2002).

The finished product was a film that did not follow the rules of traditional filmmaking whatsoever. Those who attended the premiere at El Paso's Capri Theater responded poorly to the film's substandard quality and overwhelming bizarreness. Several of those involved with the film slipped out of the theater before the film's end in order to avoid further embarrassment and having to deal with patrons angry about having wasted their money on the price of admission. The negative reception received in the town where the film was made did not bode well for the future success of *Manos*. Although Warren managed to secure a limited run for *Manos* on the Texas drive-in theater circuit through Emerson Releasing, it seemed certain that the film was to quickly fade out of memory and into obscurity forever (Ross 2005).

However, there was quite a different fate in store for *Manos* than anyone involved in the film's creation could have possibly imagined. It was during *MST3K*'s third season that *Manos* was unleashed upon the world again. Mike Nelson recalls, "Frank, Mary Jo, Paul and I watched that film from beginning to end, an extremely rare thing for a screener. We just couldn't believe what we were seeing. And though we wanted to do it, we kept turning to each other and saying, 'We can't do this movie, can we?' We had to pitch it to the rest of the people, but they were pretty easily convinced. I love that movie, because it seems to have come from another dimension — which is kind of true" (Rice 2010).

The warped vision and lack of skill displayed by Warren provided the *MST3K* crew with a wealth of riffing opportunities. As Tom Servo understates, "You know, there are certain flaws in this film." The poor cinematography and the unappealing choice of locations that contribute to the overall grimy look of the film are frequently criticized. Joel states, "every frame of this movie looks like someone's last known photograph." Crow at one point panics, asking, "Joel, is this going to turn into a snuff film?" The leaden pacing of the film is highlighted with riffs such as this exchange between Joel and Servo which occurs in the midst of the film's opening driving sequences: Servo: "So what are we, about a half hour into this movie?" Joel: "No, I'm afraid not. It's more like a minute." Later in the film, as a scene where Torgo seems to spend an eternity dragging Michael's unconscious body to a pole to tie him up, Servo comments, "You know, maybe Torgo should have let him get closer to that pole then hit him." The unbelievable aspects of the plot are noted during the riffing. For example, when Michael tries to convince Torgo that the Master would not mind if he and his family were to stay overnight, Crow points out that "the guy just buys right into the whole master thing." This comment emphasizes just how ridiculous it is that Michael senses no danger whatsoever in letting his family stay with a stranger who is behaving bizarrely while repeatedly referring to his master. As Joel asks later, "When is this guy going to start demonstrating some simple competence?" a comment which not only applies to Hal Warren's character in the film, but speaks to his lack of ability as a filmmaker as well.

The riffing provided by *MST3K*, by filling in the gaps in the sparse dialogue, gives the characters far more depth and personality than they were originally given in Warren's script. The majority of riffs are reserved for the film's most unusual character, Torgo. During a scene where Torgo startles Mike by tapping him on the shoulder, Joel remarks, "That's the playful side of Torgo right there." Tom Servo quickly agrees, stating, "He's the clown that makes the dark side fun, Torgo!" Torgo's strange appearance is repeatedly commented upon. The first moment that the camera moves from a close-up of Torgo's face to a shot that reveals his grotesquely inflated thighs unleashes a torrent of riffs. Joel states, "That's not how you wear your Depends, Torgo." Crow chimes in with, "Been hitting the Thighmaster, Torgo?" It is obvious that the attempt by the filmmakers to make Torgo appear to be a satyr failed and he instead ended up looking like a man with really big knees. The constant flow of riffs dedicated to Torgo helped to endear the character to fans of *MST3K*. Torgo became such a fan favorite that Mike Nelson would reprise his take on the character repeatedly in host segments throughout the run of the show. The character of Torgo would return in the episodes. *Operation Double 007, Village of the Giants, Danger!! Death Ray,* and *Samson vs. The Vampire Women* (Cornell, 2010).

After the airing of the *Manos* episode, fan response was immediately enthusiastic. It had been a risk for Best Brains Inc. to attempt the appropriation of a film as poorly made and obscure as *Manos*, but the gamble paid off. In an interview given for the *Onion AV Club* Jim Mallon recalls:

> I do remember working on *Manos*, and I remember watching these driving scenes and having moments where I was just like, "Is this going to...?" Most of the time I didn't question it, but on that one, I really thought, "Are we going to make it? Is this going to be okay?" ... It created a new criteria where not only were they liking what we were doing, but sometimes the worse the movie, the more they liked it. Kind of like the bigger the rollercoaster, the scarier it is, the more people are enthused about it. "Oh my God, have you seen *Manos*? It's the worst" [Phipps 2008].

The interest generated by *Manos* being featured on *MST3K* led distributors Alpha Video to make the film commercially available for purchase in its original form for the first time ever when it released *Manos* on DVD in 2003. It had been virtually impossible to obtain a copy of the film for years, even for those who had been closely involved with the making of the film (Brandt 2009). In 2004, a documentary about the making of *Manos* named *Hotel Torgo* was released. In 2005, *Entertainment Weekly* ran a feature article on the film, declaring *Manos* as "The Worst Film Ever Made" (Ross 2005). Two stage adaptations of the film were produced. Last Rites Productions, a group that specializes in producing stage adaptations of B movies, performed a version of *Manos* in Portland, Oregon, in the beginning of 2006 (Hallett, 2006). In 2007, Steven Attanasie, Jr., and Andy Grigg of the New Millennium Theater Company staged a musical version of the film titled *Manos: Rock Opera of Fate* at the National Pastime Theater in Chicago (Lowery 2007).

After enduring the horror of *Manos*, one would suspect that those involved with *MST3K* would be able to tackle any cinematic atrocity with ease. However, nothing could quite prepare anyone for the viewing experience that is the Coleman Francis "trilogy," which consists of *The Beast of Yucca Flats*, *The Skydivers*, and *Red Zone Cuba*. In a manner similar to celebrated "worst director of all time" Ed Wood, Francis would work with many of the same actors from film to film, occasionally adding well-known character actors (Bela Lugosi for Wood, John Carradine for Francis) into the mix. The two directors even shared some of the same actors, including Conrad Brooks and Tor Johnson. However, the films of Coleman Francis had none of the *joie de vivre* of the Ed Wood films. Whereas the films of Wood, technically challenged as they may be, convey a sense of the childlike enthusiasm the director had for filmmaking, the films of Francis distinctly give the viewer the opposite impression. Filmed in flat gray tones, Coleman Francis movies paint a dim and dismal portrait of the world in general and human nature in particular. Bleak landscapes are populated desperate, often ruthless, people who are fueled only by greed and coffee. Indeed, the films of Francis play out like a dirge, a lamentation against the darker side of humanity.

The first film created by Francis was *The Beast of Yucca Flats*, which saw release in 1961. The film centers on Russian scientist Joseph Javorsky, who is played by Tor Johnson. Javorsky is a Soviet defector wishing to divulge secrets about the Russian space program to the American government. While on his way to meet with an American contact, Javorsky is chased by agents from the Kremlin into the blast of a nearby nuclear test. Javorsky is then transformed into a beast that wanders the countryside killing people he encounters. Javorsky is pursued by a gunman in a helicopter, who ends up shooting at a man looking for his lost children. This scene sets a precedent for the Coleman Francis films, which all include scenes of people being hunted by aircraft. In the end, Javorsky is shot and left for dead. Vigilante justice issued in the form of a fatal gunshot would become another recurring motif in the films of Francis.

Like *Manos, Beast* was shot entirely without sound. To deal with his lack of sync sound, Francis either shot his cast in long shots or cutaway from the speaker to a shot of another actor, thus eliminating the need to try to match the dubbed sound to the movement of the actor's lips. However, there is very little actual dialogue between characters as the majority of the story is told through voiceover narration performed by Francis himself. This narration provides us with number of nonsensical observations that have nothing to do with the film unfolding in front of us, including lines like "Flag on the moon. How did it get there?" "Touch a button. Things happen" and "Nothing bothers some people, not even flying saucers."

The next film in the Francis oeuvre is the 1963 film *The Skydivers. The Skydivers* focuses on married couple Harry and Beth as they struggle to save their sport parachuting business as well as their crumbling marriage. Their efforts to create a happily married life are thwarted by angry ex-employee Frankie and his girlfriend Suzy, who also happens to be Harry's jilted lover. Things are further complicated by the arrival of Harry's old war buddy Joe Moss, who winds up falling in love with Beth. Frankie and Suzy plot revenge against Harry, pouring acid onto his parachute prior to a major group jump. The acid eats holes in his parachute, causing Harry to plummet to his death. Frankie and Suzy are hunted much like Tor Johnson's character was in *The Beast of Yucca Flats.* They are tracked down and shot to death by a group of vigilantes.

This tale of deceit, cheating, and murder is probably the most upbeat of the three Coleman Francis films, thanks in no small part to the oddball ensemble of random characters that wander in and out of the film for no apparent reason. These bit parts include a beatnik with a pet rooster, a Scotsman in a traditional kilt, a scantily clad blonde giantess with a penchant for tossing around scrawny men, and rockabilly guitarist Jimmy Bryant. Although this parade of goofy characters helps to lighten the mood of the film somewhat, *Skydivers* still retains a dreary overall feel, due in large part to the fact that it features the same unappealing settings and drab gray look that was used previously in *Beast of Yucca Flats.* Unlike *Beast, Skydivers* does feature sync sound. However, this ends up being only a slight improvement, as Francis replaced the flat narration featured in *Beast* with monotonous reading of dialogue between the lackluster actors featured in the film, something that becomes especially painful to watch during scenes featuring the exceptionally monotonous Tony Cardoza. The editing in *The Skydivers* is particularly spastic, full of jump cuts and mismatched shots. While *Skydivers* is certainly a more technically accomplished work than *Beast of Yucca Flats* and arguably the best of the three Coleman Francis films, it still falls short of being a competently made film.

The final installment came in the form of 1966's *Red Zone Cuba.* Also known as *Night Train to Mundo Fine*, the convoluted plot of *Red Zone Cuba* follows three "desperados" as they devise various schemes to obtain easy money while evading the authorities. Francis himself stars as Griffin, a hardened escaped convict who meets up with two drifters named Landis and Cook, played by Cardoza and Harold Saunders. The three men decide to join a mercenary invasion of Cuba with the promise of receiving $2,000 dollars apiece. The invasion is unsuccessful, and the Cubans capture the invading force. The trio escapes and returns to America to follow another get-rich-quick scheme devised by Griffin. They decide to travel to New Mexico to rob a tungsten mine owned by fellow mercenary Bailey Chastain, a man they left for dead back in Cuba. The group detours from their destination long enough for Griffin to kill a restaurant owner, rape the restaurateur's blind daughter, and steal their convertible. Once in New Mexico, the trio con Chastain's wife into taking them to the mine. Justice catches up to the fugitives before they can finish killing and robbing Mrs. Chastain. Like all Coleman Francis villains, Griffin is hunted and shot dead without arrest and trial.

Red Zone Cuba is a difficult movie to watch, for many reasons. A brief cameo by veteran actor John Carradine attempts to lend some legitimacy to the film, but to no avail. The movie's theme song, which is sung by Carradine in a deep bullfrog voice, is ridiculous and does not give the viewer high hopes about the quality of the film they are about to watch. The ugly locations, bleak gray look, and shoddy editing that were featured in Francis' previous films are again on display in *Red Zone Cuba*. The paper-thin plot seems to go absolutely nowhere and the story drags on with no real resolution to any of the storylines presented. There are no truly likeable characters to be found anywhere in the film. It is interesting that Coleman Francis himself would decide to take on the role of Griffin, as the character is particularly vile, greedy, and violent, with no redeeming qualities whatsoever.

Distribution of the Francis films was small and they were primarily shown on the drive-in circuit. Cardoza himself handled initial booking of *Beast of Yucca Flats*, mostly due to difficulties in finding a studio or distribution company willing to attempt promoting the film. In an interview given for *Astounding B Monster*, Cardoza recounts trying to obtain a distribution deal with B-movie production studio American International Pictures, stating "I showed it to Sam Arkoff at the Charlie Chaplin Studios on LaBrea Avenue. He got halfway through it and he said, 'Oh! I forgot! I have to catch a plane.' You know what that meant!" (Weaver 2010). Eventually, the Francis/Cardoza team found distribution for the film through Crown International Pictures. Crown continued to work with Francis and Cardoza for their next project, and *The Skydivers* became the first film that Crown not only distributed, but provided financial backing for the production of as well. However, Crown declined to participate in the production or distribution of *Red Zone Cuba*. Rather, the small and now defunct Hollywood Star Pictures handled the film. After *Red Zone Cuba*, Francis ceased directing films and his involvement in filmmaking was reduced to the occasional bit part in a Ray Dennis Steckler or Russ Meyer film. Francis eventually succumbed to alcoholism and the films that he directed quickly disappeared from public view and from memory (Woods 2001).

The crew at Best Brains Inc. elected to tackle all three of the Coleman Francis films during Season Six of *MST3K*. The experience of working closely with the dismal Francis oeuvre would prove particularly trying for the *MST3K* creative team. As Mike Nelson recalls, "I've suffered from a chronic headache for most of my adult life, and it was particularly bad when we were working on a Coleman Francis film called *Red Zone Cuba*— just a weird kind of movie that really got me wondering why I was doing this" (Nelson 2010). Kevin Murphy also recalls the Francis films as being among the worst they encountered, stating, "the Coleman Francis films were just so dreary. We did have fun with them, but I just don't enjoy watching them, because the films are so creepy" (Gribon 2005).

The Skydivers was the first of the Francis films to appear on *MST3K*. The film's many shortcomings allow for the Satellite of Love crew to get their riffs in. The slipshod editing is a focus of many riffs. During a particularly confusing series of poorly matched cuts Crow notes, "Someone with attention deficit disorder must have edited this film." During a scene where Beth is lighting candles at the dinner table, Tom Servo states, "She's setting up for a séance," to which Crow replies, "She's going to evoke the spirit of the continuity man."

The pervasive bleakness of the film is also repeatedly riffed upon. A scene of Harry and Suzy together on the beach is accompanied by the comment, "Frolicking has never been so depressing." Later, another shot of Suzy looking around is matched with Crow stating that the film had been "filmed in despair vision." Thankfully for the audience, the riffing provided by the *MST3K* crew helps to ease the feeling of despair present in *The Skydivers*.

It is interesting to note that in *The Skydivers*, most of the riffing skewers Francis' style of filmmaking indirectly, highlighting the flaws in his work without mentioning Francis by name. In *Red Zone Cuba* and *Beast of Yucca Flats,* however, Francis is called out in a more direct fashion, many of the riffs mentioning the director by name. *Red Zone Cuba* features the following riffs on Francis, "Coleman Francis makes the terrific stories" and "Have you ever read *The Total Film-Maker* by Coleman Francis?" referencing the 1971 treatise on movie making written by Jerry Lewis. A scene opening upon the image of a depressed-looking woman causes Mike to comment, "Another cheery Coleman Francis character." As Francis himself plays a lead role in *Red Zone Cuba*, many of the riffs comment on his physical appearance as well. Many of the riffs about Francis appearance focus on his resemblance to the Three Stooges' Curly Howard such as this riff supplied by Mike, "Coleman Francis is Curly Howard in *The Fugitive*." There are also several comments made about Francis' slovenly appearance in the film. When the character of Griffin mutters "Bay of Pigs" onscreen, a voice from the theater finishes the thought with "that's what they call it when I go swimming." At another point during a scene that shows a disheveled looking Francis smoking a cigarette, Crow sarcastically notes, "our auteur, ladies and gentlemen."

By the time the *MST3K* crew gets to *The Beast of Yucca Flats*, the skewering of Francis and his singular cinematic vision is in full effect. As the credits for the film roll against gray footage of a bleak airstrip, Servo quips, "This doesn't look like the Coleman Francis genre, does it?" By this point in the season, both the *MST3K* staff and fans were all too familiar with the grim look of the Francis genre. Later in the film, Servo again comments on the sense of overwhelming gloom that pervades in the films of Francis with the comment, "Coleman Francis had a dark, muddy vision ... with some cars." The cumulative effect of the repeated riffing on Francis causes him to become more than the director or an actor in the films being presented. The riffing causes Francis to himself become a character on *MST3K*, a recurring character that the audience loves to hate.

Having his films appropriated by *MST3K* most certainly brought a greater awareness of Francis' work as a filmmaker to the public. As noted by Greg Woods in *The Eclectic Screening Room*, "Thanks to the *Mystery Science Theater* crowd, Francis is better known today as a director. And despite the foreground heckling of the animated silhouettes, it is also because of this *MST3K* treatment that Francis' films are arguably better known today than ever before" (Woods 2001: 39). Like *Manos*, the work of Francis has been adapted to live theater. In the late 1990s Carmen Martella wrote and produced a stage version of a Francis film, *Red Zone Cuba: The Musical*, which was performed at the annual Philadelphia Fringe Festival (Walker 2003). Albert Walker, whose *Agony Booth* website offers *MST3K*-style snarky recaps of bad movies, often covering movies that have also been featured as episodes on *MST3K*, has stated that "*Red Zone Cuba* is one of the most requested movies, if not the most requested movie here at the *Agony Booth*" (Walker 2003). Articles analyzing the works of Francis began appearing in magazines and on the internet. In a 2005 article written for *PopMatters*, Bill Gibron makes a case for Francis' films to be considered alongside the works of neo-realist directors such as Vittorio De Sica. In the article Gibron states, "Instead of celebrating *The Bicycle Thief* or worshipping *La Terra Trema* we should point to *The Skydivers,* or *Night Train to Mundo Fine* as films that truly express the verisimilitude of the spiritless, colorless indifference that is reality. As much as we hate to admit it, Coleman Francis was in tune with the tedium of our life and times. He remains the true neo neo-realist" (Gibron 2005).

It is unlikely that the films of directors such as Coleman Francis or Hal P. Warren would have found an audience without the attention that they gained by receiving the *MST3K* treatment. *Manos* in particular has benefited greatly from its appearance on the show. Trace Beaulieu states, "We dug that up out of the graveyard and put the electrodes to the electricity. We brought that back to life. I think we can take credit for bringing that to the world" (Phipps 2008). Frank Conniff observed at the *MST3K* reunion panel at the 2008 San Diego Comic-Con that "It seems that of all the films we did that's kind of the one that we brought to the world in a big way.... I also like to think that when people talk about directors who made bad movies like Ed Wood I like to think that we contributed to the fact that maybe Coleman Francis' name comes up" (Mallon 2008). Although neither Warren nor Francis lived to see the effect of being appropriated by *MST3K* would have on their films, hopefully they would have a reaction similar to director Rick Sloane, whose film *Hobgoblins* became a fan favorite after its appearance on the show. Sloane states, "in the long run, that was what made the movie famous. There would have never been a *Hobgoblins 2* without *MST3K* and I hope one of their incarnations decides to riff on the sequel. It won't be the same without it" (Borntreger, 2008).

REFERENCES

"Appropriation." *Tate Gallery.* 2010. Accessed 2/10/10. http://www.tate.org.uk/collections/glossary/defini tion.jsp?entryId=23.

Beaulieu, Trace, et al., *The Mystery Science Theater 3000 Amazing Colossal Episode Guide.* New York: Bantam Books, 1996.

Borntreger, Andrew. "Interview with Rick Sloane." *Badmovies.org.* February 2, 2008. Accessed 2/10/2010. http://www.badmovies.org/interviews/ricksloane/.

Brandt, Richard. "Growing Up Manos." *Mimosa.* 2009. Accessed 2/15/10. http://jophan.org/mimosam30/brandt.htm.

Brant, Richard. "The Hand That Time Forgot." *Mimosa* 2002. Accessed 2/15/10. http://jophan.org/mimosa/m18/brandt.htm.

Cornell, Chris. *Satellite News.* Accessed 2/10/10. http://www.MST3Kinfo.com/.

Ferreri Guardia, Francesc. "Biranbaum, Dara." *Mediateca* 2004. Accessed 3/12/2010. http://www.mediateca online.net/mediatecaonline/SConsultaAutor?ope=2&ID_IDIOMA=en&criteri=Birnbaum%2C+Dara.

Gribron, Bill. "The Puppet Master: DVD Verdict Interviews *MST3K*'s Kevin Murphy." *DVD Verdict.* March 14, 2005. Accessed 3/15/10. http://www.dvdverdict.com/interviews/kevinmurphy.

_____. "The Outre Oeuvre: Coleman Francis—The Neo Neo-Realist." *PopMatters.* November 29, 2005. Accessed 2/04/10. http://www.popmatters.com/columns/gibron/051129.shtml.

Hallett, Allison. "Manos: The Hands of Fate." *The Portland Mercury.* January 26, 2006. Accessed 4/15/10. http://www.portlandmercury.com/portland/Content?oid=36294&category=22143.

Harvey, David. *The Condition of Postmodernity.* Malden, MA: Blackwell Publishing 1990.

Linden, Sherri. "Lost in Space—And Loving Every Moment." *Los Angeles Times* October 26, 2008. Accessed 4/25/10. http://articles.latimes.com/2008/oct/26/entertainment/ca-secondlook26.

Lowery, Tim. "Manos: Rock Opera of Fate." *Time Out Chicago.* October 11–17, 2007. Accessed 04/25/10. http://chicago.timeout.com/articles/theater/23187/manos-rock-opera-of-fate.

Mallon, Jim (director), Joel Hodgson (writer), Mike Nelson (writer) et al., *The Mystery Science Theater 3000 Collection 20th Anniversary Collection.* Shout Factory 2008,

Mallon, Jim (director), Joel Hodgson (writer), Mike Nelson (writer) et al., Episode 424. *Manos: The Hands of Fate.* Rhino, 2004.

Mallon, Jim (director), Mike Nelson (writer), Paul Chaplin (writer) et al., Episode 609. *The Skydivers.* Rhino, 2002.

Mallon, Jim (director), Mike Nelson (writer), Paul Chaplin (writer) et al., Episode 619. *Red Zone Cuba*. Rhino, 2002.

Mallon, Jim (director), Mike Nelson (writer), Paul Chaplin (writer) et al., Episode 621. *The Beast of Yucca Flats*. Shout Factory 2010.

Nelson, Mike. "10 Quick Questions With *MST3K* and RiffTrax's Mike Nelson. *Science Channel* 2010. Accessed 2/17/10. http://science.discovery.com/questions/mike-nelson/mike-nelson.html.

Phipps, Keith. "*The Mystery Science Theater 3000* reunion interview: Joel Hodgson, Trace Beaulieu, and Jim Mallon." *The Onion*. November 3, 2008. Accessed 2/20/10. http://www.avclub.com/articles/the-mystery-science-theater-3000-reunion-interview,14327/.

Rice, Forrest. "Interview with Mike Nelson." *Mystery Science Theater Review 2010*. Accessed 2/24/10. http://www.d1041111.dotsterhost.com/*MST3K*/special-events_interview_mike-nelson.html.

Ross, Dalton. "The Worst Movie Ever Made." *Entertainment Weekly*, 6/10/2005, Issue 824: 46–52.

Sontag, Susan. *Against Interpretation and Other Essays*. New York: Picador 1961.

Walker, Albert. "Red Zone Cuba." *Agony Booth*. March 20, 2003. Accessed 2/16/10. http://www.agony-booth.com/recaps/Red_Zone_Cuba_1966.aspx

Weaver, Tom. "Anthony Cardoza's Tor of the Desert." *Astounding B Monster Archive*. 2010. Accessed 2/10/10. http://www.bmonster.com/profile37.html.

Woods, Greg. "The Yucca Films of Coleman Francis." *The Eclectic Screening Room*. Issue #2 Summer 2001: 21–39.

PART THREE

Fandom

6

Becoming "The Right People": Fan-Generated Knowledge Building

by Kris M. Markman and John Overholt

In a 1992 mini-documentary produced by Comedy Central, *This Is MST3K*, show co-creator Joel Hodgson said, "We never say 'Who's gonna get this?' We always say 'The right people will get this'" (Price and Eicher 1992). This oft-repeated quote has served as a rallying cry of sorts for *MST3K* fans. It is an acknowledgment direct from the horse's mouth that they are part of a special group — they are the people who "get it." What they get, in this case, are the hundreds of often obscure jokes and references that make up the basis of the show. In carrying out the central premise of the show, making fun of bad movies, the writers call upon a wide range of cultural resources to build a highly intertextual text (Ott and Walter 2000). The references in any given *MST3K* episode reach well beyond popular culture, extending to literature, history, anthropology, and occasionally the writers' own personal lives. The writers of the show acknowledge that obscurity, rather than familiarity, is in fact the goal; in the same documentary, Kevin Murphy says, "I think we've done our job if one viewer somewhere gets the most obscure joke that we put into the show ... the obscure jokes are so much fun because there's a very small percentage of people who get those, but the ones who do say, 'My God they're inside my head. They know me. They know too much about me.'" Indeed, several fans interviewed in the documentary echo Murphy's sentiments, and note that the obscurity of many of the references is part of the appeal of the show.

The obscurity of the references, however, also serves as a potential barrier for viewers wishing to cultivate their identities as fans of *MST3K*. Research on fandom has found that fans' identities *as fans* are often closely bound up with their interactions with the texts and that, as illustrated by the Kevin Murphy quote above, fans often see themselves in the texts. In a show like *MST3K*, however, fans must do extra work to understand the references in order to fully realize their identities as fans and become "the right people." Because of the breadth of the allusions in the show, this work has to be done in concert with other fans.

This chapter examines the collaborative knowledge-building activities of *MST3K* fans as they relate to the decoding of jokes and references in the show. We first briefly discuss the previous research on *MST3K*, and then we present our framework for examining fan identities and intertextuality. We then describe the different types of references that make up the show and explore the various internet-based resources that have been constructed by fans in their attempts to decode the show's references, and discuss how these sites work as a form of collective intelligence (Jenkins 2006).

Scholarship on *MST3K*

There has been relatively little academic research on the text of *MST3K*. Royer (2000) employed a feminist reading of two *MST3K* episodes, *The Amazing Colossal Man* (Mallon 1991, Episode 309) and *The She-Creature* (Mallon 1997, Episode 808) as a means of examining how American perceptions of women and gender roles had changed over time. Royer (2000) concludes her close reading by noting that detailed watching of the show does pay off in terms of more political depth and added humor. However, she argues that the show still perpetuates common societal conventions regarding women and doesn't stray far from the norm in criticizing the 1950s conventions portrayed in the movies it skewers. Royer notes that "the humor of the observers' comments is at times productive and empowering, but is still used to bond the male critics and exclude women" (131). Finally, Royer argues that the mixed fan reactions to the character of Pearl Forrester illustrate society's unresolved feelings toward feminism and feminists. However, she acknowledges that *MST3K* has a lot to say with regard to gender roles, even if it is not all empowering or positive.

Other scholars have identified *MST3K* as an example of postmodern storytelling (King 2007; Reeves, Rodgers and Epstein 1996; Stevenson 1994). Reeves, Rodgers and Epstein use *MST3K* as a contrasting example to what they argue is the staunch anti-postmodernism of the show *The X-Files*. They position *MST3K* and the similarly formatted *Beavis & Butthead* as clear examples of ironic postmodern detachment, in which the shows "commodify oppositional reading and cash in on viewer resistance to commercial culture" (34). King (2007) focuses his analysis on the Joel Hodgson–era episodes, reading the show as an allegory for postmodernism, with its heavy use of references reflecting the saturation of popular culture into our everyday lives. King notes the heavy use of references and the range of knowledge needed to understand the jokes, including the fact that the show itself sometimes becomes the source of references. King argues that while the heavy use of references made the show incomprehensible and boring to the mainstream viewer, its self-conscious construction of *MST3K as television* served to give dedicated viewers an avenue for criticizing the media experience. King also explicitly argues against Royer's (2000) critique of the politics of *MST3K*, noting that in the episode *Jungle Goddess* (Mallon 1990, Episode 203), the show "while mired in the degraded landscape of B movies, went far out of its way to critique the politics of the films it watched, so much so that some viewers regarded the show as 'preachy'" (47). King argues that ironically, *MST3K*'s power as a mediated critique of the televised form began to weaken as the show gained popularity and began to exert its own pressure on popular culture.

Identities and Texts: The Work of Becoming a Fan

Fans and fandom have been discussed by scholars in a number of different ways and contexts. Grossberg (1997) offers three categories of investment that describe audience's relationships to popular culture: fans, ideologues, and fanatics. Fans, he says, "make an affective investment into the objects of their taste and they construct, from those tastes, a consistent but necessarily temporary affective identity" (247). The general everyday enjoyment of media texts constitutes culture for the fan, who can derive strategies for survival from fan practices. In contrast to the fan, the ideologue's investment is affective, but is based on the application of external criteria to the text. Ideologue judgments of texts may be based on content or form, but "the ideologue's taste is always measured by standards defined outside of and adhered to independently of the pleasures of everyday life" (248). Finally, fanaticism involves a totalizing, yet empty affective investment in an ideological site. The fanatic cannot step outside the object of investment, because it is lived as the totality of existence.

By contrast, Jenkins (1992) conceptualizes fans as textual poachers. Jenkins draws upon de Certeau's poaching model, but modifies it to explain the science fiction fans he studied. Textual poaching is a processual model of fandom; it emphasizes meaning making and interpretation. Textual poachers choose media texts which express their previously held commitments and interests; there is a sense of recognition and identification. In Jenkins' approach, poaching involves both reading and writing as a social process, in contrast to de Certeau's isolated readers who discard meanings when they are no longer useful. Jenkins says that for the fan, "these previously 'poached' meanings provide a foundation for future encounters with the fiction, shaping how it will be perceived, defining how it will be used" (45). Hills (2002), critiquing previous scholarship on fandom, argues that in academia fandom has generally been conceptualized as a thing, while ignoring that fandom and fan identities are also always inherently performative.

One way to understand the difference between a fan and an enthusiast is that fans often "incorporate the cultural texts as part of their self-identity, often going on to build social networks on the basis of shared fandoms" (Pearson, 2007: 102). Similarly, Harrington and Bielby (2007) argue that it is in their investment in media texts, in behavioral, psychological, and emotional terms, that fans distinguish themselves from consumers. Fans, according to Sandvoss (2005), are self-reflexive about their media consumption, and construct the object of their fandom as an aspect of their concepts of self. One common thread in these various treatments of fans and fandom is the importance of identification. This identification with the object of fandom can be enhanced by the textual strategies employed in the text. As Ott and Walter (2000) note, exercising the cultural knowledge necessary to decode intertextual references "fosters feelings of superiority and belonging.... [S]uccessful identification of parodic references allows readers to mark themselves as ... part of a selective community.... Indeed, the pleasure of recognition is often directly proportional to the difficulty of identifying the allusion" (436). Thus for fans of *MST3K*, the intertextual nature of the show, with its the rapid-fire delivery of often obscure jokes and references, is tightly coupled with their enjoyment of the text and their identities as fans.

Ott and Walter (2000) note that the term intertextuality as used in media scholarship has its roots in two different traditions. In the first tradition, dating to the 1970s, intertextuality is used as a way of describing how audiences create meaning through their interactions with texts. A second tradition, dating to the 1980s, employed the term intertextuality to describe the increasing phenomenon of television shows quoting and referencing other popular culture texts. It is this second use of the term intertextuality that we will be using in our discussion of *MST3K*, the use of intertextuality as a textual strategy.

As noted by Ott and Walter (2000), a number of media scholars have identified the frequent and intense use of intertextual references in a text as a recent phenomenon, and one that marks a text as being postmodern. Although this technique is often described as "pastiche," Ott and Walter argue that this approach is too generalized, and that more sophisticated, nuanced categories are needed to describe the range of intertextual strategies found in postmodern texts. Ott and Walter propose three categories of intertextual allusions: parodic allusion, creative appropriation, and self-reflexive reference. In parodic allusion, one text makes use of a caricature of another text, but differs from the traditional literary device of parody in that parodic allusion seeks to amuse through juxtaposition, rather than offering commentary on the original text. With parodic allusion, "the audience is, in effect, transformed into the site of critical commentary; they are judged worthy by the text and subsequently themselves if they possess sufficient cultural knowledge to recognize the popular references" (Ott and Walter, 2000: 436). Parodic allusion differs from creative appropriation in that the latter reproduces actual portions of the original text, as with sampling, and often has an explicit goal of commenting on the incorporated text (Ott and Walter). Finally, Ott and Walter describe self-reflexive reference as a stylistic device whereby authors use references to other texts as a means to comment on their own text's conditions or status. For example, Ott and Walter describe a scene from the 1996 horror movie *Scream*, where a character's direct quotation of a line from the classic horror movie *Halloween* is used to signify *Scream*'s awareness of itself as both fitting in and playing with the horror movie genre.

MST3K Fans and the Internet: Building a Collective Intelligence

To become a true fan of *MST3K*, or in Joel Hodgson's words, to become one of "the right people" (Price and Eicher 1992), is to devote oneself to the project of understanding the references. However, people attracted to the show will almost certainly not possess all of the cultural knowledge required to decode all of the references. Not only are the references sourced from a wide range of cultural domains, but some of the references are local to the Minneapolis–St. Paul area where the show was based, and thus are out-of-reach for non-local audiences, while still others are specific to the personal lives of the show's staff. Thus one fan, working in isolation, cannot hope to build the requisite knowledge to become one of the "right people," but must instead work with other fans to share information and work collaboratively to build a community of the right people. This process of knowledge sharing can be analyzed as a form of collective intelligence.

Media scholar Henry Jenkins (2006) has argued that new technologies, particularly the internet, are enabling new forms of cultural participation. Much of this participation is centered around online communities. Fans are just one of the many groups taking advantage of these new forms of community, which Jenkins says are "defined through voluntary, temporary, and tactical affiliations, reaffirmed through common intellectual enterprises and emotional investments" (27). Drawing on the work of Pierre Lévy, Jenkins defines the concept of collective intelligence as the "ability of virtual communities to leverage the combined expertise of their members. What we cannot know or do on our own, we may now be able to do collectively" (27). Collective intelligence, Jenkins notes, is not the same as the shared knowledge held in common by the group. Rather, collective intelligence refers to the knowledge held by *individuals,* which can be accessed by the group when the occasion arises. This individual knowledge then gets scrutinized by the group, and becomes added to the shared knowledge of the group only after it goes through this process. Thus, collective intelligence is as much a process as a thing.

Jenkins (2006) describes how an online community of fans of the television show *Survivor* work towards spoiling upcoming shows as example of "collective intelligence in practice" (28). Individual fans have specific knowledge, for example local information or behind-the-scenes insights, or access to specific technologies, such as geographic information systems that can provide satellite photos of potential *Survivor* locations, and they pool this knowledge in online "spoiling" forums. Jenkins demonstrates that these contributions are not accepted uncritically, however; information must be weighed, valued, discussed, and judged according to its merits and the merits of the people posting. The fans are aware that producers from the show may be planting misinformation, for example, so they work together to decide what will get added to the shared knowledge.

The Intertextuality of *MST3K*

Whereas the collective intelligence of the *Survivor* fans described by Jenkins (2006) was primarily directed towards uncovering information about upcoming shows, the primary work done by *MST3K* fans is in uncovering the meaning of the hundreds of parodic allusions (Ott and Walter 2000) employed in the show. Specifically, we have identified three main types of parodic allusions used in *MST3K*: general cultural references, callback references, and inside jokes. Most common are general cultural references, which as previously noted can cover a wide range of domains, from the popular to the very obscure. In essence, the subject matter for references on *MST3K* spans the entire gamut of Western culture. In any given episode, such as *Werewolf* (Murphy 1998, Episode 904), jokes can allude to something as plebian as the band Brooks and Dunn or commercials for Coors beer, and in the next breath reference the novel *Jane Eyre* or Bach's *Well-Tempered Clavier*. A particularly demanding joke requires familiarity with both the art of Frederic Remington and Picasso's *Guernica*. References can likewise range from the utterly mundane (Cheez-Its, Mrs. Butterworth's) to the spiritual ("I enjoyed your letter to the Philippians!"). It is not just the breadth of cultural references that makes them challenging, but the pace at which they are thrown at the audience. In *The Touch of Satan* (Murphy 1998, Episode 908), there are 62 references within the first 30 minutes of show content. Many of these play off of the movie's 1970s setting by referencing contemporary cultural artifacts: Actor Anthony Zerbe, the gas crisis, Watergate, former U.S. President Gerald Ford, streaking, football player Roman Gabriel, and the television show *Welcome Back, Kotter* all get a mention. Additional allusions in *The Touch of Satan* reference Japanese Kabuki theater, the Grant Wood painting *American Gothic*, the conductor Herbert von Karajan, and the standard legal disclaimers included in bank and credit card commercials. All of these references exemplify parodic allusion: they are there, in the text, because the writers thought they would be funny.

In general, *MST3K* places little emphasis on continuity; aside from the basic premise of the show, each episode is essentially free-standing, and the characters do not evolve over time. In fact, the insistence of SciFi channel executives that the show develop narrative arcs in the host segments was generally unpopular with both the creators and the fans. One way in which show continuity is addressed is through callback references to movies from previous episodes. The most common of these is probably "Hi-Keeba!" which originated in *Women of the Prehistoric Planet* (Mallon 1989, Episode 104). Originally the capper to a particularly weak bit of physical comedy, the odd distinctiveness of this exclamation made it easy to sprinkle throughout the show, mocking inept moments of dramatic surprise. At the same time, this brief, essentially contentless catchphrase was easily ignored by fans who did not see the original episode, and indeed, some fans mistakenly regard it as an invention of the show itself, rather than a reference. Callback references such as "Hi-Keeba!" still function as parodic allusions, because they are played for humor, not for commentary.

The furthest extension of the "The right people will get it" philosophy pursued by the show's writers comes with the occasional joke that is so specific to the experience of the writers that it is essentially incapable of being decoded by the audience without assistance. Two examples of these inside jokes of are explained in the *Amazing Colossal Episode Guide (ACEG)* (Beaulieu et al., 1996): "the Moronis' phone number" and "Stop her, she stole Mike's keyboard." In *Danger!! Death Ray* (Murphy 1995, Episode 620) Tom Servo remarks of a list of phone numbers posted on a wall "It's the numbers for the babysitters, the police, and the Moronis next door." The *ACEG* explains that this is "a reference to writer Bridget Jones's neighbors when she was a kid. This may seem really obscure, but you have to realize that in their own circles the Moronis were pretty well known" (166). Similarly, in *Gamera vs. Guiron* (Mallon 1991, Episode 312), Tom Servo responds to a shot of a girl running away on screen with, "Stop her, she's got my keyboard!" When Joel responds to this remark with "huh?" Tom Servo responds, "It's obscure." The *ACEG* illustrates just how obscure this joke was: "This completely gratuitous remark refers to a girlfriend of Mike's who broke the poor clod's heart by leaving him without a word of explanation and stealing his only possession of value, a Roland keyboard his parents had given him" (161). The *ACEG* is also slightly incorrect in the actual quote in question, as Tom Servo clearly says "she's got my" rather than "she stole Mike's" as is listed in the *ACEG*.

One problem for fans trying to decode the references on *MST3K* is that, in a time before *YouTube* and *Wikipedia*, the writers themselves were forced to rely on sometimes unreliable memories of texts to reference. A frequently recurring reference in Season 8 was in fact based on confusion between two TV commercials from the 1970s. The FAQ on *Satellite News* (Sampo and Erhardt n.d.) explains:

> [T]here was a series of commercials for Ivory dishwashing liquid, in which mothers were mistaken for their daughters — because the Mom used Ivory and so her hands were young-looking. At around the same time, there was also a commercial for Grape Nuts, in which a teenage boy mistakes teenage girl Dale's mother for Dale and utters the deathless line: "I thought you were Dale!" Best Brains only vaguely remembered these two commericials [*sic*], and apparently mixed them up in their minds. There were apparently never any Ivory Liquid commercials in which a character said "I thought you were Dale!" And the Grape Nuts commercial in which that line was spoken had nothing to do with hands. So basically they goofed. But the writers thought they were making a reference to the Ivory Liquid commericals [*sic*].

Although the references we have described thus far all fall under the rubric of parodic allusion (Ott and Walter, 2000), there are a few rare instances of the use of other intertextual strategies on *MST3K*. Specifically, the show occasionally breaks its own "fourth wall" to make a self-reflexive reference. These typically involve a character knowing something about the show that he or she is not supposed to know. For example, although Michael J. Nelson the person had been with the show since Season 1, Mike Nelson the character first appeared in *The Brain That Wouldn't Die* (Beaulieu 1993, Episode 513). A line in *The Sinister Urge* (Beaulieu 1994, Episode 613) exploits this tension when Mike Nelson makes reference to the Jet Jaguar character from *Godzilla vs. Megalon* (Mallon 1991, Episode 212). Crow picks up on the anachronism and asks, "How would you know?" Ott and Walter (2000) note that "self-reflexive references are often subtle gestures that to be appreciated require specific knowledge of the text's production history, the character's previous credits, or popular reviews" (439). Here, Crow's reaction to Mike's reference is only understandable as a joke if the viewer knows the difference between Mike Nelson the character and Michael J. Nelson the writer. A similar joke stretches the bounds of continuity even further, in *Manhunt in Space* (Mallon 1992, Episode 413), when Crow observes that a planet looks like the *Mystery Science Theater 3000* logo. Joel replies, "You're not supposed to know about that!"

Decoding the References: *MST3K* Fans Online

As luck would have it, the popularity of *MST3K* coincided with the growth of the internet, and we can see examples from fairly early in the show's run of fans using the internet to seek out information about the show and to engage in a process of collective intelligence to decode the various references in the show. In the pre-web era, Usenet groups such as rec.arts.tv.*MST3K* and alt.tv.*MST3K* were the most popular place for fans to share information about the show. An *MST3K* Frequently Asked Questions list was circulating on Usenet at least as far back as Google's Usenet archives go, to the beginning of 1992, and likely earlier. (A fuller, slightly later version can be seen in Kulawiec 1993.) That same year, a fan notes:

> About it being impossible to get ALL the references on *MST3K*—well, on rec.arts.comics, someone has been putting together a "Sandman Annotation," making ALL of the references in this comic book BRUTALLY clear. I wonder if anybody would care for an *MST3K* annotation? [Jordan 1992].

Indeed the demand was there, and the FAQ's list of explanations for obscure references continued to grow. Many of these explanations found their way into the *ACEG*, published in 1996 (Beaulieu et al.). However, as the fans themselves have noted (Sampo, 2010), and as we have shown above, the *ACEG*, seemingly the most authoritative source for information about the show, is not entirely free of mistakes. Perhaps most notably, it misidentifies the actor who says the famous line "Hi-Keeba" as Wendell Corey (it is actually Paul Gilbert). In addition, the *ACEG* is by necessity not an exhaustive compendium of all *MST3K* references, and of course does not contain any information about episodes that were produced after the book was published. Thus there continues to be a demand for a resource where fans can get their reference questions answered.

Although Usenet has largely fallen into obsolescence in recent years, many web-based discussion forums still exist for those seeking reference explanations. On *MST3K: The Discussion Board* the thread "Esoteric References VI" (Blurryeye) has been active since 2007, and now encompasses 64 pages of posts, having been viewed 45,000 times. Usenet and web-based discussion forums offer an easy path to collaborative participation; anyone with an account can contribute information. However, as an unordered and unindexed stream of posts, they work less well as a reference source. Since it is easier to repost a question that may have been previously answered than to search for the answer, they tend to accumulate redundant information.

The advent of the web made it possible for fans to construct static pages that could be easily referred back to (unlike Usenet posts) and with content far more extensive than the *ACEG* had or could have had, given its limitations as a printed book. Several sites devoted to explaining references follow a similar format: for a particular episode, each reference is quoted, followed by an explanation of the reference, and occasionally a link to an external web page or related video. The most extensive of these, *The Annotated MST* (n.d.), boasts comprehensive reference guides for 54 episodes. However, with only a handful of new episodes added in the last few years, and with the last update in October 2009, it is hard to imagine that the project will ever be completed. This is a common problem with sites run by a single person, as these usually are. The author of the abandoned site *Too Much Information: The Annotated MST3K* (Scott, n.d.) admits as much:

> Important Announcement: As you have all no doubt noticed, this project eventually screeched to a halt. Unfortunately, it all got a bit beyond me. I have other projects that are more dear to me and plenty of real life stuff going on, so I don't really have the time or energy to continue working on this project. Plus, even if I did work on TMI to the exclusion of all else, I'd still never get it done. It's too much for any one person.

Furthermore, not even the most dedicated annotator can know everything. When the author of *The Annotated MST* failed to catch the repeated references to the Fleetwood Mac song "Tusk" over the closing credits to *Werewolf* (Murphy 1998, Episode 904), she evidently received a number of emails pointing out the mistake: "About a squillion people pointed out that I missed the "Tusk" reference, although reader J.T. got there first. My bad" ("*Werewolf*" n.d.). This example illustrates the power of the collective intelligence process, where a "squillion" other fans who did have the information were able to communicate that to the annotator, thereby adding that reference to the shared knowledge of the group.

The third wave of reference-explaining sites blends the collaboration of discussion forums with the ease of use of annotation pages. By allowing anyone to contribute to the site, they avoid the problem of burnout, and draw on the broad base of knowledge of their many contributors. *The Distributed MST3K Annotation Project* (n.d.) is an offshoot of one of the most popular sites for episode trading, *The Digital Archive Project*. Although no episode is as extensively described as one of the completed episodes on *The Annotated MST*, most episode pages contain at least some information. Contributors are also able both to tag their annotations and add timecodes for the occurrence of the joke within the episode.

The *Mystery Science Theater 3000 Wiki* (2006) is broader in focus; each episode has an entry that includes plot descriptions, an account of the host segments, and the like, in addition to notes on obscure references. It also contains a few pages for recurring references, such as the aforementioned "I thought you were Dale" (2007). Although the episode descriptions and annotations on the wiki are far from complete, the mere existence of a page for each episode in an easy-to-edit format lends itself to a more comprehensive reference source. As of April 2010, 266 registered users had made at least one edit on the wiki, and 101 users had contributed five times or more. As of April 2010 the wiki is being regularly updated, and users are taking full advantage of the wiki format, for example by linking to *Wikipedia* articles or other online sources, or by adding screenshots to explain common catchphrases.

The collective intelligence process demonstrates that, even with all the resources of the web, some references may be nearly impossible to figure out without recourse to someone in the know. On the discussion forums for the *MST3K* spinoff *RiffTrax*, a puzzled poster asked "One joke I've never understood; After a string of questions, one of the three would sometimes say something to the effect of 'I ask you, Mortum Condraki' (No idea if I spelled that correctly.)" (WereSquirrel 2007). In this case, any Google search would be doomed to failure, because the viewer in question could not recognize the string of sounds as the name of the *McLaughlin Group* pundit Morton Kondracke. However, based on the phonetic spelling and other information about the episode, another forum user was quickly able to provide Kondracke's name and his information, while yet another user followed up with more specific information about that particular reference. Similarly, on *MST3K: The Discussion Board*, a poster asked: "Maybe my ears are clogged but during *Attack of the Giant Leeches*, when the scientist is smoking (at around an hour and 7 minutes into the disc), it sounds like Servo says 'Hmm, mung fo cart'?" (Blurryeye 2007). The answer provided by another user suggests that what was heard was actually "Hmong folk art," and the response notes "that this just might be a reference to the Hmong people who emigrated from Southeast Asian countries and settled in the upper midwest. The Hmong are known for their patterned tapestries." The respondent provides a link to examples of Hmong tapestries, and provides further support for his conclusion by noting that a wall painting in the background of the movie at the time of the joke was a probable source for the Hmong reference. What both of these examples illustrate is the importance of interpersonal communication in the collective intelligence process. Being able to get answers based on vague descriptions or garbled phonetic spellings is a particular characteristic of human agents.

Conclusion

In this chapter, we have looked at the intertextuality of *MST3K*, in particular, the show's use of parodic allusions as a way of creating a bond between the writers and the fans. The writers intentionally include jokes that will be difficult, if not impossible, to understand, in the hopes that "the right people" will expend the energy needed to decode these allusions. We have examined how the fans have incorporated the internet into this quest, by creating various sites for collective intelligence, where references can be listed and explained. These discussion boards, Usenet groups, and wikis form a body of shared knowledge for *MST3K* fans, and through this engagement with the text, fans deepen their identification with the show. Given the sheer number of references included in the show's 11-year run, this task of collective knowledge building might seem overwhelming. However, even though the show has been off the air since 1999, the continued fan activity online would seem to indicate that the work is worth it for the opportunity to become one of the right people.

REFERENCES

The Annotated MST n.d. Accessed 4/26/10. http://www.annotatedmst.com/.
Beaulieu, Trace, et al. *The Mystery Science Theater 3000 Amazing Colossal Episode Guide*. New York: Bantam Books, 1996.
Beaulieu, Trace (director), Michael J. Nelson (writer), Trace Beaulieu (writer), et al. Episode 513 *The Brain That Wouldn't Die* 1993.
Beaulieu, Trace (director), Michael J. Nelson (writer), Trace Beaulieu (writer), et al. Episode 613 *The Sinister Urge* 1994.
Blurryeye. "Esoteric References VI." *MST3K: The Discussion Board* July 6, 2007. Accessed 4/26/10. http://forrestcrow.proboards.com/index.cgi?board=mstchat&action=display&thread=5959.
The Distributed MST3K Annotation Project n.d. Accessed 4/26/10. http://www.dapcentral.org/ap/.
Grossberg, Lawrence. *Dancing in Spite of Myself: Essays on Popular Culture*. Durham, NC: Duke University Press, 1997.
Harrington, C. Lee, and Denise D. Bielby. "Global Fandom/Global Fan Studies." In Jonathan Gray, Cornel Sandvoss and C. Lee Harrington, eds. *Fandom: Identities and Communities in a Mediated World*. New York: New York University Press, 2007. 179–197.
Hills, Matt. *Fan Cultures*. London: Routledge, 2002.
"I Thought You Were Dale" *Mystery Science Theater 3000 Wiki* September 20, 2007. Accessed 4/26/10. http://MST3K.wikia.com/wiki/I_thought_you_were_Dale.

Jenkins, Henry. *Convergence Culture: Where Old and New Media Collide*. New York: New York University Press, 2006.

_____. *Textual Poachers: Television Fans & Participatory Culture*. New York: Routledge, 1992.

King, John. "*Mystery Science Theater 3000*, Media Consciousness, and the Postmodern Allegory of the Captive Audience." *Journal of Film & Video* 59:4 (Winter 2007): 37–53.

Jordan, Charles. "References... The Chicago Connection." *alt.tv.MST3K* February 10, 1992. Accessed 4/26/10. http://groups.google.com/group/alt.tv.*MST3K*/msg/73f26151e9e8c0a3.

Kulawiec, Rich. "*MST3K*.FAQ" *Uncensored!* November 12, 1993. Accessed 4/26/10. http://uncensored.citadel.org/amoeba-readfile.php?filename=*MST3K*.FAQ.

Mallon, Jim (director), Trace Beaulieu (writer), Joel Hodgson (writer), et al. Episode 104 *Women of the Prehistoric Planet* 1989.

Mallon, Jim (director), Michael J. Nelson (writer), Trace Beaulieu (writer), et al. Episode 203 *Jungle Goddess* 1990.

Mallon, Jim (director), Michael J. Nelson (writer), Trace Beaulieu (writer), et al. Episode 212 *Godzilla vs. Megalon* 1991.

Mallon, Jim (director), Michael J. Nelson (writer), Trace Beaulieu (writer), et al. Episode 309 *The Amazing Colossal Man* 1991.

Mallon, Jim (director), Michael J. Nelson (writer), Trace Beaulieu (writer), et al. Episode 312 *Gamera vs. Guiron* 1991.

Mallon, Jim (director), Michael J. Nelson (writer) Trace Beaulieu (writer), et al. Episode 413 *Manhunt in Space* 1992.

Mallon, Jim (director), Michael J. Nelson (writer) Paul Chaplin (writer), et al. Episode 808 *The She Creature* 1997.

Murphy, Kevin (director), Michael J. Nelson (writer), Paul Chaplin (writer), et al. Episode 904 *Werewolf* 1998.

Murphy, Kevin (director), Michael J. Nelson (writer), Paul Chaplin (writer), et al. Episode 908 *The Touch of Satan* 1998.

Murphy, Kevin (director), Michael J. Nelson (writer), Frank Conniff (writer), et al. Episode 620 *Danger! Death Ray* 1995.

Mystery Science Theater 3000 Wiki July 11, 2006. Accessed 4/26/10. http://*MST3K*.wikia.com/wiki/Mystery_Science_Theater_3000_Wiki.

Ott, Brian, and Cameron Walter. "Intertextuality: Interpretive Practice and Textual Strategy." *Critical Studies in Media Communication* 17:4 (December 2000): 429–446.

Pearson, Roberta. "Bachies, Bardies, Trekkies, and Sherlockians." In Jonathan Gray, Cornel Sandvoss and C. Lee Harrington, eds. *Fandom: Identities and Communities in a Mediated World*. New York: New York University Press, 2007. 98–109.

Price, Bill (director), Glen Eicher. *This Is MST3K*. Comedy Central, 1992.

Reeves, Jimmie L., Mark C. Rodgers, and Michael Epstein. "Rewriting Popularity: The Cult *Files*." In David Lavery, Angela Hague and Marla Cartwright, eds. "*Deny All Knowledge" Reading the X-Files*. Syracuse, NY: Syracuse University Press, 1996. 22–35.

Royer, Jessica A. "What's Happening on Earth? *Mystery Science Theater 3000* as Reflection of Gender Roles and Attitudes toward Women." Elyce Rae Helford, ed. In *Fantasy Girls: Gender in the New Universe of Science Fiction and Fantasy Television*. Lanham, MD: Rowman, 2000. 115–133.

Sampo. "Weekend Discussion Thread: *The Amazing Colossal Episode Guide*." *Satellite News* April 24, 2010. Accessed 4/26/10. http://www.*MST3K*info.com/?p=5676.

Sampo, Erhardt. "*Mystery Science Theater 3000* Frequently Asked Questions: Subtleties, Obscurities, Odds and Ends." Accessed 4/1/10. http://www.MST3Kinfo.com/mstfaq/subtle.html.

Sandvoss, Cornel. *Fans: The Mirror of Consumption*. Malden, MA: Polity, 2005.

Scott, Doug A. *Too Much Information: The Annotated MST3K* n.d. Accessed 2/1/2010. http://doctorwhochronology.com/MST3Ktmi/tmi.htm.

Stevenson, Deborah. "'If You Read This Last Sentence, It Won't Tell You Anything': Postmodernism, Self-Referentiality, and *The Stinky Cheese Man*." *Children's Literature Association Quarterly* 19:1 (Spring 1994): 32–34.

WereSquirrel "*MST3K* References I Don't Get" RiffTrax Round Table December 23, 2007. Accessed 4/26/10. http://forum.rifftrax.com/index.php?topic=3053.225.

"Werewolf" *The Annotated MST* n.d. Accessed 4/26/10. http://www.annotatedmst.com/episodes/werewolf/index.htm.

7

Converging Fan Cultures and the Labors of Fandom

by Megan Condis

The creators, writers, and performers behind the ground-breaking television program *Mystery Science Theater 3000* (*MST3K*) have spent their careers touting the benefits of what Henry Jenkins calls "convergence cultures" (Jenkins 2006). Their work bridges the gap between media elites and media consumers and empowers audiences to directly participate in shaping their experiences with media products. *MST3K* focuses on a small group of viewers who refuse a passive model of viewership, opting instead to take ownership of the programming they consume and to adapt it to their needs on the fly. The jokes that they crack from the margins of the screen enable them to amend the "bad" films they are being forced to watch to reflect their own tastes. Their devotion to a customizable, multi-media friendly format is also reflected in their business decisions. From their origins as quasi-amateur content providers on a local station in Minnesota to their endorsement of fan-centered distribution models such as tape trading, these artists mimic the virtues of grassroots media producers even as they achieve professional success on television and in Hollywood. Furthermore, their current projects, *RiffTrax* and *Cinematic Titanic*, utilize one of the most important aspects of convergence cultures: the ability to deliver content cheaply and quickly over the Internet. Michael J. Nelson's website, *RiffTrax*, even facilitates the sale of audience-created efforts, thus further blurring the line between professionals and laypersons when it comes to the production of internet-based television programming.

However, although it is tempting to emphasize the positive, democratic (and, by implication, politically progressive) characteristics of the convergence cultures that surround *MST3K* and its numerous spin-offs, it is important to recognize the unique burdens that these cultures place upon their participants. First, the mingling of independent, underground media with corporate mass media often results in a kind of exploitation, in which the ethics of the first group can be drowned out, even as their aesthetics are co-opted, by those of the second. This relationship can create a kind of imbalance in which corporate entities monetize and sell a sub-culture back to its originators, thus divesting it of much of its original cachet of rebelliousness. Also, in order for fans to fully engage with convergence cultures like the one that is fostered by *MST3K*, they must put forth a certain amount of dedication and intellectual labor, and sometimes, a significant amount of money. Finally, these commitments on the part of audience members do not always guarantee the creation of democratic and progressive utopian communities online. In fact, it is often the case that some fans, such as women, are excluded from these groups.

The Incredibly Strange Audience Who Stopped Living and Became Mixed-Up Zombies: The Perceived Threat of Television to Democracy

As the intro theme to the show explains, *Mystery Science Theater 3000* is about an average Joe who ends up becoming the subject of an experiment being conducted by a mad scientist bent on taking over the world: Dr. Clayton Forrester and his assistants, Dr. Larry Erhardt & TV's Frank. Their plan is to expose their test subjects, first Joel Robinson (played by series creator Joel Hodgeson) and then Mike Nelson (played by head writer Michael J. Nelson), to a series of the worst films and television shows ever made. In the feature film version of the series, *Mystery Science Theater 3000: The Movie*, the mad scientist Dr. Clayton Forrester broadens his test pool, telling audience members in the theater that "by observing, [they] have become a part of that experiment" (Mallon 1996). Dr. Forrester believes that a steady diet of schlock will slowly turn our brains to mush. If his experiments succeed, then he can let loose a perfect cinematic stinker on the general population, thus obliterating any potential resistance to his plot to conquer the planet.

The theory behind their experiment was born in the 1950s and early 1960s. It was nurtured by politicians and mass media scholars who feared the vast influence that the newly popular medium of television might have on the ability of the masses to effectively participate in culture and civic life. "From the very start," writes media historian John Hartley, "television attracted attention as a potential evil — it brought sex, violence, bad language and excessive or unthrifty habits into the home, and it caused vulnerable people to behave badly" (Hartley 1999: 103). For example, in 1961 FCC Chair Newton Minow made an address to the National Association of Broadcasters in which he warned that popular television was becoming a "vast wasteland" bereft of any educational or culturally beneficial content (Minow 1961).

In academia, scholars Dwight Macdonald, T. W. Adorno, and Gunther Anders led the charge against bad TV. (Media theorists also indicted television in books like Neal Postman's 1985 *Amusing Ourselves to Death: Public Discourse in the Age of Show Business*, and Jerry Mander's 1978 *Four Arguments for the Elimination of Television*.) Their primary fear was that mass produced entertainments would lead to mass produced citizens who were unable to think critically on their own and instead relied on media moguls to make decisions for them. MacDonald warned, "Mass culture is imposed from above. It is fabricated by technicians hired by businessmen; its audiences are passive consumers, their participation limited to the choice between buying and not buying," thus serving as "an instrument of political domination" (MacDonald 1957: 60). Adorno agreed, calling television's standardization of cultural production an "undreamed of psychological control. The repetitiveness, the self-sameness, and the ubiquity of modern mass culture tend to make for automatized reactions and to weaken the forces of individual resistance" (Adorno 1957: 476). He believed that television had a "nefarious effect" (Adorno 1957: 474) on the populace because it reduced complex social problems down to simple ideological lessons, a trend that favors complacency over anger and the status quo over social change:

> The ideals of conformity and conventionalism ... have been translated into rather clear-cut prescriptions of what to do and what not to do. The outcome of conflicts is pre-established, and all conflicts are mere sham. Society is always the winner, and the individual is only a puppet, manipulated through social rules.... The majority of television shows today aim at producing, or at least reproducing, the very smugness, intellectual passivity, and gullibility that seem to fit in with totalitarian creeds [Adorno 1957: 478–479].

Or, to put it another way, Adorno fears that television drains away our ability to "talk back" to elites. Anders is of the same mind; he sees the television viewer as passive and mute, happy to allow the television to speak on his behalf:

> Television viewers ... converse with each other only by accident — in so far as they still retain the will or the ability to speak.... Since the receiving sets speak in our place, they progressively rob us of our ability to speak, of our opportunities for speaking, and finally even of our pleasure in expressing ourselves.... For them words are no longer something one speaks, but something one merely hears; speaking is no longer something that one does but something that one receives. No matter in what cultural or political milieu this development toward an existence without speech takes place, its end result must be everywhere the same — a type of man who, because he only listens, will do no more than listen [Anders 1957: 361–362].

Although these theorists worried about the effects of all mass media on the public, they had a particular dread of "low-brow" entertainments, which they saw as especially crippling to the nation's collective intellect. Science fiction and fantasy, the two genres that Dr. Forrester most often uses to fuel his experiments, were particularly reviled by media critics during the 1950s and 1960s. As Lynn Spigel describes, commentators "tend[ed] to view such shows within the logic of cultural hierarchies, seeing their value in negative terms — that is as the opposite of high art. Rather than leading to knowledge, these programs are said to constitute an escape from reason" (Spigel 2001: 108).

Macdonald worried that overexposure to the simplistic stories one sees on television, and especially within "low-brow" programs, would lead to an over-all depletion of the ability of the public to see the world in a complex, nuanced way. Too much TV, he warned, would allow the "bad stuff [to] drive out the good, since it is more easily understood and enjoyed" (Macdonald 1957: 61), leading to a "narcotized acceptance of Mass Culture and of the commodities it sells as a substitute for the unsettling and unpredictable (hence unsalable) joy, tragedy, wit, change, originality, and beauty of real life" (Macdonald 1957: 72). In a sense, this view depicts the television as a Manchurian candidate that is smuggling harmful ideology inside of a harmless-looking container. As Adorno concludes,

> Meaning has been taken over by cultural industry inasmuch as what it conveys becomes itself organized in order to enthrall the spectators on various psychological levels simultaneously. As a matter of fact, the hidden message may be more important than the overt, since this hidden message will escape the controls of consciousness, will not be "looked through," will not be warded off by sales resistance, but is likely to sink into the spectator's mind [Adorno 1957: 479].

Forrester's experiment brings these fears to life by trying to reverse engineer the social concerns of the 1950s into a recipe for world domination. He floods his subjects with B-movie "bad stuff," hoping to root out all of the joy, wit, and originality inside Joel and Mike in order to more easily get them to accept *his* messages of subjugation. Even Forrester's decision to send Joel and Mike into space is an exaggeration of Anders, who noted with displeasure that television tended to isolate people from one another and from the outside world:

The mass produced hermit came into being as a new human type, and now millions of them, cut off from each other, yet identical with each other, remain in the seclusion of their homes. Their purpose, however, is not to renounce the world, but to be sure they won't miss the slightest crumb of the world as image on the screen [Anders 1957: 359].

The use of the Satellite of Love to maroon Mike and Joel in space is merely a tactic derived from Anders's belief that television was marooning the American people in their own living rooms.

Later theorists such as Stuart Hall, Roger Silverstone, and John Fiske rebelled against the dire predictions of their predecessors. They playfully described Macdonald, Adorno, and Anders's refusal to allow for any power or agency in television audiences using science fictional rhetoric referring to the trope of the "mad scientist." For example, Silverstone notes that "such arguments raise the spectre of total passivity, of views of the audience as rats in a maze, making artificial and meaningless choices under the illusion (if rats have illusions) that they are meaningful" (Silverstone 1994: 108). Hall also evokes the image of a mad doctor when he writes that "though we know the television programme is not a behavioral input, like a tap on the knee cap, it seems to have been almost impossible for traditional researchers to conceptualize the communicative process without lapsing into one or other variant of low-flying behaviorism" (Hall 1980: 131).

Luckily for Joel and Mike, these scholars argue against the prospect that audience members have *no* agency to shape and critique what they watch, making possible an escape from Dr. Forrester's plots. Taking Stuart Hall as a point of departure, John Fiske believes in "active audiences" (Fiske 2003: 49). He sets about "contradict[ing] theories that stress the singularity of television's meanings and its reading subjects" (Fiske 2003: 63), which he believes are focused too narrowly on the limitations on viewership. He argues that

Textual studies of television now have to stop treating it as a closed text, that is, as one where the dominant ideology exerts considerable, if not total, influence over its ideological structure and therefore over its reader. Analysis has to pay less attention to the textual strategies of preference or closure and more to the gaps and spaces that open television up to meanings not preferred by the textual structure, but that result from the social experience of the reader [Fiske 2003: 64].

Fiske emphasizes the freedoms taken up by the audience, such as "the viewers' ability to make their own socially pertinent meanings out of the semiotic resources provided by television" (Fiske 2003: 65). His theoretical perspective "optimistically envisions audiences as more savvy and empowered than had previously been believed" (Nakamura: 2008 34), and, as I will argue in the following section, these freedoms are what allow Joel, Mike, Tom Servo, and Crow to confound the mad scientists at every turn.

Space Mutinies: The Satellite of Love Crew as Textual Poachers

Dr. Forrester does not succeed in his experiments because his test subjects employ various viewing strategies that afford them some leeway in order to determine the meanings of a text for themselves. Henry Jenkins theorizes that these viewing strategies were developed by fans of genres such as science fiction and fantasy that were dismissed by scholars like Macdonald, Adorno, and Anders. According to Jenkins, the acts of reading performed by these fans are actually more like acts of writing in that they involve the cultivation of creative interpretations (Jenkins 1992: 62–63). As Stuart Hall would put it, "the consumption or reception of the television message" becomes, with the help of these generative viewing strategies, "also itself a 'moment' of the production process in its larger sense" (Hall 1980: 130). These reading practices are participatory. They are interactive. They require viewers to look for ways to get involved with the text, to shape and sculpt the text in order to bring it in line with their own needs. This active version of consumption is called "poaching," and it consists of "a type of cultural bricolage through which readers fragment texts and reassemble the broken shards according to their own blueprints, salvaging bits and pieces of the found material in making sense of their own experience" (Jenkins 1992: 26).

Poaching "focuses attention on the social agency of readers. The reader is drawn not into the pre-constituted world of the fiction but rather into a world she has created from the textual materials. Here, the reader's pre-established values are at least as important as those preferred by the narrative system" (Jenkins 1992: 63). In other words, readers like Mike and Joel refuse to passively accept the entirety of the text, but rather, during the act of viewing, they pick and choose the bits of the text that they want to affirm and discard the rest. They also add ideas of their own to that text. They literally "scribble in the margins," riffing in between the lines from a location on the outside border of the screen (Jenkins 1992: 152). They alter the text to suit their own tastes rather than tailoring themselves to the requirements of the text as earlier theorists feared they might.

Joel and Mike avoid the perils of media-induced isolation by choosing to conduct the experiments alongside a group of friends, though they were forced to *make* those friends out of spare parts lying around the Satellite of Love when other viewing partners did not prove to be available in outer space. According to Jenkins, participatory viewing "is not a solitary and private process but rather a social and public one" (Jenkins 1992: 75), and the camaraderie between members of various television-viewing communities is evident in the form of practices like viewing parties (Jenkins 1992: 76), the trading of VHS tapes containing missed episodes (Jenkins 1992: 71), and the creation of online communities revolving around their favorite shows (Jenkins 1992: 69). This type of viewership brings a "collective intelligence" to bear on the texts it approaches, which helps to foster multiple perspectives about a text rather than a passive assimilation of just one perspective (Jenkins 1992: 254).

The characters that Mike and Joel play use the mindset of an active audience member to survive, and as artists, Hodgson and Nelson go even further to contribute to a media environment that Jenkins believes has the potential to be democratic and anti-corporate. A convergence culture is a place "where old and new media collide, where grassroots and corporate media intersect, where the power of the media producer and the power of the media consumer interact in unpredictable ways" (Jenkins 2006: 2). The calling card of convergence is "the flow of content across multiple media platforms, the cooperation between multiple media industries, and the migratory behavior of media audiences who will go almost anywhere in search of the kind of entertainment experiences they want" (Jenkins 2006: 2). As a result, "Consumers will be more powerful within convergence culture ... if they recognize and use that power as both consumers and citizens, as full participants in our culture" (Jenkins 2006: 260).

Mystery Science Theater 3000 and its various spin-off programs exemplified the spirit of today's convergence cultures, even before Jenkins coined the term, in that it never settled on a single distribution platform but instead constantly expanded onto new platforms throughout its broadcast history. *MST3K* also epitomizes a particular mindset often found within convergence culture enthusiasts which reject[s] the idea of a definitive version [of a text] produced, authorized, and regulated by some media conglomerate. Instead, fans envision a world where all of us can participate in the creation and circulation of central cultural myths. Here, the right to participate in the culture is assumed to be the "freedom we have allowed ourselves," not a privilege granted by a benevolent company, not something they are prepared to barter away for better sound files or free Web hosting. Fans also reject the studio's assumption that intellectual property is a "limited good," to be tightly controlled lest it dilute its value. Instead, they embrace an understanding of intellectual property as "shareware," something that accrues value as it moves across different contexts, gets retold in various ways, attracts multiple audiences, and opens itself up to a proliferation of meanings [Jenkins 2006: 256].

Of course, Nelson and Hodgson add value to bad movies by riffing on them, and once outside of their on-camera personas, they also thumb their noses at corporate ideas about intellectual property by maintaining a healthy disrespect for the notion of copyright when it comes to participatory fan practices like tape trading. During the first four seasons of the show, the final credits sequence for each episode ended by telling fans to "keep circulating the tapes" (Cornell and Henry 1992b), though this was amended by Trace Beaulieu in an interview with *The Onion's AV Club* after Rhino Home Video began selling VHS tapes and DVDs of certain episodes to "keep circulating *some* of the tapes" (Phipps, emphasis added). Even so, several of those Rhino Home DVD releases gently mock the FBI warnings against piracy and unauthorized distribution by adorning them with an image of J. Edgar Hoover that has been festooned with graffiti, a choice which is yet another example of their tendency to "scribble in the margins" (see Figure 1). They have even turned a blind eye to the virtual tape traders using peer-to-peer sharing software at the *Digital Archive Project*, so long as episodes that are available for purchase on either DVD or VHS remain unavailable for download ("Digital Archive Project FAQ" 2002).

In some cases, these freedoms afforded by participatory convergence cultures can nurture progressive, democratic political content. Dr. Forrester hoped that the terrible movies he forced upon Mike and Joel would drain them of their will to resist, but he was actually unwittingly providing them with the makings of an underground counter-cinema dubbed "paracinema" by its enthusiasts (Sconce 1995: 374). Paracinema is a fairly "elastic" category of film that includes "entries from such seemingly disparate subgenres as 'badfilm,' splatterpunk, 'mondo' films, sword and sandal epics, Elvis flicks, government hygiene films, Japanese monster movies, beach-party musicals, and just about every other historical manifestation of exploitation cinema from juvenile

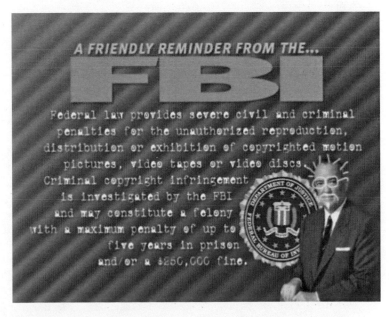

Thumbing their nose at copyright law (Murphy 1999, Episode 1002).

delinquency documentaries to soft-core pornography," a list which fans of *MST3K* would likely find quite recognizable (Sconce 1995: 372).

According to Jeffery Sconce,

> Paracinema is thus less a distinct group of films than a particular reading protocol, a counter-aesthetic turned subcultural sensibility devoted to all manner of cultural detritus. In short, the explicit manifesto of paracinematic culture is to valorize all forms of cinematic "trash," whether such films have been either explicity rejected or simply ignored by legitimate film culture. In doing so, paracinema represents the most developed and dedicated of cinephilic subcultures ever to worship at the "temple of schlock" [Sconce 1995: 372].

Paracinema enthusiasts place their favored "trash" films under the same kinds of intense scrutiny that is usually reserved for "high-brow" cinema, which allows for a more critical audience position than theorists like Macdonald, Adorno, and Anders supposed possible for mass produced entertainments. By mixing high-class critical know-how with low-class entertainments, paracinema enthusiasts declare that the tastes of the masses are just as worthy of academic attention as those favored by elites (Sconce 1995: 375).

In addition to being well-versed in academic and critical discourses, participants in convergence cultures are usually very well-read. They use this pool of knowledge in order to "read intertextually as well as textually and their pleasure comes through the particular juxtapositions that they create between specific program content and other cultural materials" (Jenkins 1992: 37). For fans of *MST3K*, this intertextual reading style is primarily actualized through allusions and references to an amazingly diverse set of texts ranging from the classics of cinema and literature to more esoteric cult films to other episodes of *Mystery Science Theater 3000* itself. This allows viewers to demonstrate their "competence among codes and conventions [as well as], the knowledges, skills, and differences (real and imagined) which make up the mosaic of contemporary culture" (Silverstone 1994: 115). In fact, the competency that a viewer demonstrates via their understanding of these references determines one's status in the paracinematic community. Michael J. Nelson's latest project, *RiffTrax*, allows viewers to demonstrate this competence even further by empowering them to take on the role of the riffer themselves. Community members can create iRiffs, homegrown audio commentary tracks for movies and shorts that are hosted and sold for them on the *RiffTrax* website. iRiffs are the ultimate outgrowth of convergence cultures in that they allow audience members to participate in (and profit from) the production of new texts and the creation of new readings of old texts, as some of them are simply new takes on the films that *MST3K* and *RiffTrax* have already riffed.

The Final Sacrifice: The Consequences of a Convergence Culture

Despite the enthusiasm that this description inspires, it is important to keep in mind that a fan who participates in a convergence culture carries special burdens above and beyond those required of a more passive audience member. First, the mingling of corporate and underground sensibilities that occurs within convergence cultures always runs the risk of creating "sell-outs," as corporate entities re-package and market a sub-culture back to its grassroots creators in order to make a profit. By "making it big" on cable and in theaters, *Mystery Science Theater 3000* exposes paracinema's underground culture, which originated in do-it-yourself 'zine publications such as *Psychotronic Video, Zontar, Subhuman, Trashola,*

Ungawa, Pandemonium, and the RE/Search volume, *Incredibly Strange Films,*" (Sconce 1995: 372) to a "paradox" (Jenkins 2006: 62):

> Commodification is also a form of exploitation. Those groups that are commodified find themselves targeted more aggressively by marketers and often feel they have lost control over their own culture, since it is mass produced and mass marketed. One cannot help but have conflicted feelings because one doesn't want to go unrepresented — but one doesn't want to be exploited, either [Jenkins 2006: 62–63].

In cases like these, access to a sub-culture that has been taken up by the mainstream media is actually restricted as the cost of participation rises from the negligible cost of VHS tape trading between generous and enthusiastic fans to the cost of a cable subscription, and later, the cost of a personal computer, an Internet connection, and an ever-expanding collection of books and DVDs.

Thus, participation in a convergence culture like the one that has grown up around *MST3K* requires a significant outlaying of both labor and funds. As discussed above, one proves one's fanhood by demonstrating a mastery of the references tossed out by the riffers, some of which are extremely obscure. For example, *The* Mystery Science Theater 3000 *Amazing Colossal Episode Guide* contains a list of the fifty most obscure references in the show (Beaulieu, Chaplin, Mallon, et al., 1996: 161–171). Many of them are intended only for Minnesota locals and one or two of them are inside jokes for the cast and crew alone. Knowledge of these riffs necessarily demonstrates ultimate mastery, but it is nearly impossible to obtain without conducting additional research on the show. This forces "newbies" to invest a great deal of money and labor into the show by catching up on missed episodes on DVD, reading official episode guides, and visiting the websites of Mike and Joel's current projects to keep themselves apprised of new developments. These websites, in turn, lead fans towards still more purchases. The *RiffTrax* business model is a bold example of the potential for the commodification of community membership within convergence cultures. While the website trades in movie mockery, it is also an advertising hub for DVDs; when a fan buys a *RiffTrax* download, they are almost always given a link to an Amazon.com page for the film that they want to see torn apart. Even the iRiffs program commodifies fan participation. While fans create the content and set their own prices within a certain range, *RiffTrax* takes fifty percent of the profits made by each iRiffs installment as a hosting fee (Nelson 2009).

Furthermore, models of convergence cultures on the Internet often exaggerate the extent to which fan participation is democratic by ignoring the experiences of female fans and fans of color. According to Lisa Nakamura,

> Jenkins's argument that audiences of the digital age demand and deserve the right to participate in the formation of media texts to put in dialogue with those that they see around them, thus resulting in productive forms of "textual poaching," puts much faith in the notion that this is a desirable outcome because it will result in "better," or at least more diverse and democratic art [Nakamura 2008: 50].

Nakamura argues that utopian visions of the Internet pre-date Jenkins's discourse around fan cultures. The medium itself has been praised since the early 1990s for its supposedly liberatory ability to transfer the authority of the author to the reader. Such praise for Internet technology has

> been around since the early days of text-only Internet and hypertext theory, which posited that readers could choose their own endings to digital narratives and thus exercise their postmodern

subjectivities and literalize the notions of readerly resistance to authorial intention by becoming co-authors of a work [Nakamura 2008: 50].

On the contrary, Nakamura's research into the visual cultures of the Internet demonstrates that it "is anything but a space of utopian humanism where differences between genders, races, and nationalities are leveled out; on the contrary, it is an intensely active, productive space of visual signification where these differences are intensified, modulated, reiterated, and challenged" (Nakamura 2008: 34).

To be fair, Jenkins does briefly address these issues in his discussion of the "participation gap" (Jenkins 2006: 258). Typically, the term "participation gap" refers to a disparity of access to the types of computer technologies that make convergence cultures possible.

Though Jenkins does not mention gender in his evaluation, a cursory examination of the experiences of many women on the Internet will demonstrate that there is a digital divide between men and women online. From the catcalls, harassment, and stalking they may experience in online gaming environments like *World of Warcraft* and Playstation 3's *HOME* (a few isolated examples pulled from gaming forums and blogs can be found at Hikani October 17, 2009, Verena November 24, 2008, and Kevi21 November 23, 2008) to the constant insistence from men in chatrooms and on male-dominated forums like 4-chan and somethingawful.com that female posters upload a picture of their "tits or GTFO," or "get the f**k out" (Disgruntled Pumpkin October 22, 2009), women are definitely treated like second-class citizens in many parts of cyberspace. Although the numerical divide between male and female users has essentially closed, by 2003 the percentages of women and men online reached a stable equilibrium (Nakamura 2008: 154), and women in general were late adopters of online technologies (Nakamura 2008: 136). So, while men may not currently have "greater access" to Internet technology, their head start in the digital race affords them with the privilege of greater confidence in their abilities to work with that technology.

Unfortunately, this confidence often translates into the assumption that female users lack these abilities, causing some male users to look down upon female users or to single them out for "griefing" or online harassment. This means that, although fans in general have a greater amount of control over content in a convergence culture such as the one that has grown up around *Mystery Science Theater 3000*, an inclusive environment for all fans is not guaranteed merely by the existence of freedoms online. On the contrary, a "boys club" atmosphere can easily be shaped by fan-produced content that objectifies women and makes light of women's issues. Such content is like a neon sign saying "women are not welcome here."

A precedent for the distinction between male and female fans was set back in the early days of *Mystery Science Theater 3000*. Jessica A. Royer notes that, during the early seasons, there were no female writers on the show, which means that sexist jokes occasionally made it onto the air (Royer 2000: 120–125). Even after Mary Jo Pehl joined the writing staff in 1992 (Cornell and Henry 1992c), the crew of the Satellite of Love still subtly communicated the notion that women should not be riffers. There is only one robot (excluding Magic Voice, who is not listed in the opening credits as one of Joel and Mike's "robot friends"), Gypsy, who identifies as female. Gypsy "is a cartoonishly feminine robot with a squeaky 'bimbo' voice and bright red lips" who has "few lines and little screen time in comparison with her male counterparts (human and robot)" (Royer 2000: 118). Gypsy is typically unable to set aside her other duties and join the boys watching the movie. Instead, she runs the ship, takes cares of Joel and Mike's everyday needs, and makes sure that everything runs smoothly while they play in the theater. She is built from practical household goods, including an infant's car seat, while Tom Servo and Crow are made up mostly of sporting goods and toys (Cornell and Henry 2002), a bodily difference which points to a "mothering" type of functionality for her. In addition, Gypsy is portrayed as a bit ditzy during the host segments because her brain function is drained by the millions of tasks that she must do to make the Satellite of Love habitable to Joel and Mike (Cornell and Henry 2002). She is "kept silent by her duties, which are the traditionally feminine roles of nurturing and being responsible for the lives of everyone on the ship" (Royer 2000: 125). Her example is not encouraging to female fans who might want to try their hand at the types of textual play afforded to fans in a participatory culture. Rather, the show suggests that such play is reserved for male participants.

And although there are several female iRiffs creators on *RiffTrax* and *RiffTrax Presents*, some fans on Nelson's site are producing content that makes female fans, the author of this essay included, feel unwelcome. For example StephenInReston's SharpShooter Productions iRiff on the 1950s educational short about sexual consent, "How Much Affection," opens with a trivialization of rape. In the first scene of the movie, a young woman jumps out of a car and flees to the front door of her home. Her date follows after her. The riffer speaks for him, "Look, I didn't think no meant *no*" (StephenInReston November 17, 2009). In the same riffer's "The Gossip," StephenInReston cuts directly to the chase by musing aloud to his audience, "Women... They suck" (StephenInReston February 14, 2009). A fan named Mr. B Natural is slightly less subtle. He says in the opening moments of his iRiff of *Cat Women of the Moon* that he chose this particular film because "it explores one of [his] favorite subjects: women and their pussies" (Mr. B Natural May 29, 2009). It is not difficult to imagine female fans of *Mystery Science Theater 3000* feeling put off by these "jokes."

Mystery Science Theater 3000 and its current iterations exemplify both the virtues and the faults of Jenkins's convergence cultures. As Jenkins notes, "the power of participation comes not from destroying commercial culture but from writing over it, modding it, amending it, expanding it, adding greater diversity of perspective, and then recirculating it, feeding it back into the mainstream media" (Jenkins 2006: 257). These powers are the key strengths of the cultures of riffing ushered in by *MST3K*. One thing is for certain: we need not fear falling victim to Dr. Forrester's nightmare vision of a docile American television audience as long as we utilize the reading strategies modeled for us by Joel, Mike, and the 'bots. However, convergence cultures are not so divorced from corporate profit motives that we can safely label them as uniformly populist, and although these reading techniques allow for great freedoms of creation and interpretation, they do not guarantee the existence of inclusive communities. We can best actualize our dreams of a democratic media environment when we are realistic about the limitations of convergence cultures even as we work to expand their strengths, and so it is important to take into account the experiences of marginal groups of fans, such as women, even as we sing the praises of participatory fandom.

REFERENCES

Adorno, T. W. "Television and the Patterns of Mass Culture," in Bernard Rosenberg and David Manning White, eds. *Mass Culture: The Popular Arts in America*. Glencoe, IL: Free Press, 1957.
Anders, Gunter. "Phantom World of TV," in Bernard Rosenberg and David Manning White, eds. *Mass Culture: The Popular Arts in America*. Glencoe, IL: Free Press, 1957.
Beaulieu, Trace, Paul Chaplin, Jim Mallon, et al. *The Mystery Science Theater 3000 Amazing Colossal Episode Guide*. New York: Bantam Books, 1996.

Cornell, Christopher, and Brian Henry. "Cancellation and its Aftermath." Mystery Science Theater 3000 *Frequently Asked Questions. Satellite News* 1992a. Accessed 12/05/09. http://www.mst3kinfo.com/mst-faq/cancel.html.

_____ and _____. "East Meets West (1991–92)." *The Almost but Still Not Quite Complete History of* Mystery Science Theater 3000. *Satellite News* 2002. Accessed 12/01/09. http://www.mst3kinfo.com/history/page 6.html.

_____ and _____. "Legalities." Mystery Science Theater 3000 *Frequently Asked Questions. Satellite News* 1992b. Accessed 12/01/09. http://www.mst3kinfo.com/mstfaq/legal.html.

_____ and _____. "Parts: The Bot Building Horror." Mystery Science Theater 3000 *Frequently Asked Questions. Satellite News* 1992c. Accessed 12/05/09. http://www.mst3kinfo.com/mstfaq/bots.html.

_____ and _____. "The Sci-Fi Channel (and Sci*fi)." Mystery Science Theater 3000 *Frequently Asked Questions. Satellite News* 1992d. Accessed 12/05/09 http://www.mst3kinfo.com/mstfaq/scifi.html.

_____ and _____. "Where Are They Now?." Mystery Science Theater 3000 *Frequently Asked Questions. Satellite News* 1992e. Accessed 12/5/09 http://www.mst3kinfo.com/mstfaq/wbrains.html.

"Digital Archive Project FAQ (Frequently Asked Questions." *Digital Archive Project* 2002. Accessed 11/14/09 http://www.dapcentral.org/.

Disgruntled Pumpkin. "Know Your Meme: Tits or GTFO." *Know Your Meme* October 22, 2009. Accessed 01/06/10. http://knowyourmeme.com/memes/tits-or-gtfo.

Fiske, John. *Television Culture* 12th edition. New York: Routledge, 2003.

Hall, Stuart. "Encoding/decoding," in Stuart Hall, Dorothy Hobson, Andrew Lowe, et al., eds. *Culture, Media, Language: Working Papers in Cultural Studies, 1972–79*. London: Hutchinson and Co., 1980.

Hartley, John. *Uses of Television*. New York: Routledge, 1999.

Hikani. "Stalking help, please?" *World of Warcraft Forums* October 17, 2009. Accessed 01/06/10. http://forums.worldofwarcraft.com/thread.html?topicId=20565927325&sid=1.

Hodgson, Joel and Josh Weinstein. "Theme Song Lyrics: For episodes 101 through 512." 1989. Christopher Cornell and Brian Henry. Mystery Science Theater 3000 *Frequently Asked Questions. Satellite News* 1992. Accessed 12/01/09. http://www.mst3kinfo.com/mstfaq/lyrics.html.

Jenkins, Henry. *Convergence Cultures: Where Old and New Media Collide*. New York: New York University Press, 2006.

_____. *Textual Poachers: Television Fans & Participatory Culture*. New York: Routledge, 1992.

Kevi21. "HOME problem needs to be sorted!" *Playstation Home Forums* November 23, 2008. Accessed 01/06/10. http://community.eu.playstation.com/t5/PlayStation-Home/HOME-problem-needs-to-be-sorted/m-p/6020439.

Mander, Jerry. *Four Arguments for the Elimination of Television*. New York: Morrow, 1978.

MacDonald, Dwight. "A Theory of Mass Culture," in Bernard Rosenberg and David Manning White, eds., *Mass Culture: The Popular Arts in America*. Glencoe, IL: Free Press, 1957.

Minow, Newton N. "Television and the Public Interest (Lecture at the National Association of Broadcasters, Washington D.C.)." May 9th, 1961. *American Rhetoric* 2009. Accessed 12/01/09 http://www.americanrhetoric.com/speeches/newtonminow.htm.

Mr. B Natural. "Mr. B Natural: *Cat Women of the Moon*." *iRiffs. RiffTrax* May 29, 2009. Accessed 11/29/09 http://www.rifftrax.com/iriffs/mrbnatural-cat-women-moon.

Mallon, Jim (director), Joel Hodgeson (creator), Michael J. Nelson (writer), et al. *Mystery Science Theater 3000: The Movie*. Image Entertainment, 1996.

Murphy, Kevin (director), Michael J. Nelson (head writer), Paul Chaplin (writer) et al. Episode 1002 *The Girl in Gold Boots*. Rhino, 1999.

Nakamura, Lisa. *Digitizing Race: Visual Cultures of the Internet*. Minneapolis: University of Minnesota Press, 2008.

Nelson, Michael J. "iRiffs FAQ." *RiffTrax* 2009. Accessed 11/05/09 http://www.rifftrax.com/iriffs-faq.

Phipps, Keith. "The *Mystery Science Theater 3000* Reunion Interview: Joel Hodgson, Trace Beaulieu, and Jim Mallon." *The AV Club* November 3, 2008. Accessed 10/31/09. http://www.avclub.com/articles/the-mystery-science-theater-3000-reunion-interview,14327/.

Postman, Neal. *Amusing Ourselves to Death : Public Discourse in the Age of Show Business*. New York: Viking, 1985.

Royer, Jessica A. "What's Happening on Earth? *Mystery Science Theater 3000* as Reflection of Gender Roles and Attitudes Towards Women," in Elyce Rae Helford, ed. *Fantasy Girls: Gender in the New Universe of Science Fiction and Fantasy Television*. Lanham, MD: Rowman and Littlefield Publishers, Inc., 2000.

Sconce, Jeffery. "'Trashing' the Academy: Taste, Excess, and an Emerging Politics of Cinematic Style." *Screen* 36:4 (Winter 1995): 371–393.

Silverstone, Roger. *Television and Everyday Life*. New York: Routledge, 1994.

Spigel, Lynn. *Welcome to the Dreamhouse: Popular Media and the Post-war Suburbs.* Durham, NC: Duke University Press, 2001.

StephenInReston, SharpShooter Productions. "The Gossip." *iRiffs. RiffTrax* February 14, 2009. Accessed 11/29/09 http://www.rifftrax.com/iriffs/sharpshooter-productions/gossip.

_____. "How Much Affection." *iRiffs. RiffTrax* November 17, 2009. Accessed 11/29/09 http://www.rifftrax.com/iriffs/sharpshooter-productions/how-much-affection.

Verena. "Playstation Home is Not for Women." *Verena's Welt: An Australian in America* November 24, 2008. Accessed 01/06/10. http://www.verenaswelt.at/2008/11/24/playstation-home-is-not-for-women/.

8

"Consume excrement and thus expire": Conflict Resolution, "Fantagonism," and alt.tv.mst3k

by Jeremy Groskopf

On October 30, 1993, Comedy Central premiered the 13th episode, of its fifth national season, of *Mystery Science Theater 3000: The Brain That Wouldn't Die*. On this day, the legions of MSTies across the country were treated, for the first time, to the work of new host Mike Nelson (played with an "everyman" simplicity and rambunctiousness by Michael J. Nelson). Original host Joel Robinson (played as a sleepy-eyed father figure by series creator Joel Hodgson) had officially departed the show at the end of the previous week. A change in central character would send shockwaves through the fan base of any successful show, but this change resulted in such a groundswell of anger and infighting that the young internet could barely contain the vitriol — or so the fans' own historicizing would have us believe. The semi-official website *Satellite News* recalls the moment in a tone reminiscent of wartime remembrance:

> The online communities created around the series ... [developed] two factions, one cheerfully celebrating [the change], the other dolefully condemning it. It was clear that both sides were not prepared to tolerate the presence of the other, and neither faction felt in any way disposed to depart a community they felt was their "home" in the online world. It was a recipe for disaster.
>
> The two factions began to argue, and in short order these arguments escalated into *The Great Joel vs. Mike Flamewar of 1993*, which raged, to varying degrees, everywhere in MSTie cyberspace. In each place ... the same thing happened: Polite discussions and reasonable critiques turned into angry exchanges ... [which] evolved into personal attacks.
>
> Harsh and angry words were exchanged and almost everywhere things got very personal and very mean, each side accusing the other of intolerance and much worse. Pretty soon, the TV show that had started the arguments faded into the background as petty personal feuds were brought into the open, and a broader and extremely bitter debate about censorship and free speech and rights vs. responsibilities in the on-line world raged. [...]
>
> The shouting did not subside for months [Cornell and Henry, "Part 9: Schism"].

The implication here is that there was a unified fan base which then split, resulting in a pitched battle for dominance. As the fan base still existed in order to historicize itself, we must also assume that the split was eventually healed, though no reasons are given for how or why such a thing happened. What we purportedly have, then, is a blip on the radar of an otherwise unified fanbase. But there are problems with this history: it is written by the fans themselves, with no reference to specific events or other evidence.

Democratic unity, rather than all-out war, is clearly evident in at least one of the online newsgroups for *MST3K* — alt.tv.mst3k — active during the late 1993 and early 1994 "Flame-war." A perusal of the posts to this group reveals a fight that was significantly less combative, far less long lasting, and almost entirely devoid of "intolerance." Repeated attempts by some fans to turn aesthetic debates (casting, writing, character relations, and the "meaning" of the show) into a consensus persistently failed to generate much more than the comment "they're just different; neither era is better." Indeed, it seems that an assumption of unity in the fan group — along any line — is far more pronounced than its actual practice.

In the pages that follow, I will lay out a general history of roughly six months' worth of newsgroup messages at alt.tv.mst3k. The selection of this particular group is one of convenience. Though many *MST3K* centered newsgroups existed at the end of 1993 — including the Compuserve group, widely believed to be the one most often visited by the Best Brains themselves — only the alt.tv.mst3k group is readily available via archiving (thanks to Google's "Groups" search) and of a suitably large size to be analyzed. The analysis of the statements posted to this group will show a clear distinction between the type of factional conflict implied in the accepted history of the moment and the comradeship in evidence in actual group discussion. Over the course of this history it will become clear that, at least in the case of *MST3K*, fan behavior — even in the most trying of times — operates in a way consistent with interpretive openness, not interpretive consensus, and tends towards a use of humor that parallels *MST3K* itself: as a form of teasing between the members of the group.

Fandom, Fan-tagonism, Humor, and Hegemony

It is not uncommon, in the published critical disdain for *MST3K*, to read assumptions similar to this one by noted film critic Jonathan Rosenbaum: "the filmmakers were clearly counting on audiences believing that any science fiction movie made in the 1950s is idiotic by definition." Rosenbaum goes on to refer to the selection of the film as a quest for a "stinkburger" and chides the writers for coming up with lame jokes simply to "prove how smart [they] are" (Rosenbaum, 1996). Such assumptions about the perspective of the show are undoubtedly commonplace and, to be fair, are not entirely in disagreement with *MST3K*'s own image; for example, it is pretty difficult to persuasively argue that the endless parade of fat jokes in *Mitchell* (Murphy, episode 512) is affectionate rather than cruel. However, to simply accept that the program takes an elitist or aggressive stance towards its material as a matter of course — or even that a joke must be one or the other, affectionate *or* cruel — is to turn the show's philosophy into a "straw man." Such a perspective is grounded in the old theory that laughter is, by its very nature, only one step removed from aggression. Henri Bergson, for example, believed that laughter and compassion were effectively antithetical, claiming that the comic "goes his own way without troubling himself about getting in touch with the rest of his fellow beings" as comedy represents a "callousness to social life" (Bergson, 1980: 147). To take up such a perspective is to ignore the distinction between "laughing at" and "laughing with" — ridicule and teasing. In order to understand humor — and, for that matter, any dialectical interaction — one must remain cognizant of the fine gradations between the poles of aggression and affection.

One can hardly fault cultural scholars and critics in general, and Rosenbaum in particular, for such a failing, as broader cultural theorizing often falls prey to this same issue — presuming that aggression and affection are easy to isolate. Fan studies in general tends to stress only one of the two poles at a time. Henry Jenkins, with his stress on the value of a "participatory culture" (in which consumers become creative producers in their own right by rethinking and recreating the culture which they enjoy), stresses the individuality of fans, but ultimately leaves implicit the notion that fans uncritically support and encourage creativity that comes from within the group — as though fandom itself is a utopian realm of "folk culture" (Jenkins 2006). Jonathan Gray nuances this perspective a bit in his exploration of the anti-fan — "those who hate or dislike a given text, personality, or genre" (Gray, 2005: 841) — but still leaves fan groups as, ultimately, a united whole under attack from outsiders. Classical fan studies did virtually nothing with in-group conflict.

Derek Johnson does some of the groundwork to allow us to examine fan interactions such as the "Great Joel vs. Mike Flamewar," as he focuses specifically on group infighting and fracture — the blurry zone between Jenkins' fan utopia and Gray's fans under siege. Johnson's "fan-tagonism" concept adds to the discussion a notion of fandom as eternally in conflict over the meaning and value of its text. Johnson's point — that "divergent fan interests" produce a proliferation of preferred readings of a given text (Johnson, 2007: 286) — is well taken, but his further contention that fandom is, therefore, a small-scale hegemonic power game is more problematic. Specifically, his contention that "[a]lternative positions and tastes must somehow be silenced so that divergent interests within a community can be unified as hegemonic interpretative consensus" (Johnson, 2007: 287) is no less totalizing and problematic than Jenkins' eternally united fans.

The problem is two-fold. Firstly, Johnson's analysis, centered as it is on *Buffy the Vampire Slayer* and fan hopes for the future progression of the story, hopelessly entwines fandom with narrative (specifically, attempts to predict plot twists and the concomitant stratification of any series into eras more or less in line with the hoped for ending). This cannot work in *MST3K*, as it is a program with little, if any, narrative development; without a dramatic story arc of any particular relevance, the *MST3K* fan has little narrative future upon which to hang their hopes — aside, perhaps, from choosing between a fatherly relationship (Joel and the Bots) and a "brotherly" one (Mike and the Bots). Secondly, we must be wary of conflating two types of hegemony theory: the political and the aesthetic. Political hegemony theory, expressed clearly by Celeste Condit (1994) in her conception of "concordance," is one in which individuals who have stakes in society may be convinced to take up beliefs that are seemingly against their own interests. Bordwellian aesthetic hegemony, meanwhile, is an almost "passive," victimless argument for why the Classical Hollywood style might have developed; Bordwell leaves the politics of hegemony aside and makes Hollywood into little more than a machine which repeats particular meanings and approaches for no reason other than streamlining and simplicity. To imply that fan debates are reconciled by political hegemonic power struggles is to assume that "victory" is the point of any argumentation, and that "social control" is the necessary outcome of any majority opinion. However, this is an unfair extrapolation which — much like the correlation of humor with aggression — privileges the notion of conflict over any notion of camaraderie. Any study of fandom must surely be forced to admit that a fan group is based far more strongly in camaraderie than conflict, and must take pains not to over-stress the behavior of a very vocal, but nonetheless minority group of participants. However, the fans' history of their "war" commits both of these potential errors: over-stressing the difference between Joel and Mike's relationship with the Bots, and leaning towards conflict and victory as the only plausible model for dis-agreement.

The humor philosophy of the Best Brains themselves offers a strong counterargument to such overly politicized approaches to fan activity. Using a metaphor attributed to original cast member Trace Beaulieu, it is common, in interviews, to hear any given Best Brains member compare the relationship of Joel/Mike and the Bots and the films to the relationship between the Marx Brothers' and their co-star Margaret Dumont (Wolinsky 2009). The implication is that, although the Marxes/riffers might appear to mercilessly mock Dumont / the films with their humor, in actuality, Dumont and the films must hold a reasonable amount of viewer interest on their own. The humor comes from a collaboration of talents, not a one sided display of comic brilliance in the face of ineptitude. This "Dumont and the Marx Brothers" example may, in fact, be the best way to think not just of the show, but of the fans relationships to each other. When a commentator loses sight of the value of the perspective of the object or individual under discussion, the commentary itself comes across as arrogant. An integrated, collaborative fan community is more functional as, even when one raises points of disagreement, the value of the other's perspective is affirmed in the same breath as it is critiqued. To argue within a group when one wishes to remain part of that group, one is beholden to see those with which one disagrees in the same light as the Marx Brothers saw Margaret Dumont: as worthy adversaries.

For a wider analysis of fandom, then, the truth seems to lie somewhere in between inclusiveness and hegemonic assertions — between argumentativeness and unity. At times a particular reading (likely already a politicized one) is beaten down or rendered invisible in a hegemonic power game. On most occasions, however, fandom seems to simply "agree to disagree," nullifying the possibility of power struggle by respectfully foregrounding a variance of taste. It does so because there are often no particular stakes to any argument, unlike in wider cultural hegemony in which one particular identity trait "may seem to disappear when individuals align along other markers of difference" (Staiger, 2005: 80) and support one belief at the overt expense of another. Rather than "ongoing, competitive struggles," then, online fandom most frequently works as a respectful, integrated society. In fact, it is those very members who behave in ways that might be described as politically hegemonic, and who clearly believe that "alternative positions and tastes must ... be silenced" (Johnson, 2007: 287), who most strongly annoy the group. It is these combative personalities who are ultimately the victims of the only clear "power struggle" to take place in a fan group. The remainder of the fan community refuses consensus in the name of multiple interpretations and only playful "fantagonism" — a culture which "riffs" its own arguments.

The "War" of '93

The time period of the "Flamewar," in this newsgroup, is book-ended by complaints about the station, Comedy Central. These consist of various gripes by the fans about the show's treatment by its station. Complaints range from the use of a station identifier "bug" (dubbed the "obnoxicon" by fans), to voice-overs during the end credits, to scrolling jokes, all in some way obscuring part of the program. The argument was nearly always about the fans and the show being disrespected by the network, which consistently failed to leave it alone; the goal was simply to fight for less irritating station advertising, or pine for a shift to another network, never to criticize the show or changes within it.

A single message to the group should be enough to clarify exactly how such complaints were approached. A fan named Sean McAfee, in the wee morning hours of February 12, 1994, was the first to complain about the then new "News Bites" crawl, in a message entitled "ARGH! Comedy Central, BITE ME!" His message was little more than a litany of sins:

> When will Comedy Central learn?
> They use the obnoxicon, MSTies complain, obnoxicon is removed.
> Penn does voiceovers over the ending credits, MSTies complain, Penn is removed.
> So tonight, I'm taping "The Killer Shrews" ... and during the opening sketch, what do I see? One of those damn scrolling newslines (or whatever the hell they call it), making a really lame joke about Steven Spielberg!
> If this keeps up, I think it's time for a roadtrip to CC headquarters so I can disembowel whoever approved this stupid idea with a dull spoon [McAfee 1994].

The post was followed with 14 other messages of unanimous condemnation over the next five days.

Clearly the bulk of the complaint here rests on an assumed superiority of a fan's sense of humor, which they see as uniformly different from the "lame" employees at Comedy Central, and the channel's assumed greater interests in profit and self-promotion than the integrity of the text. The fans clearly felt that they were defending their show from mishandling, and that the actual producers of the show at Best Brains, Inc., would have been happy for their support. This is an obvious instance of what Johnson refers to as a fan effort to "delegitimize institutional authority" over the text, as the interests of the fans and the creators are being set in sharp contrast to the interests of the station (Johnson, 2007: 291). As such, a consensus is built that all negative aspects arising from the "necessary evil" of the show's presence on a profit-driven television station are the result of exploitative network meddlers, while the show itself is unsullied by discussions of money. The humor of Best Brains is rendered pure and superior to "commercial humor" in a clearly hegemonic act, giving the fan base a sense of unity behind its show, regardless of what each fan's individual take might be on capitalism and corporate freedom. Here we have a clear instance of hegemonic conflict over the meaning of the show, and one which, though the "villains" are placed outside of the fan group as corporate stooges, is otherwise in line with Johnson's overly combative notion of fan-tagonism.

However, in actual conflict within the group at this time, what stands out is the persistent failure of arguments to ignite into anything like this type of divisiveness — to the type of "intolerant flame war" that has been described in the history. During the period described as the "Flamewar," posts to the newsgroup fall into a pattern of: (1) actual debates about thematic changes to the program and worries that Joel was "fired"; (2) a sense of finality and touchiness to the issue; and (3) a sense of irritation at those who persist in bringing up the topic, resulting in a wave of silly misinformation. The first section of the pattern consists of two concrete disputes and a number of smaller "Joel vs. Mike" threads which ultimately come across as inconsequential. The two major battles were centered on sexism (specifically whether or not it was more prevalent now that Mike had taken over), and on whether or not Joel was being slighted by the show by being referred to on one occasion as "the other guy" rather than by name.

The debate over whether or not the show was sexist began on December 16, when Mike's work as host was tied to "puerile, sexist humor" via the song "Tubular Boobular." The song, directed towards the quantity of skin on display in the film *Outlaw* (Beaulieu, episode 519), was effectively a string of sexual-innuendo nonsense (for example: "It's breasticaboobical, chesticamammical, pendular globular fun!"). The argument, though it burned very brightly, lasted only about a week, ending by roughly December 22 (with some straggler comments for a week thereafter). The argument, spanning a few threads, comprised more than 40 posts in 7 days.

Begun by a fan calling himself jfox, the argument started with a direct attack on the change, with the claim that "Mike STINKS!! Since his advent on the show, the robots have doubled their quota of jokes related to sex, and Mike is so sniggering and childish I can't bear to watch him" (jfox 1993–4). A few posts followed which clarified that there were no elements of his criticisms which were technically new to the show since Mike took over hosting (Mike had always been a writer, Gypsy had always been stupid, etc.)—posts which explicitly took the debate out of the realm of a Joel vs. Mike dispute and therefore, it should be noted, technically out of contention for inclusion in the supposed "Flamewar." Freed as the thread was from a "Joel vs. Mike" dispute, Amanda Lowry French attempted to take the debate to a higher level of gender theorizing with a long and complicated critique of the show as being organized around male oriented pop culture rather than female, arguing that the riffing was more frequently about science fiction and airplanes and Easy Bake Ovens and thimbles.

Though there were some extremely well reasoned counter-opinions to French's critique, the tone of the opposition became more and more dismissive as the dispute wore on. A regular named Bruce Gilbert provides a clear example; he opened his post with a list of fourteen "other viewpoints MST3K is not told from," including African Americans, Jews, Southerners, and "Fans of Michael Bolton." Though Gilbert followed this brush-off with a long and complicated counter-argument of his own, later posters began to echo the snark-iness of his opening joke, but without any larger rationale. The more patronizing and brief tirades by later posters simply brought other members of the group to French's defense. French's supporters argued that the critique was not "a criticism so much as an observation," and that the group had become far more upset than her analysis warranted. Within four days of the first post, Michael L. Sensor, brought the argument to a head by using the one and only phrase which actually seemed to trigger a return volley of antagonism from this group: "If you don't like MST3K … TURN IT OFF! WATCH SOMETHING ELSE!" (lenn, Frauwirth, et al. 1993) Over the course of the threads, the assumption became stronger and stronger than any gender critique of MST3K was effectively an attack on the show itself, with those who opposed the argument treating French and her supporters more and more as outsiders — as "anti-fans" rather than fellow fans. The skirmish finally ended when Gordon Dahlquist stated, in a gesture of inclusivity rather than consensus, "It is so irritating not to be able to even talk about issues of gender and culture without provoking these ground level rebuttals" (Dahlquist 1993).

Effectively, those who came to the defense of French's statement weren't defending her analysis — which almost everyone had a point of disagreement with — but were instead defending the value of her input to begin with. As such, the group was advocating an atmos-phere of debate and interpretive freedom. Here we have a clear instance in which one inter-pretation of the show was perceived as so in conflict with another interpretation, that a certain subset of the group deemed their own viewpoint "more correct." As Johnson would point out, battles such as these seem to become battles over "'true fan' status," in which only "one prescribed evaluative relationship to the text" can be sanctioned (Johnson, 2007: 290). Note how rapidly such arguments degenerated into statements like "if you don't like it, watch a different show!"

Upon further scrutiny, however, this example actually takes us into fuzzier realms ignored by Johnson — specifically, the acceptability of variance of opinion. A certain amount of hegemonic consensus generation was inevitable in this fight; the question of whether or not it was even possible to criticize the show as substantially gender biased had to be answered. However, in the final tally, we do not see any consensus form in the group as to what that ultimately means: the charge of sexism remained unsettled — was it a problem with the show, a problem with culture, or did a slant towards one gender's culture constitute no problem at all? Nor do we see any attempt at reaching such a consensus. Viewers who chose to believe that such a "male dominated" perspective was a problem for the show seem to have been content to carry on participating in a newsgroup in which other viewers chose to believe that the predominance of this perspective was not a problem. Such discussions did not become off limits, nor were they ended in victory of one side over the other — evidenced by the fact that one further exchange took place after Dahlquist's post (Ienn 1993).

The second major conflict — and the only one to clearly revolve around a distinction between the Joel era and the Mike era — occurred around a skit in the Christmas episode, *Santa Claus* (Mallon 1993, Episode 521), in which Gypsy gives Mike a handmade sweater that reads "JOIKE" across the front, which she explains by saying "I started making it for the other guy and, well, you know." The thread began with Arshavir Blackwell getting very irritated that Joel's name was never spoken in the episode, and assuming this meant "he *must* have left on pretty bad terms" (Blackwell 1993). Though Robert J. Granvin tried repeatedly to keep the peace, this dispute began to get out of hand and drift towards an attempt at condemning all non–Joel episodes through an insinuation of conspiracy. Though most of the posters here continued to be in agreement with the original poster, the villain became James Craig Lowery, who implied that the differences in the program could be attributed to the greed of Michael J. Nelson — "he's been head writer ... and has probably felt frustrated that all he got were bit parts in the host segments."

Lowery elaborated on this argument the next day under the title "Mike is a frustrated musician who now has an outlet" (Lowery 1993), a post which attempted to use formal analysis of the show to justify the conspiracy theory. This dispute, in a scant 15 messages (five of which were by Lowery himself), swirled through many of the previous debates in the group, bringing them all together into one relatively aggressive argument. Lowery, who disliked the musical numbers proliferating in the show, was almost immediately attacked by Lynsa for spreading "conspiracy theories" and, in an act clearly designed to marginalize Lowery's viewpoint, was then told "If you don't like Mike ... Circulate the Tapes through your VCR." Much like the sexism debate, then, we do have an instance here of one participant attempting to shut the other out of debate, as dissent is described as outdated fandom. Lowery persisted throughout this fight to argue that he was the one being rational (which, aside from the silliness of the accusation and the conspiratorial tone he took in the title to his message, he was), but he was — to be fair to the notion that there was a "Flamewar" — persistently attacked by everyone else in the group.

It was Judex who, on January 3, in an otherwise pretty snide response, finally reoriented this aggressive debate back to the group's stock posture of inclusiveness with the statement "It's all a matter of opinion. And nobody's opinion becomes more valid through endless repetition." By that point the group's other means of fostering inclusive harmony had also been deployed — the argument had moved offline and into email exchange between Lynsa and Lowery, where they settled their differences in whatever way they chose, leaving the group dynamic a place of openness rather than fighting. So, ultimately what we have here is evidence that when fighting does actually flare up, and threatens to enter into the realm of "interpretative consensus" ("Watch something else!" or "Watch your videos!"), it moves out of public view, leaving no need for consensus of interpretation. In the group, all opinions are valid; disputes that could eventually lead to the need for a hegemonic interpretation are moved into the private sphere of one on one interaction.

Interestingly, both of the major battles here represent a fanbase that is arguably anything but intolerant of other viewpoints. The only people being "shouted down" in these disputes, or any other threads, are those who are themselves trying to "win" the dispute. Had there been, therefore, a suitably large number of hard-line group members of the type that Cornell and Henry describe as "intolerant" (which there may well have been in other newsgroups), then the "Great Joel vs. Mike Flamewar" might well have happened. However, in actual fact this particular group consisted of a very small number of "intolerant" fans and a vast majority of keepers of the peace.

Following this era of open disputes, if two arguments can make an era, the period of the "Flamewar" saw a distinct shift towards a moratorium on aggressiveness. Interestingly, however, considering our analysis of the previous two battles, this moratorium appears to have had no clear instigating factor — a fact which perhaps provides us with a notion of the origin of the myth of the Flamewar (if indeed it is a myth). At this point, the group began to treat the "Flamewar" as though it had already happened, despite the fact that little evidence of it exists.

As of December 10, "Kirk versus Picard" (a *Star Trek* reference) was still the touchstone for a flame war for poster Hal Prentice (Prentice 1993). The follow up to his post of that date produced four reply assertions that one could not really compare Joel to Mike — they were "just different." The flame war persistently failed to happen in this thread and in similar ones prior to it. By December 15, a month and a half after Mike's first televised appearance, Scott M. Fabbri's list of "Top Ten Annoying Threads" in the newsgroup did not even include "Joel vs. Mike" as an option; the closest option was "Hey! Who's the new guy? Where'd Joel go?" (Ienn, Fabbri, Gilbert 1993). Somehow, however, by the 28th of December, responses to James Craig Lowery's critique of the musical numbers on the show began to rely on an implicit link between Mike criticism and Mike hatred — or, what Lowery referred to as the "'yer fer me or agin me' attitude." The things which occurred between these two points, however, had little to do with an actual flame war over host-preference. There was only the sexism battle in the interim — a discussion which, thought it got heated, even being referred to as "the flames and thunder rumbling through the newsgroup" (McNamara 1993), had had nothing much to do with Joel versus Mike after the initial post.

The actual drawing of lines in the sand and fracturing of the group into "two factions ... that ... were not prepared to tolerate the presence of the other" never really happened — at least not in public correspondence. It was simply assumed. It is interesting to note, therefore, that on August 5 — three full months before the airing of Mike's first episode — preemptive strikes were being made against a potential fan schism over the transition. Matthew Duhan requested that the FAQ be amended to include the line "please do not waste bandwith by repeatedly bringing up this [Joel vs. Mike] topic" (Schwartz 1993). It seems that the expectation became a truism simply due to the passage of time; no actual fighting on the topic was necessary. By late January, assumptions would fly in posts which referred to a difference between the Joel era and the young Mike era. An exchange between Keith N.I. and Phil Mueller between January 28 and 30 is a perfect case in point, as Keith N.I. leaped to the assumption that Mueller did not like Mike, forcing Mueller to respond:

"Where did you get the idea that *I* didn't like Mike! [...] I believe most people would not love Mike because of his dark side [but] I didn't say *I* didn't love Mike" (bk5491 1994). On January 26, Pam Von Krosigk made perhaps the most remarkably simple deceptive statement in the entire newsgroup along this line: "I don't want to get this Mike vs. Joel thing started again, but..." (Von Krosigk 1994). There was arguably no "thing" in the first place, as the Lowery fight was a misunderstanding; how could she "restart" it?

It seems, then, that other conflicts — sexism and conspiracy theorizing — gave the group the feeling that a bitter split had occurred, when no such thing is in evidence in the historical record. By far the most common sentiments expressed are in support of discussion and different opinions. No matter how heated a discussion might have been, the only time a line was really drawn in the sand was when one individual tried to "autocratically declare an end to all debate ... in a futile attempt to preempt anyone who would rebut them" (lenn 1993), usually with a "watch your old tapes and go away" retort. It was only these assertions which sparked a clear fracture and drew actual flames.

The Satire of '94

By far the more interesting — and, to my mind, the more exemplary — phase of the "war" was the final piece: the self-referential "fan fiction" wave of misinformation that erupted during the first two weeks of February, in which the group turned the "conflict" into a joyous construction of nonsense. Though Ben Scott would later claim that he'd "been spreading 'Joel is dead' stories by Email reply since early January" (Denkewalter 1994), the public stories began with Harlan Freilacher's tale of Joel being killed in a botched Invention Exchange (a regular occasion on the show during which first Joel and the Bots, and then the Mads, each reveal a silly invention to the other group):

> Joel Hodgson left the show because he's decided to continue his education. His character was killed off in an accident with the invention exchange; his latest Gizmo exploded. So no, he won't be coming back. Mike plays Joel's cousin, who came looking for Joel, and found Deep 13. The Mads, seeing the opportunity to replace Joel, hired Mike as a temp, supposedly so he could earn enough money to continue his search for Joel. [...] The robots, who always thought of Joel as their father, accepted Mike as family, but of course they don't show him the level of respect they showed Joel (Kendall 1994).

Despite the misinformation being, in Freilacher's own words, "so damn blatant," his tale was apparently picked up and spread by a few members who had not seen the episode in which the transition occurred. By February 6, the group was off to the races, with several alternative stories being offered by other members.

- Robert F. Denkewalter claimed that the switch was made without warning, "like the time they switched the husband ... on Bewitched"; this rash action was necessary because Joel had been abruptly fired after he "decided that the [next] show ... would be the one where he went public with his homosexuality" (Denkewalter 1994).
- Amanda Lowry French claimed that Joel's "real-life" desire to spend more time with "his wife and brand-new baby daughter," resulted in a fiction of "the Mads experience[d] guilty pangs when Joel told them about his dying Sea Monkeys down on Earth; they allowed Joel to escape from the SoL as long as he agreed to hunt down and kill Yahoo Serious." In this story, Mike was actually a "Mad scientist in training" who was a rival

with Dr. Forrester, which was supposedly justification for "why the experiments are so much darker; he's really evil" (Kendall 1994).

- JPope offered that Gypsy, having gone crazy with the notion that "Joel was going to kill her and hook the SOL up to his Amiga," had killed Joel "ala 2001" after Joel had left the ship to perform repair work. Mike, having been unfrozen from hibernation as a replacement for Joel, had to "retrieve Joel's dead, lifeless carcass" (Burkholder 1994).

- Keith N.I. claimed that Tom and Crow "flushed" Joel out of the Satellite after he ate "a stale hamdinger," which ultimately resulted in Joel becoming CEO of Gizmonic Institute (via a "hostile takeover") and "sending out assassin squads to hunt down Deep 13"—all of which was supposedly revealed in "episode 425, 'Home Alone 3: The Destruction of Jared Zid'" (Burkholder 1994).

- Dave Setty, in the first overtly self-referential fan-fiction, returned to the notion of a botched Invention Exchange and stated that the "Freilicherizer" that Joel had invented—a clear reference to instigator of the misinformation fad, Harlan Freilacher—had malfunctioned, and "when the lights came back on, Joel lay on the floor with a knife protruding from his back"; Mike, an assassin hired by the Mads to kill the Bots, eventually takes over the Satellite and—in another bit of fan-group self-reference—reprograms the Bots "to have no memory of ... 'the other guy'" (Setty 1994).

- Matthias Ferber claimed that Joel was fired by Comedy Central when they discovered that he was doing bit parts on *Seinfeld*, which resulted in the loss of "his income, his family, and his home." The evidence for this story was that Joel was currently living in Ferber's parents' basement. Hodgson's plans for the future consisted of plastic surgery and a "talk show on the Fox network" (Pruden 1994).

- Erin Cash took the blurring of fantasy and reality to the greatest extreme, arguing that Joel was killed in real life by Mike and Trace Beaulieu for "getting too much credit and attention"; Mike and Trace then circulated the story that Joel had left "to try new things" in order to cover up their crime (Pruden 1994).

A common theme running through the lies seemed to be the direct contradiction of public statements by Best Brains. Of the three things listed as "what we know so far" all the way back in August of 1993—"It will not be an unnoticed swap as with the Darren's from *Bewitched*," "Joel will not die," and "Gypsy will be instrumental in the switch" (Pohlman 1993)—at least one is contradicted in most of the stories, sometimes, as in the case with Denkewalter, very explicitly. A further theme was the assumption of antagonism between Joel and Mike, blurring James Craig Lowery's conspiracy theory and the argument that Mike's type of humor was more aggressive and sex-obsessed.

JPope added a second layer to this joyful noise with a false announcement that *MST3K* would be moving to HBO for its sixth season (JPope, Ferris, et al. 1994), which resulted in a wave of similar claims about *MST* moving to QVC, the Weather Channel, C-SPAN, and similar nonsensical stations (TV's Spatch 1994). By February 8, the games had become so widespread that frequent contributor Jon P. LeVitre proposed a "creative writing contest" in which wild explanations for "Why Joel isn't on the Show Anymore" were to be judged by "creativity, originality, lack of accuracy, and penmanship" (LeVitre 1994). On February 10, a further renegotiation of argument toward wry and complicated humor arose, as John Mechelas replied to one of the stories with the brilliantly comic "Standard Boneheaded Reply Form"—consisting of a vast number of check boxes for the responder to list their grievances against a post in a simple and streamlined manner (JPope, Mechelas, et al. 1994). Via use of this form, one could conveniently tell a poster that one "took exception to" their post, due to it being "lame," "stupid," or "much longer than any worthwhile thought of which you may be capable," and culminating in "recommendations" like "find a volcano and throw yourself in," "consume excrement," or "consume excrement and thus expire."

What we have here, then, is a fan group which, when faced with a situation in which a deep and serious rift was supposedly about to form, responded with humor instead of fighting. Granted, this was somewhat derisive humor: the lies were directed at "newbies" who kept asking the group where Joel had gone, and the "Standardized Bonehead Reply Form" strongly implied that the poster in receipt of said form had said something stupid. However, neither of these things was really malicious or intended to provoke hostile reactions or fracture the group. Indeed, one could argue that they were actually acts of inclusivity rather than exclusivity. The lies were concocted as a game; not only did they defuse any potential rift that might have been occurring by providing a distraction from arguments, but they gave the group something to rally around — perhaps the program had taken a step out of their comfort zone, but that very step could be used to prove that the group dynamic itself had not changed. Likewise, the "Bonehead" form was laced with humor, as is evidenced in the previously quoted portions. As such, it allowed a poster to criticize another group member without causing much of the defensiveness that had mounted around discussions of Mike's character.

Conclusion: Consensus versus Community

Most examples of conflict within the group appear, upon deeper examination, to be examples of civility rather than discord. Actual fighting was avoided as often as possible, as fans allowed variance of opinion to exist peacefully within the group. It seems, then, to be quite impossible to assume that the bulk of the fan base was "not prepared to tolerate the presence of the other," as the semi-official history claims. The only subgroup to whom they were intolerant was the group that was actively fostering a schism.

In point of fact, fans seem to be extraordinarily aware that hegemony — though they may not refer to it by name — is not part of the way their subculture works. In fact, it is often those who are intolerant of other perspectives that are chastised. It is those very fans who believe that "alternative positions and tastes must ... be silenced" (Johnson 2007: 287) who most strongly annoy the group. So, Johnson's "fantagonists" are not always the norm; they are sometimes the outliers.

The norm, in this fangroup, is the type of person who replies to an argument with which they disagree with the exhortation "consume excrement and thus expire" — a phrase which, in its very silliness ("eat shit and die" spoken with pomposity) can do nothing to end any debate. It is designed for laughs and brotherhood, not divisiveness and "victory." In this case, then, fans actually fight only for their perspective *not* to be hegemonically drowned out. They do not fight to "win" — but to preserve the safety of the space. And in doing so, they may argue, but they also joke, tease, and "riff" their own foibles and conflicts.

REFERENCES

Newsgroup Threads from alt.tv.mst3k

Anderson, Jenny, and Vanessa S. "Re: Tubular boobular." *alt.tv.mst3k* December 29, 1993 — January 4, 1994. Accessed 5/17/2010. http://groups.google.com/group/alt.tv.mst3k/browse_thread/thread/ed 833618a603474/.

bk5491, Gerson V Koenig, Jason Cohen, et al. "Valley of the giants.." *alt.tv.mst3k* January 25–31, 1994. Accessed 5/17/2010. http://groups.google.com/group/alt.tv.mst3k/browse_thread/thread/ebf85f0b61 84e8b1/.

Blackwell, Arshavir, Douglas Carroll, Kevin Podsiadlik, et al. "Joike????" *alt.tv.mst3k* December 27, 1993 — January 7, 1994. Accessed 5/17/2010. http://groups.google.com/group/alt.tv.mst3k/browse_thread/ thread/95d821f01b5472e2/.

Burkholder, Troy, Mike Cohen, Klyfix, et al. "An old fan. What's going on?!" *alt.tv.mst3k* February 5–11, 1994. Accessed 5/17/2010. http://groups.google.com/group/alt.tv.mst3k/browse_thread/thread/9ec32 ec2eb17040a/.

Dahlquist, Gordon, terry r lenn, and Lynsa. "tubular flames." *alt.tv.mst3k* December 20–23, 1993. Accessed 5/17/2010. http://groups.google.com/group/alt.tv.mst3k/browse_thread/thread/7bd90ffe654d2cb0/.

Denkewalter, Robert F., Thomas Servo, Diane Thorne, et al. "What happened to Joel?" alt.tv.mst3k February 6–19, 1994. Accessed 5/17/2010. http://groups.google.com/group/alt.tv.mst3k/browse_thread/ thread/31a719a64099b3a8/.

jfox, Ian "THE ARM" Whitney, Rebecca R Ferris, et al. "Tubular Boobular." *alt.tv.mst3k* December 16, 1993 — January 1, 1994. Accessed 5/17/2010. http://groups.google.com/group/alt.tv.mst3k/browse_ thread/thread/48279bda505070ea/.

JPope, Rebecca R Ferris, Ander, et al. "MST3K Moving to HBO!!!!!" alt.tv.mst3k February 8–18, 1994. Accessed 5/17/2010. http://groups.google.com/group/alt.tv.mst3k/browse_thread/thread/39cffb6 dea436e89/.

JPope, John Mechelas, Matthew Moss, et al. "The Demise of CC!!!" *alt.tv.mst3k* February 10–26, 1994. Accessed 5/17/2010. http://groups.google.com/group/alt.tv.mst3k/browse_thread/thread/44029da 2729049de/.

Kendall, Jon P LeVitre, Tammy Davis, et al. "Where's Joel?" *alt.tv.mst3k* February 4–14, 1994. Accessed 5/17/2010. http://groups.google.com/group/alt.tv.mst3k/browse_thread/thread/886173d351539852/.

lenn, terry r. "Here we go again..." *alt.tv.mst3k* December 22, 1993. Accessed 5/17/2010. http://groups. google.com/group/alt.tv.mst3k/browse_thread/thread/7b8806015852cf6/.

lenn, terry r, Scott M. Fabbri, and Bruce Gilbert. "Top 10 Annoying Threads." alt.tv.mst3k December 11– 16, 1993. Accessed 5/17/2010. http://groups.google.com/group/alt.tv.mst3k/browse_thread/thread/ca0 de69d25fdd482/.

lenn, terry r, Ken Frauwirth, brenda olsen, et al. "Toobular Boobular." *alt.tv.mst3k* December 18–23, 1993. Accessed 5/17/2010. http://groups.google.com/group/alt.tv.mst3k/browse_thread/thread/d1f3d3ffc659 df08/.

LeVitre, Jon P. "Creative Writing Contest": *alt.tv.mst3k* February 8, 1994. Accessed 5/17/2010. http://groups. google.com/group/alt.tv.mst3k/browse_thread/thread/ddc30a4e20e3cfb4/.

Lowery, James Craig, Lynsa, STAR, et al. "Mike is a frustrated musician who now has an outlet." *alt.tv.mst3k* December 28, 1993 — January 4, 1994. Accessed 5/17/2010. http://groups.google.com/group/alt.tv. mst3k/browse_thread/thread/2e0da0cf4870d16f/.

McAfee, Sean, Pat Walsh, Petrea Mitchell, et al. "ARGH! Comedy Central, BITE ME!" *alt.tv.mst3k* February 12–16, 1994. Accessed 5/17/2010. http://groups.google.com/group/alt.tv.mst3k/browse_thread/thread/ 7d58ae1623c9627/.

McNamara, Bob, brenda olsen, fRiNgE, et al. "Greatest MST promo spot." alt.tv.mst3k December 22– 26, 1993. Accessed 5/17/2010. http://groups.google.com/group/alt.tv.mst3k/browse_thread/thread/3d 0231f80626598e/.

Pohlman, Matthew M., Greg Galcik, David J., et al. "images and sounds." *alt.tv.mst3k* August 7–18, 1993. Accessed 5/17/2010. http://groups.google.com/group/alt.tv.mst3k/browse_thread/thread/3e3d1e7876 61f0f0/.

Prentice, Hal, Rebecca R Ferris, Chuck Usul, et al. "I Like Mike!" *alt.tv.mst3k* December 10–12, 1993. Accessed 5/17/2010. http://groups.google.com/group/alt.tv.mst3k/browse_thread/thread/fd720088045 ebacb/.

Pruden, LeeAnn, Matthias Ferber, Amanda Lowry French, et al. "WHERE IS JOEL NOW??" *alt.tv.mst3k* February 14–18, 1994. Accessed 5/17/2010. http://groups.google.com/group/alt.tv.mst3k/browse_ thread/thread/5b0605e78be22ba5/.

Schwartz, Bruce V., Matthew Duhan, mark_flores, et al. "Joel leaving: when???" *alt.tv.mst3k* August 5–11, 1993. Accessed 5/17/2010. http://groups.google.com/group/alt.tv.mst3k/browse_thread/thread/b8cff 3da0d36cab2/.

Setty, Dave. "The *truth* behind the host change." alt.tv.mst3k February 11, 1994. Accessed 5/17/2010. http://groups.google.com/group/alt.tv.mst3k/browse_thread/thread/1d21d283d5e7470b/.

TV's Spatch, Dan Bell, Matthias Ferber, et al. "MST3K moving to QVC." alt.tv.mst3k February 10–18,

1994. Accessed 5/17/2010. http://groups.google.com/group/alt.tv.mst3k/browse_thread/thread/9fbb0935af55c10e/.

Von Krosigk, Pam. "MST3K not as good as before?" *alt.tv.mst3k* January 26, 1994. Accessed 5/17/2010. http://groups.google.com/group/alt.tv.mst3k/browse_thread/thread/1b22aeb2f80b6628/.

Secondary and Video Sources

Beaulieu, Trace (director), Michael J. Nelson (writer), Trace Beaulieu (writer) et al., Episode 513. *The Brain That Wouldn't Die*, 1993. Rhino, 2000.

Beaulieu, Trace (director), Michael J. Nelson (writer), Trace Beaulieu (writer) et al., Episode 519. *The Outlaw*, 1993.

Bergson, Henri. "Laughter." In Wylie Sypher, ed. *Comedy*. Baltimore and London: Johns Hopkins University Press, 1980.

Bordwell, David, Janet Staiger, and Kristin Thompson. *The Classical Hollywood Cinema: Film Style & Mode of Production to 1960*. New York: Columbia UP, 1985.

Condit, Celeste. "Hegemony in a Mass-mediated Society: Concordance about Reproductive Technologies." *Critical Studies in Mass Communication*. 11.3 (Sept. 1994): 205–230.

Cornell, Christopher, and Brian Henry. "The Almost But Still Not Quite Complete History of *MST3K*— Part 9: Schism (1993)." *Satellite News* 2002. Accessed 3/1/2009. http://www.mst3kinfo.com/history/page9.html.

_____. "The Almost But Still Not Quite Complete History of MST3K — Part 12: Raise Your Freak Flag High (1995)." *Satellite News* 2002. Accessed 4/16/2009 http://www.mst3kinfo.com/history/page12.html.

Gray, Jonathan. "Antifandom and the Moral Text: Television Without Pity and Textual Dislike." *American Behavioral Scientist*. 48.7 (March 2005): 840–858.

Jenkins, Henry. *Convergence Culture: Where Old and New Media Collide*. New York and London: New York University Press, 2006.

Johnson, Derek. "Fan-tagonism: Factions, Institutions, and Constitutive Hegemonies of Fandom." In Jonathan Gray, Cornel Sandvoss, and C. Lee Harrington eds., *Fandom: Identities and Communities in a Mediated World*. New York and London: New York UP, 2007.

Mallon, Jim (director), Michael J. Nelson (writer), Trace Beaulieu (writer) et al., Episode 521. *Santa Claus*, 1993. Shout Factory, 2009.

Murphy, Kevin (director), Michael J. Nelson (writer), Trace Beaulieu (writer) et al., Episode 512. *Mitchell*, 1993. Rhino, 2001.

Rosenbaum, Jonathan. "No Joke: *Mystery Science Theater 3000: The Movie*." Chicago Reader April 18, 1996. Accessed 5/15/2010. http://www.chicagoreader.com/chicago/no-joke/Content?oid=890287.

Staiger, Janet. *Media Reception Studies*. New York and London: New York University Press, 2005.

Wolinsky, David. "Cinematic Titanic's Joel Hodgson Demystifies Movie Riffing." *The Onion A.V. Club* September 9, 2009. Accessed 5/14/2010. http://www.avclub.com/chicago/articles/cinematic-titanics-joel-hodgson-demystifies-movie,32238/.

9

Cinemasochism: Bad Movies and the People Who Love Them

by David Ray Carter

In the late 1940s, American cinema's mode of operation changed significantly from that of previous decades. The Paramount Case of 1948 had dealt a crushing blow to the cinematic monopoly held by "the Big Five"—Fox, MGM, Paramount, RKO, and Warner Bros. No longer would five corporations dictate the viewing habits of an entire nation and Hollywood's star-laden blockbusters were, by law, now required to share marquee space with films from smaller production companies such as American International Pictures (1956), Crown International Pictures (1959), and Lippert Pictures (1948).

The three new studios, as well as the dozens like them, were able to make films faster and cheaper than their Hollywood counterparts. Thus, it was easier for them to make films about current topics of interest — the "exploitation" film — and to adjust more quickly their target audience when the primary cinemagoer in America became the teenager. The independent studios populated their films with rubber-suited monsters, teenage delinquents, and mad scientists, representing a wholly different type of cinema — if not a different America — from the urbane sophistication of Hollywood productions.

By the first years of the 1960s, the gulf between Hollywood and the independents was too vast to ignore. Consider that *West Side Story* won the Academy Award for Best Picture in 1961. The same year, Crown International released *The Beast of Yucca Flats*, AIP released *The Phantom Planet*, and Exploit Films released *Rocket Attack U.S.A.* It was clear that America's "second cinema" was fixated on topics far removed from the musicals of Hollywood and concerned with entertaining a different brand of cinephile.

West Side Story's Oscar victory implied it was somehow "better" than the other films made that year. This may only be a question of degrees when speaking about its fellow nominees, but there can be no doubt that the members of the Academy would have considered it superior to the output of AIP, Crown, and their ilk. The consensus between critics and major studios was that AIP and Crown made "bad" movies; movies that lacked the technical aptitude, coherent narratives, and overall quality of work on display in mainstream films.

Indeed, the technical limitations of a film like Crown's *The Creeping Terror* are hard to overlook, but certain type of movie fans love the film for reasons beyond the scope of the Academy's selection process.

Institutionally dismissed but often commercially successful when released, these "bad films" would later find renewed attention from fans that prized their intangible qualities over the accomplishments of those films deemed good. The bad cinema fan finds enjoyment in these films in spite of— or as often is the case, *because* of— their technical limitations. Such a fan engages in cinemasochism, finding pleasure in cinema others have deemed too painful to endure. The cinemasochist takes the same approach to film that Susan Sontag does in her "Notes on 'Camp'" (Sontag 2008: 46). To paraphrase Oscar Wilde as she applies him to film studies: there are no good or bad movies; they are either charming or tedious.

For the cinemasochist, bad film viewing is a type of sport; a cinematic variation on the game of "chicken" often seen in juvenile delinquent films. "How much can you take?" is often the key question in cinemasochistic circles, with being able to stomach the worst that cinema has to offer a badge of honor among initiates. One should not make the assumption that the cinemasochist views these films through gritted-teeth and half-closed eyes. On the contrary, implied by cinemasochism is an inherent love of bad film, a preference for the flawed works of cinematic neophytes over the pristine results of Hollywood's artisans. Finding bad cinema "charming" rather than "tedious" is the central tenet of the cinemasochistic lifestyle.

The American television show *Mystery Science Theater 3000* (*MST3K*) perfectly embodies both the literal and metaphorical meanings of cinemasochism. *MST3K*'s premise is based on the assumption that bad cinema can be physically and mentally debilitating. A rotating cast of sadistic mad scientists subject our heroes — and by extension, the audience — to a sampling of some of the most technically inept cinema from the 1940s through the 1990s. The show deals with films that encompass practically every genre and a wide array of topics, with the sole unifying factor being that all of the films possess a certain charm that transcends their status as "bad cinema."

The intangible charm of these films is enhanced by the "riffing"— witty comments made during the showing of the film — of the human host and his robot companions. Extending the idea that these films are intrinsically harmful, riffing is the coping mechanism that allows those subjected to them to survive. The technique has the dual purpose of both simultaneously pointing out aspects of the film worthy of ridicule and celebrating them for the added entertainment value such moments provide. When our hosts point out that a character that has yet to speak is told to "shut up and sit down" in *Teen-Age Crime Wave*, the audience is made aware of both the narrative flaw and the humor it brings.

Mystery Science Theater 3000 was not the first instance of cinemasochism, nor was it the first time such films had been used as the basis for riffing or other forms of comedy. Bad film appreciation has a history spanning much farther back than *MST3K*'s 1988 debut yet the show was — and remains — the most widely known vehicle of cinemasochism. The fact that it did not create the cinemasochistic attitude or aesthetic but rather synthesized ideas from various pre-existing traditions and fan-groups is perhaps key to the esteemed place that the show holds in the minds of many fans. Bad film culture had been growing for some time and *Mystery Science Theater 3000* disseminated and popularized many of the opinions that had previously been exclusive to either underground cineastes or film academics. In doing so, the program ushered in a new wave of bad film appreciation — creating 21st century cinemasochists molded in its image.

Precursors to *Mystery Science Theater 3000*: Style

The premise of *Mystery Science Theater 3000* involves the commenters-cum-filmmakers recontextualizing an existing film into a new work, one that contains their running commentary. Horror, melodrama, science fiction and even educational films become comedies through the riffing of the cast. Anyone who has seen the original version of *Manos: Hands of Fate* can attest that the film is something wholly new after the *MST3K* treatment. In the extreme case of *Manos*, not only does the horror film become a comedy, the unwatchable becomes enjoyable and what is generally considered to be one of the worst films of all-time becomes what many *MST3K* fans consider to be the show's finest work.

The practice of re-contextualizing existing films has its origins decades before *Mystery Science Theater 3000*. The use of stock footage to pad out a film was a common technique by both major studios and the independents and it is fitting that so many films featured on *MST3K* use stock footage. Stock footage would often be recontextualized to fit the need of the particular film but the first complete recontextualization of an entire film was Woody Allen's 1966 debut *What's Up Tiger Lily?* Allen combined two entries of the Japanese spy series *International Secret Police* into a single film, replaced all of the dialogue and changed the scene order. The result was to turn an action film into a comedy, replacing whatever goal the original filmmaker had with Allen's unique brand of humor.

Dialogue replacement and montage manipulation can both be seen as forms of riffing but one in which the original work is completely transmuted through the construction of a new narrative. *Tiger Lily* is completely a Woody Allen film in the sense his re-contextualization created a third unique film, wholly separate from the two existing films used to create it. One is unable to form an opinion on *International Secret Police* from it, and it is impossible to determine whether or not it would qualify as a bad film, or if Allen considered what he was doing in any way cinemasochistic. It is, however, one of the most well known ancestors of the *Mystery Science Theater 3000* spirit in that it replaced an existing film's sensibilities with those of a new group of artists. Hodgson, Nelson, Mallon, et al. would transform the narratives of dozens of films with their comedy in precisely the same way Allen does in *What's Up Tiger Lily?*, albeit with less manipulation of the original material. The year 1973 would see the *Tiger Lily* technique used for vastly different means: political propaganda. French Situationalists redubbed the martial arts film *The Crush* into *Can Dialectics Break Bricks?*, replacing the plot with a variety of revolutionary messages and critiques of capitalism. *Can Dialectics Break Bricks?* is far removed from the lighthearted humor of *Mystery Science Theater 3000* but proved that dialogue replacement alone could significantly alter a narrative without the need for montage manipulation as well.

A far less known but closer relative to *Mystery Science Theater 3000* can be found three years before Allen's film. *Rocky & Bullwinkle* creator Jay Ward's episodic television show *Fractured Flickers* debuted in 1963 and featured silent films dubbed with comic dialogue. While the show shared *Tiger Lily*'s use of replacement narratives, it comes closer to the *MST3K* style of riffing through its use of non-sequitur humor and pop culture references. The *Fractured Flickers* style of humor would draw attention to the technical limitations of some of the films it was lampooning but occasionally used footage from more acceptable fare such as 1923's *The Hunchback of Notre Dame*. Though it is now considerably less remembered than Allen's film, *Fractured Flickers* appears to have had a greater influence on the style of other early examples of riffing than *What's Up Tiger Lily?*

Mystery Science Theater 3000's truest ancestor is the 1982 film *It Came from Hollywood*, a *bona fide* cinemasochistic work in that it is a celebration of films historically perceived as bad. The film is comprised of dozens of clips from B-movies from the 1920s through the late 1970s and there is considerable overlap between the films showcased in *It Came from Hollywood* and those that would later appear on *MST3K*. There are few instances of direct riffing but the film approaches the mixture of ridicule and celebration of bad cinema found in *MST3K*. *It Came from Hollywood* spawned a *Tiger Lily*-esque film of its own, 1983's *What's Up Hideous Sun Demon*. A direct riff on *The Hideous Sun Demon*, the film is in many ways a bawdier, counterculture version of the *MST3K* format.

Many of the films that would later appear on *MST3K* had already garnered new audiences by the mid-eighties as staples of late-night television and as features on regional and syndicated "horror host" programs, the format of which would later be appropriated by *MST3K*.

Epitomized by characters such as Zacherley, Ghoulardi, Vampira and her early eighties reincarnation in the form of Elvira, the horror host had long been the champion of cinemasochism, providing audiences with Z-grade features and glibly derisive commentary since the early 1950s. Many future *MST3K* films would appear on horror host programs or as late-night filler on local television stations. *Manos: Hands of Fate, The Amazing Colossal Man*, and similar films were regular features of weekend "All Night Movies" during the seventies before being rescued from obscurity by *Mystery Science Theater 3000*.

When *Mystery Science Theater 3000* began airing in 1988, it would be a synthesis of the influences outlined above. It took the structural format of the horror host show and combined it with the direct riffing found in *What's Up Tiger Lily?* and *What's Up Hideous Sun Demon*, then added the contemporary pop culture obsessions of *Fractured Flickers* with the trash-culture archeology of *It Came from Hollywood*. The combination of these influences would make *Mystery Science Theater 3000* a unique experience but one grounded in enough of pre-existing culture that viewers would more readily accept it.

Precursors to *Mystery Science Theater 3000*: Theory

By the late 1980s, much of the stylistic groundwork for *Mystery Science Theater 3000* had been laid. The intellectual ideas behind cinemasochism had already existed both in the public's consciousness and in film scholarship for some time as well. Critic J. Hoberman would be one of the first to give the cinemasochist a voice in his 1980 essay "Bad Movies." In the essay, Hoberman succinctly declares what could be the cinemasochist's creed, "it is possible for a movie to succeed *because* it has failed" (Hoberman 2008:517). Hoberman later singles out the film *Robot Monster*—a first season feature of *Mystery Science Theater 3000*—as a "supremely bad movie — an anti masterpiece —[that] projects a stupidity that's fully as awesome as genius" (Hoberman 2008:520).

Hoberman goes on to find praiseworthy elements in the films of Ed Wood and other filmmakers in the same vein as those shown on *MST3K* before beginning an extended defense of Oscar Micheaux. Micheaux is considered by many, Hoberman included, as one of the least talented filmmakers of all time. In keeping with the spirit of cinemasochism embraced by *Mystery Science Theater 3000*, Hoberman examines the multitude of flaws in Micheaux's work as if they are evidence of his genius. Where others see the litany of mistakes, errors, and poor technique in Micheaux's films as evidence of poor quality, Hoberman, as a cinemasochist, is entranced by them. He finds value in Micheaux not because his films fail on some level but because they fail on every level, becoming a type of anti-cinema as rare and as valuable as a cinematic masterpiece.

An even more apt summation of the cinemasochistic position would be found in Hoberman's collaboration with critic Jonathan Rosenbaum, *Midnight Movies*. This time Rosenbaum elucidated cinemasochism in his assessment of the 1978 box-office bomb *Sextette*. He states, "To appreciate the humor and charm of one of the world's worst movies requires, however, a certain sympathy for and empathy with the hapless participants — not to mention a sense of irony about the very processes of cinematic illusion" (Hoberman 1980:272). Again, Rosenbaum finds *Sextette* fascinating because it fails at every requirement typically expected of cinema, espousing the same "so bad it's good" viewpoint that is central to *Mystery Science Theater 3000*. Additionally, there are several instances in *Mystery Science Theater 3000* where a sympathy or empathy for the cast and crew is directly expressed by the commentators, evidence that they are in line with Rosenbaum's assessment of a viewer that appreciates, rather than hates, bad cinema.

Hoberman and Rosenbaum's book investigates the midnight movie phenomenon, another early example of a cinemasochistic tendency, this time in a cultural context. Midnight movies and cult film fandom in general are predicated on an appreciation for cinema that is outside of the parameters of the mainstream. The cult surrounding *The Rocky Horror Picture Show* is of particular relevance to *Mystery Science Theater 3000* for two reasons. First, it is evidence of a large group of people appreciating a film that was critically and commercially unsuccessful upon its release, who willfully "subjected" themselves to it with a fetishistic fervor. Secondly and perhaps more importantly, the call-and-response audience participation aspects of the film — not intended by the filmmakers and wholly created by the fans themselves — are direct precursors to *MST3K*'s riffing. *Rocky Horror*'s audience participation was heavily standardized as opposed to the ad-libbed improvisations of Hodgson, Nelson, and robots but the similarities in the spirit of such reactions are not insignificant. The pointing out of flaws and criticizing of poor dialogue are shared traits of the *Rocky Horror* audience and the crew of *MST3K* and in both cases the chiding is done from a position of celebration rather than derision.

Mystery Science Theater 3000 would be in full swing when critic Jeffery Sconce pointed to it as an example of the "ironic reading strategies" employed by bad cinema fans in his 1995 essay "Trashing the academy: Taste, excess and an emerging politics of cinematic style." Much of Sconce's argument is an academic reinterpretation of the positions taken by several cinema fanzines of the eighties such as *Psychotronic Video*, *Subhuman*, and *Zontar*, a 'zine of particular use to Sconce despite decrying the very type of highly intellectual project he undertakes. Sconce uses the term "paracinema" to describe the types of films to which the cinemasochist is drawn. He describes the culture by pointing out that films which are "unwatchable for most mainstream viewers," for the cinemasochist, "have assumed an exalted status" (Sconce 2008:115). Fanzine culture is an important precursor to *Mystery Science Theater 3000* for both the identification of films that lend themselves to cinemasochism and the establishment of a hierarchy and canon within those films.

Sconce's placement of cinemasochism under the academic microscope further brought to light something that Rosenbaum identified: a recognition of the sophistication of cinematic knowledge possessed by the cinemasochist. Rather than having bad taste, the cinemasochist has a very refined and specific type of taste. A cinemasochist has a greater knowledge of cinema than the typical fan and chooses to watch such films as an act of rebellion against the mainstream assumption that such films are intrinsically bad. Sconce believes that the cinemasochist "represents the most developed and dedicated of cinephilic subcultures" (Sconce 2008:101). Joan Hawkins identifies that cinemasochistic fanzines often cover highly praised "art" cinema and low-budget schlock with equal frequency and fervency, "making no attempt to differentiate among genres or subgenres, high or low art" (Hawkins 2008:120).

The makers of *Mystery Science Theater 3000* possessed both the extensive cinematic knowledge and populist view of cinema that Sconce, Rosenbaum, and Hawkins identified. Any given episode of *MST3K* shows that the creators had an impressive knowledge of cinematic clichés, the filmmaking process, and the past and future careers of the cast and crew of the film in question. Furthermore, the meta-references in the series make it clear that the creators expect that their audience possesses the same level of knowledge so that they are sharing in the humor. Humor and an encyclopedic knowledge of film are the two bedrocks of *Mystery Science Theater 3000* and, by extension, the forms of participatory cinemasochism that followed the show.

Beyond *Mystery Science Theater 3000*

As the popularity of *Mystery Science Theater 3000* grew, so did the practice of cinemasochism. *Laserblast*, *Mitchell*, and *Racket Girls* had previously only been known to a select group of initiates but *MST3K* had exposed them to society *en masse*, reintroducing them into the pop culture lexicon at the same time. Bad cinema's rehabilitation in the nineties owes no small debt to the popularity of the show and its ability to bring pre-existing ideas about dismissed or forgotten films to the mainstream via comedy. Only in a post–*Mystery Science Theater 3000* culture could a film about Ed Wood, Jr., the maker of so much of the cinemasochistic canon, win several Academy Awards. The irony of one of 1994's best films being about one of history's worst filmmakers is something that could not have existed prior *MST3K*'s almost evangelical espousal of cinemasochism and the wider cultural recognition of such films.

One of *Mystery Science Theater 3000*'s largest contributions to cinemasochism is the establishment of a cinemasochistic canon of film. To this end, *MST3K* sparked a renewed interest in an inversion of the typical critic's poll: the "worst" list. Singling out particularly egregious violations of cinematic convention had existed since the beginnings of institutionalized film criticism but had become an institution of its own through a series of books by Michael Medved, the most known of which being *The Golden Turkey Awards*, and the annual anti–Oscars, the Razzies (Medved 1980). Containing a wealth of overlap with the *Mystery Science Theater 3000* selections, these institutions of bad taste became useful guides to the worst cinema has to offer for neophyte cinemasochists who had developed a taste for bad cinema from *MST3K*. Such "worst lists" continue in a more populist form via the *IMDb* Bottom 100 List (*imbd.com* 2010). Practically all of the *MST3K* films appear on the list, which is a tally of the hundred worst reviewed films by users of the site. *MST3K* favorite *Manos: Hands of Fate* occupied the top position for some time and has, as of this writing, been replaced at the top by *Red Zone Cuba*, another *MST3K* film.

The influence of *Mystery Science Theater 3000* can also be seen in the growing number of cinemasochists collaborating and communicating via the Internet. In search of new additions to the "worst movie" canon, like-minded cinemasochists compare recent viewings on several film websites' message boards, both of the general cinema and cinemasochist specific varieties. Such communities played a large role in the revival of 1990's *Troll 2*, a film that many place alongside *Manos: Hands of Fate* and *Plan 9 from Outer Space* at the top (bottom?) of the cinemasochistic hierarchy. Due in large to pre-existing fan networks that grew out of an appreciation of the *Mystery Science Theater 3000* brand of cinema, *Troll 2* quickly developed a large cult following, even spawning a documentary on the phenomenon with the hyperbolic and debatable title *Best Worst Movie*.

The Internet now serves as the primary breeding ground for new forms of riffing and cinemasochism. *BadMovies.org* humorously reviews bad films of all genres and ends its reviews with a "Stuff to watch for" section, giving the times of moments worthy of particular ridicule so that the reader can be prepared to do their own riffing when appropriate. Other sites offer similar guides to cinemasochism-friendly films in varying degrees of seriousness. Sites such as *Bad Movie Planet*, *B-Movie Graveyard*, *Oh the Humanity!*, and *Braineater* all apply the *MST3K* approach — humor mixed with an impressive cinematic knowledge — to their written criticism.

Taking a different approach but one that is in keeping with *Mystery Science Theater 3000*'s spirit of ridicule and celebration is blogger and author Cleolinda Jones. Jones is the creator of the "Movies in Fifteen Minutes" concept and the book of the same name in which she uses a screenplay format to riff on the plots of popular films. In the same vein as *MST3K*, Jones' parodies contain a multitude of pop culture references and use many Internet specific running gags and in-jokes, in much the same way that the series developed its own self-referential humor over time. When asked about her selection process for parodies, Jones espoused a view similar to ones given by *Mystery Science Theater 3000*'s creators in interviews. "Some movies are too awful to be any fun; some are too good," she states, echoing the sentiments of *MST3K*'s creators when they were asked about why they never featured Ed Wood's *Plan 9 from Outer Space*.

Jones also gives insight into the relationship that the cinemasochist, particularly the cinemasochistic artist, has with the subject of their work. She states that she attempts to begin her parodies "from a position of affection," regardless of her individual opinion about the work, "because just being mean is too easy." The creators of *Mystery Science Theater 3000* shied away from outright condemnations of films as well, with the show's riffing rarely becoming mean spirited or delving into personal attacks. Finally, Jones admits to being a fan of *Mystery Science Theater 3000* and credits part of her technique to the show's riffing format. "If you have enough jokes, you'll be okay," she says about what she learned from *MST3K*, adding, "If someone doesn't get this one, they'll get the next one" (2010).

Mystery Science Theater 3000 Forever

With a litany of obsessively detailed sites honoring the show and a number of unrelated sites carrying on its spirit, it is fitting that *Mystery Science Theater 3000* would find a new life on the Internet after its cancellation in 1999. Various incarnations of the show's performers and writers carry on its legacy in Internet exclusive forms. Original creator host Joel Hodgson helms *Cinematic Titanic*, the group that comes the closest to *MST3K*'s original intent by using a scientific experiment plot device and focusing solely on riffing on B-movies. The sporadic release schedule of *Cinematic Titanic* often corresponds with live performances and occasionally features films previously shown on *MST3K*, such as fan-favorite *Santa Claus Conquers the Martians*. By continuing to focus on older films, *Cinematic Titanic* closely represents traditional cinemasochism and its obsession with documenting and re-evaluating forgotten films of the past.

Much more frequent are the releases by second host Mike Nelson's project *RiffTrax*. The *RiffTrax* are downloadable files containing Nelson and company's riffing which then must be synced with the movie being parodied. The elimination of the need to purchase the rights to the film has allowed Nelson's *RiffTrax* to riff on any film they desire, leading to many installments dealing with mainstream films and even current DVD releases. Rather than being a departure from the cinemasochistic ideals, *RiffTrax*'s focus on mainstream film proves that there is an element of bad cinema in all levels of film and represents the inversion of the cinematic hierarchy the cinemasochist embraces by treating "good" films to the same ridicule as "bad" films.

Mystery Science Theater 3000 did not change the way in which films are made but one could make the argument that it had a significant influence on how films are viewed, however. *MST3K* drug cinemasochism out of the closet, so to speak, and in doing so created the "recreational cinemasochist," someone who flirts with bad cinema but does not devote his or her life to it. It allowed the ideas of cinemasochism to disseminate to the mainstream without being watered down and gave the curious and the already initiated a place to experience films once believed to be too painful to watch. Perhaps nowhere is the influence of *Mystery Science Theater 3000* on film viewership and film culture more evident than on the user-driven film site Internet Movie Database. As of this writing, almost twenty-thousand individuals had voted on the quality of 1966's *Manos: Hands of Fate*, a full eight thousand more than reviewed *A Man for All Seasons*, that year's Academy Award winner for Best Picture.

REFERENCES

Hawkins, Joan. "Sleaze mania, Euro-trash and high art: the place of European art films in American low culture," in Ernest Mathijs, and Xavier Mendik, eds., *The Cult Film Reader*. Berkshire: Open University Press, 2008.

Hoberman, J. "Bad Movies," in Phillip Lopate, ed., *American Movie Critics: An Anthology from the Silents Until Now*. New York: The Library of America, 2008.

Hoberman, J., and Jonathan Rosenbaum. *Midnight Movies*. New York: Da Capo Press, 1983.

"IMDB Bottom 100 List." *The Internet Movie Database* Ongoing. Accessed 03/15/10. http://www.imdb.com/chart/bottom.

Jones, Cleolinda. Personal interview. 15 March 2010.

Medved, Michael, Harry Medved. *The Golden Turkey Awards*. New York: Putnam, 1980.

Sconce, Jeffery. "Trashing the academy: Taste, excess and an emerging politics of cinematic style," in Ernest Mathijs, and Xavier Mendik, eds., *The Cult Film Reader*. Berkshire: Open University Press, 2008.

Sontag, Susan. "Notes on camp," in Ernest Mathijs, and Xavier Mendik eds., *The Cult Film Reader*. Berkshire: Open University Press, 2008.

Part Four

Media Texts, Audiences,
and the Culture of Riffing

10

Double Poaching and the Subversive Operations of Riffing: "You kids with your hoola hoops and your Rosenbergs and your Communist agendas"[1]

by Ora McWilliams and Joshua Richardson

Imagine: you are sitting in a theater with the lights down low. The previews are over, and a solemn, churchlike silence has descended over the space. The film begins. Suddenly, a voice rings out — loud, clear, distinct. It is the voice of a viewer, commenting on the movie. This person breaks the enforced quiet of the viewing space, and in doing so reclaims the theater for the viewer, at least until another member of the audience yells at them to be quiet.

Welcome to Viewership, Post–*Mystery Science Theater 3000*

Running from 1988 through 1999 on three different networks, *Mystery Science Theater 3000* (*MST3K*, or simply *MST*) is one of the most important programs in the canon of postmodern viewership, due to its incisive wit and clever viewpoint on notions of spectatorship. The model presented by the show is one of interaction, situating the text in the center of the entire history of popular culture through its clever "reference" structure. This construction proved an enticing formula for audience emulation, evolving "movie talking" from the heckling common to the underground of horror film and the grindhouses into the new form of "riffing."

At first blush, the riffing seems like a simple methodology — the viewer watches and comments. Upon closer examination, the process' complexities emerge, and point to a few vital facts: first, that the process of riffing is a method of fan interaction that both reflects existing practice and invites reenactment by the viewer; second, that this interaction is situated in a generational "sweet spot" that resonated with its Generation X viewership on multiple levels; and thirdly, that the spread of this practice from the institutional hegemonic television construct *Mystery Science Theater 3000* to the everyday viewing lives of its audience was an inevitable evolution of the process itself.

110

"My first lobotomy kit"[2] — Identifying Fandom and the Commercial Existence of Rebellion

Fandom studies draw from the distinction Michel deCerteau makes between strategies of the producer/creator elites and tactics of the non-elite audience. The elites have the power to plan and the non-elites "make do" (deCerteau 29–35). Fandom represents the empowerment of the non-elite by appropriation through collective actions, which creates a voice for the masses.

The fan culture of the show *Mystery Science Theater 3000* defines the text as much as the show itself. *MST3K* was not about consumption, at least not in the way that its contemporaries were. Few toys and few shirts were made, and most of those were created and distributed through a fan club and not the program itself. If one compares *MST3K* to other 1980s shows that existed solely to "move merchandise" (such as cartoons like *G.I. Joe*), the differences in the respective aims of *MST* and its competitors are quite obvious.

One category of item would prove an important part of the *MST* legacy: the sale of episodes. In an era in which most television shows being aired did not sell episodes to viewers, *MST*, through a deal with nostalgia merchants Rhino Entertainment, released videocassettes to the emerging home video market. The show was not selling the ethos or idea; it sold the model, not the behavior, as the behavior was broadly owned and not truly commodifiable.

There is also evidence for fan consumption external to the text. The show notably re-popularized and recycled many older cultural artifacts and gave them new life. The fan culture which surrounds the show played an important role in the growth and success, not just of the show itself, but also for the texts being riffed, creating new audiences for films as diverse as *Gamera, This Island Earth,* and *Hobgoblins*.

Mystery Science Theater 3000 was also unique among television shows of its time due to its emphasis on fan participation and interactivity. Fan participation came in two forms: official and unofficial. There were several official channels of fan participation, the most prominent being the *MST3K* Information Club, the direct method for producer interaction with members. Membership's benefits included a biyearly newsletter. Another channel was the "Viewer Mail" segments, where the actors would read some fan letters on the air, answer questions and occasionally riff fan art and letters, a practice reminiscent of the way that comic companies would print fan mail in the back of their publications and respond to fan queries.

A third official encouragement of fan culture was the "exchange the tapes" campaign in the early days of the show. To circulate and create new fans people were encouraged to disseminate videotaped copies of the show (a practice the Grateful Dead allowed which helped the band become one of the most successful and popular touring acts). As the show became more successful and the marketing of videotapes through Rhino expanded, the practice became a liability to *MST*'s marketing strategy and was discouraged. There were also two official MSTie (or *MST* fans) conventions in 1994 and 1996; the latter featured a live performance of *This Island Earth*, which would later become *MST3K: The Movie.* Lastly, during the Sci-fi Channel era, the network's web site had a section entitled "Caption This …," in which a still of the live feed of the network was taken every few minutes (or so) and fans were encouraged to create their own riff.

In addition to the "official" fan communities there were also several "unofficial" (although not necessarily unsanctioned) communities as well. One example of this is the

Rec.arts.tv.MST3K newsgroups where producers and actors involved with the show would interact regularly with fans; this group was responsible for the "save our show" campaign which moved the show from Comedy Central to Sci-Fi channel. Additionally, there were other internet outlets such as the AOL Message boards and Satellite News.

Fan involvement was especially strong with *Mystery Science Theater 3000*; one reason for this is the immersion suggested by the show's format. *MST3K* had a flexible relationship with the fourth-wall, an imaginary space which enforces the separation between viewer and creator.

Within *MST3K* the viewer occupies various roles: "third person" omniscient and "first person" point-of-view. The omniscience and point-of-view of the viewer simultaneously allows the viewer to be sadist and masochist in the terms of the experiment — the perceived torture of the "crappy movie." Then the torturer shares the pain with us, the viewer. More often the view is that of a particular character: in most instances we see what the silent but observant robot Cambot sees. Some hybrid scenes also exist in which character appears to address the viewer directly, even though the character's gaze is addressing his torturer, while cuts back and forth also show the viewer looking from the point of view of the torturer. In other scenes the character is actually addressing the audience, such as during the fan mail segments. This complex process works in practice because of suturing mechanisms.

The term suture literally means "stitched into." In the theories of Lacan and those that followed him, such as Jacques-Alain Miller, it has come to mean "standing-in" or "taking-the-place-of," that is, the moment that a viewer comes to feel themselves in a text (Silverman 195–207). The suture mechanism used in the opening of *MST3K* leads the viewer through several layers of reality disguised as hatches serving as a decompression zone, which effectively allows the viewer a moment to adjust before the program begins. Being in a particular space (such as the "theater" in which the film is shown) radically changes the suture, the sound and, at times, the coloring — to black and white. The frame mechanism of "movie sign" signals the switching of the view to seeing the movie frame. The suture is changed because for the viewer, he or she is no longer omniscient, but in fact, a viewer with the robots and the protagonist. This is created visually when the television viewer is shown the back of the heads of the "riffers," which creates the illusion that you are in the audience with them and should partake in the actions of the characters.

Here, in the show's suture mechanisms, lies a key to fan participation. Sometimes the viewer can stand outside of the experiment such as watching the laborer (Joel or Mike) and boss argue; other times the viewer is plunged into the experiment, such as while watching the film; and still other times the viewer is being told the show is made for his or her benefit, as in the fan mail segments. The viewer of *MST3K* must multitask, as they are viewing a movie and at the same time viewing a second text: that of the creators of the television program *Mystery Science Theater 3000*. Riffing adds a vital second level of significance to the text.

"I can't wait until they start the Internet"[3] — The Function and Taxonomy of Riffing

The most basic unit which film commenting can be reduced to is the" riff," a single comment made by the viewer concerning the text. The riff itself is a versatile thing, serving many functions over the course of an extended "riffing," or set of riffs commenting on a text. This practice seems similar at first glance to "heckling," an old method of text inter-action, and the roots of riffing certainly seem to lie in the heckle. Important differences exist, however. Examining the origins of the word "heckling" reveals one vital difference: the term was originally used to describe a process of finding fault in cloth (OED). Heckling is also often associated with live performance: theater and stand-up comedy. The heckler tries to destroy the text and establish dominance. The riffer, on the other hand, seems more influenced by the jazz technique it takes its name from; a riff settles over an existing text, creating a new thing, dependent on the previous work, but greater than it. The distinction is one of harmony versus discord.

A brief framework of riff types, as well as a discussion of their individual purposes, is crucial to a dissection of the methodology demonstrated by *MST3K*. We have divided riffs into three loose categories: Riff On Action, External Reference, and Internal Reference. It is vital, however, to remember that riffs are capable of serving multiple purposes and can often fit into multiple categories:

1: Riff On Action — "Beep! Plot point!"

The most basic form of riff is the Riff On Action, which serves as a direct commentary on the screen action-taking place. For instance, in *Tormented* (#414), Joel and the bots shout, "Plot point!" to underline the film's rather obvious classical narrative structure and clumsy plot advancement. These riffs also close the gap between program and audience practice most effectively; it mirrors the pre–*MST* horror-viewing cliché of the audience member shouting instructions and warnings to the on-screen protagonist.

Riffs On Action occur in many forms. Sometimes the riffer simply comments on the occurrences on screen ("Beautiful maidens in the hands of hideous beasts. This is my kind of movie!" #107, *Robot Monster*). In other instances, the riffer refers to non–diagetic elements such as background music ("Any movie with 'wok-a-chicka wok-a-chika' in it is okay by me," #512, *Mitchell*). In still other examples, the riffer's remark re-contextualizes the screen action by suggesting potentially different events or meanings behind them ("Now pull your pants up and get out of my office," #1005, *The Blood Waters of Dr. Z*).

The primary function of the Riff On Action is as a bridge to audience experience. By highlighting the elements the audience is perceiving, either directly or through contradiction, the program establishes a common space with the viewer/potential riffer. This space, con-structed from the common experience of watching the film, begins to break down the walls between viewer and participant established by the format of the show.

2: Exterior Reference — "In cars"

The second category in our hierarchy of riffs is the exterior reference. Here, the com-menter makes mention of a text other than that currently being consumed. In *Pod People* (#303), the cast begins singing a stilted version of electronic musician Gary Numan's song "Cars" as stop-motion animation (of Alf-like alien Trumpy using his powers to animate his young friend Tommy's toys) is on screen. Such a reference is often also something of a com-mentary on the action — most likely, in the aforementioned instance, the cast is riffing on the background score's similarity to the music of early keyboard rockers such as Gary Numan.

The exterior reference performs a vital function in the construction of *MST3K*'s meaning — it situates the program in the center of a web of texts, interrelating it to the entire history of popular culture. Such a web is enticing to active fan communities, as it gives them license to perform similar rearrangements in their own media lives in order to increase their comprehension and control. As Henry Jenkins writes, "Fans often find it difficult to discuss single programs except through references and comparisons to this broader network" (Jenkins, 40).

Furthermore, the constant external reference serves as a gatekeeper to exclusivity, letting the culturally literate feel superior for their knowledge. This is a concern of particular import to the members of Generation X that formed the core of the audience. In 1993 Douglas Rushkoff wrote of Generation X culture, "the flippancy with which we regard the very spine of the boomer movement has, unfortunately, provoked outsiders to attack [Generation X] … Defiance toward our elders … keeps our world of recycled, self-referential imagery and post-moral understanding out of the reach of anyone but children" (Rushkoff 7). The Xer constructs a media reality out of specific detritus that tends to restrict older viewers from participation, and *Mystery Science Theater*'s constant parroting of the accumulated pop knowledge of its hyper mediated creators led the way to a "reference space" in which the understanding of Hanna-Barbera cartoons is put on a level with comprehensive literacy in the classics.

3: Internal Reference —
"By this time my lungs were aching for air"

The final variety of riff is the internal reference, the callback to an earlier episode of *MST3K*. For instance, episode 201, *Rocketship X-M*, begins a reference repeated several times throughout the run of the show — the quote "by this time my lungs were aching for air," a reference to the television program *Sea Hunt*. This variety of riff often begins its life as a different type; our example is an External Reference. The recurrence of the line in several other episodes (for instance, #204, *Catalina Caper*) transforms it into an entirely different thing.

The purpose of the internal reference is to create a privileged, referential universe for its most dedicated fans. Such a system of connections encourages fandom, by giving a form of insider knowledge that lionizes fan devotion and text consumption, hooking an audience into the reality formed by the program. The viewer who is familiar with *Catalina Caper* laughs at the callback, prompting less experienced viewers to ask why. The knowledgeable fan then explains the reference, and perhaps offers the neophyte a taped copy of the older episode, thus perpetuating viewing cycles.

As an aside, another means by which the program *Mystery Science Theater 3000* inserted its own text over the film being riffed was the use of changes to the silhouettes of the characters watching the films. Several times over the run of the program, Joel, Mike, Tom, or Crow would alter their visual image (such as by putting on a hat), which would be reflected in their shadowy, representative form in the Satellite of Love's theater. Using such means, *MST3K* was able to "push in" its own reality over that of the creators of the material to be riffed.

"The family of shame!"[4] Audience Positions and Riff Categories

Stuart Hall identifies three positions from which a text can be decoded in his article "Encoding, Decoding." They are the Dominant/Hegemonic, the Negotiated, and the Oppositional. The Dominant reading accepts the worldview and signifiers of the work as intended by the producer. The Negotiated accepts the larger ideas of the piece but quibbles over the specifics, creating a contradictory and inconsistent version. The Oppositional deliberately re-contextualizes the piece, understanding the signs of the work in a new framework and disregarding the original intent (Hall 515–516).

Riffing, as an act, seems to involve an Oppositional reading, and on a very real and important level it does. The riffer acts against the interests of the creator/producers (though without destroying the original piece, as in the act of heckling), taking their work and framing it in a larger context never intended by its makers. Once a film has been viewed in a riffed condition (either through the "professional" avenue provided by *MST3K*, or the "amateur" experience produced by riffing with one's friends, it is often permanently altered in the viewer's mind; having seen the *MST3K* episode *Manos: The Hands of Fate* (#424), it is difficult to imagine engaging with the film in a non-satirical context.

On deeper study, the process of riffing can be understood to operate in all three positions; moreover, these positions roughly connect to the framework of riff types established above. The Riff On Action corresponds to Dominant readings, by commenting directly on the diagetic and non-diagetic reality of the artwork. Even when the comments themselves are snarky, they reinforce the text's values in a global sense simply by accepting the film within its own framework; for all of its sarcasm, the "Plot point" comment in *Tormented* reminds us that the producers control the content of the film through existing, formulaic modes of creation, leaving us in a passive position. The possible exception to this occurs during a counter-action comment, in which the riffer straddles the line between Dominant and Oppositional understandings, both reinforcing the hegemonic construction and rejecting its literal interpretation. By suggesting that Dr. Z "pull [his] pants up" in the riff on *The Blood Waters of Dr. Z* mentioned earlier, Mike and the Bots are reconstructing the verbal flashback over which their comment is situated, altering the scenario from a rejection of Dr. Z's work to a suggestion of socially inappropriate behavior; the audience may then choose their own interpretation of the work.

The External Reference, on the other hand, provides a deeply Oppositional reading to the text, rejecting the closed reality of a producer-controlled piece in favor of a fan-oriented, "open" construction. In this version of things, the text ceases its existence as an isolated and closed unit, as the riffer reminds the viewer that these works operate within a larger framework of other, similar pieces. The External Reference creates a new universe in which the intent of the producers is situated as only one form of intent in a system of others, with no more value than that of the rest. The creators of *Pod People* mean us to view the visuals representing Trumpy's psychic shenanigans in one way; the riffer, invoking Gary Numan, directs us to another point of view, leaving us to create our own version of the scene.

An Internal Reference can be hard to classify, as it often is a callback to a riff of another sort. The Negotiated position, however, best reflects the overall purpose of these references, which typically have little contact with the subject matter at hand but instead create a local and discrete reality independent of the world of the current text. Here we once again notice the creation of an alternate space; this time situated in the retreat from the text into the meta-text created by the riffing framework itself. This reading rejects even the larger universe created by the external reference in favor of a localized, carefully arranged set of meanings. When the on-screen riffers of *MST3K* shout "Mitchell!" in various episodes, the reference calls less to the film *Mitchell* (episode #512) and more to the shared text space of *Mystery Science Theater 3000* itself and the understanding of its fans.

Still another level of reading is present in *MST3K* itself, however. The positions are those of the creator/producers of the show, reacting to the texts made by other creator/producers, in a closed loop of cultural elites. Moreover, although most of the body of reference in the show is to popular entertainment, occasional mention of rather obscure works affiliated with hegemonic forces slip in, such as the reference in *Catalina Caper* (#204) to the experimental film *Koyaanisqatsi*. The fan riffer is not a part of the cultural discourse, but the staff of a cable television program are a part. Despite the populist origins of *MST3K* in cable access and the Midwest, the very process of broadcasting on a national level makes the program into the very thing it tries to mock: a producer-oriented television program in which meaning is provided to its audience to be directly, Dominantly decoded in a unidirectional channel of communication.

Members of the show's audience were bound to find this unsatisfying. After all, their watching signified their willingness to transgress against rigid modes of text reception. The existence of *Mystery Science Theater 3000*, positioned in time as it was, made inevitable the creation of fan communities and the explosion of the riff idea into the larger culture. In other words, *MST* and Generation X would prove a perfect match.

"Oh no: Raid!"[5] — Textual Poaching as the Institution

The classical model of media involves a creator, distinct from his audience, building the artifacts of culture, to be consumed by a muted audience. The viewer is left with no recourse for changing the program; his choice is between spectatorship and avoidance. Unfortunately, neither allows for influence on the product itself; such a construction fails to account for modern fan communities. A quick glance at today's internet fan groups reveals a feeling among fans that the media they consume is, at least in part, theirs, and that their opinions on what should occur in the programs going forward, as well as which elements can be properly construed as canonical, have an importance all their own. The old model gives us no tools to understand this attitude — surely these fans should realize their own insignificance in the process of text production? Why would these people think their opinions would matter?

Henry Jenkins helps us reorient our understanding of media to include these fan communities in his book *Textual Poachers*. Referencing and extending the works of Michel de Certeau, Jenkins refers to a process of "poaching," in which fans violate the boundaries between media artifact and producer, appropriating elements of text found to be to their liking. In this view, the canons of fandom are seen to be even more important than those of the creators; by rejecting the dictated means of understanding meanings, the poachers claim the realm of meaning for themselves.

The riffing illustrated in *MST3K* proves itself to be a potent mechanism for this kind of poaching. The space created by various kinds of riffs can be appropriated to the use of the poachers, filled with reference and critical dissections. Again, we can see the way that different riff varieties contribute to the process. Riffs On Action serve to demystify the arcane methods of text creation, bringing faults in the logic behind a work's construction to the fore. The External Reference appropriates text by reducing it, bringing out the commonalities between various works and allowing the construction of a fan canon. The Internal Reference adds the final touch: by insisting on the importance of the riffing framework, this riff brings the framework itself to the same level as the text being riffed. The net result of a complete set of riffs is a fan-created artwork, dependent on the text being riffed but independent of its structure of controlled meanings and unidirectional communication.

Mystery Science Theater 3000, though a primary source for the fan's adopting of this behavior, is an imperfect model at best. The first problem, already discussed, concerns the institutional nature of the television program *Mystery Science Theater 3000* itself, which involves a production process that excludes the audience (although, notably, the show attempted to reduce the effect of this through the reading of viewer mail and the emphasis placed on the fan club). The second, and greater, problem is that of text quality. *MST3K* riffed "bad" movies; its methodology assumed the low quality of the films that it commented. This introduces a subjective aesthetic element to the practice, restricting the wide applicability of riffing to the realms of "trash" culture and the "cult classic." A truly universal, truly subversive riffing technique should be capable of appropriating any text that the poacher using it desires. To find such a process, independent fan action would prove necessary.

"Dear Agent Scully, I did not appreciate your lawyer's tone"[6]— Double Poaching and Fan Empowerment

From the early days of *MST* fan communities, one common query fans had for one another was that of which film the fan would most like to see riffed. An important trend that emerged was the desire of MSTies to see films often deemed aesthetically "good" (such as the original *Star Wars* films) get riffed. This desire clearly operated outside of the scope of the television program—*MST* needed clearances for the films that received its riffing treatment, and the high cost and controlling producers of many commercially successful films restricted *MST* from being able to access them. The fan community suffered no such restrictions. Soon, "fan riffs" on popular works began turning up on the internet.

This fan practice of emulating the methods of *MST* in a wider, legally unencumbered sense has such far-reaching implications that it deserves a close examination. We have dubbed such practice "double-poaching," in recognition of the work of de Certeau and Jenkins. A double-poach occurs when a fan appropriates a method of textual appropriation from an institutional text. Although the method itself is of elite origin, the repurposing act by the fan community democratizes the process, bringing marginal and excluded consumers under its umbrella and empowering them to own rearranged forms of text. This hybridized "riffed" text is itself validated by the institutional nature of the program being emulated—the show justifies the fan practice, and the fan practice legitimizes the illusion of the outlaw status of the show. Thus, double-poaching creates a truly symbiotic relationship between producer/creator and fan enactor.

The scope of fan practice extends riffing into territory that no program could reach. As mentioned above, a fan riffing can encompass any text, regardless of producer/creator desire. Moreover, a fan riffing exists more or less apart from the censoring structures attached to typical means of broadcast; a riff made in the comfort of one's home may be as obscene as one wishes. Finally, a fan riffing is more dogmatically flexible. The central authority in control of *MST3K* inescapably expresses the agenda of its constituents; for example, the program often criticized its older films from a modern perspective on gender and race. A fan riffer can express a different set of political or social beliefs. By doing so, the riff space is made democratic in an absolute sense, as only the availability of any position on a cultural artifact can really make it democratized.

"I can't stop. I don't know how it works!"[7] — Riffing After *MST3K*

After the end of *Mystery Science Theater 3000*, its creators involved themselves in various other ventures — book publishing, video game creation, comic writing, and, eventually, other riffing projects. Two successors to the program eventually coalesced, each formed around one of the show's hosts. The first project was *RiffTrax*, the brainchild of head writer and host Mike Nelson. *Cinematic Titanic* was later created by Joel Hodgson, the original host and co-creator of *MST3K*. Both efforts involve riffing, but beyond that, they differ greatly in purpose.

Cinematic Titanic operates much as *Mystery Science Theater 3000* did, producing "episodes" of B movies and exploitation pictures with commentary by Joel and others. The program uses a visual superimposition process similar to the "Shadowrama" of *MST* (though, notably, the *CT* viewer no longer shares a conventional movie theater with the riffers, perhaps due to the increased emphasis on home viewership in the digital media age). There is a metaplot of sorts, with the riffers working with a corporate/military force to preserve films, but it seems to be placed in the background in comparison to *MST3K*'s elaborate set-up. *RiffTrax* hardly seems to bother with recurring plot, although it features occasional fictional riffers such as "DisembAudio." *RiffTrax*, rather than licensing movies, records audio files meant to be played over a viewing of a specified text, thus freeing Nelson and his compatriots to deal with a wider variety of films.

Of the two, *RiffTrax* seems to be trying to emulate the fan practice more; their web site even features a mechanism by which fans may record and market their own riffs, with a portion of the proceeds going to *RiffTrax*. *Cinematic Titanic* focuses more on the institutional traditions of *Mystery Science Theater 3000*, essentially marketing a kind of nostalgia, although the films used tend to be more contemporary than the "classic" B films of *MST* (most *CT* films are from the sixties and seventies, as opposed to the forties and fifties). *CT* also features an emphasis on live performance, thereby linking the audience to the act of riffing. Each tries to capture the former *MST* audience in its own way, and each is successful, filling different, but equally important, niches in the post–*MST* riffing world.

"Goodnight, sweet crustacean"[8] — Conclusion

When a group of local comedians and filmmakers formed in Minnesota in the late eighties, it would have been difficult for them to foresee the far-reaching effects of the program they produced. Their effort would alter viewing practices around the world, providing a model of defiance of entrenched authority to fans seeking a piece of intellectual territory all their own. Although the show itself was institutional, and denied fans the agency they desired, by enacting of the behaviors of the show's stars (via the double-poach process), *MST*'s loyal legions of viewers were able to find a voice all their own. Riffing is not always an oppositional practice, but it is always a grab for ownership, a vital tool in the struggle for the meaning of texts.

The authors would like to thank the libraries at the University of Kansas.
Ora McWilliams would like to thank Joy Bancroft, Rabbie Najjar, and the staff of the KU Writing Center.
Joshua Richardson would like to thank Dorthea for editorial aid and for putting up with him in general.
Finally, all thanks to the authors of the first amendment. KEEP CIRCULATING THE TAPES!

Notes

1. *Mystery Science Theater 3000*, episode 906, *The Space Children*.
2. *Mystery Science Theater 3000*, episode 417, *Crash of the Moons*.
3. *Mystery Science Theater 3000*, episode 910, *The Final Sacrifice*.
4. *Mystery Science Theater 3000*, episode 608, *Code Name Diamond Head*.
5. *Mystery Science Theater 3000*, episode 310, *Fugitive Alien*.
6. *Mystery Science Theater 3000*, episode 910, *The Final Sacrifice*.
7. *Mystery Science Theater 3000*, episode 310, *Fugitive Alien*.
8. *Mystery Science Theater 3000*, episode 404, *Teenagers from Outer Space*.

References

deCerteau, Michel. *The Practice of Everyday Life*. Berkeley: University of California, 1988.

Hall, Stuart. "Encoding, Decoding." *The Cultural Studies Reader*. in Simon During ed. 2nd ed. London: Routledge, 2006. 507–17.

Hodgson, Joel (director), Mike Nelson (writer), Kevin Murphy (writer) et al., Episode 424 *Manos: The Hands of Fate* 1993.

Jenkins, Henry. *Textual Poachers*. New York, NY: Routledge, 1992.

Mallon, Jim (producer), Trace Beaulieu (writer), Joel Hodgson (writer) et al., Episode 107 *Robot Monster* 1990.

Mallon, Jim (producer), Michael Nelson (writer), Trace Beaulieu (writer) et al., Episode 201 *Rocketship X-M* 1990.

Mallon, Jim (director), Michael Nelson (writer), Trace Beaulieu (writer) et al., Episode 204 *Catalina Caper* 1990.

Mallon, Jim (director), Michael Nelson (writer), Trace Beaulieu (writer) et al., Episode 303 *Pod People* 1991.

Mallon, Jim (director), Michael Nelson (writer), Trace Beaulieu (writer) et al., Episode 310 *Fugitive Alien* 1991.

Murphy, Kevin (director), Mike Nelson (writer), Trace Beaulieu (writer) et al., Episode 417 *Crash of the Moons* 1992.

Murphy, Kevin (director), Mike Nelson (writer), Trace Beaulieu (writer) et al., Episode 404 *Teenagers from Outer Space* 1992.

Murphy, Kevin (director), Mike Nelson (writer), Trace Beaulieu (writer) et al., Episode 414 *Tormented* 1992.

Murphy, Kevin (director), Michael Nelson (writer), Trace Beaulieu (writer) et al., Episode 512 *Mitchell* 1993.

Murphy, Kevin (director), Mike Nelson (writer), Trace Beaulieu (writer) et al., Episode 608 *Code Name: Diamond Head* 1994.

Murphy, Kevin (director), Mike Nelson (writer), Paul Chaplin (writer) et al., Episode 906 *The Space Children* 1998.

Murphy, Kevin (director), Mike Nelson (writer), Paul Chaplin (writer) et al., Episode 910 *The Final Sacrifice* 1998.

Nelson, Michael (director), Paul Chaplin (writer), Bill Corbett (writer) et al., Episode 1005 *Blood Waters of Dr. Z* 1999.

Silverman, Kaja. *The Subject of Semiotics*. New York, NY: Oxford University Press, 1983.

11

Frame Work, Resistance and Co-optation: How *Mystery Science Theater 3000* Positions Us Both In and Against Hegemonic Culture

by Michael Dean

When I was a kid, my little brother and I used to perform parodies for the mic of a small audiocassette recorder. Our script was a paperback collection of the TV, movie and comic-strip parodies done under Harvey Kurtzman's direction for the early issues of *Mad* when it was still a comic book. There was something about the frantic but artful comic pacing of stories like "Superduperman" and "Flesh Garden" that cried out to be translated for the ear, so we turned them into radio sketches, with my brother and myself each taking multiple roles and providing sound effects. If movies tended to entrance the average adult viewer, the spell they cast over juvenile audiences was ten times more powerful, but *Mad* showed us that we didn't have to take movies — or even the adult world, for that matter — as seriously as they seemed to want to be taken. From that scripted beginning, my brother and I moved on to a new phase of production: We set the tape recorder in front of the TV during an afternoon broadcast of the 1952 movie *Heidi*, intermittently muting the TV speakers and substituting the characters' dialogue with our own improvised comical impersonations. We kept ourselves in stitches, and from that point on, the experience of watching movies — especially the pompous, the treacly and the melodramatic ones — was never the same. We had, in effect, made ourselves critics and, at the same time, part of the show.

The history of cultural criticism in the 20th century follows a shifting focus from the author to the text to the audience. It was a focus that came close to bestowing sovereignty, so that when the author wore the crown, traditional criticism was felt to have no higher calling than to ferret out the true meaning of a text as it was conceived by its creator. In the case of cinema, the auteurism of Andrew Sarris (1962/1970) and his colleagues was not so much a delineating principle as a basis for criticism in the first place. If the key to understanding and appreciating a work art lay in the intentions of the author, then movies could only be considered art if a movie author could be identified. The film director had barely been fitted for that role when critics came to the conclusion that the author had "died," that the author's intent was unknowable and largely irrelevant. Certain codes circulated within and between classic Hollywood and television texts regardless of the author's intent or consent, and they went a long way toward fixing and defining the viewer's identity as citizen of the political, economic and psychological hegemonies that pervaded Western society. From this point of view, audiences were simply receptors, the mental screen on which the cinema projected its social coherence. The late-20th-century school of criticism that grew partially out of the work of Stuart Hall and the Birmingham Center for Contemporary Cultural Studies turned the previous model on its head, effectively locating the relevant result of a cultural expression in the audience as a site of resistance and redeployment. Far from being a passive reflection of cinema's social programming, by the end of the century, the audience was where the action was, the place where multiple cultural perspectives contextualized, interpreted and repurposed the experience of cinema and television.

In 1988 Joel Hodgson unveiled *Mystery Science Theater*, a television series in which the re-visionary activity of the audience was seen to invade the hitherto hermetic frame of the cinematic screen. In a way, *MST3K* can be seen as emblematic of the late-20th-century celebration of individual agency and the powers of the audience, but it also illustrates some of the limits of those powers. What I want to do here is directed less toward a close examination of the show or its episodes, than the kinds of questions that arise if we take *MST3K* and its offspring as an example of the ways that power and point of view are negotiated between a pop cultural work and its audience.

Even if the riffing done by the *MST3K* hosts aims largely for laughter rather than a specific political or historical critique, its willingness to violate the sanctity of a movie's frame and challenge the movie's terms of engagement can be seen as setting an empowering example for all audiences. However, there are also elements of its audience surrogacy—including its lack of specificity—that undermines or displaces the potential for a fully critical, adversarial or alternative audience perspective and leaves in place certain assumptions of the movies as products of Western hegemony. There had been earlier attempts to join satirical commentary directly to its object (e.g., the short-lived syndicated TV series *Mad Movies*, Firesign Theatre's *J-Men Forever*, Woody Allen's *What's Up, Tiger Lily?*) but the approach taken by *MST3K* was unique and drew the attention of a large and devoted audience for more than a decade. Through its offshoots, the *MST3K* concept continues to evolve in ways that both adapt to and react against developing technologies. All of which makes the show an instructive case history of the dialectical push and pull by which pop-cultural works and their audience inform and respond to one another.

In its initial incarnation, on a local UHF Minneapolis channel, *Mystery Science Theater* was modeled closely on a staple of local programming: the afternoon horror or science-fiction movie broadcast. With names like *Shock Theater*, *Chiller Theatre* and *The Vampira Show*, those broadcasts traditionally were fueled by old movies that were cheap for the station to acquire but so cheesy and arcane that it was necessary to build a bridge from the movies to the only audience that might forgive their corniness: kids (and potheads). The movies themselves, made for earlier generations, were often slowly paced, with low-budget sets, awkward, melodramatic acting and barely surviving prints, but local stations created an inviting doorway into them by using host characters in a role similar to carnival barkers. These framing segments involved a host costumed in some form of horror drag who had the job of establishing both a lurid anticipation for the movie and a camp, comical, over-the-top atmosphere that young viewers often found more captivating than the movies themselves. The deficiencies of the movies combined with local skits performed at virtually every commercial break by the host and other secondary characters made for the kind of alienation effect Bertolt Brecht would have longed for.

The first obligation of the afternoon horror-movie host was to draw audiences into the movie, but the framing skits also acknowledged the movies' generic absurdities. If you were watching these broadcasts with fellow viewers who were as young or stoned as you were, you could not help but talk back to the screen, pointing out predictable clichés, continuity blunders and various instances of unintended humor on the part of the narrative. Under these circumstances, the source of entertainment lay less in the movie than in the participatory performances of you and your friends; the movie was a kind of straight man feeding you opportunities for sarcasm and parody.

MST3K took that basic formula and made some important shifts. First of all, the host was no longer a host as such. Whereas the traditional afternoon horror-movie host was there to "invite" us into the movie-watching experience, which the "host" was seen to be in control of, the Joel Robinson character played by Joel Hodgson is not in control. According to the *MST3K* framing narrative, he is forced to watch the movies against his will. He is a surrogate for the audience, not the broadcaster, and therefore has no obligation to promote the movie. Joel is free to take an entirely critical position. This also distinguishes *MST3K* from audience participation events like the *Rocky Horror Picture Show* experience in which the audience response is ritualized and appended to the film as a kind of extra-diegetic, interactive performance. In the case of *Rocky Horror*, the audience activities are invariably cued by the movie — effectively extensions of the film that function as a kind of participatory homage rather than a critique.

Second, what was merely a temporal frame (that is, occupying episodes of time before and after segments of the film) in the traditional afternoon horror broadcast is extended in *MST3K* to include a literal spatial frame during the showing of the movie. As Erving Goffman observed in *Frame Analysis: An Essay on the Organization of Experience* (1974) the boundaries of a movie screen are an explicit instance of how frames literally and abstractly position us with respect to a given social experience. While appearing as a silhouette along the margin of the lower frame of the film screen, Joel comments on the movie while it unfolds and from a position that is analogous to our position as an audience in a theater. *MST3K* is premised — literally and figuratively — on a fabrication of the relationship between a theatrical-movie and its audience. In fact, it is a fabrication of a fabrication, since the screening room that imitates a theatrical environment is itself a fiction. Furthermore, the layering of frames within frames extends to the boundaries of the satellite, in which Joel is held as captive audience. (Goffman's work would be the best guidebook for carrying the current paper's analysis further.)

Insofar as Joel plays a coerced role within a larger governing mechanism (the Gizmonic Institute) the *MST3K* framing narrative reflects the mid-20th-century critical model, which fixes the audience in place as receptor of the cultural text. But Joel also represents the audience in its resistance to the text, which makes him ultimately the hero of a dramatization of the late-20th-century audience-centric critical model. Furthermore, in its invocation of the audience environment, *MST3K* does not fail to recreate the kind of group dynamic that encouraged you and your friends to talk back to the TV screen. It isn't just Joel watching, but Joel and robot friends Crow and Tom Servo. It is a staging of the audience as a community of critics interacting with the movie and with each other.

The paradox of this is quickly evident. Joel is not the audience but a dramatization of the audience's role. Even as he is commenting on the show, he *is* the show. He is positioned as an outsider in relation to both the movie and the conditions of its screening (which are out of his control), and, by allowing that position to literally intrude into the frame of the movie, *MST3K* provides for a subversive disruption of the movie's integrity — but at the same time, Joel's critical perspective is absorbed into the frame. There is a sense in which *MST3K*'s widening of the movie's frame to include the critical audience is less a subversion than an inoculation.

MST3K is both a reflection and a reinforcement of our impulse to criticize and mock the flaws and phony elements of a movie when it appears on our living-room television, but what happens when an audience gathers around a living-room TV to watch *Mystery Science Theater 3000*? Do we interject our own comments in relation to the target movie as we would if we weren't watching it in the context of *MST3K*? Do we ridicule shortcomings in the *MST3K* episode itself? Or do we respond by proxy, letting the silhouettes of Joel and the bots do our talking back for us? In the spirit of Cultural Studies, it would be interesting to see the results of a genuine survey on this question, but, anecdotally, my experience and that of people I've spoken with, suggests that we interject only laughter, consistently ceding the critical role to our audience surrogates when we watch *MST3K*.

If the movie has become essentially a narrative within a narrative, then Joel is no more than a character in the external narrative. The presence of his silhouette and those of Crow and Tom, in effect becomes a classic over-the-shoulder point-of-view shot by which the audience's gaze is filtered through the perspective of a particular character or group of characters. Arguably, we see the movie through the eyes of Joel et al. Although we began by saying that Joel is us, the audience, it may be truer to say that the audience becomes him, his point of view.

And what is that point of view? If Joel represents the audience as character, then what sort audience do we become in identifying with him? All audiences are not alike, of course. It makes a difference when you and your companion critics gather around the livingroom TV set if you are sharing the sofa with, say, Roland Barthes and Christian Metz or with Kaja Silverman and Donna Haraway or with Antonio Gramsci and Walter Benjamin or with Spike Lee and Stanley Aronowitz or with me and my brother. Different communities will find different elements of a movie to comment on, different observations to make and different jokes to crack. Ostensibly, Joel's character is defined by the framing narrative. His companions, Tom Servo and Crow, are a false community in that they are actually extensions of Joel — robots that he has pieced together out of spare parts. Joel himself is established as a relatively nondescript "little guy," Everyman as blue-collar worker. He has a caring parental relationship with the robots, modeled on the human/puppet relationship in shows like *Kukla, Fran and Ollie*— also a local-station afternoon staple. He has apparently been victimized and used as pawn by powerful corporate and governmental interests. Ideologically, therefore, we might expect the premise of *MST3K* to be setting us up to view the films from a working-class, perhaps even Marxist, perspective. That viewpoint never materializes, however. All the characteristics that are given to Joel are ultimately there to serve a single purpose: to make us identify with him. He is essentially a white, male, nerdy, wage-earning, nice-guy schlub — the embodiment of what must have been projected to be *MST3K*'s dominant demographic. He invites audience sympathy also in the way that he has been manipulated by institutional forces larger them himself. As the introductory theme song tells us, the sinister Powers That Be don't like him, which means, of course, that we must like him.

Any hint of political commentary or dystopian institutional critique is limited by Joel's essential passivity toward his situation and is further eroded as the series progresses when it is clarified that the scientists who have imprisoned Joel are not representative of the Gizmonic Institute that employed him, but rogue mad scientists who are relocated from their initial organizational environs to a subterranean hide-out called Deep 13.

When a critic working from a Cultural Studies model locates a source of agency in the audience, it is based on the audience's ability to reappropriate mass-cultural material for its own particular uses. Joel, as a fictional figure, represents the audience, but only as a largely empty vessel for identification. To identify with his position is to abandon all the particularities that might define a specific audience in opposition to or in an alternative relation to mass culture. Why are the *MST3K* screenings located aboard a satellite? To some degree, the satellite can be seen as evocative of the cheesy sci-fi trappings of the movies on view, but the framing storyline is not, after all, set in a future any more advanced than "next Sunday." A not insignificant effect of the off-planet setting is that it both isolates and universalizes the viewing experience. The movies are not being watched in, say, an inner-city slum or a Middle Eastern women's shelter, but in a kind of neutral zone. Joel and *MST3K*, therefore, represent the audience not in its potential range of multicultural and gendered perspectives but as a centralized, context-less point of view.

A full character profile of the fictional Joel based on a tracking of the framing narrative from episode to episode is beyond the scope of this paper, but, in a sense, such a profile is irrelevant to an understanding of the point of view that he brings to the *MST3K* audience. For one thing, Joel's abducted janitor character is replaced early in the 10-year run of the series by Mike Nelson's similarly kidnapped temp-worker character with little effect on the show's concept or tone. Mike's character is initially a little more rebellious toward his captors, but quickly settles into the routine. In any case, once the "Movie Sign" appears and the film begins to roll, *MST3K*'s framing narrative is virtually set aside in much the same way that the host segments of *Chiller Theatre* would be forgotten while the movie was running. Joel and the robots comment in character (Trace Beaulieu, for example, delivers his gags in Crow's cartoonish voice) but only in a superficial sense. In most episodes, little or no reference is made to the framing narrative's backstory during the screening of the movie. The gags and observations are informed throughout by the pop-culture acumen and comedic skills of Hodgson and his fellow performers. These actors' sense of irony and wry detachment really define the parameters of the point of view through which we watch an *MST3K* movie, much more so than any fictional perspective invented for the characters they play.

In this ensemble of performers we do see a kind of community such as might gather in our imaginary living room if we were blessed with a group of friends who are professional comedians. But there is an important difference: Presumably, the *MST3K* commentators have viewed each episode's movie numerous times and, while there was undoubtedly a stage of spontaneous improvisation by the writer/performers, that moment has long passed by the time an *MST3K* episode is broadcast. At that point, we are watching a performance that has been honed and scripted out of the funniest of the gags brainstormed by the actors and writers during rehearsal. The fumbles, unsuccessful jokes, ill-timed responses, misremembered names, etc. have all been ironed out, and if any crop up on camera, it's a simple matter to edit them out. It's worth remembering that, although we view the *MST3K* movie in all its varied shots and cuts, the movements and gestures of the movie-riffing silhouettes are carried out in long takes broken only by the show's intermissions. The connection between this shadow play and the gags we hear on the audio track, however, is entirely flexible. With the exception of Crow's flapping lower jaw, we can't see the performers' lips move, so there's nothing to prevent the audio commentary from being erased, dubbed and redubbed as needed.

That's not the case, of course, in our living room. Here, when a joke falls flat, it is met with silence, and when it works, we provoke laughter from our fellow viewers. On

MST3K, the performers rarely laugh at one another's gags, partly because the jokes are no longer new to them and partly because there's no time for that kind of spontaneous response when they have to be constantly alert for cues from the movie to their next scripted wisecrack. According to the show's own official estimate, each episode contains an average of 700 interjected humorous comments.

In 2007, Hodgson and ex–*MST3K* cast members Beaulieu, J. Elvis Weinstein, Frank Conniff, and Mary Jo Pehl launched a similar concept in the made-for-DVD series *Cinematic Titanic. CT* follows the formula of *MST3K* in its framing science-fictional backstory, which also involves coerced viewing of bad movies as part of a study by a controlling higher power. But this framing device is only faintly observed. There is no expository theme song to orient the viewer to the back-story. It is virtually ignored during the movie and it doesn't require Hodgson and the others to be anything other than what they are: sarcastic, pop-culture-savvy humorists. The actors, playing themselves, even make reference to their former gigs on *MST3K.* During the screenings, the cast again appears as silhouettes, but this time posed along the lower right and left sides of the screen either seated or standing against railings on what are apparently meant to be decks of a ship. The effect of seeing some of the performers standing rather than looking up from the seats of a theater audience is suggestive of the performative nature of the riffing. They are no longer down in the audience with us but up on a kind of multi-tiered stage. That combined with the increased number of riffers tends to underscore the artifice of the situation as each performer awaits his or her turn to deliver a scripted interjection.

The reference to the *Titanic* reflects the status of the films on view as disastrous aesthetic failures, but it also evokes the sinking technological context of the original *MST3K* conceit. The idea of heckling bad, low-budget movies from theater seats was already a scene from a vanished venue: the old grindhouse movie-watching experience. Although one *MST3K* performance targeting *This Island Earth* was packaged for theatrical distribution, the series lived its life primarily through afternoon cable TV. With its peanut gallery limited to a small group (rather than an entire theater audience), *MST3K* could be seen as an effort to transfer the grindhouse experience to the living-room TV. But even that communal living-room circle may be a fading cultural moment in the face of onrushing technologies.

Another *MST3K* offshoot, *RiffTrax,* which features the involvement of Mike Nelson and the remaining faction of former *MST3K* performers, is more cognizant of contemporary modes of entertainment. Although audio commentaries were nonexistent at the time *MST3K* began, their omnipresence today on DVDs and Bluray discs has made audiences well-accustomed to consuming anecdotal, humorous, historical, technical, and aesthetic narrations of a film in a parallel track alongside the subject narrative of the movie itself. Present-day viewers are also increasingly prepared to encounter visual narrative through various computerized platforms. *RiffTrax* has adapted to these evolving technologies — and the exigencies of securing rights to the movies — by offering the audio riffing separately from the movie via Web downloads. The viewers are left to rent or download the movie and synchronize it with the audio commentary provided by *RiffTrax.* Freed from the necessity of obtaining rights, *RiffTrax* is able to target much more high-profile movies than *MST3K* ever was.

By this time, the viewing experience has come a long way from the communal environment of a grindhouse theater or a group gathered around a living-room television set. The various platforms available to audiences today emphasize the individual, who is more likely to stream a visual narrative via a laptop or an iPhone or a portable DVD player than to view it in a room with other individuals. For the individuals who download a *RiffTrax* commentary, the disembodied voices do not so much evoke the communal audience experience as displace it.

Nevertheless, even the definitions of audience and community are undergoing radical changes in the wake of the Internet's radical reimagining of society. The audience of the World Wide Web is both dispersed and focused into infinitely variable nodes of interest. The Web's technical possibilities combined with the iconoclastic attitudes fostered by projects like *MST3K* and *RiffTrax* (not to mention Harvey Kurtzman's *Mad* and other *MST3K* forebears and siblings) have generated guerrilla pop-cultural critique/interaction in the form of DIY YouTube parodies, mash-ups, remixes, re-dubs, sound samples, re-captioned comic strips—and the cult phenomenon known as MSTing, which directly applies the *MST3K* technique of interjected commentary to written pop-cultural fiction. For corporate-owned properties, copyright laws have provided the greatest defense against *MST3K*-style satirical commentary. Most MSTers confine their "riffing" to original fan fiction rather than scripts from corporate-owned entertainment properties, which renders such twice-removed MSTing somewhat toothless: the cannibalizing parody of a pastiche. There's no denying, however, that among the MSTers, a strong sense of community persists, as well as an equally strong dedication to reappropriating pop-cultural concepts and texts.

With its premise of critiquing mainstream narrative from the margins based on an obsessive mastery of pop-culture allusion, *MST3K* has always had an attachment to fan subcultures and it has continued to be a presence on the Web and at comics and science-fiction conventions. Trace Beaulieu (1997) has even written a comic book called *Here Come the Big People*, satirizing our willingness to be controlled by technology.

Meanwhile, even as *RiffTrax* has attempted to accommodate new modes of delivery, both it and *Cinematic Titanic* have taken another step backward toward the live grindhouse experience that inspired *MST3K*. The *CT* performers have taken their act on tour, commenting alongside screenings of movies before live audiences. The added spontaneity of that format allows the performers to ad-lib more, responding to each other and to the audience. The *Cinematic Titanic* DVD releases are now including recorded live performances and RiffTrax also offers DVD releases of some live RiffTrax events.

We can see in the evolution of the *MST3K* concept the shifting strategies and technologies of the modes and media of mass-culture narrative in its attempt to seize and address the social consciousness in a hegemonic point of view, but we can also see the resilience of the audience in the way that it absorbs and adapts the narrative experience to its own purposes. As much as narrative may bind an audience to it, as much as modern technology and mass culture may hold us each prisoner in our respective satellites, they can also lay the foundation for our escape. My brother and I learned from *Mad* the same spirit of resistance that flourished in the grindhouse theaters and *MST3K* learned from the grindhouse experience about how to play to that resistance.

REFERENCES

Beaulieu, Trace, Jimmy Palmiotti, and Amanda Conner. *Here Come the Big People*. Ottawa, IL: Event Comics, 1997.

Goffman, Erving. *Frame Analysis: An Essay on the Organization of Experience*, New York: Harper & Row, 1974.

Saris, Andrew. "Notes on the Auteur Theory in 1962," in P. Adams Sitney, ed., *Film Culture Reader*. New York: Praeger Publishers, 1970. 121–135.

12

"Not too different from you or me":
The Paradox of Fiction,
Joint Attention, and Longevity

by Michael David Elam

One of the interesting phenomena of observing comedy — on television, in a club, at the office — is the experience of watching someone say what you've always wanted to, perhaps even better than you could. For many people *Mystery Science Theater 3000* (*MST3K*) does just that. Its entertainment rolls out in the form of quips and cracks, i.e., riffs, that often provoke one to think, "I wish I had said that" or "That's exactly what I was thinking."[1] While it situates bad films within a larger narrative framework in order to underscore and criticize glaring defects, what sets *MST3K* apart from other shows with the primary goal of criticism or satire is its appeal to the audience. Not *appeal* as an object, but an action that proffers something of itself and elicits responses. Indeed, knowing that someone else thinks that what one watches is poorly done — in many cases absurdly so — helps create the feeling that one is actually participating in the tortuous experiment. In this way *MST3K* draws its viewers into the program, providing them with an experience based on more than observation alone. The show also provides a vicarious experience: being forced to watch bad movies and learning to cope with it. One doesn't simply watch the characters stranded on the Satellite of Love (SoL) suffer through watching bad movies; one suffers with them. What the show itself provides is a way to help viewers negotiate through the experience by supplying them with a mechanism by which to respond to the films: the riff. The riff allows the viewer to connect with the riffer, in this case the inhabitants of the SoL, by pointing to the object being riffed upon in order to suggest a possible response to the thing being observed. Joel Hodgson in fact explains this dynamic's basic structure in a trailer for *Cinematic Titanic*'s live show: "Most jokes are a straight line between a comic and an audience. A riff is a triangle. It's between the person riffing, the screen, and the audience" (Hodgson "Live Tour" 2010).

While watching *MST3K*, then, one feels a powerful connection to the characters stranded on the SoL, the nature of which connection closely parallels that of joint-attention learning and also resembles very much the experience of emotional connectedness with fictional characters portrayed on television and in other media, referred to by some scholars as the paradox of fiction.[2] This chapter hopes to introduce its readers to the basic concepts of the paradox of fiction and of joint attention, focusing on how these models help explain why *MST3K*'s unique expressional mode lends itself to connecting with its audience; show how the show draws viewers into shared experience with its characters; and suggest that part of its increasing longevity lies in its ability to connect to viewers by way of this shared experience. It is also hoped that this article might stimulate more in-depth studies by researchers and specialists in areas of expertise within and beyond the arts and humanities in order to more fully explain the affect of *MST3K*'s unique format.

The Paradox of Fiction[3]

Perhaps the best and most succinct overview of the paradox of fiction's characteristics, and the theories that attempt to explain it, is Jerrold Levinson's "Emotion in Response to Art: A Survey of the Terrain" (1997). In the article, Levinson reduces the philosophical components concerning emotional responses to works of art down to five questions, the second of which addresses the matter here: "How can we intelligibly have emotions for fictional persons or situations, given that we do not believe in their existence? (This query relates to what is known as 'the paradox of fiction')" (Levinson, 1997: 21).[4] With respect to the paradox of fiction itself, Levinson writes that it comes about by holding three propositions which cannot be maintained together: "(a) We often have emotions for fictional characters and situations known to be purely fictional; (b) Emotions for objects logically presuppose beliefs in the existence and features of those objects; (c) We do not harbor beliefs in the existence and features of objects known to be fictional" (Levinson, 1997: 22–23). The paradox of fiction may be reformulated thusly: Observers of fictional works have powerful emotional reactions to them even though they know such works to be representations of the non-real, and these feelings appear to be genuine. That is, one might feel as deep a grief for the death of a fictional character as for a real person despite knowing that the former does not exist in reality.

How, then, does the paradox of fiction work, if at all, in *MST3K*? After all, the situation presented to its viewers seems a conscious fabrication; there is no attempt to hide the absurdity of its own premise. It presents itself in a number of ways that seem conventional of comedy: over the top premise, deliberately bad special effects, silly looking characters, etc. Where, then, can one emotionally connect to the show — a way in which so many seem to have connected so far — especially since its premises lend themselves to creating a greater chasm between the show's fictional situation and the typical viewer's reality? It appears that *MST3K* invites such a connection from its almost imperceptible, and somewhat unusual use of second person interaction — somewhat unusual because although the kind of second person interaction employed by the show isn't uncommon in shows of fiction (being found often in children's television programs such as *Sesame Street, Dora the Explorer, Super Why*, etc.), it is uncommon to find it used in such a show ostensibly for adults, or at least a show not specifically for children.[5] What distinguishes *MST3K*'s second-person interaction, then, is its level of informality, its conversational tone, inviting viewers to connect to the program's characters as if they have a kind of personal friendship. Here the assumptions concerning the paradox of fiction are stretched to their limits, because not only are the fictional characters of *MST3K* non-existent, but these non-existent, fictional characters also directly address their viewers as if they have a real connection to them.

A very good example of this dynamic being played out presents itself in the opening to *Hercules Unchained* (Mallon 1992, Episode 408), with Tom Servo yelling from inside a yellow wash and wax machine being operated by Joel, the principal character on the SoL. At this point, the show attempts no second-person interaction with the viewer, using instead about twelve seconds to establish that, despite Joel and Gypsy's exhortations the wash is good for him, Tom Servo is in distress, shouting that he's tasting soap while in the machine. At this point, however, an interesting second-person interaction between characters on the show and its viewers commences. Crow appears close-up and addresses the audience directly: "Hey everybody," he says, "It's a bad day around here. It's annual wash and wax day — the most dreaded day of all. You can't go near Joel, or he'll scrub you into a pink pulp." The warning to viewers to stay away imbues the emotional address with a kind of intimacy, although viewers are clearly in no danger of suffering the fate about which Crow warns. In the very next moment, after Crow flees from in front of the camera, another second-person address follows from Joel: "Oh, hi everybody; welcome to the SoL. It's really lucky you happened by. It's our annual wash and wax day. It's one of the funnest days of all!" This is followed by Joel's warning to Tom Servo to close his mouth since the buffers are coming, after which Crow pops into view again, exclaiming, "Isn't it horrifying!"

What emerges appears to possess a strong resemblance to the paradox of fiction — that is, the audience makes an emotional connection to the characters they know are not real (even if the emotional connection is not the one desired by Crow). The scene also contains elements by which the show seeks to connect in a certain way to its audience. The scene, which portrays something similar to the familial interactions many experience, is loaded with domestic energy. Indeed the domesticity of the scene, coupled with the lightness of mood on the part of the ostensible parent figure (Joel), Crow's panic, and both of their respective addresses to the audience, serves to connect viewers to the characters in a way they might not have done otherwise had the show simply depicted the situation in an exclusively third-person manner. This charm, as it were, suggests that part of *MST3K*'s success and longevity is largely due to good-will built between it and its audience, something the program maintained throughout its eleven-year run. The show attempts to present scenes with which its audience could essentially relate, even if their particulars differ from those of viewers' experience.

The attempt to link to viewers in ways with which they would likely be familiar, however, is not explained so easily in the context of the paradox of fiction. The show's use of second-person address complicates the matter. Such use is not enough *per se* to negate the possibility that what is being experienced is in fact what examinations of the paradox of fiction attempt to explain using first- and third-person models, but, interestingly, in *Emotion and the Arts* (Hjort and Laver 1997), an entire section of which is devoted to discussing the paradox of fiction, there is no examination of the role second-person interaction might play in explaining this phenomenon. For that, one should examine the phenomenon known as joint attention.

Joint Attention[6]

Joint attention, roughly speaking, is the way in which two individuals participate with each other in order to observe a third phenomenon, and is usually understood in terms of a way in which children acquire language through cognitive development (Tomasello 2006). The process is interactive and set within relational activities (Tomasello 2006). Ingar Brink points out, "Joint attention is based on the ability of two or more subjects to focus their perception simultaneously, as a consequence of attending to each other, on a shared attentional object" (2001: 267). This gives rise to the possibility, furthermore, as Carpendale et al. imply (2005), that particular situations of perception-sharing potentially create unique social relationships.[7] Indeed, *MST3K* situates itself as a kind of joint-attention experience, proceeding rather systematically. Viewers are addressed directly, establishing a connection between them and the show's characters. The show simulates being sucked into the theater along with the characters that they might be subjected to watching painful movies together. Both audience and characters proceed to jointly attend to the movie foisted upon them, now with the characters providing a running commentary, i.e., riffs. The riffs, being rehearsed by the characters who have established an initial connection with the show's audience (now watching with them), become a manifestation of the jointly shared frustration directed at the poorly made films. In riffing, the characters on the show simultaneously perform the audience's frustration and relieve it through various conventions of comedic discourse. It's quite a complex feat, but this is part of what sets *MST3K* apart as a show that, through providing a shared experience, appears genuinely to care for and involve its audience.

A number of techniques help the show authenticate and sustain this connectedness. *MST3K* has effectively ritualized the process of establishing itself as a shared experience from the beginning, when Joel was the principal character stuck on the SoL. There is no possibility that members of the *MST3K* audience are understood to be alone in their viewing experience. The theme song's use of second-person references, instead, recognizes the implied presence of the show's audience, and a viewer hearing the words understands that he or she is being situated alongside the show's characters in order to participate in the program with them. All elements of the experience will be shared.

Another ingredient in creating and maintaining this shared experience comes in segments of the program when characters are not watching films, one example of which is given above. While instances of this kind of second-person address occur most often in the opening segments of the show, usually before the first commercial, there are other instances in which connections to the audience are seamlessly, almost imperceptibly, interwoven into other parts. An example of such second-person acknowledgement happens during the first break in *Space Mutiny*, during the show's later run on the Sci-Fi Channel (Murphy 1997, Episode 820). Here, Mike Nelson has just emerged from the theater holding a tea cup and saucer. Interestingly, the subtle recognition of the audience occurs not in the form of verbal address, but in deliberate eye-contact, indicating that he is happy to have a moment to himself. While trying to listen to a classical record and enjoy his cup of tea, Mike makes additional eye contact at other points, connecting himself to viewers and implying that they enjoy a quiet moment alone as well. His repose is interrupted, of course, as Crow and Tom crash into the SoL, and the finale of the segment employs a recognizable stock television address to the audience from Mike, "We'll be right back." Again, the audience doesn't simply observe the segment, they experience it *via* Mike's multiple referential glances to viewers and direct address to them. The connection built at the show's outset is reinforced, and the audience continues to participate as the show unfolds.

Perhaps, though, the most enjoyable shared-experience of *MST3K* is jointly attending to the bad films shown on the SoL. As viewers watch, they may be aware of three things happening at once: (1) they are watching a show in which an audience is watching a bad movie; (2) they are watching the internal audience's response to the bad movie; and (3) they are watching the bad movie with the internal audience. The first action does little to differentiate the experience of watching *MST3K* from that of any other show. However, due to the second-person interaction used at the show's outset, there is a potential connectedness between audience and show in the second action. Due to such connectedness, established as the show begins with direct addresses to the audience, the third action takes on a relational quality — the audience interacts with a bad movie in tandem with the characters on the SoL. The metaphor may be banal, but it's as if one is right there with Joel/Mike and the Bots as they navigate their way through the wreckage of bad films.

The characters' responses to the films express what the audience feels, offering even additional insights into the level of badness these films reach and ways to respond further. In this context, *MST3K*'s riffing becomes a way for members of the audience to develop and interpret their own reactions in a communal setting. The riffing helps viewers feel connected through shared knowledge and privileged communication. This is the triangular quality of the connection that Joel Hodgson delineates in the quote above. In this sense, a viewer may potentially feel smarter, as it were, and more self-aware through his or her connection with the show. It is, to venture another banal metaphor, like growing together. The potential growth resulting from the connection resembles very much that resulting from jointly attending to an object in an interpersonal, interactive context (cf. Clark 2005). Powerful feelings rise from sharing such insights and information, which results in a greater understanding of what is being observed — in the case of *MST3K* comprehension elucidating the absurdity of the film jointly observed.[9] This strengthens the bond between viewer and show, and bolsters the relational experience of watching it. Furthermore, viewers don't simply relate to the characters on *MST3K*, as if the characters merely resemble something appealing to members of the audience. They share experience with them, and this connection suggests a significant reason why *MST3K* has been able to sustain its popularity and reach out to additional viewers, drawing them in to share in the pain of watching bad movies together.

This is not to suggest, though, that in watching *MST3K* one necessarily feels connected to the program, nor that its second-person address affects all viewers in the same way. Such universal claims would be false. One should be able to find a demographic of viewers for whom this usage is off-putting. Nevertheless, many people continue to enjoy the show, and current releases of it on DVD, as well as current releases of *RiffTrax* and tour dates for *Cinematic Titanic*, both featuring writers and performers from *MST3K*, bear witness to the enduring legacy of the show. Many shows only dream of achieving and maintaining such sustained longevity. Joseph Jon Lanthier's review of the sixteenth volume of collected *MST3K* episodes beautifully and succinctly expresses this fact and is worth quoting at length:

> Quite possibly the most "cultish" cult hit of all time..., the show remains an irreproducible, madcap blend of highbrow, camp, and giggle-inducing potty humor, as well as the most effective distribution method of esoteric cultural references this side of *The Simpsons*.
>   Why more cinephiles don't adore its gut-busting, self-effacing acumen is inexplicable: *MST3K* captures the tetchy, irreverent glory of a film buff forced against his will to endure subpar on-screen antics with only slicing wit and the memories of legitimate cinematic art to mollify his anguish (and who hasn't been there?). Perhaps it's the fact that indulging in the comedy requires one to sit through reels and reels of shlocky F-grade horror and sci-fi. Or maybe it's the equally cheap-o (albeit lovingly so) narrative premise that pits a marginally educated everyman (first creator Joel Robinson, and then later the more punchline-centric head writer Mike Nelson) and his snarky robot pals against interstellar trailer trash and their mad scientist momma's boy offspring [2009].

Indeed, Lanthier's terms "self-effacing" and "everyman" characterize much of *MST3K*'s successful second-person connection with viewers. The show doesn't impede connection with snobby characters portraying themselves as above the bad movies they watch. Instead it promotes connection to characters who are "regular Joe[s]"—"not too different from you and me" (Hodgson and Weinstein, The Brains 1988–1999). *MST3K* invites viewers to suffer with its characters, helplessly being force-fed cinematic refuse together. Such a thing might be hard to do in isolation, or even in bad company, but on the SoL one is among friends.

"Epilogue: Where you always get to see Lee's gut" (Mallon 1992, Episode 324)

The original plan for this chapter was to examine *MST3K*'s potential for longevity with respect to the currently available research on the program. The question for readers of this collection was originally: Is *MST3K* worthy of *academic* study and, if so, for what reason(s)? While an affirmative answer may be assumed by those contributing to or reading this collection, it is dangerous, as one retail maintenance man pointed out to me many years ago, to assume anything (many will know why). In fact, since the airing of the first episode of *MST3K* on KTMA in December 1988, through its final run on the Sci-Fi Channel, which ended in August 1999, only two articles addressing the series appear in a subject-search of the MLA International Bibliography, and only one of those focuses solely on the show itself.[10] By contrast, a subject search of *The Simpsons*, which began its own run in 1989 (and continues at the time this article is being written), yields fifty results. From this one may be tempted to conclude that fruitful academic study of television series focuses more on shows such as *The Simpsons* than *MST3K*—at least the possibility of serious study seems more limited in light of these MLA search results.[11] Such a conclusion, however, would be a mistake. The potential for the serious study of *MST3K* seems vaster than current MLA International Bibliography search results suggest, and, I believe, the longevity of *MST3K* may benefit from such attention (see notes 5, 6 and 9 below).

To that end, this piece closes by attempting to suggest even further avenues of inquiry for future researchers of *MST3K*. These needn't be limited only to spotting and deciphering seemingly obscure pop-culture references, although this should be done. Rather, researchers might also provide insight into matters of convention and innovation of form and structure in *MST3K*, as well as in the materials being riffed. It has come to my attention, for example, that the movies being riffed on might be explored as characters (or character types) in their own right. Additionally, other studies could focus on the artistic performances of characters on *MST3K*, or look into what common features characterize performances subjected to the show's riffing. It seems, in fact, that many of the show's qualities extend beyond the realm of literary and film research. Investigation might extend, as this piece suggests, into areas of cognitive and social research in order to explain better other characteristics and components of this unique show—propelling research well into A.D.: next Sunday.

NOTES

1. Hearing someone say better what one wants to say is the initial premise introduced by Penn Jillette in the 1992 Comedy Central documentary *This Is MST3K!* (Bill Price 1992).
2. This link between joint-attention learning and the paradox of having emotional feelings for known fictional characters was first suggested to this author in a graduate philosophy seminar at Saint Louis Uni-

versity, a course that examined the phenomenon of beauty as a way to understand the existence and nature of God. The problem being addressed at this point in the course was why people, knowing that fictional characters and situations don't exist, have powerful, emotional reactions to them anyway.

3. This terminology is taken from the first part of Hjort and Laver's *Emotion and the Arts*. The volume is very useful for understanding the various ways in which artistic works present themselves to audiences and ways in which individuals respond to them. The discussions in the volume are not limited to a single theoretical methodology or disciplinary paradigm. The volume instead provides a sample of the competing views addressing the paradox of fiction and offers readers a primer for studying philosophically the interplay between emotion and art.

4. The others are: (1) What kind or type of emotions are had in response to works of art? ... (2) How and why do abstract works of art, especially musical ones, generate emotions in audiences, and toward what do audiences then have these emotions? (3) How can we make sense of the interest appreciators have in empathetically experiencing art that expresses negative emotions? (A particular form of this query is "the paradox of tragedy.") (4) Is there a tension or conflict between responding emotionally to art and what aesthetic appreciation of art demands? (Levinson, 1997: 20–21).

5. Deliberately excluded are shows featuring second-person interaction as part of variety content, examples of which are monologue sequences on shows like *Saturday Night Live*, stand-up routines on talk shows, etc. Another example of second-person address that doesn't fit the *MST3K* model would be narrative elements in shows such as *The Wonder Years, Everybody Hates Chris*, etc. These types of second-person address, while acknowledging an audience, serve an almost purely narrative function; they are not concerned with creating a conversational environment or fostering potential interaction with the audience. With respect to narrative models used by children's television shows, it seems that from studies of these much can be brought to bear on understanding how *MST3K* connects to viewers, and should be included as another potential avenue of study by experts in the fields of children's communication and other related areas. Two particularly helpful starting points may be found in works by Shalom M. Fisch (esp. chapter six) and Deborah K. Wainwright, listed below.

6. As mentioned above, this examination of joint attention as a means by which to understand how audiences recognize and react to works of art, including, but not limited to, fictional narratives, rises from philosophy lectures, which suggested that emotional reactions to literature, the conundrum posed by the paradox of fiction, might find their explanation in the reader's ability to properly interpret the archetypal emotional stances embodied in fictional characters or situations. An apophatic approach was taken based on research showing how children with autism are unable to "read" emotional postures. I do not pretend to be an expert in matters of cognitive development, but from my brief examination of the topic I do believe that the phenomenon of joint attention has implications for understanding the unique relationship between television shows and their audiences — indeed, for understanding how audiences react to fictionalizations generally. It is hoped, therefore, that others in fields such as philosophy, cognitive theory, etc., will apply their expertise in order to explain better the relationship between performance and audience, particularly that of *MST3K* and its viewers.

7. Herbert H. Clark also points out that communication is not merely based in language use; it comes about in complex social interactions (2005). While joint-attention seems most relevant in discussions of how children develop their communication skills, it seems particularly useful in discussions of interaction with fiction, indeed with art generally, because of the limited ability of the audience to exchange information with what is observed. In fact, it is impossible for a work of art to receive anything from its audience, but it may be that the producer of the art, in a way, interacts with the recipient in order to communicate some idea that both presumably understand.

8. The bracketed "than" comes from the theme song used during the show's run on KTMA-TV from 1988 to 1989. Although the authorship of the song's lyrics changed halfway through season five, when Mike Nelson replaced Joel Hodgson as the human stranded on the SoL, and with it the lyrics, the majority of the song remained the same across all seasons of the show: i.e. from "We'll [I'll] send him cheesy movies..." onward.

9. This is not an uncommon feature of literature, and one example that comes to mind is that of Mark Twain's "Fenimore Cooper's Literary Offences," in which the audience is invited to share insights into why James Fenimore Cooper's fiction is not worth reading. In fact, one might look to this work as a type of the kind of riffing one sees in *MST3K*, and it would be interesting to trace a genealogy, if you will, between *MST3K* to other works of satire in literary history.

10. In "Talking out of School: Academia Meets Generation X," Traci Carroll contrasts how *MST3K* and *Beavis and Butthead* employ a similar mode of criticism as they draw from two very different assumption bases: (according to Carroll) "highbrow" for the former, and "low-brow" for the latter. In "What's Happening on Earth? *Mystery Science Theater 3000* as Reflection of Gender Roles and Attitudes toward Women,"

Jessica A. Royer focuses her inquiry on the social attitude towards women in the 1990s as understood in light of *MST3K*'s treatment of *The Amazing Colossal Man* (Mallon 1991, Episode 309) and *The She-Creature* (Mallon 1997, Episode 808).

11. Searching the MLA International Bibliography's database for other prominent television series that feature satire as a major element yielded the following number of hits: *M*A*S*H*, 5; *Monty Python's Flying Circus*, 7; *South Park*, 33. Other searches for studies of more traditional television sitcoms yielded these hits: *Friends*, 11; *Seinfeld*, 42; *The Cosby Show* 16; *Cheers*, 3.

References

Brinck, Ingar. "Attention and the Evolution of Intentional Communication." *Pragmatics and Cognition* 9: 2 (2001): 259–77.

Carpendale, Jeremy I. M., et al. "Constructing Perspectives in the Social Making of Minds." *Interaction Studies* 6: 3 (2005): 341–58.

Carroll, Traci. "Talking out of School: Academia Meets Generation X." In John M. Ulrich, and Andrea L. Harris eds., *GenXegesis: Essays on "Alternative" Youth (Sub)Culture*. Madison, WI: University of Wisconsin Press; Popular Press, 2003. 199–220.

Clark, Herbert C. "Coordinating with Each Other in a Material World." *Discourse Studies* 7: 4–5 (2005): 507–25.

Fisch, Shalom M. *Children's Learning from Educational Television*. Mahwah, NJ: Lawrence Erlbaum Associates, 2004.

Hjort, Mette, and Sue Laver, eds. *Emotion and the Arts*. New York: Oxford University Press, 1997.

Hodgson, Joel. "Live Tour" *Cinematic Titanic* 2010. Accessed 4/29/10. http://www.cinematictitanic.com/live tour.php.

_____, and Josh Weinstein; The Brains. "Love-Theme from MST3000." Cornell and Henry. "Theme Song Lyrics." *Satellite News* 2010. Accessed 4/26/10. http://www.mst3kinfo.com/mstfaq/lyrics.html.

Lanthier, Joseph Jon. "*Mystery Science Theater 3000*: Volume XVI." *Slant Magazine* December 1st, 2009. Accessed 4/30/2010 http://www.slantmagazine.com/dvd/review/mystery-science-theater-3000-volume-xvi/1642.

Levinson, Jerrold. "Emotion in Response to Art: A Survey of the Terrain." In Mette Hjort and Sue Laver, eds. *Emotion and the Arts*. New York: Oxford University Press, 1997. 20–34.

Mallon, Jim (director), Michael J. Nelson (writer), Trace Beaulieu (writer), et al. Episode 309 *The Amazing Colossal Man* 1991.

Mallon, Jim (director), Michael J. Nelson (writer), Trace Beaulieu (writer), et al. Episode 324 *Master Ninja 2* 1992.

Mallon, Jim (director), Michael J. Nelson (writer), Trace Beaulieu (writer), et al. Episode 408 *Hercules Unchained* 1992.

Mallon, Jim (director), Michael J. Nelson (writer), Paul Chaplin (writer), et al. Episode 808 *The She Creature* 1997.

Murphy, Kevin (director), Michael J. Nelson (writer), Paul Chaplin (writer), et al. Episode 820 *Space Mutiny* 1997.

Price, Bill (director), Glen Eichler (writer), *This is MST3K!* 1992.

Royer, Jessica A. "What's Happening on Earth? *Mystery Science Theater 3000* as Reflection of Gender Roles and Attitudes toward Women." In Elyce Rae Helford, ed., *Fantasy Girls: Gender in the New Universe of Science Fiction and Fantasy Television*. Lanham, MD: Rowman & Littlefield, 2000. 115–33.

Tomasello, M. "Social-Cognitive Basis of Language Development." In Keith Brown, Anne H. Anderson, et al., eds. *Encyclopedia of Language and Linguistics*, 2nd ed., vol. 11. Amsterdam; London: Elsevier, 2006. 459–62.

Twain, Mark. "Fenimore Cooper's Literary Offences." *Huck Finn; Pudd'nhead Wilson; No. 44, The Mysterious Stranger; and Other Writings*. Literary Classics of the United States. New York: Penguin, 1982. 669–81.

Wainwright, Deborah K. *Ready to Learn: Literature Review, Part 1: Elements of Effective Educational TV*. Philadelphia: Annenburg School for Communication; University of Pennsylvania, 2006.

13

Mystery Science Theater 3000: A Media-Centered Exploration

by Zachary Grimm

While satirical television today provides examples like *The Daily Show with Jon Stewart* and *The Colbert Report*, one must wonder why, after its birth in 1988, *Mystery Science Theater 3000* (*MST3K*) only lasted a short time. Because of its eventual cancellation, even on the Sci Fi network, with which it was associated in its later seasons, the show seems to have been deemed unpopular in some way. However, using its real-world implications, *MST3K* can be a valuable tool to examine our modern views on perceiving the world around us.

One of the many things that make *MST3K* an interesting text is its duality in terms of the kind of medium that it is, as well as the larger medium in which it is contained, and likewise influences. It is a medium that uses three characters, Joel (or Mike), and robots Tom Servo and Crow, all of whom position themselves inside a movie theater setting (or what appears to be one) and verbally poke fun at old "B" science fiction movies using both situational humor that reacts to the plot of the movie, but also interjecting verbal references to popular culture at exactly appropriate times. Barry Brummet, in *Rhetoric in Popular Culture,* makes the argument that a medium must take into account its social uses (Brummet 2006), and an episode of *MST3K* does some interesting things with the concept of social uses.

As a text, the episode seems to somewhat answer the question of what would happen to the possibilities for interpretation if the technology of watching a movie were connected to different social uses. It does this by simply presenting itself within a different social context than that to which we as an audience for movies are accustomed. By doing this, *MST3K* seems to interrupt those "normal" social uses to which a movie tends to adhere.

MST3K does indeed possess its own kinds of media logic, as termed by Altheide and Snow, who said that a technology grounded within certain social uses then causes its audience to have certain perceptions both within and without the text (Altheide 1979).

The "mechanics" (structure) of the show are nestled within the context of a movie theater, reinforced (most obviously) by its title, *Mystery Science Theater 3000* (one can't help but notice the similarity to the title of the 1950s program *Science Fiction Theatre*). By creating this idea, the audience should then have some common expectations of how to think about and react to the film which we expect to be shown at some point during our time in that darkened theater. As the movie starts, those expectations of the mechanics of a theater are fulfilled. We see in front of us the silhouette of a row of connected theater seats, coupled with the silhouetted figures of Joel, Tom Servo and Crow actually sitting in front of us, reinforcing the idea of a movie-going experience as a social event.

What's interesting is that, as an audience, we're not *really* in a movie theater watching a movie, and yet, simply because of the visual conventions of a theater (silhouetted figures and seats in front of a screen on which the movie is projected higher in height than the three characters), we as an audience automatically take into account, on our side of the screen, the attitudes of a movie theater audience. One of the most acceptable (and widely shared) attitudes is to keep quiet during the theatrical showing, which I would argue is a convention that we carry into our own homes while watching movies in a vastly different environment than the movie theater.

While we should note these observations we've made of the structure of the theater as predictive of the experience, it isn't long before our expectations as an audience are interrupted, and continue to be. While the aspects of the theater, were, to borrow Brummett's term, "designed" to look like an actual movie theater, the fact that, almost immediately, the three silhouetted figures "in the front row" begin talking amongst themselves about the opening credits of the movie (and perhaps even about how they would much rather be doing something else) should give us pause.

At this point, then, the media logic of a movie within a movie theater has been interrupted, because we have internalized certain expectations of the experience — one of those being that we assume that once the movie begins, the viewers will remain quiet. But, in keeping with the disruption of media logic, what we get is the complete opposite.

To those familiar with the context of *MST3K*, perhaps some have come to internalize a different set of perceptions that allow them to see this interruption from the front row as not problematic. For those who haven't, the fact that their viewing experience becomes progressively devoid of their expected power to interpret the B movie as they see it might be problematic. What happens is that the three individuals in that front row largely govern the interpretation.

If we accept this perceptual change, what is even more interesting is that our minds soon begin to watch the B movie in an entirely different way as it progresses, simultaneously accompanied by the banter from Joel, Tom Servo, and Crow. We seem caught up in a dual notion of watching a horrible B movie, and yet we are simultaneously immersed in a much more entertaining comedy happening just a row of seats in front of us, narrated and "acted out" by the three silhouetted critics.

So, rather than turn the "bad" movie off, we continue watching. Because of that perceived distance, what may have originally been a largely innocuous experience of watching an old movie suddenly turns into a strange multi-dimensional experience akin to a live stand-up comedy performance in which we as an outside audience wait in anticipation to hear what one-liner Joel, Crow, or Tom will utter in response to the action (or lack thereof) within the movie. We forget what is happening in actual black-and-white, veritably more interested in the meta-movie much closer to us both in perceived distance as well as importance. Not only that, but because we have chosen to immerse ourselves in this new kind of experience, it is possible that we have thus begun a journey which could change the ways we watch movies on television, now that we are able to do so outside a movie theater.

We can see moments of this change whenever we make satirical comments while watching a movie within our own homes. *MST3K*, though, seems to silence us (willingly, if we are familiar with the context of *MST3K*) via the three characters in front of us, while we wait for their irresistible one-liners. But, the fact that we make our own comments in our own environments suggests that we have internalized the effect of being silenced during a public viewing, and that this silencing is "appropriate" within *that* context. However, the projected satire involved during that silence seems to push us to perform our own commentary within our *own* homes, because we cannot comfortably comment while in the larger public setting.

Another point that Brummett makes when discussing TV as a medium is that it helps push viewers to think about their environment in certain ways (Brummett 2006). What's interesting is that with *MST3K*, we are dealing with three interconnected realities. There is the world within the 1959 movie, the manufactured world of *MST3K*, and there's our world, in which we must make sense of both. The show, by using the 1950s world and its contrived set, also illuminates how we as viewers think our world "should" be. In an ideal world, each of us predominantly has our own voice, whereas in the world dominated by television that bombards us with advertisements and "reality" shows, our voice either gets lost, or television successfully makes a commodity of it. The commentary from Mike, Tom and Crow seems to illustrate this fact, because we take their words as more "important" than the 1959 movie right in front of us, which exists in a specific time and space.

It's like when, on *The Daily Show*, Jon Stewart shows us a clip of a speech by George W. Bush. The speech itself exists both in the moment in which we watch it, but also existed in the moment in which he said it. Clearly, it is real. While our perceptions of Bush's words and actions *may* be similar to the satirical interpretation Stewart makes, the fact that his interpretation exists within the context of the mediating culture of satirical television allows us viewers to briefly hold Stewart's interpretation of Bush's speech as the final (often satirical) say, thus seeming to forget Bush's message, *plus* our own original interpretation of whatever it was that Bush had to say.

However, the whole point of satire is to help audiences realize that whatever the message of the *real* text, its purpose is to call attention to both interpretations. Once we recognize that both exist, our job as fans of satire is to distance ourselves mentally from the humorous perception, ideally recognizing it as humorous, which allows us to laugh, because we're not then taking it as the intended serious interpretation.

Fluidity is a characteristic of media-centered criticism that seems to have implications in this episode of *MST3K*. Considering the structure we often associate with watching movies inside a movie theater (and our expectations of that experience), it should affect us *somewhat* negatively when we discover that those expectations have been interrupted. Brummett suggests that it's like moving from a printed book to a book online. The tools are different, but the mental processes are similar enough to not be overly disruptive (Brummett 2006).

The same seems to be true of this episode of *MST3K*. We move from a vehicle of a movie theater experience, to one in which those expectations are interrupted — largely by humor. It is because of that humor that the move from one experience to another seems less disrupted. What's interesting is that, although the structure of *MST3K is* different from another kind of show, as an audience, we generally accept it as a reasonable form of discourse, mainly because of the satirical elements.

A very important element of that satire is based on countless references to popular culture. Before the targeted movie, *Earth vs. The Spider*, begins, we are first asked to watch, alongside Joel, Crow, and Tom, a "short" (a piece of cinema at the beginning of a feature film that is significantly shorter in duration). This particular short is designed to instruct us on the proper ways of public speaking—which, of course, has nothing to do with the plot of the feature film. In the credits of this "short," Joel notices that one of the names is "E.C Buehler." Utilizing the show's way of calling up references to popular culture, Crow immediately pipes up after Joel observes the name, and says, "Oh, must've been his day off." This refers, as the laughing minds of today's popular culture should recognize, to the 1986 film, *Ferris Bueller's Day Off.* Since, this *MST3K* episode was made between 1991 and 1992, audiences savvy enough to catch that reference would certainly have the opportunity to laugh.

Like any satirical text, not everyone is going to get *all* the jokes *all* the time, and the same is true for *MST3K.* Some of the quips and one-liners succeed with some audiences, and the same references pass by others, unappreciated. For example, toward the beginning of *Earth vs. The Spider,* two of the main characters have a scene on a street corner, and the young man says something to the young woman to upset her. As the young woman walks away, the young man is left alone for a moment, but then he turns around to follow the woman down the street. At this moment, the three commentators start to sing the words "Doh-oh-Bee" while humming a distinct tune. While younger audiences may not see the reference as amusing, older viewers may assume a *supposed* reference to the character "Dobie Gillis," which existed in 1959, around the same time that *Earth vs. The Spider* was produced. I say "supposed," because neither Joel, Tom nor Crow explain their references, leaving us to interpret. As a member of the younger generation, I *can* laugh at this reference, but it is a laugh more of recognition than of true understanding. With a more recent reference like Ferris Bueller, I can appreciate it because I *am* of that particular generation.

The same can be said for several other references in the film, all of them considered "popular" in their own respects. During the credits of the feature film, the graphics are in the foreground, while a superimposed spider web is in the background. As the credits "fly" back to fade out past the web graphic, Joel says "Look, Charlotte, it spells out a word." Those who were children and adults in the 1970s would understand the reference to the movie *Charlotte's Web,* noticing the riff on a particular line from the movie. As was true with the reference to Dobie Gillis, some audiences may not appreciate the joke, while others would. What popular culture has the ability to do, however, is span across generations. So, while I was *not* alive during the 1970s, I *was* still able to watch *Charlotte's Web* as a child a decade later, and thus was able to appreciate the reference in today's culture, almost 40 years after its original conception.

Still other references are popular in nature, but, like *Mystery Science Theater 3000* itself, they are popular only to certain groups, like making references to *Star Trek* or perhaps even *Harry Potter* might be. At one point in the film, Crow watches as the two young kids we saw in the beginning of the feature film wander through a cave. The female character stops, and looks at one of the walls of the cave. Almost instantly, Crow says, "Hey wait, this wall says 'Arnie Saaknussen!'" Those of us who have seen the older version of the science fiction film *Journey to the Center of the Earth* are able to laugh out loud at this reference, while others who aren't fans of similar science fiction movies would probably scratch their heads.

In another unrelated moment of the feature film, one of the characters, while staring in horror at the giant spider offscreen, screams, "It's one of *them!*" Tom Servo then replies, "Oh, but I don't mean the 'giant ants' 'them,' that is...." Die-hard fans of classic science fiction movies would surely understand Tom's allusion to the earlier sci-fi thriller *Them,* from which the idea of using real insects in superimposed "process shots" was taken for the production of *Earth vs. The Spider.*

Popular culture also relies (sometimes heavily) on sexual innuendos and connotations, and in the "short" before the feature film, the three commentators call upon this use of sex to satirize the moment. In the "short" on public speaking, the main speaker uses the phrase, "Make sure to use plenty of lip and tongue action." Immediately, Tom Servo chuckles. Here, by having Tom noticeably amused, the writers of *MST3K* are calling upon our irresistible tendency to sometimes view things in a sexual way — provided we laugh: which I did. Since I laughed, as an audience member I am acknowledging the altered connotation as acceptable, discarding the fact that the real intentions of the original "short" film were to use that line to refer to the proper ways to speak in public. Because I laughed, the popular sexual connotation overshadows the original denotation of the short film, and the satire has succeeded in its quest to distance me from the text.

The feature film itself, at one point toward its conclusion, strives for the quick and easy joke in this same manner. One of the characters suggests that, to kill the giant spider, the best way is to electrocute it. As part of the plot, the male character says to another, "Want to go at it in the truck?" Again, all three commentators find this moment irresistibly funny. Since I am accepting of their humor, I did as well. Just as in the "short" film, the sexual connotation wins out over the real meaning, and again the satirical nature of *MST3K* gets its point across.

Clearly, as a text, *Mystery Science Theater* is *much* more than a simple satire of an old movie. If we explore it, we can see that its writers have designed it to serve as a new kind of genre, and, because of that, it has the liberty to function on many different levels, while still using certain conventions of popular culture — sometimes to call attention to those conventions, but also to turn them on their edges and allow us the opportunity to explore them and enjoy the text much more than we would otherwise.

REFERENCES

Altheide, D.L., and R.P Snow. *Media Logic.* Beverly Hills, CA: Sage, 1979.
Bummet, Barry. *Rhetoric in Popular Culture: Second Edition.* Thousand Oaks, CA: Sage, 2006.
Mallon, Jim (director), Mike Nelson (writer), Trace Beaulieu (writer), et al. Episode 313 *Earth vs. The Spider* 1991.

14

Authorship and Text Remediation in *Mystery Science Theater 3000*

by Kaleb Havens

[D]o you think that such as these see anything of themselves, or of one another, but the shadows formed by the fire falling on the opposite part of the cave?
— Plato, from the "Republic," Book vii

In the above quote Plato suggests a metaphor for education by comparing the audience to subjects trapped in a cave, forced to interpret the nature of their existence only through shadows. Through this exercise Plato inextricably links our understanding of the world with perspective and illustrates how even simple tricks of light can fool our senses, implying that all human understanding should be constantly re-evaluated. The lecture is titled "Truth and Its Shadow," and how fitting that the visual palette *Mystery Science Theater 3000* employs on the canvas of old media to reveal new truths consists entirely of shadow. Namely, the silhouettes of Joel/Mike, Crow, and Tom Servo as they pick apart, prod, and "riff" relics from a bygone era of motion pictures. Their commentary on preexisting texts is a form of media interpretation and participation known as "Remediation," and as we explore theories of authorship and audience throughout media history, *Mystery Science Theater 3000* emerges as a paradigm of the changing shape of authorship in first the Broadcast Era, and now the new audience culture of the Digital Media Age.

Remediation Defined

Termed by Jay David Bolter and Richard Grusin in their book of the same title, "Remediation" is the process by which new media (in this case, broadcast and digital) "repurpose" artifacts of old media and reintroduce them to the media-consuming culture. Bolter and Grusin make the case that this process does not, as some in their field had suggested, seek to make old media obsolete, but rather pays homage to works preceding the remediatee. Citing examples as far back as Biblical accounts depicted in paintings and stain-glass windows, Bolter and Grusin contend that new media has always been constructed on the foundations of human communication that came before it:

The process of remediation makes us aware that all media are at one level a "play of signs," which is a lesson that we take from poststructuralist literary theory. At the same time, this process insists on the real, effective presence of media in our culture. Media have the same claim to reality as more tangible cultural artifacts; photographs, films, and computer applications are as real as airplanes and buildings [18].

The permanence of certain media artifacts, then, is categorized by their repetition in our culture through remediation. Remediation has gone on since the first human communications, but new media of the broadcast and digital ages have brought about, by the rapid nature of their development in contrast to the performative or print medias, a proportional surge in the process of remediation; Bolter and Grusin cite the adaptation of Jane Austen novels as just one example of a media culture hungrily repurposing old media; "The contemporary entertainment industry calls such borrowing "repurposing": to take a "property" from one medium and reuse it in another. With reuse comes a necessary redefinition, but there may be no conscious interplay between media" (45). One needs only to look at the staggering number of novel and play adaptations produced in film and television each year to observe this trend. But the distinction between *MST3K* and the most recent BBC production of *Pride and Prejudice* is twofold; the focus of *MST3K* on new media, and the transparent nature of the remediation.

The first distinction, a focus on "new media" is simple enough; instead of drawing from literary or otherwise older media works, aside from allusions and references in "riffs" or character dialogue, *MST3K* is sustained by films created during the broadcast era of entertainment; *MST3K* remediates artifacts from its own media era, so recent that the term "artifact" is practically a misnomer. Aside from remakes of old films and "movie tie-ins" with existing television or radio serials, new media drawing on itself is rare within the broadcast era, and even rarer is the transparency of the remediation: *MST3K*'s abandonment of the story-telling convention known as "suspension of disbelief." Although it was not the first attempt on television to do so, *MST3K* was certainly the most commercially successful program (having existed for a decade on one cable station or another) to focus almost exclusively on a conscious remediation of other media; conscious because the *MST3K* text directly references the existence of the media it repurposes, contrary to the efforts of most remediations such as film adaptations of Austen works: "Acknowledging the novel in the film would disrupt the continuity and the illusion of immediacy that Austen's readers expect, for they want to view the film in the same seamless way in which they read the novels" (44). Comparatively, *MST3K* always directly names the films in question, going so far as to name the titles of the episodes after the films being screened. This focus on the repurposed media sets *MST3K* apart from most instances of new media remediation, such as film adaptations, which seek to preserve the continuity of the pieces. Indeed, the internal continuity of *MST3K* is dismissed in the lyrics of the opening theme song: "If you're wondering how he eats and breathes and other science facts, (la la la) Repeat to yourself it's just a show, I should really just relax" (Mallon, et al. 1991–1999, Episodes 101–1013). This direct communication with the audience, a stylistic hallmark of *MST3K*, will be addressed further in the next section. For now, the distinction that the show is so integrally connected with the texts it remediates sets it apart from most pieces of broadcast media. Digital media is a separate but equally intriguing comparison, especially concerning RiffTrax in relation to the *MST3K* canon, and will be addressed fully in the final section.

So not in remediation itself, which occurs throughout all media, but in the topicality and transparency of the process does *MST3K* carve out a unique niche in new media. But the show does much more than participate in a tradition of remediation; by the nature of its self-referential transparency in the realm of new media, it works towards redefining the relationship between creator and consumer of media.

The Fourth Wall: Authorship and Text

The name Bertolt Brecht may be new to those in the field of media studies, but students of the theater will recognize it as readily as a proscenium arch. Brecht was a 20th century German playwright, director and author of numerous dramaturgical essays outlining his theories on the relationship between a piece of theater and its audience, namely that plays should challenge audience passivity. He was not the first to suggest compromising the fourth wall or, as many suppose, to have employed the terminology. But his techniques and theories persist as a paradigm for avant-garde theater, which often seeks to remind audiences of the constructed nature of their media. He was known to criticize naturalistic theater, which unwaveringly preserved the fourth wall: "the audience is tacitly assuming that it's not in a theatre at all, since nobody seems to take any notice of it. It has an illusion of sitting in front of a keyhole. That being so it ought not to applaud till it starts queuing for its hats and coats" (*The Messingkauf Dialogues*, 1977: 51).

On the next page Brecht concludes, "We want to demolish the fourth wall" (52). The act of removing that barrier between the media and its audience has sweeping implications. Media texts, such as printed works or operatic stage performances, had always maintained a sacrosanct status as unalterable regardless of what space in which the media was consumed. Removing the fourth wall, Brecht posits a dialogue, a "bi-directional discussion" (Bennett, 1997: 24) in which the audience as well as the text is engaged. He would position actors amidst the audience (Bennet, 1997: 24) in just one of many techniques that sought to open the media to contribution from the audience. By projecting the shadow of theater seats onto films, *MST3K* shatters the fourth wall and galvanizes this dialogue between audience and text employing a methodology unlike any other television show. The visual metaphor suggests that, just as Crow, Tom Servo, and Mike/Joel contribute their own content to the media, the audience is entitled to heckle or "riff" the media artifacts as well, becoming contributors in their own right. Not only the visuals, but the riffs themselves work towards this end; by categorizing input which in most other contexts such as theaters or movie viewing spaces would be considered affronts to the reverent silence a movie or theater audience would habitually show during the viewing of the piece, audience participation of the same kind is suddenly legitimized because the media has turned a critical eye on itself. Furthermore, since the theater seats would suggest that the characters of *MST3K* are audience members rather than constructors of media, Brecht's bi-directional dialogue would seem to be initiated in this instance not by the creators of media but by the consumers. Although their performances may be more scripted and rehearsed than those of the film they critique, the writers and cast of *MST3K* were once audience members, consuming the media artifacts in question and seeking to engage in a bi-directional dialogue. The distinction, then, is whether *MST3K* should be categorized as the refined contributions of audience members to this dialogue or a series of new media artifacts in their own right.

Host segments notwithstanding, the vast majority of each episode is devoted to the screening of largely uncut, unaltered originals of the media artifacts in question, not to mention that *MST3K* episodes are always named after the films being screened. As a general rule media theorists don't categorize televised films, which are often edited, introduced and commented on by hosts, and supplied with lower third graphics championing the sponsor network's programming as new media artifacts. Yet no audio is provided by the host during the movie itself in such instances, although they often imply that you and he or she are "watching the film together." The distinction is certainly a fine line, but the fact that the characters' dialogue in *MST3K* is a regular, direct contribution may be argued to inherently alter the fabric of the media artifacts until the repurposing yields an entirely new media product. However, the process necessitates the producers to be audience members at some point during the generative stage of the *MST3K* program, and the fidelity of that process to the performance of the actors during the screenings of *MST3K* is too sharp to deny that the Brechtian dialogue between producers and consumers of media is in action. The establishment of this relationship within the text is a crucial component to *MST3K*'s role in redefining the author/text/consumer relationship through remediation, perhaps making it accurate to categorize *MST3K* as one of the longest running, if not the only, commercially successful television show of the avant-garde movement.

Rereading

With audience participation occupying such a key role in the fabric of *MST3K*, it's important to consider not only whether or not the audience engages with a text, but with what methods and to what ends. Reader response theory, a school of thought originating in literary criticism, explores how viewing texts through a variety of critical lenses can reshape our understanding and connection with them. To pull a particular case study for comparison, Annette Kolodny applies a feminist lens to several pieces of canonical literature and stories written by women which she believes to be their ideological counterparts, and the resulting sets of observations in her article "A Map for Rereading," "challenge(s) the ... authority [that] has traditionally wielded the power to determine what may be written and how it shall be read..." (464). By applying modern lenses to media artifacts, in this case literary works, Kolodny unearths new meaning in the realms of gender studies in a process which she inextricably links with reader and text similar to Brecht's bi-directional dialogue: "those most recent theorists of reading ... combine an increased attentiveness to the meaning-making role of the reader in the deciphering of texts with a recognition of the links between our 'reading' of texts and our 'reading' of the world and one another" (460). As an observer with a different worldview than the author of the text, the reader unlocks new meaning by interpreting the media artifact and holds as much power by "reading" as the written text itself. Since the inception of the printing press, mass media has worked as the great equalizer in the balance of power between producers and consumers of media, blurring the lines by disseminating the power to create new media. Similarly, *MST3K* assaults the pulpit of media moguls by adapting their throwaway products into new media artifacts merely by the act of viewing. Remediation, repurposing, breaking the fourth wall, the rereading of media texts; whatever terminology employed, *MST3K* applies the critical lens of satire and reawakens new meaning from all but abandoned media artifacts.

The Digital Age

The act of remediation has never been so alive as it is today on the world wide web. Millions of users daily upload their own edits of Hollywood films on video sharing sites such as YouTube, Daily Motion, and Vimeo, changing the meaning of the texts for satirical purposes. Internet "memes" based on popular media spring up seemingly out of thin air, and entire cultures exist devoted solely to creating content, based on popular media artifacts, generated entirely by fans. It is in this climate that some of the creators of *Mystery Science Theater 3000* have released "RiffTrax," or audio tracks recorded to be synced with popular motion picture blockbusters as well as public domain short films from the mid to late 20th century. The creators of *MST3K* independent of broadcast cable networks choose as their object of ridicule, rather than obscure pieces that studios would sooner forget than defend, major studio releases, lampooning movie franchises such as *Star Wars, Indiana Jones, Harry Potter, Jaws, Twilight,* and many more.

This trend represents two important aspects of "Riffing" as mass media evolves beyond the broadcast and into the digital age. Firstly, the focus of RiffTrax on popular rather than obscure films indicates a shifting appeal of the direct, transparent remediation techniques characteristic of *MST3K* towards a greater mass media audience. Based solely on the internet, RiffTrax circumscribe consent licensing from studios by producing the synchronized audio independent of the original media artifacts. Secondly, by requiring the target audience to assemble the components of the intended viewing experience themselves, namely the original film and the RiffTrax audio, the creators encourage the audience to initiate the media consumption and remediation themselves. While seemingly minute, this distinction simultaneously reflects Bolter and Grusin's Remediation, Brecht's bi-directional dialogue and Kolodny's rereading in a relationship between audience and text that goes beyond even the scope of *MST3K*; although merely assembling prepackaged components, the application of critical lens to media artifact has never been more in the hands of the audience as it is with RiffTrax. These satirical, supplementary audio tracks are indicative of the new digital age of media where meaning is fluid and the interpretation of media is linked to the dynamic state of media beyond its initial conception and mass media release. Whatever advances the digital age brings to methods of remediation (since it has certainly already contributed, along with media saturation, to remediation frequency), it's impossible to conceive *MST3K* and RiffTrax as anything but representations of cutting edge Broadcast and Digital era remediation.

At the 1993 Peabody Award ceremony, *MST3K* was honored with an award in the broadcast entertainment category. It was said "With references to everything from Proust to *Gilligan's Island, Mystery Science Theater 3000* fuses superb, clever writing with wonderfully terrible B-grade movies." The cultural significance of *MST3K* is due in no little part to this willingness to incorporate the width and breadth of the media canon in its satire, speaking to the rich tradition of remediation that preceded the program. For over a decade audiences appreciated the witticisms of characters subjected to experiences all media viewers can relate to — the interpretation of texts. By turning the eye of media on itself, *MST3K* empowers audiences to engage with texts in a discourse of critical interpretation that yields meanings as numerous as the shadows of audience members at the feet of screens around the world.

REFERENCES

Bennett, S. *Theatre Audiences*. 2 Park Square, Milton Park, Abingdon, Oxon, OX14 4RN, UK. 1997.
Bolter, David Jay, and Richard Grusin. *Remediation: Understanding New Media*. MIT Press, 2003.
Brecht, Bertolt. *The Messingkauf Dialogues*. Translated by John Willett. London: Methuen, 1977.
Kolodny, Annette. "A Map for Rereading: Or, Gender and the Interpretation of Literary Texts." *New Literary History*, Vol. 11, No. 3 (Spring, 1980): 451–467.
"*Mystery Science Theater 3000* awarded for Excellence in Broadcast Entertainment." 1993 Annual Peabody Award Ceremony. University of Georgia. 1993. Speech.
Rolleston, T.W. *Selections from Plato, from the Translation of Sydenham and Taylor*. London: Walter Scott, Paternoster Square, 1891.

PART FIVE

Mental Hygiene:
The *MST3K* Shorts

15

"People were whiter back then"[1]:
Film Placement and In-Theater
Commentary as Sociopolitical Dialogue

by Erin Giannini

Social guidance films would not have existed had America been like *Leave It to Beaver*.
Instead, they thrived in a nation traumatized by war, fearful of communist witch
hunters, terrified of nuclear annihilation, and rocked by fears of a generational rebellion.... Mental hygiene films were popular because they showed life not as it was but
as their adult creators wanted it to be.
— Smith 1999: 25

In his analysis of the representation of whiteness in culture, Richard Dyer relates an
anecdote about his perception of his own whiteness while dancing; that is, the association
of "white" with tightness and lack of rhythm (Dyer 1992). While making no overt references
to Dyer's analysis, the association of whiteness and "tightness" informs the ironic commentary
by Mike, Crow, and Tom Servo of the short film "A Date with Your Family." "A Date with
Your Family" (Simmel 1950), part of the genre of "mental hygiene" films shown in schools
attempts to elucidate the appropriate ways in which a family should interact at the dinner
table, including the proper order in which each family member should be seated and served
and, most importantly, the tenor of the conversation while eating. In particular, the narrator
emphasizes that dinner table conversation should be "pleasant" and "calm." "Pleasant,
unemotional conversation helps aid digestion," to which Tom responds: "I cannot stress
unemotional enough" and Crow with: "Emotions are for ethnic people."

While the focus of this essay is not an analysis of the representation of whiteness in
either *Invasion USA* (Green 1952) or "A Date with Your Family," it does represent one of
the many correspondences between the short film and subsequent feature in this episode of
Mystery Science Theater 3000 (Murphy 1994, Episode 602). Indeed, this is not a rare phenomenon within the context of the series. While some correspondences may be more obscure
than others (such as the conflation of the Chevrolet industrial film "Hired" [Handy 1940]
with the horror film *Manos: The Hands of Fate* [Warren 1966] [Hodgson 1993, Episode
424], connected through the fact that the first 20 minutes of the film featured an extended
sequence with nothing but people driving), by looking at the episode in its entirety, rather

than its individual parts, it is clear that there is an intelligence at work with regard to the selection of these short and feature-length films. Further, the selection of these films, as well as the in-theater commentary itself, represent opportunities, on both a micro (commentary) and macro (selection of films) to engage in a sociopolitical dialogue with regard to the subject matter of the films themselves. Thus, the focus of this article will be an analysis of the use of both film selection and in-theater commentary in this manner, particularly in "A Date with Your Family"/*Invasion USA* as well as its use in *Teen-age Crime Wave* (Sears 1955) and "Assignment: Venezuela" (Tobin 1956). The latter two films are examined primarily to elucidate that such commentary remains remarkably consistent whether it is a feature film only, or an unaired extra, respectively. That is, while the stand-alone feature and stand-alone short represent a different presentational context, the opportunity for relevant social commentary is still possible.

As the quote by Smith that opens this chapter contends, mental hygiene films such as "A Date with Your Family" had an express purpose in directly influencing children's and teenagers' behavior. In *Mental Hygiene: Classroom Films 1945–1970*, Ken Smith argues that these films operated with the remit to scale back children's independence and freedom gained during the Depression and Second World War when parents' attentions were more focused on survival and/or aiding the war effort (Smith 1999). Such films would thus help parents avoid their teens rebelling in a similar fashion to the previous generation. In a brief historical overview, Smith traces how, as far back as Thomas Edison, film as a method of teaching had been considered as a possibility, in order to engage students on a more "fun" level. Further, as the Television Institute declared in 1946, when discussing the power of the moving image to sell goods: "Action plus animation create a stepped-up emotional drive lacking in all other forms of advertising art" (Samuel 1999: 9). While they were speaking primarily of television and advertising, the idea of the moving image creating a "stepped-up emotional drive" could be equally applied to this sub-genre of films used primarily in small classroom settings. Indeed, it would not entirely stretch the point to find something of a mirror image in the Satellite of Love's audience of three or even the fan practices of viewing the series' episodes in how these mental hygiene films were initially screened. This point will be addressed in greater depth below.

Despite the focus, within many of the films, on convincing youth to conform to a strict code of behavior, their initial genesis was grounded in a more progressive view of pedagogy; that is, to make learning enjoyable, to stimulate discussion, and allow students to think and sort through issues themselves. That being said, the pressure to conform and engineer a more well-behaved youth population situates such films as both a quaint relic of the past and a disturbing glimpse at social engineering. As H. M. Barr, research director for Portland, Oregon's public school system, claimed in 1947: "All education is indoctrination. The real question is whether indoctrination shall be confined merely to the mores and taboos of the past, or whether it shall be directed toward solving the problems of the future. In time, parents will recognize that the hope of a better world lies in such a new curriculum" (quoted in Smith 1999: 25).

While such attempts at social engineering are perhaps to be expected within a mental hygiene film like "A Date with Your Family," the choice to pair it with the feature-length, moderately successful *Invasion USA*, released two years after "A Date with Your Family" was made, highlights that film's equally blatant attempts to influence audience behavior. In brief, *Invasion USA* uses a framing device of a group of individuals in a bar — a socialite, a reporter, a rancher, a manufacturer, and a shadowy figure swirling a glass of port — and how they respond to the invasion of the United States by a country that is never named. The shadowy figure with the port is revealed at the end to be a hypnotist, and the majority of the narrative of the film an induced "might-have-been." The result is that each character shifts his behavior to help fight the impending "threat" that, while unnamed throughout the film, is clearly represented as Russian. The end of the film even echoes the paternalistic tenor of "A Date with Your Family" by including a narrative voice-over for the only time in the film, quoting George Washington's admonition that "To be prepared for war is the most effectual way of preserving peace." Such a moment underlines the ultimately didactic nature of the film, and ties it explicitly with the short film that precedes it within the episode, in which the actors themselves had no audible dialogue in favor of an overlying narration by Hugh Beaumont.

Thus, the "flow" (Williams 2003) of the episode, in terms of how these two films were scheduled and shown within a single episode, can lead the viewer to find correspondences between the "mental hygiene" genre of the short, and the only slightly less obvious propagandizing of *Invasion USA*, regardless of any commentary provided by Mike, Tom Servo, and Crow T. Robot. This is not to suggest that such commentary is unnecessary; as in each episode, the commentary provided within the theater — and often by the host segments — makes explicit any absurdities, satirizes over-earnestness, and provides multiple layers of contemporary and obscures references. John Storey articulates it thusly: "[W]e can identify this in the way that television, in a effort to fill the space opened up by the growth in satellite and cable channels, recycles its own accumulated past, and that of cinema, and broadcast these alongside what is new in both media" (Storey 2006: 144). This is clearly at work within the commentary for both "A Date with Your Family" and *Invasion USA*. Comments such as referring to "A Date with Your Family" as "The Woody Allen Story" or responding to *Invasion USA*'s president's claim that America will "Make war on any nation anywhere" with "I think Peggy Noonan wrote this speech" ties these 1950s productions with a more contemporary response. It represents one particular approach within a postmodern context, in which an older text is mobilized either in an educational or ironic sense. In a similar vein, *Teen-Age Crime Wave* is easy to read as a feature-length propaganda piece of the dangers of juvenile delinquency; indeed, more than one of the selected shorts during the run of the series dealt with the "problem" of juvenile delinquency. Yet the subtext of the film itself is flagged up in one of the host segments. Mike, Tom, Crow, and Gypsy parody the then-popular Mentos commercial with a mint called "Mystos." While the repeating chorus "Youth is great, old is stupid" of the song (set to the Mentos theme music) is ostensibly parodying the Mentos commercials' content, it also serves to bring to the surface the subtext of *Teen-Age Crime Wave*. As Jim Collins writes:

> The Christian Broadcasting Network and Nickelodeon both broadcast series from the late fifties and early sixties, but whereas the former presents these series as a model for family entertainment the way it used to be, the latter offers them as fun for the contemporary family, "camped up" with parodic voice-overs, supergraphics, reediting designed to deride their quaint vision of American family life, which we all know never really existed even "back then" [Collins 1992: 334].

The use of Hugh Beaumont as the narrator for "A Date with Your Family" — he would subsequently become famous for playing Ward Cleaver on *Leave It to Beaver* — is not addressed in the in-theater commentary. It does, however, undersore the "quaint" nature of both "A Date with Your Family" and *Leave It to Beaver*'s view of family relations.

As for *Invasion USA*, the film itself represents a kind of brokerage between its component parts. As previously mentioned, the film uses the "It was all a dream" type of framing device, in a similar fashion to the proto-noir film *The Woman in the Window* (Lang 1944). Several minutes of the film are devoted to the main characters watching television in a bar; further, nearly all the battle scenes within the film (that is, those that do not directly involve the central characters, such as the aftermath of the atomic bombing of Manhattan) rely on World War II stock footage. As Crow notes: "World War 3 is a lot like World War 2." The commentary by Mike also questions the visual ethics of the film's use of stock footage of the London Blitz by speculating on how the survivors of the Blitz might have felt about its use within *Invasion USA*, that is, the properness of appropriating such scenes of destruction within the context of the film. The central (and explicit) message of the film was the dangers of complacency in the face of the Communist threat, a message no more hidden than the social engineering of family relations undertaken by "A Date with Your Family." One of the host segments within the episode elucidates this quite obvious theme: Mike, Tom, and Crow comfort and advise an atomic bomb (played by Mike Dodge, staff writer) who is bemoaning his uselessness in the current era.

CROW: Things aren't all bad, Mr. Bomb. Take North Korea, for instance.
TOM: Or the instability in Eastern Europe.
MIKE: There's always a despotic dictator looking for Mr. Goodbomb.

It is only after the bomb has said goodbye, cheered by their words, that all three realized the dangers of their own complacency and sympathy for the redundant nuclear weapon. "Did we just do something horribly wrong?" Mike's question is left unanswered; it has no need to be answered, as the function of the narrative of *Invasion USA* does the job of providing one particular answer: Yes, they did.

The structure of a series like *Mystery Science Theater 3000* allows this kind of dialogic commentary regarding the past (the highest percentage of films screened during the series were made in the 1950s, often due to rights issues; notable exceptions include the *Gremlins* knock-off *Hobgoblins* [Sloane 1988], *Soultaker* [Rissi 1992], and *Merlin's Shop of Mystical Wonders* [Berton 1996]). Indeed, as Collins noted above in his analysis of cable channel Nickelodeon's use of '50s and '60s programs, it allows the series to not only "deride [these films] quaint vision of American ... life" but also connect this initial vision with current social or political or cultural issues.

This was abundantly clear in the VHS/DVD-only release of the short film "Assignment: Venezuela." Produced by the Creole Oil Company as a corporate training video, its *Mystery Science Theater* version existed only as a DVD extra or special VHS tape direct from Best Brains. It debuted at Conventio-Con 2 and had initially been planned to be part of a CD-ROM project released by Voyager, which would have included not only a MST-inspired video game, but optional additional commentaries for "Assignment: Venezuela." The project fell through as *Mystery Science Theater* transitioned from Comedy Central to the Sci Fi Channel, and thus lost Trace Beaulieu, the project's biggest advocate, as well as because of financial difficulties at Voyager.

"Assignment: Venezuela" and its status as a non-broadcasted short seemingly allowed more latitude to Trace, Mike, and Kevin in terms of the subject matter of their commentary. Tracing the "adventures" of an oil company employee newly transferred to Venezuela, and his attempts to familiarize himself with the setting and the language, there is an inherent colonialism to his viewpoint; not the least being that the white narrator, his wife, and his children are the primary voices heard within the short film, despite his constant interaction with Venezuela residents and Creole employees. The only exception is an uncomprehending porter at the airport on whom the narrator attempts his self-referred "guide-book Spanish." The Venezuelan porter responds with a "no habla English." While the commentary itself does not explicitly address this colonialism, the awareness of such informs their reactions. When the narrator's wife shows their children Lake Maracaibo, Venezuela, on the map, she begins by pointing out the United States, to which Crow responds: "The best country ever." When the narrator explains that the Venezuelans correct him when he refers to himself as American, indicating he should more properly say "Norté American," Tom responds with: "Or white devil." In the two most politically explicit examples, Mike's commentary on the narrator's description of the off-shore oil wells' "geometrically exact" placement to maximize production, is: "The pattern nicely doubles as a pentacle to Satan"; Tom's response to the narrator's paean to the "prosperity oil has brought to Venezuela" is "Oil is a loving god."

While corporate training and publicity films comprise a fair number of the short films riffed by *Mystery Science Theater*— including Chevrolet's "Hired," C. G. Conn's "Mr. B Natural" (Patton 1956), Union Pacific's "The Days of Our Years" (Miner 1955) and "Last Clear Chance" (Carlisle 1959), and General Motor's "Design for Dreaming" (Beaudine 1956)— few are as potentially politically fraught as that of an oil company, particularly one showing drilling in a foreign country for export to the United States. While, unlike every other short featured on the series, "Assignment: Venezuela" is not paired with a feature-length film, it nonetheless shares features with mental hygiene films such as "A Date With Your Family" as well as the overt propagandizing of *Invasion USA*. While "Assignment: Venezuela" attempts to sanitize the environmental and racial issues inherent in oil drilling in Venezuela, as well as serve as positive publicity for Creole, the film itself has been viewed by some as operating nonetheless as an historical document of 1950s era Venezuela.[2] Mike, Tom, and Crow's commentary serves as the same kind of bridge between the modern and postmodern eras as it does in "A Date With Your Family" and *Invasion USA*.

Of course, the most important difference between the short/full-length feature construction of the typical *Mystery Science Theater* episode must be addressed. That is, the decontextualization of "Assignment: Venezuela" both from airing on television and the lack of any of the usual framing devices used within the context of the series. There is no Dr. Clayton Forrestor/TV's Frank or Pearl Forrester/Brain Guy/Bobo element within the presentation of "Assignment: Venezuela." While this may seem an obvious point, the contextualization of each episode as a form of "torture" for Joel, Mike, and the robots means that there is a purpose behind the selection of features and shorts: maximum pain or, as Dr. Forrester puts it: "Deep hurting." Yet since Dr. Forrester — and later, Pearl — act as "scheduler" within this context, they thus operate as the start point of the "flow" of each episode. Raymond Williams argued that the point of flow is to engage the audience in the "central television experience," which in the current era represents a "replacement of a programme series of timed sequential units by a flow series of differently related units in which the timing, though real, is undeclared, and in which the real internal organization is something other than the declared organization" (Williams 2003:66–67). Applying this definition to the "scheduling" of shorts/feature-length films, as well as the host segments that often relate back or reconceptualize what has just been viewed, the undergirding structure thus becomes more prominent. That is, the correspondence between shorts and the features are the overt "schedule" imposed by Dr. Forrester or Pearl. The "real internal organization," it could be argued, is the ironic commentary that Joel, Mike, and the 'bots overlay on the films, as well as the host segments. Indeed, after viewing "A Date with Your Family," Mike, Tom, Crow, and Gypsy attempt to incorporate the lessons of the short into their own shared meal. After several attempts at vague and unemotional conversation, Gypsy finally interrupts with: "Mike, this sucks! Can we just eat?" at which point the meal devolves into a free-for-all. Thus, the sarcastic commentary on the film within the theater is further ironized by the skit outside it, highlighting its inapplicability in a more "realistic" context.

Such a reading of flow's organizational elements is in line with John Fiske's interpretation of the same. Fiske argued that the network scheduling thus serves as flow's "author"; that is, that the scheduling policy for a night of programming was the "internal organization" that Williams sought in his analysis (Fiske 2006). In this view, Dr. Forrester's pairing of shorts and full-length feature operates as its own special kind of flow. They can thus be read as his attempts to elicit a particular reaction from his small group of viewers; that is, to find the film that would be Joel (and later Mike's) breaking point. Yet, Fiske further argues that the "sequence and flow" of a night of programming prizes associative rather than logical relations; this open-ended structure allows the viewer to make the connections between the component parts, rather than closing down all contradictions within the scheduled material and thus disempowering the viewer.

Within the diegesis of *Mystery Science Theater*, Joel, Mike, and the 'bots are themselves "viewers"; they have no influence on what material will be screened for them, and no choice but to watch it. What they can do is to reconfigure, re-interpret, connect, and ironize the content of the films. What simultaneously connects and separates the viewer/inhabitants of the Satellite of Love from the at-home viewer is that none of them are viewing or commentating on the films by themselves. That is to say, mirror-like, the three-fold commentary of Mike, Tom, and Crow (unheard by Dr. Forrester or Pearl) is similar to the potential commentary by the viewer of *Mystery Science Theater* unheard by Mike, Tom, and Servo. Further, the occasionally obscurity of references (both historical and regional) made within the Satellite of Love's commentary, and parsing of same by the home viewer, connects both in a "knowledge community" (Jenkins 2006).

The positioning of Mike or Joel and the 'bots as an "empowered" viewer, in the Fiskian sense of the term, thus allows them to not only survive the films but to provide the at-home viewer with additional knowledge or flag up the problematic (on a social, political, or cultural level) content or world-views that the films are espousing. Particularly with regard to both intended and non-intended mental hygiene films, their commentary, whose original function had been to persuade both youth (actual mental hygiene films) and adult (feature films such as *Invasion USA*) audiences of proper behavior or local/global threats, the knowledge community on the Satellite of Love undermines the film's original purpose while simultaneously undermining Dr. Forrester/Pearl's purpose to torture them with bad cinema.

Thus we can see, within *Mystery Science Theater 3000*, there are at least three operative levels of commentary at work within each episode. There is Dr. Forrester's/Pearl's selection of films that will be sent to the Satellite of Love. There is Joel or Mike and the 'bots' analysis/commentary of the film, both inside the theater and within the host segments. Finally, the third part of the triangle, the at-home viewer, who is similarly free to make (or not make) connections between the component parts and overall flow of the episode they are watching. While it is easy to view "watching" as a passive activity, and thus only view the overt scheduling aspect, as represented by Dr. Forrester/Pearl, as the only active element within this matrix, both sets of viewers are tacitly encouraged to commentate on their own. As per example, the 24-hour "B-Fest" at Northwestern University, Evanston, Illinois, despite having existed previous to the debut of *Mystery Science Theater 3000* (the first B-Fest was November 13, 1981) was and is now publicized as "an audience participation version of an episode of Mystery Science Theater 3000." While the audience's commentary on films *Plan 9 from Outer Space* (Wood 1959) can end up sounding more like the audience participation culture around the *Rocky Horror Picture Show* (Sharman 1975) rather than the scripted commentary of *Mystery Science Theater*, such an assumption on the part of the B-Fest organizers falls prey to the assumption that the viewers of the series are not in fact active participants. While events such as B-Fest represent one particular kind of viewer response, albeit mostly absent of the sociopolitical dialogue that can (and does) occur within the televised series itself, it still indicates active, and indeed group, participation in the consumption of these films themselves. While little has currently been written on the fan culture surrounding *Mystery Science Theater*, and indeed, that is not the intention of this article, they do represent one of the earliest online fan cultures (known as MSTies), interacting with one another through tape trading and message boards.[3] Such an interaction was tacitly approved and encouraged by Best Brains during the first four seasons of the series, with the ending tag "Keep Circulating the Tapes." While Derek Kompare, in his analysis of television's transition from a flow model to a published model with the introduction and boom of television on DVD, argues that the VHS format did not lend itself to being archived and collected by the average viewer, due to both the limited storage capabilities of VHS and the issues of space for numerous tapes (Kompare 2006), he clearly seemed unaware of the thriving archiving and tape-trading culture of the MSTies. This tape trading culture represents its own kind of dialogue between fans of the series and the series itself, both in acquainting newer viewers with the full canon as well as serving as publicity for both *Mystery Science Theater* and the fledging comedy network for which it was an early flagship series. Regardless of the fact that after the fourth season of the show on Comedy Central, that line in the credits had to be eliminated due to legal concerns, that does not mean that such recording and trading practices stopped among the fan culture around the series. Indeed, the Digital Archive Project runs on a similar barter system to the original practices of MSTie fandom, "embracing the ancient art of 'tape trading'" in order to "facilitate the digital capture and storage of high quality video archives of television shows that either have been or are in danger of being taken off the air forever." Nor was "Keep Circulating the Tapes" excised from the credit roll when earlier episodes of the series were released on DVD.

While such a discussion may not seem entirely germane to a discussion of the social and political content of film selection and in-theater commentary, such practices that disseminate the episodes, ape the practices of the series in another context, or archive them for personal viewing are, I argue, a part of the dialogue that occurs both in and around *Mystery Science Theater 3000*. The film selection and commentary set up a dialogue that can bring to the surface the problematic elements of features and shorts (including racial and gender politics, among others) for the at-home viewer. This viewer can then potentially extend this discussion beyond the boundaries of the scheduled viewing context. Perhaps this was the intention behind Best Brains credit roll "thank you" to the authors of the First Amendment; the ability to start a dialogue that questions the celluloid assumptions, perversions, and propaganda of our past.

NOTES

1. Taken from the commentary of the short "Body Care and Grooming" (Beaulieu 1993, Episode 510).
2. "Assignment: Venezuela" has been released on DVD as part of the box set: "World History: South

America" by Quality Information Publishers and billed as a "great historical film about the Venezuelan oil industries in general and how it was built from the ground up."

3. Satellite News dates the emergence of the MSTies around 1991 to 1992, as well as enumerating the numerous fan initiatives and feedback to Comedy Central, including petitioning for the removal of the Comedy Central logo from the screen, as it blocked Crow in the theater, and complaints about the Penn Gillette voice-overs that often occurred over any ending credit host segments. Many of these complaints were due to the aforementioned tape trading culture of the MSTies, and voice-overs and logos were felt to diminish the quality of the archived episode. Penn Gillette later issued a personal apology to the MSTies, although presumably it was a network decision when the voice-overs aired.

REFERENCES

Beaudine, William (director), Tad Tadlock, Marc Breaux, et al. *Design for Dreaming*. MPO Productions, 1956.

Beaulieu, Trace (director), Michael J. Nelson (writer), Joel Hodgson (writer), et al. Episode 510 *The Painted Hills* 1993.

Beaulieu, Trace (director), Trace Beaulieu (writer), Paul Chaplin (writer), et al. Episode 522 *Teen-Age Crime Wave* 1994.

"B-Fest History." B-Fest: A&O's annual festival of b-movies! Accessed 1/15/2010. http://www.b-fest.com/history.html.

Berton, Kenneth J. (director), Ernest Borgnine, et al. *Merlin's Shop of Mystical Wonders*. Monarch Video, 2004 (originally released in 1995).

Carlisle, Robert (director), Leland Baxter, William Boyett, et al. *Last Clear Chance*. Wondsel, Carlisle, and Dunphy Productions, 1959.

Collins, Jim. "Postmodernism and Television," in Robert C. Allen, ed., *Channels of Discourse, Reassembled*. London; Routledge, 1992.

"Digital Archive Project FAQ." Digital Archive Project. Accessed 1/15/2010. http://www.dapcentral.org/modules.php?op=modload&name=FAQ&file=index&myfaq=yes&id_cat=17&categories=Digital+Archive+Project&parent_id=0.

Dyer, Richard. *White: Essays on Race and Culture*. London: Routledge, 1992.

Fiske, John. *Television Culture*. London: Routledge, 2006.

"Frequently Asked Questions: Other Media." *Satellite News*. Accessed 12/01/2009. http://www.mst3kinfo.com/mstfaq/book.html.

Green, Alfred E. (director), Robert Smith, Franz Schulz, et al. *Invasion USA*. Synapse Films, 2002 (originally released in 1952).

Handy, Jamison (director). "Hired." Jam Handy Organization, 1940.

Hodgson, Joel (director), Michael J. Nelson (writer), Joel Hodgson (writer), et al. Episode 424 *Manos: The Hands of Fate* 1993.

Jenkins, Henry. *Convergence Culture: Where Old and New Media Collide*. New York: New York University Press, 2006.

Kompare, Derek. "Publishing Flow: DVD Box Sets and the Reconception of Television." *Television and New Media* 7:4 (Winter 2006): 335–360.

Lang, Fritz (director), Nunally Johnson, Edward G. Robinson, et al. *The Woman in the Window*. MGM Video, 2007 (originally released in 1944).

Miner, Allen H. (director), Joe Ansen, Herman Boxer, et al. *The Days of Our Years*. Dudley Picture Corporations, 1955.

Murphy, Kevin (director), Michael J. Nelson (writer), et al. Episode 602 *Invasion USA* 1994.

Murphy, Kevin (director), Paul Chaplin (writer), Bill Corbett (writer) et al. *Assignment: Venezuela and Other Shorts* 2000.

"Part 6: East Meets West (1991–92)." *Satellite News*. Accessed 12/01/2009. http://www.mst3kinfo.com/history/page6.html.

Patton, Phil (director), Marvin David, Betty Luster. *Mr. B Natural*. Kling Film Productions, 1956.

Rissi, Michael (director), Vivian Schilling, Eric Parkinson, et al. *Soultaker*. Image Entertainment, 1999 (originally released in 1990).

Samuel, Lawrence R. *Brought to You By: Postwar Television Advertising and the American Dream*. Austin: University of Texas Press, 2001.

Sears, Fred F. (director), Ray Buffum, Tommy Cook, et al. *Teen-Age Crime Wave*. Clover Productions, 1955.

Sharman, Jim (director), Richard O'Brien, Jim Sharman, et al. *The Rocky Horror Picture Show*. 20th Century–Fox, 2000 (originally released in 1975).

Simmel, Edward G (director), Arthur V. Jones, Hugh Beaumont, et al. "A Date with Your Family." Simmel-Meservey, 1950.

Sloane, Rick (director), Rick Sloane, Tom Bartlett, et al. *Hobgoblins*. Micro Werks, 2009 (originally released in 1988).

Smith, Ken. *Mental Hygiene: Classroom Films 1945–1970*. New York: Blast Books, 1999.

Storey, John. *Cultural Theory and Popular Culture: An Introduction, Fourth Edition*. Essex, England: Pearson Education Limited, 2006.

Tobin, Jack (director). "Assignment: Venezuela." Quality Information Publishers, 2004 (originally released in 1956).

Warren, Harold P. (director), Tom Neyman, John Reynolds, et al. *Manos: The Hands of Fate*. Alpha Video, 2003 (originally released in 1966).

Williams, Raymond. *Television: Technology and Cultural Form*. London: Routledge; 2003.

"World Histories: South America." Quality Information Publishers. Accessed 12/02/2009. http://www.qualityinformationpublishers.com/8dvdboxsetsouthamericahistorypeopleandculturefilmsfeaturingbrazilpuertoricoperuchileguatemalavenezuelaboliviauruguayandoth.aspx.

16

The Endearing Educational Shorts

by Amanda R. Keeler

When most people think of *Mystery Science Theater 3000* they remember the show's riffs of numerous B-grade science fiction, horror and exploitation films. But over the years the program screened a number of shorter features, including educational and industrial films. Like the B movies and independently produced films that headline *Mystery Science Theater 3000* episodes, these shorter films grew out of their own tradition, a concurrent trajectory alongside more mainstream Hollywood films. Many of the short films featured on *Mystery Science Theater 3000* typify the educational films that people of a certain age most often think of when they remember the health and science class filmstrips they watched in middle and high school.

If there is such a thing as an "average" *Mystery Science Theater 3000* fan or viewer, these may or may not be the film lovers that go to the art cinema and worship films by canonized European and Hollywood directors, but they film lovers nonetheless. They love watching "bad" movies, making fun of them these films and hearing the Satellite of Love crew quip comedic at them as well. Perhaps *Mystery Science Theater 3000* is the place where viewers learned not to take media so seriously, that it is okay to poke fun at movies, and that films can be used for any number of purposes, even against the grain of their intended audiences or messages.

Though these B movies and shorts educational films populate most *Mystery Science Theater 3000* episodes, both genres were historically overlooked in academic discourse until the last two decades. Scholars like Jeffrey Sconce, Joan Hawkins and others have made a place in academic film studies for what is termed "paracinema," an umbrella term for films that fall outside of mainstream tastes. As well, the short-form, exemplified by the many different types of films that often begin *Mystery Science Theater 3000* episodes, have historically been difficult to study. Because these short films are not often available through feature-length distribution channels, they were nearly impossible to locate, though this has been remedied in the last decade through online sites like *Youtube, AVgeeks, Academic Film Archive,* and *Internet Archive*. With improved distribution networks, scholars have been able to approach and re-examine these texts in detail and reignited interest in these films.

One genre in particular — educational films, also known as classroom films or mental hygiene films have over the past several years elicited a great deal of attention from scholars interested in nontheatrical films, meaning, films designed and produced for school, church or community use, rather than for theatrical exhibition. These films were produced by companies like Jam Handy Organization, Coronet Instructional Films and Encyclopædia Britannica. To explore these educational films featured on *Mystery Science Theater 3000* more closely, this chapter will explore three avenues: First, it will briefly examine the history and trajectory of educational films in the United States leading up to the 1950s, the decade during which many of the educational shorts shown on the show were produced. Second, it will discuss what type of education these films attempted to convey, in particular in the three films: *What to do on a Date* (Coronet Instructional Films 1951), *Body Care and Grooming* (McGraw-Hill Text Films 1947) and *Are You Ready for Marriage?* (Coronet Instructional Films 1950). Finally, it will examine what aspects of these films garner the riffs from Joel (and Mike), Crow and Tom Servo. I argue that, despite the satirical treatment that these films were shown via the Satellite of Love crew, these films enjoyed a renaissance through the television show. By featuring these educational films on *Mystery Science Theater 3000*, decades after their original productions, these films entertained, and possibly educated, a new generation of viewers. Further, the ribbing these films receive from Joel (and Mike), Crow and Tom Servo, in essence, can be viewed as a loving, gentle skewering, as the characters (and actors) wax nostalgic about having watched these films as teenagers in high school.

Educational films were and are a part of a long tradition of media used for educational purposes in the United States, from magic lanterns, to phonographs, to film, radio and television, all employed in the classroom in a variety of ways. In terms of film, many of the genres typically associated with educational uses are bound loosely with one another because historically they have been considered nontheatrical, and thus, are not as widely known or seen as popular theatrical films. The films that conjure up this term today are usually associated with the types of films many students watched in their classrooms from the 1940s through the 1970s, when their teachers rolled in 16mm film projectors, loaded up the reels, and the students sat back and enjoyed, films that told the lifecycle of the monarch butterfly, or the inner-workings of a Ford automobile, or the proper way to brush and floss your teeth. These films, usually considered science films, industrial films and health films, respectively, are often lumped together as educational film, and were often used to supplement teacher instruction in classrooms in the United States over the last several generations.

These educational films that many students grew accustomed to seeing occasionally in school grew out of a tradition that dates back to the first years of the twentieth century, when people like Charles Urban, George Kleine, and Thomas Edison tried to interest the public in the idea of educational moving pictures. All three of these men worked in the film industry that would later become Hollywood, and thus had a stake or a personal interest in helping to make moving pictures viable fore educational purposes. Urban, a film supplier and independent producer, worked tirelessly to promote and popularize science films. In 1907 he published a booklet, titled "The Cinematograph in Science, Education and Matters of State," which touted the educational potential of moving pictures. George Kleine, a successful importer and distributor of "high-class" European films, published his 300-plus page *Catalogue of Educational Motion Pictures* in 1910. The most well known of the three, Thomas Edison, frequently discussed his feelings about the educational potential of moving pictures in newspaper and magazine articles. He was quoted frequently with having plans to "revolutionize education" by replacing school textbooks with moving pictures (Needham 16). To help bring this agenda to fruition, Edison heavily promoted his latest invention, a portable projector he called the Home Projecting Kinetoscope, designed "for education and entertainment at home, in schools, Sunday-schools, clubs lodges, etc." (Edison 1913).

To some, educational film was a way of creating additional markets outside of the theatrically run films in the United States. To others, educational film meant an alternative to the "salacious" dramas, the unsophisticated slapstick comedies, and the corrupting effects of pictures featuring people in opium dens and involved in the "white-slave" trade (see 1913's *Traffic in Souls*). For educators, in the midst of radical changes to the theories of education in the early twentieth century, moving pictures in the classroom freed students from the one-dimensional images and ideas in textbooks. Moving pictures could bring education to life. Showing educational films in the classroom could help educate young people in ways that a textbook alone could not by allowing students to see the people of Japan, the pyramids of Egypt, or the inner workings of the human body, via motion pictures, rather than the flat, static images in outdated textbooks.

By the late 1900s and early 1910s reformers working outside of the film industry, like John Collier and Jane Addams felt strongly about the theoretical potential of educational moving pictures. Popular magazines and motion picture trade journals were convinced as well, avidly promoting films for use in churches and schools — spaces that Edison's catalogue had suggested. Collier, who worked for a prominent reform group in New York City, the People's Institute during the 1910s, and helped form the New York Board of Censorship/ Review, worked tirelessly not only to make theatrical moving pictures more suitable for children and families, but also to bring educational moving pictures into the same spaces that Urban, Kleine and Edison promoted. John Collier writes, "The prevailing view at the People's Institute ... was that the cinema was 'the people's theater,' and held great potential for education and for life" (Collier 1963: 71–72). Likewise, in 1907 Jane Addams opened a nickelodeon at her Chicago settlement house, Hull House. Though this film theater experiment proved short-lived, Addams continued to see nickelodeons as inexpensive entertainment for working class patrons and as a way of educating audiences. The progressives, in general, were aware of the power and the draw of cinema, and wanted to help reform moving pictures into a respectable, family-friendly amusement that could be used for the greater good.

Film historian Ben Singer writes, "Education by movies became a favorite theme because it provided a topic custom-made for the needs of popular journalism at the time. It tapped into a pervasive set of 'buzz words' and 'buzz issues,' i.e., those composing the forward-looking enthusiasm of the Progressive Movement" (Singer 1988: 52). Concurrent with the growing interest in educational film were a number of reforms taking place in schools in the United States. Many of the reforms sought during this time came under the umbrella of homogenization: making the schools in America consistent between rural and urban places, rich and poor neighborhoods, and making education available and mandatory for *all* children and young adults. Historian Michael McGerr writes that many of the proposed changes to education in the early twentieth century came from people associated with progressivism, like educator and educational theorist John Dewey (McGerr 2003: 109–11). Dewey himself wrote, in 1913, that moving pictures might prove educational for schoolchildren, as long as there was "careful discrimination" in producing and implementing them in the classroom (Dewey 1913: 692).

But despite the time, energy and money that men in the film industry put towards the promotion of educational film as a viable alternative to theatrical moving pictures, by the early 1920s it was clear that their efforts never captured the public as fully as many had hoped. Paul Saettler writes, "The rigid classification of films as either educational or entertaining [had] proved detrimental" to the promotion of these films as an alternative to the "crass" fare of the moving picture house (Saettler 2004: 97).

But this early failure did not derail the push to bring this technology into the classroom. By the late 1910s and early 1920s the discussions on educational moving pictures had spawned a peripheral industry to theatrical films, where the promotion of these films defined the scope of publications like *Reel and Slide, The Screen,* and *Visual Education.* The popular press continued its preoccupation with educational films as well, continuing to promote them in widely circulated magazines like *Christian-Science Monitor, Newsweek,* and *Science.* The first wave of individuals who attempted to promote the idea of educational moving pictures may have given up the fight, but they sparked the interest of many more, who gladly picked up where they left off.

With the advent of non-flammable safety film in the 1910s, and Eastman Kodak's smaller gauge 16mm stock in 1923, it was safer and cheaper for teachers to bring films into classrooms. Companies like Bell & Howell, Electrical Research Products, Inc. (ERPI), and Victor Animatograph developed portable and inexpensive 16mm cameras and projectors, which further helped with the ease and implementation of visual education in schools. With the commercial feasibility of sync sound film technology in the late 1920s, a whole new avenue of educational film production emerged. These improved technologies facilitated the next wave of companies producing educational films, like Encyclopædia Britannica, Coronet Instructional Films, McGraw-Hill Text-Films, and many others. The production of these films peaked in the 1950s-1960s, during which time thousands of films were produced for all manner of educational purposes, ranging from science, music and art appreciation, driver's education, health and well-being, to sexual education. School districts and university libraries bought these films, and loaned out their collections of 16mm educational film prints to other institutions, forming distribution networks that kept these films in regular circulation, in schools and in pupils' minds.

Education as a "buzz" word also ties in to the utopian notions that spring up around new media, with oft-repeated hopes and dreams that the movies, or the telegraph before them, or radio after them, will be the saving grace of modern civilization. Mary Gray Peck sums up this sentiment in 1917, writing, "Motion pictures are going to save our civilization from the destruction which has successively overwhelmed every civilization of the past" (Peck 1917: 57). Her hyperbolic language illustrates how deeply moving pictures were tied to ideas of improving education and making the world a better place.

The 1950s and 1960s were the height of educational film production and use in the United States. As video technologies became less expensive and more viable in the 1970s and 1980s, the use of film shifted to video for the purposes of classroom media. The educational media remained the same, but film soon became a "quaint" and expensive technology, replaced by the user-friendly VCR, which soon became a permanent fixture in the classroom. The switch in media platforms did not erase film's influence in the classroom, but merely altered its delivery. Today, media in classroom continues to proliferate, thanks to the shift to inexpensive computers and Internet technology.

With this history in mind, I would now like to transition to the other side of this study, and think about three of the educational films that *Mystery Science Theater 3000* has featured over the years. Simply put, many of these older 16mm educational films have not aged well. It is easy to look back at these films and poke fun at them in a number of ways, and that is precisely what the show did. To think about these films I will first discuss what type of education these films attempted to convey. As well, I will examine what aspect of these three films garners from the riffs from Joel/Mike, Crow and Tom Servo. As difficult as it is to re-approach these films when they teach outdated social modes and gender roles, or long-since debunked scientific theories, these films remain fascinating, as time capsules of a moment in time. As well, these films in the classroom meant a break from the usual teacher lectures. And they remain fun, which explains why they were chosen for *Mystery Science Theater 3000*. What follows is a short textual analysis of three educational films featured on the program over the years.

What to Do on a Date (Coronet Instructional Films 1951)

The film *What to Do on a Date* is a ten-minute long film produced by Coronet Instructional Films in 1951. Like many health education films from this era, the film was made in conjunction with "educational collaborator" Evelyn M. Duvall, Ph.D., from the National Council on Family Relations. The film features two young men, Jeff and Nick, who discuss how Nick is going to ask Kay, "a swell girl," out on a date. The Satellite of Love crew, picking up on the creepy 1950s vibe of the film, make one of their many references to Alfred Hitchcock's *Psycho*. As the boys are hanging out in Nick's foyer, and perhaps because they exude that creepy teenager-ness of a young Norman Bates, Jeff raises his tennis racket and Crow begins a chorus of *Psycho*'s shrieking violins.

Nick is not only worried about asking Kay out on a date, but also about what they should or should not do on their date if she says yes. Kay agrees to go out with Jeff, and the two end up at a scavenger sale. Instead of enjoying the date as it progresses, and getting to know Kay better, Jeff fixates on what they will do on their next date. Jeff spots a bulletin board, on which he finds a list of coming group activities in the next few weeks. The film's narrator suggests that these group activities, like bike trips, bowling, weenie roasts, square dances, picnics and baseball games are a sure bet "if you plan for what she enjoys." Tom Servo decides that this is the perfect opportunity to jokingly insert the calling card of 1970s pornography and exploitation film music, singing "bam-chica-bam-bam."

The Satellite of Love crew also finds ways to poke fun at the overly-enthusiastic and eager teenagers that populate this film. While decorating for the scavenger sale, Kay hangs cardboard elephants. As Kay hammers a nail through one of the paper elephants, while smiling, Joel says, "Kay worked on the kill floor, she knows where to deliver the blow." His comment seems as appropriate to the context of the film as the hanging of paper elephants. Soon after their hard work, the teenagers are treated to a refreshments table. What looks like a normal bunch of teenagers helping themselves is soon overshadowed by a chorus of "mmm sausages" from Crow, Tom Servo, and Joel. Remember, teenagers are very hungry animals.

In general, since many of these types of health education films were created for classroom use, their lengths vary, but often run from five to thirty minutes. *What to Do on a Date* comes in at ten minutes, which begs the question of most educational films: How do you teaching "dating," or another complicated social interaction, in ten minutes? The film does an excellent job of capturing the timeless awkwardness of teenagers attracted to one another, who wonder how they are to act on their teenage impulses appropriately, while reinforcing the general chaste nature of the 1950s. It does also direct teenagers to "safe" activities, which might seem quaint now, but were likely suitable group activities for young people in this era.

Many of these health educational films, like *What to Do on a Date*, take on a sense of awkwardness themselves, in that they attempted to teach a complicated social lesson or moral, while sidestepping and hovering around "touchy subjects." This film would never directly say, "Don't have sex," but this is implicitly built into the context of "group dates are preferable," a stance that inherently speaks volumes to keeping paired-off teenagers from the back seats of cars or other disreputable spaces. Joel and the robots pick up on this sense as well. The film opens with Joel stating, Joel, "this is like having your mom tell you about sex," to describe the process of learning about dating protocols from your inexperienced friend in a classroom film.

What to Do on a Date ends with the narrator reminding the viewers that it is easy to have fun on dates. He says, "Yes, there are lots of things to do on dates" and now, after watching the film, "you'll know what to do on your date." But Tom Servo disagrees. He reminds the viewers that this advice is not for everyone: "If you're an AV geek, don't even kid yourself," meaning that for the high school nerds, there will be no question of where to go on a date, but rather, no date at all.

Body Care and Grooming (McGraw-Hill Text-Films 1947)

At the beginning of *Body Care and Grooming*, a ten-minute McGraw-Hill Text-Film from 1947, Crow asks what many original viewers of this film were probably thinking: "Oh, is there going to be a test?" Per the titles of the film, *Body Care and Grooming* was part of a Health Education Series, "Correlated with Textbook of Healthful Living by Dr. Harold S. Diehl." The narrator begins: "Ah, spring," to which Crow answers, "Filthy, shameful spring," in response to the cute (and again) chaste young heterosexual couples enjoying themselves around their college campus. Noticing the absence of anyone but white teenagers, Mike says, "You know, people were a lot whiter back then."

In this ten-minute film, the narrator tells the audience that, "clothes are important," and shows the proper grooming of the "important" parts, "hands, hair, teeth, skin," to which Crow adds, "and your naughty bits." The narrator's next task begins by picking out a woman walking through campus, fixating the camera on her, and looking her up and down to examine her body and clothing. The narrator is disappointed that the young woman has not been properly grooming herself, and proceeds to tell her that her blouse, skirt and socks are completely inadequate. The narrator also suggests, frequently, that the way to show that you have spent time and energy on your appearance is to look exactly like everybody else. Crow remarks, "Expressing individualism is just plain wrong."

The film ends with the young woman, fresh from her shower (having survived another round of Crow's *Psycho* shrieking violins). The young woman then prepares to go to bed, after she has showered, brushed her teeth, and put on clean "lingerie." The narrator adds, "and so the end to a perfect day" to which Joel replies, "an entire day spent grooming." From the context of this film, it would seem that most teenagers spend approximately three-quarters of their day showering, grooming and brushing their hair and teeth. By attending class, changing a tire, or reading books, these teenagers demonstrate the acceptable ways in which they are allowed to "get dirty" in their daily lives, and what *must* be done to remedy that immediately.

This type of educational film works on two levels, teaching both socially acceptable behaviors and grooming, with a smattering of science and anatomy. While it stresses the importance of proper grooming and hygiene, it also features several visual aids that focus on science lessons: Detailed cutaway diagrams of human skin, hair follicles, oil and sweat glands. This might have afforded a film like this to be used in two different classrooms, in both health and biology classes. At the same time, the "acceptable" behaviors that these films try to teach and convey are firmly rooted in middle-class American (harkening back to Victorian) sensibilities. These films are teaching not only a certain set of middle-class values, acted out entirely with white, middle-class teenagers, who seem to have ample time, energy and money with which to purchase nice clothes, shoes, and hoards of personal soaps and shampoos.

Again, this film, like *What to Do on a Date* does an excellent job of capturing the awkwardness of teenagers, particularly here by reminding them endlessly that they must groom and primp many hours each day in order to be acceptable human specimens. This film was produced in 1947, and looking back, it captures nicely the zeitgeist of the moment: pushing the teenagers toward conformity, telling them that appearances mean everything, and holding everyone to the standards of white, middle-class culture that was at the height of its cultural dominance here, soon after the end of World War II.

Are You Ready for Marriage? (Coronet Instructional Films 1950)

In the 1950 Coronet Instructional film *Are You Ready for Marriage?* viewers meet Sue, who is 18, and Larry, who is 19. This educational film was produced in conjunction with consultant Reuben Hill, Ph.D., Research Professor in Family Life at the University of North Carolina. *Are You Ready for Marriage?* is slightly longer than the previous two ten-minute films. If you can learn to date and groom yourself in ten minutes, surely you can prepare yourself for marriage in fifteen fact-filled minutes.

The film opens with the couple kissing. Tom seems to agree with the title, saying, "The tepid embrace tells me they are ready for marriage." Mike replies, "Welcome to as far as you are going to get." Larry and Sue have been dating for "three months, one week, two days and seventeen hours." They want to get married before Larry graduates from college. Sue's parents balk at the idea, and send the young people to the marriage counselor at "State U." The counselor has a wealth of information to share with the young couple, including a number of highly "scientific" visual aids. First is "Cupid's Checklist," designed to gauge if two people belong together. The counselor asks Sue and Larry to see if they have "similar backgrounds," questions if they are "real friends," and decide whether or not they really "understand" marriage. Mike reminds them of at least one of the most important pre-marriage question: "Are you from the same family?"

The counselor sends Sue and Larry through a "marriage development quotient," that "represents the psychological distance between a man and his wife from the time they are born until the time they die." Again applying hard scientific facts to his counseling of young people, he also explains to Sue that there are "masculine" and "feminine" ways of looking at things in the world. Sue replies, "but I don't want to marry a girl like me, I want to marry a *man* like Larry," to which Crow retorts: "Oh no you don't."

The counselor produces yet another visual aid, the "Chance for Happiness" chart that tells that the length of engagement will have a direct result on the later marital happiness. Sue is finally beginning to understand the type of work that she and Larry have ahead of them. She asks, "Do we have similar backgrounds? Do we have the same religious beliefs?" After several meetings with the counselor, Sue's parents have come around. Her fathers says,

"If you want to Sue, your mother and I, we can make arrangements for you to begin school at State U this fall with Larry, instead of at the Junior college. Then, if you two get along, in school that is, you continue to reduce the psychological distance, then perhaps at Christmas vacation, or Easter vacation, we'll be glad to announce the engagement." In celebration of this, the young couple hug and smile. The counselor ends by saying: "I think you've made a good start towards getting ready for marriage."

Like *Body Care and Grooming, Are You Ready for Marriage?* mixes both social training and "science" to educate its viewers. The multiple visual aids attempt to convey to Sue and Larry the "scientific" principles behind the counselor's views on successful marriages. But for as much as this film banks on seemingly made-up terms like "psychological distance" it presents a very level headed assessment of young people and marriage. The film was produced in 1950, and seems progressive for the time frame. In it, it attempts to guide young people and help them make important decisions before they marriage. The counselor in the film encourages the young people to get to know one another better before they marry at such a young age. Sue's parents like the idea of the young couple seeking advice outside of the family with the professional counselor, but they also appreciate being involved in the conversation. In light of the many quick marriages that occurred before and after World War II, the film seems to be telling young people to slow down, and think long and hard about the life-altering changes that will occur if two people marry before they are ready. With that in mind, however, both Sue and Larry are portrayed a vacuous and spacey individuals who are looking to jump into marriage quickly. Thankfully, by the end of the film, Sue and Larry are properly schooled, and are ready for enter into a long engagement waiting period.

It is nearly impossible to know what audiences thought of these films at the time of their initial release. Modern audiences take delight in pointing out the outdated social norms and scientific principles of these films. In this light, it is easy to dismiss the influence that these films might have had on audiences, and the place that educational films had in the daily lives of millions of school children and teenagers in the United States. But there is no denying that these films, despite their sometimes awkwardness, were a part of American students' lives over the last century, and that they stuck around mentally, enough so that programs like *Mystery Science Theater 3000* took the time to revisit them, and point out what makes them unique and fascinating as artifacts of a time long since past.

Does the Satellite of Love treatment qualify as a gentle riffing? In a word, yes. The satirical riffing that the crew shows these films illustrates a few things. As mentioned, it is likely that the rights to these educational films were easy to obtain, as the films long since abandoned by their filmmakers and film companies. As well, in the earliest days of the show, the writers helped themselves to whatever films they could locate around their public access station, where they found many educational shorts. Availability, then, might account for the presence of a number of these educational films in the *Mystery Science Theater 3000* oeuvre.

Furthermore, as discussed in the introduction, many MSTies were likely instantly transported back to their childhoods when watching these educational features. Reliving the trials and tribulations of being a teenager, and surviving the occasionally misguided advice of these films would mean that you quite possibly successfully made it out of your awkward teenage years intact. Who has not felt out of place because they did not know how to act on a date, or felt like they were not going to ever get a date because their hair was messy, or their clothes were not perfect? And then when they finally found someone they wanted to be with, did it not help that they had a film to tell them the traits that would help them have a successful marriage?

By showcasing a number of educational films over its years, *Mystery Science Theater 3000* has kept alive the tradition of these prolific films, and helped to honor their original producers. Some of them might be "cheesy" movies, but why ignore the silly moments. The Satellite of Love crew celebrates, instead, and keeps these films alive in the public consciousness, and at least for the last fifteen years or so, delighted the fans of *MST3K* enough to keep coming back for more. The post *MST3K* group *RiffTrax* continues to riff on these educational shorts to the delight of fans.

REFERENCES

Are You Ready for Marriage? Coronet Instructional Films, 1950. In *Mystery Science Theater 3000* Episode 613. Jim Mallon (director), Mike Nelson (writer), Trace Beaulieu (writer) and Kevin Murphy (writer). Original Airdate 26 November 1994.

Body Care and Grooming. McGraw-Hill Text-Films. In *Mystery Science Theater 3000* Episode 510. Jim Mallon (director), Joel Hodgson (writer), Trace Beaulieu (writer) and Kevin Murphy (writer). Original Airdate 26 September 1993.

Collier, John. *From Every Zenith.* Denver: Sage Books, 1963.

Dewey, John. "Cut and Dry School Methods," "Edison vs. Euclid: Has He Invented a Moving Stairway to Learning?" in Winthrop D. Lane, ed. *The Survey* (6 September 1913) 691–92.

Edison, Thomas A. "Motion Picture Films for Use on the Edison Home Kinetoscopes." Catalogue. 1913.

Freeman, Frank N. "Requirements of Education with Reference to Motion Pictures." *The School Review* 31:5 (May 1923): 340–350.

McGerr, Michael. *A Fierce Discontent: The Rise and Fall of the Progressive Movement, 1870–1920.* New York: Oxford University Press, 2005.

Needham, Mary Master. "Going to School at the 'Movies': An Interview with Thomas A. Edison." *Saturday Evening Post* (30 November 1912) 16–18, 42.

Peck, Mary Gray. "As Miss Peck Sees It." *Photoplay* (February 1917) 57.

Saettler, Paul. *The Evolution of American Educational Technology.* Greenwich: Information Age Publishing, 2004.

Singer, Ben. "Early Home Cinema and the Edison Home Projecting Kinetoscope." *Film History* (1988): 37–69.

What to Do on a Date. Coronet Instructional Films, 1951. In *Mystery Science Theater 3000* Episode 503. Jim Mallon (director), Joel Hodgson (writer), Trace Beaulieu (writer) and Kevin Murphy (writer). Original Airdate 31 July 1993.

17

Writing History with Riffs: The Historiography of the "Shorts"

by Miranda Tedholm

The *Mystery Science Theater 3000* shorts were originally conceived as filler to supplement films whose length did not completely fill the show's time slot. Eventually released as a VHS compilation in 1998, the "shorts" (as I will refer to them in this essay) present a different spectator dynamic than most *Mystery Science Theater* episodes, and, for many, provided their only access to these otherwise-lost educational films. The riffing and engagement with ephemeral media objects that had been designed for a very specific purpose puts the shorts in a slightly different position than the other *Mystery Science Theater* episodes, which focused on edited versions of "B" movies.

The shorts transverse different kinds of spectatorship, viewing practices, and temporalities, enacting a sophisticated call-and-response to the source text that sutures the temporal gap between the source texts and the viewing present. This is done by creating and re-situating the source films into an affected, constructed time (i.e., "the not-too-distant future") that exists neither in the present day nor in the time of the source text.

This essay considers the *MST3K* shorts as both temporal rupture and a practice of ironic consumption done as a historiographic act of writing and rewriting the past. The riffing on the shorts creates a document that unifies the past and absorbs it into what is understood to be the present; although the framing conceit of Joel and the robots is meant to be "in the not-too-distant future," we understand them to inhabit a present roughly akin to our own through signaling devices such as hairstyles, clothes, and speech patterns that inscribe this part of the show as part of the late 20th century.

The shorts provide access to an ephemeral, largely forgotten object, but resituate it in the present in order to read the original film-texts as incorporated into the present moment. It is clear through this practice that these context-less objects can only be understood through the lens of sarcasm as practiced in the moment of the films' second consumption.

The shorts riff on ephemeral educational films, often the notorious "mental hygiene" subgenre. It is the riffs on the mental hygiene films that will be the concern of this chapter, specifically "A Date with Your Family" (Mallon 1994, Episode 602/ Simmel-Meservey, 1950) "Cheating" (Mallon 1993, Episode 515/Centron Corp. for Young America Films, 1952), and "The Home Economics Story" (Mallon 1991, Episode 317 / Iowa State College, 1951). These films, targeted at young adults and adolescents, used didactic tactics in order to frame and illustrate correct behavior.

According to Ken Smith in 1999's *Mental Hygiene,* these films reflected Cold War anxieties about youth more than they reflected anxieties about the Space Race, which is curious given that their production was contemporaneous with increased science funding. Many of the films were created in order to prevent another "flapper" generation as the students who came of age during the time in which these films were made had grown up without significant adult supervision, due to World War II (Smith, 1999: 18). Ken Smith writes, "the general feeling of the [immediate postwar] time ... was that this new generation was spinning out of control" (1999: 22). Therefore, educators and others felt that using media — often via discarded equipment that had been used to train soldiers in the war via other educational films — in order to establish correct behavioral guidelines in school was an effective means of preventing juvenile delinquency. The mental hygiene film is "the marriage of a philosophy-progressive education — and a technology — the instructional film" (Smith, 1999: 19).

These low-budget films were produced for use in American classrooms for several decades in the mid–20th century, and often focused on non-academic "citizenship" and "life skills" topics such as dating, honesty, substance abuse, and personal hygiene. The prototypical mental hygiene film is narrated by a didactic, usually male authority figure and features low-budget actors and actresses, who portray dramatic tableaux related to adolescent struggles such as dating, friendship, honesty, popularity, and manners.

The tableaux used in mental hygiene films share several salient characteristics. First, they are heavily influenced by traditional melodramas in that they rely on emotional (over) reaction, made even more ripe for riffing in that these dramas are enacted by actors who could generously be described as amateurs. These small melodramas are used to create an "emotionally derived learning" experience (Smith, 1999: 23). Peter Brooks describes melodrama as "a form of theatricality which will underlie novelistic efforts at representation — which will provide a model for the making of meaning in fictional dramatizations of existence" (1985: 13). Therefore, the emotional reactions were used in order to augment the "meaning-making," even for things as banal as hand-washing or dinner manners. The implication is that without an emotional draw (or manipulation, if you prefer), the lessons in the films have no meaning.

Second, mental hygiene films often employ fairly traditional narrative structures that focus on people's reactions to problems, which are sometimes resolved by the end of the film. A common structure found in mental hygiene films is the development of a narrative but no resolution, and instead an invitation for student "discussion." There is little character development, but the *plot* grows as generic children or adolescents enact stories related to common issues.

Finally, these traditional narratives contain resolution that often takes the form of either tragedy or quick repentance, as in "Cheating" (Episode 515/Centron Corp. for Young America Films, 1952), in which young John loses credibility, grades, and a coveted student government position. The film augments his personal frustration and failure with expressionistic shots of ticking clocks and nearly-empty rooms, before the narrator opens up the "discussion" with leading questions that further indict John. Other mental hygiene films not addressed by the "Shorts" feature endings that involve teen death or social isolation, sometimes ending with shots of teenage girls sobbing while the narrator eviscerates them for character flaws.

Often, the youth in the films discover that acceptance and happiness come hand-in-hand with conformity and agreeableness, sacrificing individuality for the concerns of the group, such as the adolescents in 1950's "Date with Your Family" (Episode 602), who embody the narrator's didactic suggestions for maintaining domestic harmony at the expense of sharing personal news and individual struggles. The narrator states, "the children greet their dad as though they are genuinely glad to see him." Tom Servo states, "They're not, of course," which opens up the interpretive possibility to the narrator's specific word choices and their obsolescence forty years on. The narrator further intones, "This is the time for pleasant discussion and a thoroughly relaxed mood." That statement seems at odds with the sarcastic statements uttered by the films' viewers, and again makes reference to the world of possibility denied by the framing of the film tableaux.

The surviving documents related to the films' actual use within schools focus on rental and print statistics. Other surviving documents include suggested lesson plans and discussion questions that were part of the teachers' guides often rented or sold with the films. Most of these guides focus on simplistic educational goals such as remembering facts from the films or guiding the students through a discussion structured to foster agreement with the films' argument, rather than the critical thinking and analysis usually privileged in American classrooms.

The films were discarded, usually after years of viewings in schools, churches, and other institutions, and few have been preserved. Therefore, their resurgence via different means of circulation such as YouTube and Rick Prelinger's Archive.org has changed their place in the culture. Previously, substantial privilege was required in order to access these films: most extant copies reside at university libraries or have been rescued from the trash by enterprising collectors. When most people discussed these films, there was little corroborating evidence as the films themselves had largely vanished; they were objects that existed in cultural memory more than cultural archives. However, new means of circulation, including the films' broadcast as part of *Mystery Science Theater* and their availability online has decreased the amount of specialized knowledge and access previously necessary to experience these films. The Shorts' use of riffing and camp maintain specialized positions for some viewers in that knowledge about the films is used to construct the commentary, and strategically withheld from the audience. The privileged spectators become the silhouetted crew whose commentary is married to the film.

The riffing on the Shorts appears to be a form of call and response: the source text is the call, and the riff is the response, in the tradition of *Rocky Horror*–style fandom. However, unlike *Rocky Horror*, the response is neither uttered in unison nor is it part of an iterative tradition. Moreover, the commentators are imbued with superiority, rather than becoming part of an experience shared by all viewers. It becomes a type of camp, as described by Susan Sontag, who states that camp is "alive to a double sense in which some things can be taken," that "the essential element is seriousness, a seriousness that fails," that "things are campy, not when they become old — but when we become less involved in them, and can enjoy, instead of be frustrated by, the failure of the attempt" and that "camp rests on innocence" (1964: 281, 283, 285, 283). I read the shorts as closer to this definition of camp than the "feature" episodes of the show due to the educational shorts' failed seriousness and mediated innocence. Unlike many of the feature films, the educational shorts took themselves very seriously and sought to depict an innocent world of weenie roasts, family dinners, and wholesome vocational training. The films' lack of self-awareness situates them even further in the moment contemporaneous to their production because it betrays the filmmakers' inability to see the "double sense" present in many of the films.

The spectators watching the show experience two layers of the media event: related to both interest in the source text and the reaction articulated in the response-text. Therefore, it may be more appropriate to classify the *Mystery Science Theater 3000* experience as call, response, and response. The response that occurs in the unmediated final layer — the home viewer — remains undocumented.

The educational films that the show presents are targeted at naïve viewers with little of today's media sophistication; however, it is also worth noting that many mental hygiene films employ rudimentary interactive features through moments of narrative address that break the fourth wall and direct the audience to discuss or consider something. The films demonstrate no self-reflexivity or awareness, which heightens their characterization as sincere or naïve cultural objects. They were produced in and for a specific time period and had no pretenses of lasting past their intended use period. However, new media technologies related to both circulation and preservation have enabled these films to re-circulate, particularly on the Internet, and newfound academic and cultural interest has re-situated them into people's consciousness via events such as the Orphan Film Symposium. Injected unchanged into the late 20th and early 21st century, the films seem to be understood only ironically: viewers can understand them only as objects of camp or mockery. In *Mystery Science Theater 3000*, this "riffing" involves allusive statements meant to draw attention to the gap between the source-text's innocence and the viewer's sophistication.

The films themselves work as documents meant to change the future, yet are inherently situated in the present moment of their production. Of the Shorts I am discussing, most have futural themes, either espousing ideas for children's educational futures or describing agricultural breakthroughs. For example, "The Chicken of Tomorrow" cheerfully describes early attempts at factory farming and agricultural science research for "the chicken of tomorrow." Since the Shorts are being riffed upon in what could be considered yesterday's tomorrow, the film's vision of the future is both critiqued and assessed in terms of its correctness. The viewer, as well as the commentators, is left assessing how much of the film's vision has come to fruition.

Another example is "The Home Economics Story," in which an intrusive narrator follows a young girl through her decision to attend college and her educational career at Iowa State College. The original source text is constructed such that the narrator knows Kay's fate from the beginning, although he introduces the moments that come closest to this film's idea of narrative tension: when she introduces the idea of attending college to her parents, when she decides on a major, etc. The narrator is privileged because he presents the outcome of the story, frames it, and establishes authority, but the commentators are further privileged because they interpret his narrative. The implication of "The Home Economics Story" is that due to the women's training in home economics, the story is really only just beginning when it ends — by extent it espouses the idea that film can change the future. The narrator's use of direct address, assuring the viewer that these educated young women will affect your life, must be accounted for in a future viewing: again, the viewer must assess whether the narrator's statements are true. The context of late 20th-century viewing, occurring after second-wave feminism and the obsolescence of many programs of home economics study, provides the humorous context for many of the comments made by Joel, Tom Servo, and Crow as they situate the film's vision of empowered young women working with the cultural truth of female oppression, sexism, and hegemony.

The source texts are used to situate and ostensibly, influence or shape the future. A strange lacuna is created when the present-situated robots comment with sophistication on these naïve films, making remarks that require a broad understanding of cultural texts.

Moreover, the comments made refer to atemporal cultural texts. For example, Joel says during "The Home Economics Story" that Kay is going off to a Godard film festival (it is also worth noting that Godard's films themselves contain significant numbers of references); later he mentions *Carrie* (1976). Godard had not yet begun filmmaking at the time "The Home Economics Story" was filmed; the short also pre-dates *Carrie* by more than twenty years.

The union of the innocent, humble film with the multiple references to other cultural objects causes it to transcend its origins and become a nodal hypertext that points to other texts. This practice also locates it within the network of culture. The unification of the naïve past with the "sophisticated" present gives validation to the source text by locating it within the network of cultural texts. Simultaneously, the educational films gain cultural validation and become inextricably linked to other, more sophisticated texts. The pastiche narrows the demographic of the ideal viewer to one who understands the riff and requires a certain experience with media culture and active media viewing.

Because most of the educational shorts were originally shown in what could be considered coercive viewing contexts (in which a person who held power required subordinates — namely, students — to watch films) (Smoodin, 2004: 160–202), the viewing practice is changed during the event of the *Mystery Science Theater 3000* short. Moreover, it is re-enacted within the framing conceit of the mad scientists forcing Joel to watch the films: itself a coercive viewing practice if there ever was one!

The riff does something more than react to the source text; it changes the viewing dynamic from one of coercion to one of pleasure and consent, in which the viewers or readers of the film transform it into a writer-ly act that absorbs the iterative film event into a practice that rewrites it as part of everyday life: part of a practice of ironic consumption. This practice is imposed on the viewer because the unadulterated versions of the shorts are inaccessible, or were largely inaccessible at the time the Shorts first aired: a viewer who wanted to see the films without commentary or without the commentators' silhouettes would have been sorely disappointed.

In this practice, the viewer-writers align their viewpoint with those of the naïve viewers intended as the ideal audience. Armed with the amassed cultural knowledge of the past half-century, these sophisticated viewers perform a created identity: an amalgam of the naïve students for whom the films were intended and the sophisticated media consumers who are able to make humorous, entertaining connections between the stilted educational shorts and other media objects. The *MST3K* riffing responds to the proto-interactivity of the educational films' invitations for discussion by taking it further and discussing outside the strictures of the film.

While the specific structure of the educational mental hygiene films seeks to limit discussion patterns by funneling youths into acceptable behavioral patterns, the *Mystery Science Theater 3000* riffs work both with and against that impulse. The films seek to shut down responses in youths and the riffing works in order to illustrate a plenitude of potential outcomes. The original source-text and the riffs work here to demonstrate two extremes for youth behavior, one overly controlled and the other overly free. For instance, in "The Home Economics Story," the film espouses a traditional skills-based education for young women, and many of the riffs are related to the excesses of campus life and anxieties related to school. When Kay writes a letter to her parents, Crow "speaks" for her and creates a reference to *Carrie* (1976), stating that "tonight, everyone will die." When the women that the film follows meet together, jokes are made about marijuana smoking or binge drinking — exactly the types of behaviors that mental hygiene films wanted to discourage.

As mentioned above, the adolescents in "A Date with Your Family" are encouraged by the narrator to engage in very specific and banal conversation with their own family. The narrator's suggestions imply that certain topics or ideas not be broached with one's own family, ever; yet the statements made by the Tom Servo stand in direct contradiction to this directive as he speaks for the oldest girl in the family: "Mom, I'm pregnant." This statement not only provides an absolute opposition to the instructions of the film, but plays along with the melodramatic heritage of many mental hygiene films. By utilizing a cliché statement that works as a plot point in many melodramas, the *Mystery Science Theater 3000* commentators defy the narrator's directive about acceptable conversation for families while still riffing on the genre heritage of many mental hygiene films in order to unite and transverse several texts. In doing so, the film presents a way to understand the source-texts, their place within culture, and their links to other media-texts, and ties them to specific temporal moments, thus writing their history.

The source-texts of the shorts espouse a recitation or reading reaction from their audience, whereas the riffing interpolated into the source-text demonstrates an act of writing, a defiant re-situating and injecting of the text into the present day. This is historiography in practice: rewriting the past in order to understand the present and to provide documentation for the future — a future that, doubtless, will re-situate and re-write the texts as its own act of understanding.

REFERENCES

Brooks, Peter. *The Melodramatic Imagination*. New York: Columbia University Press, 1985.

De Certeau, Michel. Trans. Steven Rendall. *The Practice of Everyday Life*. Berkeley: University of California Press, 1984.

Indiana University Audio/Visual Department. *1960 Educational Motion Picture Catalog*. Bloomington: Indiana University, 1960.

Mallon, Jim (Director), Joel Hodgson (writer), Mike Nelson (writer) et al., *Shorts*. Rhino, 1998.

Smith, Ken. *Mental Hygiene*. New York: Blast Books, 1999.

Smoodin, Eric. *Regarding Frank Capra: Audience, Celebrity & American Film Studies 1930–1960*. Durham, NC: Duke University Press, 2004.

Sontag, Susan. *Against Interpretation*. New York: Noonday Press, 1964/1966.

PART SIX

Satire and Gender

18

Robot Roll Call: Gypsy! (Hi Girls!)

by Michele Brittany

From 1988 to 1999, *Mystery Science Theater 3000* (*MST*) entertained television viewers with comedic commentaries or riffs on typically subpar older movies. The host, Joel or Mike, along with his four robot friends, also acted out skits during breaks in the movie known as host segments, creating a 90-minute episode. Ten years since the show's cancellation from the Sci-Fi Channel (renamed to SyFy in 2009), *MST*'s third home, the popularity of the show has continued to thrive through periodic DVD box set releases. Of four robots, Gypsy was the one female robot, controlled all the higher functions (life support systems, piloting, etc.) of the Satellite of Love (SOL), the space ship where the host and the robots lived. As the only consistent feminine presence throughout the show's life — the villainous Pearl was a later addition — Gypsy's representation of "woman" is problematic. She appeared to confirm feminine stereotypes typically found in mass media, but did Gypsy also challenge these tropes? To date, there has been little study completed on Gypsy's character in the field of cultural studies. To fill this gap, this study will explore the entire host segments commercially released in DVD box sets (currently seventeen volumes) and single DVD issues (eleven), a total of 77 episodes spanning the show's national broadcast period (1989–1999). Utilizing a textual/semiotic approach in conjunction with statistical figures, the data — host segments — will be compared and contrasted in two ways: (1) the impact of the host, Joel (1988–1993) or Mike (1993–1999); and (2) the impact of the show's broadcast station, Comedy Channel/Comedy Central (1989–1996) to Sci-Fi Channel (1997–1999). The channel comparison is of particular interest because while *MST* was shown on the Sci-Fi Channel, the show's creative was tasked with creating an overarching continuity to the host segments. This analysis will result in a comprehensive study of the complex yet probable role of Gypsy on the show as a nurturer (mother-type), which is stereotypical of women's roles in television.

History and Era Statistics for Commercially Released Episodes of MST on DVD

MST started broadcasting nationally in 1989 with the newly formed cable station, The Comedy Channel, and is considered "season one" although *MST* was broadcast on the local public access channel KTMA from Minneapolis/St. Paul the year before, from November 1988. The show had a successful run for seven seasons, until being cancelled because of the channel's shift in programming direction. A contract was secured with Sci-Fi Channel and from 1997 through 1999, *MST* was broadcast for seasons eight through ten. At The Comedy Channel, thirteen episodes were aired for each of the first two seasons and then, for seasons three through six, MST aired 24 episodes each season, with only seven episodes for season seven. A total of 129 episodes aired and at time of writing, there were 57 episodes available on DVD, or 44 percent of The Comedy Channel represented. During the Sci-Fi Channel era, MST aired 22 episodes in season eight and only 13 episodes each for seasons nine and ten. A total of 48 episodes aired at Sci-Fi Channel and of those, 20 episodes are represented with DVD releases, or 42 percent episodes available.

While being split by broadcast channel eras, *MST* was also split by hosting duties. Joel Hodgson, the brainchild behind the series, played Joel Robinson from 1988 through 1993, and then head writer, Michael J. Nelson, played Mike Nelson from 1993 through 1999. Joel completed 129 episodes, all with The Comedy Channel, and of those, 57 or 44 percent were available, while Mike completed 92 episodes, split between The Comedy Channel and all of the Sci-Fi seasons, and of those, 40 or 42 percent were available. The result is that between broadcast station eras and host eras, the representation is almost equal. However, comparing broadcast stations and host eras by the number of host segments per episode, then broken down by the appearance of each robot per segment, a different picture emerges.

There were four robots on the show: Tom Servo, Crow T. (The) Robot, Gypsy, and Cambot. Cambot was the "eye" by which the viewer watched the show unfold and was only shown in the "Robot Roll Call" and for statistical purposes was counted as having "appeared" in the segment if the host and/or any of the other robots cued Cambot. For the other robots, they had to physically appear on screen at some point during the segment in order to count as an appearance. The number of segments per episode was standardized to five, based on the early structure noted in *The Mystery Science Theater 3000 Amazing Colossal Episode Guide* (1996) as follows: from season one through five, the prologue and invention exchange were counted as one segment and then there were four additional segments, and from season six through ten, the prologue was tacked onto segment one and then there were four additional segments. With those perimeters in mind, there was a total of 385 host segments (77 episodes times 5 segments), 285 at The Comedy Channel and 100 at the Sci-Fi Channel. All segments taken together garnered the following statistics: Tom and Crow appeared 371 times or 96 percent of the time in comparison to Gypsy who appeared 110 times or 29 percent of the time and Cambot with 61 references for 16 percent representation.

During The Comedy Channel era, Tom appeared 275 times representing 96 percent of the segments, Crow 276 times representing 97 percent, Gypsy 100 times for 35 percent, and Cambot 57 times for 20 percent of the 285 segments. Alternatively, during the Sci-Fi Channel era, Tom appeared 96 times representing again 96 percent of the segments, Crow 95 times for 95 percent, Gypsy 10 times for 10 percent, and Cambot 4 times for 4 percent of the 100 segments. So, Gypsy was represented 25 percent more of the time during The Comedy Channel era than with the Sci-Fi Channel.

When comparing robot appearance by host, both hosts are almost equally represented between Joel and Mike with 190 and 195 segments respectively. During Joel's era, Tom and Crow appeared 182 times each for 96 percent, Gypsy 62 times for 33 percent, and Cambot 39 times for 21 percent representation. In comparison, during Mike's era, again Tom and Crow were equally represented with 189 appearances for 97 percent, Gypsy 48 times for 25 percent, and Cambot 22 times for 11 percent of the total segments. Hence, Gypsy found 8 percent more representation with Joel, than with Mike, when comparing host segment representation. What does all these numbers mean? Initially, the figures show that Gypsy, as the consistent feminine presence on the show was limited to begin with and declined between both the broadcast and the host eras. What follows is a textual analysis to give flesh to the figures and provide a fuller picture of Gypsy as "woman" on *MST*.

Robot Roll Call

According to the show's theme song during Joel's hosting era, Joel Robinson, a janitor at Gizmonics Institute, was shot into space to the Satellite of Love by the evil Dr. Clayton Forrester and his assistant, Dr. Larry Erhardt (known as The Mads), in order to conduct an experiment to identify the movie that creates the most depressing, disheartening response in Joel. To have companionship, Joel built four robots from a variety of parts on the SOL, a homage to Bruce Dern's cult movie *Silent Running* (1972) where Dern's character had robots to keep him company, but also served to complete tasks assigned by Dern. Tom Servo, a stocky red 'bot with a clear gumball head, and lanky, golden boy, Crow T. Robot, accompany and engage in riffing movies alongside Joel in the theater, as well as participate in the majority of host segments with Joel and later Mike. Cambot serves as the eye for the viewer and the scientists: as the camera eye, glimpses of Cambot are rare throughout the series. Typically the host or the bots requested Cambot to cue a particular camera on SOL to see outside the satellite or to help with lighting or music for skits during the host segments, or to record their activities. (The roll call line up implies that Cambot was created by Joel, but the brief description in *The Mystery Science Theater Amazing Colossal Episode Guide*, makes it ambiguous as to Cambot's origins). Gypsy, with a long, black tubing apparatus supporting a large purple head with contoured light blue foam lips and a single eye, was tasked with running many of the higher functions of SOL and hence, did not participate in the movie riffing and was sometimes a participant in the host segments. In the final segment of *Mad Monster* (Mallon, 1989, Episode 103), Joel explains that Gypsy was created as a peripheral character to be responsible for the important functions of the ship so that Tom and Crow could focus on and work out their free will issues. Gypsy rounds out the robot roll call.

Voiced and handled by J. Elvis Weinstein during the very first year at KTMA, Gypsy was portrayed as a masculine robot in at least the pilot episode, however when *MST* went national in season one, Jim Mallon took over the voicing and handling of Gypsy and the change in handing marked the change in gender of Gypsy from male to female. Mallon would relinquish duties to Patrick Brantseg during mid eighth season and Patrick finished with the series in 1999. With the gender switching, Gypsy became the only "female" on SOL as well as the only consistent on-screen "feminine" presence throughout the *MST* series (Mrs. Forrester moved in with Dr. Forrester in season seven and replaced him in season eight). Starting out as a skeletal head frame with a single eye on the head, Gypsy's head was replaced with a Century baby seat turned upside down and painted purple, the lower jaw with the inner lining from the baby seat, foam tubing for her lips, an Eveready flashlight as her eye and some sort of clear small plastic tubing dangled from the back of her head during the first nationally broadcast season. Her body was made of black tubing and lots of it, as revealed in the third host segment of *The Crawling Eye* (Mallon, 1989, Episode 101) when Gypsy develops a diode rash on a section of her body's vertebrae. In that segment, Tom asks Joel why her body is so long and Joel responds that he got caught up in connecting the tubing together, similar to addicting paper clip rope. By second season, the tubing was gone and her eye had taken on an amber-red glow, similar to HAL 9000 from Stanley Kubrick's seminal *2001: A Space Odyssey* (1968), a movie that the creative force of *MST* would reference a number of times in relation to Gypsy.

Given that Gypsy was probably the most intelligent robot on SOL, it seems odd that it was so difficult to understand Gypsy's dialogue, especially early on in the series. During the opening segment of *Wild Rebels* (Mallon, 1990, Episode 207), Joel comforts a moaning Gypsy. Joel relates that because Gypsy is responsible for running and maintaining so many of the higher functions on SOL, her speech abilities suffer and hence her garbled, mumbling speech, usually limiting her to short phrases that tend to include single syllable words. When Joel shuts down some of her higher functions, a commercial break disrupts the segment and the viewers only catch the tail end of Joel and Gypsy's conversation. Her dictation is greatly improved — coherent and intelligent sounding. Gypsy belittles and attributes her depression to being just one of those days. She thanks Joel for listening since she knows that Joel is very busy. She marks and does a short countdown until she reinitiates the functions, including the flow of oxygen, since Joel is about to pass out from lack of oxygen. When the systems come back online, Gypsy blurts out the name "Richard Basehart," the star that played Admiral Nelson on the sixties series *Voyage to the Bottom of the Sea*, the man who she adores, although the reason for her admiration is never really explained.

Boy, Girl, Woman: Finding Gypsy

Gypsy is a problematic feminine presence on *MST* for a number of reasons. Her beginnings as a boy or male robot coupled with her nondescript body shape the majority of time — none of the bots wear clothing except during certain skits — and her masculine grunts and handling by men, often left the viewers confused as to what Gypsy was. For instance, Joel reads a viewer's letter in the closing segment of *The Crawling Hand* (Mallon, 1989, Episode 106), in which Gypsy is referred to as a "him." Joel corrects the writer by reminding viewers that Gypsy is a "her." And in the closing segment of *The Sidehackers* (Mallon, 1990, Episode 202), Joel shares a viewer's letter in which the writer requests a non-gendered robot be added to the line and includes a rendering of what the proposed "it" robot should look like. Joel responds that the viewer's proposed robot looks very similar to Gypsy. Apparently, Gypsy as the "token female" seemed to be falling short of the femininity presence in the first season of *MST*.

Midway through the second season, Gypsy's first costumed appearance in the third segment of *Ring of Terror* (Mallon, 1990, Episode 206), portrayed her as a nurse complete with the white nurse's cap, dress, and long eyelashes applied above her eye. However, it was in *The Wild Rebels* (Mallon, 1990, Episode 207) that Gypsy got a lot of screen time, in three of the five episode's host segments. Michael J. Nelson reflected on Gypsy's role up until that point: "The revelation about Gypsy's character was a conscious effort on our part to expand her function on the show. Weighing on our minds was the fact that we had one female character and she was a dim-witted, cowlike creature played by a man" (Beaulieu, Chaplin, et al., 1996: 26). It seemed to be a turning point to add depth to Gypsy's character. Not an easy feat since Gypsy was not part of the riffing crew in the theater and only so much time during the host segments to fill with skits, reflections of the episode being riffed, letter reading activities, interactions between SoL's crew and the Deep 13, and the Mads themselves.

Even with a female role was included during a segment, in the tradition of early theater, Crow or more often Tom, due to his hover apparatus looking like a skirt, would don female clothing and complete a skit, therefore leaving Gypsy unseen. For the skits in which Gypsy did appear in costume, she wore formal dresses, feminine uniforms (most often as a nurse), dangly earrings, flower accents, blonde wigs, red foam lips, and on a couple of occasions, she had breasts.

While costuming helped engender Gypsy as female as the series progressed, Joel's relationship with Gypsy as a father figure, greatly influenced Gypsy's evolving feminine presence, particularly beginning with season two. As mentioned before, *Wild Rebels* (Mallon, 1990, Episode 207) was pivotal for Gypsy development, but it also showed just how much Joel cared for her as a surrogate daughter and his protectiveness towards her and her feelings. In segment one of this episode, after their heart-to-heart conversation, Joel gives Gypsy a fatherly hug and tells her how much appreciates their talk as being "warm and wonderful." In segment three, Joel tells Gypsy that they are alike and that sometimes they need to let off steam. Joel tells her he considers her his mistral and breaks out in a song to which she croons in response and says that she feels special from the attention that Joel gives her, especially given in the open sequence, viewers find out that she is most likely depressed by her affections for Richard Basehart. As her fatherly figure, Joel is always there for her, giving her a supportive hug when she sings out of tune to everyone else as in *The Sidehackers* (Mallon, 1990, Episode 202), caresses her when she cannot answer simple questions as in *Mad Monster* (Mallon, 1989, Episode 103), and refers to her with pet names such as "pumpkin" as in *Wild Rebels* (Mallon, 1990, Episode 207).

Joel, as host, solidified Gypsy's position on the show, but midway through season five, Gypsy, in a humorous nod to when HAL 9000 read the lips of Drs. Dave Bowman and Frank Poole, sent Joel back to Earth to save him after listening in on a Mads conversation to terminate who she believes they are referring to Joel when in actuality, they were discussing temp worker Mike. Without Joel, a new host, the temp worker Mike (and longtime head writer for the show) joined the SOL crew. The change in hosts did not appear to shift the dynamics of the group. In fact Gypsy appeared in all the host segments of *The Wild World of Batwoman* (Mallon, 1993, Episode 515) when Mike has to referee the ramifications of cheating that emerges when Crow plagiarizes verbatim Gypsy's essay. However, it is in opening segment of *The Creeping Terror* (Mallon, 1994, Episode 606), that viewers get to see Gypsy's intellectual maturity as she speaks out poetically against the oppression by white men in a coffeehouse skit. Gypsy's outburst surprises her and has the avid support of Crow. However, when Mike conveys his remiss with the Mads for creating poseurs of the bots (the Mads had sent up the coffeehouse props to the SOL crew), Gypsy admonishes him by stating "a white, male, middle-class power holder would say that Mike" (Mallon, 1994, Episode 606). It was a moment that would have rivaled Helen Reddy's "I am woman, hear me roar" lyrics that is readily defined with the early seventies feminist moment. It may be one of Gypsy's defining moments as a woman.

The statistical data also supports Gypsy's emerging presence in season two through season six. Discounting season three for only 17 percent episode availability (4 out of 24), and season seven for a lack of sufficient number of episodes (only 7 episodes aired that season for which 3 are available on DVD), Gypsy had a strong appearance ratio — season two 23 percent; season four, 45 percent, season five, 34 percent; and season six, 38 percent — in comparison to the first season, in which she appeared only 17 percent of the time. When *MST* was aired on Sci-Fi Channel, Mrs. Forrester was introduced to replace Dr. Forrester, who had become a cosmic baby at the end of season seven. Gypsy's appearance on the show declined to 9 percent in season eight, 0 percent in season nine, and finished off at a dismal 16 percent in the final season. The overall decline of Gypsy could have been the result of two decisive decisions: Mrs. Forrester as an evil woman bent on world domination (now we know where Dr. Forrester got his ambitious aspirations) presented the show with a new feminine presence on the show, and Sci-Fi Channel's mandate to *MST* creators to write in an overarching story to tie the host segments together from one episode to the next. Mrs. Forrester was a particularly strong female character and the story possibilities, along with her cronies Dr. Bobo and Brain Guy, presented new opportunities. The growth of Gypsy was stunted and her relegation to a peripheral character, similar to Cambot was imminent.

In Closing, Ram Chips

We have only scratched the surface of Gypsy's complexity as the consistent feminine presence throughout the *MST* series. As the only female on the series, until the permanent story inclusion of Mrs. Forrester, Gypsy was portrayed as a nurturer of life to the others on SOL because of her responsibilities for running many of the crucial higher functions that kept the SOL operational. Her sacrifice for the others — truly the loss of her ability to speak coherently and access her superior intelligence — is made apparent to the other bots and the viewers in season two. As Joel's creation, Gypsy fills the role of daughter, often emphasized by the gentle and caring support that Joel conveys to her during his hosting era. And while her sex was initially questioned at the beginning of the series, the various feminine and gender-defining costumes that adorned the Twiggy-esque frame of Gypsy removed doubt from the viewer's mind, as did her flirtation with feminism in season sex. While the introduction of Mrs. Forrester provided the MST writers new storyline opportunities as well as confirming to Sci-Fi Channel's mandate for the presence of an overarching storyline, Gypsy's character growth suffered. With more commercial releases forthcoming, this is not the end of Gypsy's story — it is really the beginning.

REFERENCES

Beaulieu, Trace, Paul Chaplin, Jim Mallon, Kevin Murphy, Michael J. Nelson, and Mary Jo Pehl. *The Mystery Science Theater 3000 Amazing Colossal Episode Guide*. New York: Bantam Books, 1996.
Mallon, Jim (director), Michael J. Nelson (writer), Trace Beaulieu (writer), et al. Episode 101 *The Crawling Eye* 1989.
Mallon, Jim (director), Michael J. Nelson (writer), Trace Beaulieu (writer), et al. Episode 103 *Mad Monster* 1989.
Mallon, Jim (director), Michael J. Nelson (writer), Trace Beaulieu (writer), et al. Episode 106 *The Crawling Hand* 1989.
Mallon, Jim (director), Michael J. Nelson (writer), Trace Beaulieu (writer), et al. Episode 202 *The Sidehackers* 1990.
Mallon, Jim (director), Michael J. Nelson (writer), Trace Beaulieu (writer), et al. Episode 206 *Ring of Terror* 1990.
Mallon, Jim (director), Michael J. Nelson (writer), Trace Beaulieu (writer), et al. Episode 207 *Wild Rebels* 1990.
Mallon, Jim (director), Michael J. Nelson (writer), Trace Beaulieu (writer), et al. Episode 515 *The Wild World of Batwoman* 1993.
Mallon, Jim (director), Michael J. Nelson (writer), Trace Beaulieu (writer), et al. Episode 606 *The Creeping Terror* 1994.

19

What's the Difference?
Satire and Separation in
That "Little Puppet Show"

by Alana Hatley

Introduction

"Satire" is a word that is used to describe a wide range of humor, including everything from *The Colbert Report* to *Space Balls*, with *Mystery Science Theater 3000* falling somewhere in the middle. Critical study of satire will probably lead many to eliminate *Space Balls* from the satire category, citing it instead as a parody, since *Space Balls* pays homage to *Star Wars* rather than suggesting the film's "correction." But how exactly can scholars and critics distinguish between the motives, purposes, and effects of *The Colbert Report*, in which the satirist himself enacts an exaggerated version of the satirical target, and those of *MST3K*, in which the satirist seems to sit apart from the target and ridicule it from a distance? Are these approaches actually so different? How are they related to 18th-century satire, called the "Golden Age" of satire, which critics have tended to focus on when examining satiric traits and motives? The traditional understanding of satire is not sufficient to allow us to answer these questions, so our first task will be an attempt to begin redefining satire.

The discussion of *MST3K*'s satire is further muddied by the difficulty of pinning down which aspects of the show are satirical. There is a vast difference between the humor of the "riff" segments and that of the "host" segments. At first glance it would seem that the riffs are more satirical than the host segments, since they are directly mocking the target: bad films. However, "pure" satire is generally structured in such a way that the speaker embodies the target, as the speaker of "A Modest Proposal" embodies those who "feed" off the Irish poor, or as Stephen Colbert's character on *The Colbert Report* embodies extreme conservatism. This is very different from a speaker who simply makes fun of the target. A closer analysis will show that the host segments are actually the satirical foundation of *MST3K*, which allows the riffs to work. In order to judge the effectiveness of the particular satire created in *MST3K*, though, we must be able to determine that there exists a difference between the satirist and the target; without such a difference, satire cannot exist. (Note: Since the particular qualities of *MST3K* here discussed remain consistent between the show's various writers, the show itself will be considered the satirist for the sake of expediency).

Redefining Satire

As a starting point for rethinking the nature of satire, I looked up glossary definitions of the word that are given on the websites of some of the leading literature textbook publishers, since textbook glossaries tend to demonstrate concepts that are well-established or "traditional." The poetic glossary on McGraw-Hill's website offers this definition of satire: "a literary work that criticizes human misconduct and ridicules vices, stupidities, and follies." This doesn't really tell us much; according to this understanding, Jeff Foxworthy is in the same category as Alexander Pope. The definition provided on Bedford/St. Martin's *Meyer Literature Site* gives us a bit more to work with by adding a motivation, and succinctly covers the traditional understanding of satire: "the literary art of ridiculing a folly or vice in order to expose or correct it." However, along with the previous one, this definition needs an update; any definition that still uses words like "folly" and "vice" to convey its major concepts is about a hundred years too old for our purposes. I therefore turn to Norton, to see what they have come up with. *The Norton Introduction to Literature Website* defines satire as "a literary work that holds up human failings to ridicule and censure." Here, although the diction has been updated, the assumption remains that satire is created when the satirist recognizes some repellent Other and chooses ridicule as the means of correcting the Other's "failing." This view of the satiric impulse paints a picture of authors of satire as morally self-righteous, angry, or bitter egotists whose only motivation is the desire to rant about other people and perhaps to correct them. At the very least, this view of the satire implies that the satirist must hold a strict distinction between good, equated with him- or herself, and bad, equated with the Other who is being targeted.

While many critics in the past have done in-depth analyses of satire and have created more complex versions of this kind of definition, for many years the basic idea that satire seeks to ridicule and correct some repellent Other has been the standard. The reason for the static definition is most likely the fact that critique of satire as a literary genre has primarily focused on 18th-century authors like Alexander Pope. When focusing on this time period, the traditional definition makes sense because Pope and his contemporaries do seem to deride some Other in order to correct that Other's deviation from the norm, or from what ought to be the norm. However, while the 18th century is still often referred to as the "Golden Age" of satire, our own time period is seeing a proliferation of satiric works, like *MST3K*. To attempt to understand these works without a theory of satire that considers our postmodern, poststructuralist creative atmosphere is to hinder the progress of criticism. Fortunately, some critics have already begun the process of moving toward a new understanding of satire.

Redefining Satire: Part II

In working toward a theory of satire in the postmodern world, it quickly becomes apparent that the old definitions simply will not work. When critics try to use them, the result can easily be a conclusion that does not seem to be well-founded. For instance, Earl B. Brown, Jr., decides that satire has become impossible. He believes this conclusion is necessary because he recognizes that postmodern authors no longer feel comfortable drawing strict lines between good and bad; deviation from the norm is no longer clear because the division between self and Other is no longer clear. This is a common theme in postmodern works, and since Brown accepts that satire is defined by absolute distinctions between good and bad, self and Other, he concludes that satire can no longer be achieved (Brown 1980: 87). The problem with his conclusion is that we can look around and see all kinds of postmodern satire being created and recognized as such. The answer to Brown's categorization conundrum is not to do away with the satire category, but to rethink it. A new perspective will help us understand not only postmodern satire like *MST3K*, but all satire.

Kathryn Hume sees a particular kind of satire being written in the twentieth century. She terms it "diffused satire," because it does not have an Other as a specific target, and does not necessarily seek to correct. She considers this kind of satire to be "more essentially ambiguous than the traditional kinds of satire found at the hot center of the mode" (Hume 2007: 325). While stating that satire is not only still possible but is currently very active, this theory of a new kind of satire continues to assume that "traditional kinds of satire" do in fact target the Other and unambiguously seek to correct it through denunciation and judgment. It does not consider the kind of satire that we find in *MST3K*: the sharp-edged, biting critique that does have a specific target but that does not seek to "correct" it and does not seem to be very different from it on the surface.

Frederic V. Bogel puts forth a theory that that goes further than any of these in its attempt to rethink the motivations and purposes of satire. Not only does he challenge the assumption that *contemporary* satirists must utilize a strict distinction between good (self) and bad (Other), he challenges the assumption that *any* satirists must necessarily hold a clearly defined view of good and bad. He therefore reexamines 18th-century satire while keeping in mind the possibility that the writing process was a way of creating distance between themselves and their satiric objects, rather than an expression of a preexisting difference (Bogel 2001). By this he means that the impulse to satirize a particular target is motivated by the desire to say, "I am not like them; I differ," rather than "They are bad and should be corrected." This sheds light on *MST3K*'s satire by allowing us to discuss it as a way of creating recognizable difference, rather than a tool for correction.

Reconciling the Hosts and the Riffs

But if the satire within *MST3K* is motivated by the desire to establish difference between itself and its target, doesn't that mean that the satire is located within the riff segments? After all, those segments are the ones that attempt to directly show how "bad" the target films are, thereby implying their contrast with the satirist. While this is true, simply making fun of something does not in and of itself constitute satire. For satire to exist, the satirist must be sufficiently *like* the target to be in a position to judge it. For instance, if an English professor makes fun of Siberian peasants, we would not call it satire; we would probably simply call it mean. But if an English professor makes fun of *English professors*, especially those who are poor English professors, then such humor has the basic characteristics intrinsic to a satirization. If the English professor also pretends to *be* the type of poor English professor he or she is targeting, then the categorization of the humor as satire is certain.

Consider that paragon of satire, "A Modest Proposal," in which the speaker is a genteel cannibal, bent on feeding off of his own people even while treating such behavior as helpful and community-minded. Obviously, Swift is targeting absentee landlords and others who take advantage of the Irish poor, or "feed" off them. But in order to satirize the target, Swift must *become* the target, and in this case the speaker of the essay occupies the position between these two opposing viewpoints — that is, Swift on the one hand and his target on the other. By occupying the space between Swift and his target, the speaker performs the dual function of seeming like the target while simultaneously ridiculing the target. This would not be feasible if Swift himself was not also very much like his target in most regards.

Because of all this, the host segments of *MST3K* are necessary, and necessarily cheap and cheesy. The riffs constitute the primary vehicle of opinion and humor in the show, but they are not well-suited to establishing the likeness that gives any satirist the ability and the right to create satire. In order for them to work, there must be some other aspect of the show that sufficiently demonstrates this likeness. The host segments perform precisely this function.

What's the Difference?

Of course, Swift was not entirely like his target; unlike those he wished to correct, he believed that the Irish poor could and should be cared for. The satirist must be sufficiently like the target to gain the ability and right to satirize it, but must also establish difference in a crucial area. So what is the crucial area of difference that separates *MST3K* from its bad movies? The show focuses the bulk of its attack on the poor quality of the acting, dialogue, character development, storyline, and effects, all of which can be caused or at least made worse by the low budgeting of nearly all the movies featured on the show. Here's the kicker though: *MST3K* is itself guilty of all of those things. The low-budget origins of the show meant that the host segments necessarily utilized cheap sci-fi effects and non-professional actors, and the writing of them — well, let's be honest. None of us fans watch this show for the creative storyline or witty dialogue of the host segments, although they are often both creative and witty. The riffs are the reason we watch; the riffing is what spawned its own culture.

However, the riffs are so clever that it almost seems out of place for the writing of the host segments to be so cheesy. Further, budgeting became much less of an issue as the show became more popular, but the "cheapness" of *MST3K*'s early days was deliberately maintained. As stated earlier, this is because cheap and cheesy are necessary for the show to establish its likeness to its targets. Because of all this, the difference established by the riff does not reside in the particular faults of the targeted movies, but in the *awareness* that they are faults. If *MST3K* were simply a show about some guy trapped in space with robots, the host segments could validly be called low quality or "bad" film. However, since the show is a satire of bad film, and since it is necessary for it to establish a likeness with bad film before it can establish a difference, the host segments must therefore be called good art. It's good art because its various writers have recognized that it must appear "bad," and each of the writers has maintained that standard.

Conclusion

Although low budgeting can be an obstacle for a filmmaker or screenwriter, good artists can create good art anyway. The mark of a good artist is that he or she can create something of quality with whatever medium or material is around to be used. If you don't have the money normally required to make a good space movie, then you must either find a new and creative way to achieve the effect you're after or make a different kind of movie. If you can't afford to hire quality actors, then you do something different like animation — or puppets. In fact, narrow budgeting can be an opportunity to innovate because it is a constraint, and just as meter constrains the poet, narrow budgeting causes the artist to think around corners and find new approaches. *MST3K* does not criticize movies for being low-budget; it criticizes movie-makers for their lack of recognition of what constitutes a good movie. By so doing, the show makes a powerful statement about what does constitute a good movie, and it has nothing to do with money. It is this awareness of film as art and of the qualities that make good art that gives *MST3K* the ability, and the right, to satirize others in its field. The rhetorical statement made by this satirization is not an attempt to "correct" these low quality movies, but to situate *MST3K* in relation to them: we make cinematic art just like you, and we have very little money just like you, but we are different from you in that we produce quality anyway.

REFERENCES

Bogel, Frederic V. *The Difference Satire Makes: Rhetoric and Reading from Jonson to Byron.* Ithaca: Cornell University Press, 2001.
Brown, Earl B., Jr. "Kosinski's Modern Proposal: The Problem of Satire in the Mid-Twentieth Century." *Critique: Studies in Modern Fiction* 22.2 (1980): 83–87.
"Glossary." *LitWeb: The Norton Introduction to Literature Website* 2005. Accessed 3/13/10. http://www.ww norton.com/college/english/litweb05/glossary/welcome.htm.
"Glossary of Literary Terms." *The Meyer Literature Site: Bedford/St. Martin's.* Accessed 3/13/10. http://www. bedfordstmartins.com/literature/bedlit/glossary_p.htm.
"Glossary of Poetic Terms." McGraw-Hill Online Learning Center 2002. Accessed 3/13/10. http://high-ered.mcgraw-hill.com/sites/0072405228/student_view0/poetic_glossary.html.
Hume, Kathryn. "Diffused Satire in Contemporary American Fiction." *Modern Philology: Critical and Historical Studies in Literature, Medieval Through Contemporary* 105.2 (2007): 300–25.

PART SEVEN

Technology and Episode Collecting

20

The Design and Speculative Technology of *MST3K*: Joel Hodgson and Trace Beaulieu at MIT

by Jason Begy and Generoso Fierro

On January 17, 2009, Joel Hodgson and Trace Beaulieu came to the Massachusetts Institute of Technology to discuss their time on *Mystery Science Theater 3000* and the recently-formed Cinematic Titanic. They were interviewed onstage by Jason Begy and Generoso Fierro of the Comparative Media Studies department. The following is a transcript of the interview.

GENEROSO: Comparative Media Studies at MIT is very proud to present Joel Hodgson and Trace Bealieu.

TRACE: There will be a test!

GENEROSO: Thank you for coming, very much. This is all very last minute, and you flew out this morning and we've been tormenting you for the last five hours, but you're here, and everyone else is here, so again, on behalf of myself, MIT Comparative Media Studies, thanks again.

JOEL: Are you going to pray now? It sounds like you're going to pray.

GENEROSO: … No!

JOEL: What should we do?

GENEROSO: I think we should talk, maybe I can ask you questions about what you've done. You had something you wanted to ask them, didn't you Jason?

JASON: I had a couple things. Well first of all, we were wondering how you guys met originally.

TRACE: This is the first time actually. Hi. (shakes Joel's hand)

JOEL: Hi. Well, we all started in the Minneapolis comedy scene in the 80's. I knew Trace just peripherally; I would see him on stage occasionally but we hadn't really met. Eventually we both ended up in a writing group for comics that was meeting at the library. This could only happen in Minneapolis, a bunch of comics, who are usually very cynical people who don't hang out together, but in Minneapolis they do. We're really grateful for that. So we met there. Josh Weinstein was in it as well.

So we were in this writing group and it was about time to do *Mystery Science Theater*. I had built the robots and the sets, and we were about to shoot the pilot. I had just met

Trace and really liked him, I thought he was funny so I invited him to come to the first day. And I had known Josh, so I invited him too. Trace grabbed Crow and Josh grabbed what was to become Tom Servo.

GENEROSO: And everything was basically built by the time they got there? What was the initial set like, for example?

JOEL: Well we wanted to talk today about some of the ideas behind *Mystery Science Theater*. I don't know if you know this, but we kind of based it on *Silent Running*, which was this very weird movie with Bruce Dern. He played a guy in space running from, I don't know, the people that wanted to destroy his spaceship. And he had three robots, Huey, Dewey, and Louis. So can we just show a little of that trailer? If you've never seen it, it's actually a slow moving movie, but it's interesting science fiction. [plays a brief clip from the trailer] So anyway, I just wanted to show that because we got the idea for the geodesic domes that the Satellite of Love was built out of from those spaceships in the movie.

GENEROSO: We could have seen them if you'd let the trailer run longer!

TRACE: Check it out from your local video store.

JOEL: And so that was kind of the premise. And we could show the pilot...

TRACE: Yeah show a little bit of that.

JOEL: You can see I'm trying to look a little bit like Bruce Dern with the jumpsuit.

TRACE: It's a frightening copy. It's an amazing rip-off.

JOEL: It is really, truly fantastic. [waiting for the pilot to start] Ok that's good! Now this is really the proof-of-concept to show to KTMA what we were talking about. So we don't really riff on movies but it's setting up the world of the show, and the robots. We just kind of pieced it together. [watching pilot] So it just goes on like that.

TRACE: For two hours!

GENEROSO: What is up with the doorway sequence? Why is that there? What was the motivation behind it?

JOEL: In the early Mickey Mouse club, the black and white one, they had a safe where the cartoons were kept. You had to go to the safe and open it, and I always liked that, that the video existed somewhere. There's kind of a disconnect when people introduce a movie and it just starts, like, where or what is it, why? So the idea that you have to go to the movie was just a simple idea. There was also the premise that there was a ball of air that stayed around Joel wherever he was on the ship, so supposedly there was a column of air going all the way down to the theater and coming all the way back. That was how the Mads [mad scientists] made me go to the theater, otherwise why would I go. Right?

GENEROSO: Makes sense.

JOEL: So anyway, I wanted to say that this shows just really the very beginnings of it. My idea was only how radical it would be to have theater seats and a couple of pilots and a guy watching a movie with you, and not the six hundred jokes per show that it became. That had a lot to do with Trace and Josh. We did 22 shows locally at KTMA, and as time went on they started to say "hey, we can put more and more jokes into it."

TRACE: As you watch the trailer, you're kind of screaming for something to be said about those space ships. You knew where those spaces were, and we know where they were, and over time it was just desperation to fill the time and to entertain ourselves, really. Because we truly were trapped in this crappy television station, sitting a foot off a green screen wall, with very little feedback. We'd occasionally hear someone laughing in the control room but they didn't want to wreck the take. It was a perfect metaphor for the spaceship.

JASON: Can you tell us about the sale to KTMA? Was this what convinced them to pick up the program?

JOEL: Well here's basically how it happened. I used to make robots out of found objects. I made like a hundred of them locally in Minneapolis and sold them through a store called Props. While I was doing that I was in a warehouse space, and Jim Mallon was editing a movie called *Blood Hook*. So that's where I met him. And it wasn't until well after that that he approached me. He was at KTMA, and he was production manager, or general manager, or something.

TRACE: Something like that.

JOEL: And he wanted to do a standup comedy special. He thought it would be good to do like a gong show with standup comics. He knew I had done standup, but I had just gotten done doing standup for three years and I thought it was kind of a pedestrian idea. So I said, "here's the guy you want to talk to, and I can make like a trophy or something but I don't really want to get involved." Then when I got home, I thought "oh wait a minute, here's a guy in Minneapolis who wants to make TV." I had had this idea for a show called "You Are Here," which was kind of based on a scene in *The Omega Man* with Charlton Heston. It's like a zombie movie; it's the end of the world but he can come out during the day. He's watching a movie about Woodstock and he's alone saying "look at all the people, oh my god that was so great." So my original idea was to base it on that scene: it was the end of the world and I was watching a movie with a robot, but it was just too bleak for a comedy show.

So I transposed that idea onto *Silent Running*, and I knew how to make robots so I brought that to Jim Mallon and he really liked it. He basically said "yeah we could do this," and I mentioned that I knew there were these public domain movies we could use, but he said we could use the movies that were at KTMA. That was how it got going. The pilot was to demonstrate to the boss ... do you remember his name?

TRACE: I don't ... the boss of KTMA?

JOEL: The boss of KTMA. I think it was to demonstrate to him what the show would be like and to try get all the elements together. And for ourselves, just to see it. The other thing that this demonstrates is that Beeper became Tom Servo. We could just tell right off the bat that this robot was awful. It really was a simple as me going home, popping the head off, looking around, grabbing a gumball machine. It was already rigged up with a string, so I just ran a thread down. It moved and was animated, so that really became Tom Servo.

If you watch the KTMA shows on YouTube you can see Josh creating who Tom Servo is, because I didn't really know. He was just Servo, and Josh gave him the moniker Tom because he was kind of like an FM DJ. So over the course of KTMA Tom Servo emerges.

GENEROSO: Where did Dr. Forrester come from?

JOEL: That came from the theme song. Jim Mallon showed a friend of his the tape, and this guy goes, "this needs a theme song." And you look at it and you just go "oh it's so laborious, all the exposition, 'I'm Joel Robinson, I built this ship, these are my robots,' it's awful."

And I couldn't have gotten to that, I just didn't think that way. But once it was suggested I thought "oh yeah now we can do that, now we know what this is so it's easy to arrange it." So we wrote "his bosses didn't like him and they shot him into space" and then...

TRACE: And I was already there doing a puppet, and they said "ok stand over here." We had absolutely no budget at KTMA for this, so when you see the Mad Scientists, the art direction is "the clothes we came in with." I think eventually we got lab coats. You can see us reading our scripts because we had no time to rehearse.

And there was a lot of pressure when we were doing the Mad Scientists in those days because we did them right before lunch. It was like all of you [gesturing towards the audience] are getting your keys, and jingling them, getting your coats on going "c'mon, we're going to miss Denny's!" So that was our motivation.

I came in one day, and they said "oh now we have this theme song that explains the whole thing," and we lip-synched to it. You can see it in those early KTMA's, I'm way out of synch because I couldn't even hear the music, I didn't know what was going on. I'm going "what? I'm a mad scientist now?" I don't know.

JOEL: We also figured out that the premise is going to be much more effective if Joel is being made to watch these movies against his will. So the story emerged and for that to happen, these guys are the ones who made it happen.

Josh and I wrote the lyrics to the theme song and that exercise helped us understand how to put it all together. I'm not exactly a storyteller. I think it seems fairly obvious to people, how to get to that point, but I think we wanted to just get everything up and running visually and then make it make sense. Fortunately we had time and resources to do it. It just wouldn't have happened if Jim Mallon was not at KTMA and he somehow was able to swing us getting in there and shooting these elements to make it happen.

And then we were able to start doing it in Minneapolis, and people in Minneapolis are so great they loved what we were doing and were really encouraging. So really *Mystery Science Theater* was created from that day until our last show on KTMA where we really figured out how to riff on movies, what that was, what the story was, and yeah.

JASON: So you can tell us about the Satellite of Love, and you came up with its shape? I'm sure more than one person has noticed its resemblance to a dog bone.

TRACE: The dog bone shape, there's a picture here [looking for something on the laptop connected to the projector] ... click on that ... click ... click ... and then uh ... let's see ... demon dog ... go back up ... ahh, that one.

GENEROSO: I went to school and everything!

TRACE: There was an episode, wasn't it the pilot for the channel? When we moved to cable, the ship is attacked by these demon dogs ... — demon dog picture on screen —... Joel had like about a billion of these things, and they're "Battle Bones."

JOEL: Right, they're from *He-Man and the Masters of the Universe.*

TRACE: This is the thing you carry all your figures with, and Joel made them into dogs. You can't see them too well but they have ears, and they attack the ship and we could never figure out why they attack the ship. Then we get an exterior view and we realize it's shaped like a dog bone. And that's why the Satellite of Love looks like that.

The other reason it looks like that is I had to build it in a night, and I wanted to make it look like a bone, but I had no sophisticated equipment to make curved surfaces. Then I remembered there were patterns in an old copy of *Popular Mechanics* to make a buckyball, so I went home with my exacto knife and made it out of foam core. It's about four feet long. I walked in the next day after crunching it in the car door, and left little pieces of model kit all the way down the hallway. And that became the ship.

It's kind of based on, like Joel said, the *Silent Running* modules that were on the sides. And there was this film called *First Men in the Moon*, I don't know if you remember that...

JOEL: A Harryhausen movie.

TRACE: Yeah. There was this ball and it's painted with like an anti-gravity paint, and I liked that shape too. [laughter] Hey, it works!

JOEL: I want to mention too that we had just talked about Buckminster Fuller; we both really liked the geodesic dome idea. Also there's a theater in L.A. called The Cinedome, which is exactly that shape. So we thought that it would be fun to reference that too in the shape. But the thing I really liked, and this is another thing that Trace came up with, it's kind of like that moment in *2001* where he throws the bone into the air, and it becomes a spaceship, so it was kind of a reference to that too.

TRACE: We're pulling from a lot of stuff. Like the kids on the Internet are doing!

GENEROSO: KTMA, you're there, you're drawing from their film collection but you're making fun of these films. And as you start to progress word gets out about what you're doing. Something I've always wondered is, how hard was it for you to get more films? Whoever is sending them to you knows you're skewering them. What was the acquisition like? How were you able to get films after that point?

TRACE: It wasn't really that hard.

JOEL: Well, for Cinematic Titanic right now we're actually talking directly to the people. Whereas we just used the film library at KTMA, which was no problem. When we did it for Comedy Channel and Comedy Central they had a film acquisition person who really dealt with that, we never got involved. That's partly why we can't get rights to some of the movies, because they made deals that we can't amend now.

So it wasn't that bad, and for a lot of these movie people it was all about exploitation. They're putting this movie out because the kids will like it, and now they're going "oh they like it for a completely different reason? They like it because they think they're stupid? Ok!"

It's not like they're saying, "come on, what are you saying? What are you implying by making fun of our movies?" They're like, "yeah! Give me that money!"

GENEROSO: That's the thing though, KTMA at that point had these crappy movies, they're probably getting screened four or five times by KTMA. And then all of a sudden like KTMA is asking for every crappy movie out there. Somebody has to start thinking, "Hey, I wonder if it's those guys that are making fun" and then they're going to jack up the price.

JOEL: Well, it didn't really happen at KTMA. From the time we started to the time we were done, it was only twenty-two movies, and so that wasn't really a thing. And then when we went to Comedy Channel, I don't know if behind the scenes that was meaningful. The way they usually did it was they put thirteen great movies and put it with thirteen bad movies. And we just wanted the bad movies. So it turned the whole industry upside down. "We don't want your good movies, and we don't want to pay for your good movies, we just want these movies that you usually put in to fill out the package."

GENEROSO: The filler movies.

JOEL: Yeah, so I think they were more confused than anything when that started.

TRACE: We were always pretty much under the radar, too, we could get these crummy movies. Even to this day no one has really complained to us, the people that have worked on these films.

JOEL: Yeah, I've heard Jordan Fields, who was our guy at Rhino Home Video, and has since moved to Shout Factory and is working with *Mystery Science Theater* at Shout Factory, he said that occasionally he runs into a distributor who might complain a little bit and say "I know it's not *Citizen Kane*, but come on!" But at the end of the day, you know, they want to get a check.

TRACE: They still want a check.

JOEL: So some of the distributors we're dealing with now, they're saying "you know, as long as it's making money I'm doing what I was meant to do as a producer," and they seem pretty content with it. As for my experience with the actors who were in the movies, it was just something they did for a couple of days. They know that it wasn't great. I think it's only the audience that worries about it. — to Generoso — You got a look on your face like you're positive they're angry at us.

GENEROSO: Three words: Joe Don Baker.

JOEL: Ok.

TRACE: Two words: find him.

JOEL: Are you riffing on us man? You know, I don't really know. The Godzilla stuff and the Japanese stuff he was distributing, all the rights have reverted back. He was just a distributor, I think. Wasn't he?

GENEROSO: He was all over the Gamera films...

JOEL: But I always felt like he was just kind of a middle-man in America who redistributed the titles and put his name in them.

GENEROSO: This isn't Fellini, I can't imagine he would get that mad at what's happening. But it just seemed like you were constantly, "oh it's a Sandy Frank film!" Let's get him!

JOEL: Another thing too about Sandy Frank is, I have to say, when we were at KTMA, I felt like our whole thing solidified around the Gamera movies. Once those happened we found our place in the universe, we knew that this was going to work. And there were five of them?

TRACE: There were a lot of them.

JOEL: Maybe a fifth of all the movies we did, or a fourth, were Gamera movies. They just kept coming in and they were so perfect for what we did. And we did any number of things, I think we did a disaster movie *SST Death Flight*, there's some of that in our cell tape.

At the end of twenty-two weeks of doing the show at KTMA, this is what we used to sell it to the Comedy Channel. I think it demonstrates us figuring our way out, basically on camera developing the show. As you saw, when we first started it just wasn't all there. I think this gets closer to what you know as *Mystery Science Theater*.

TRACE: This is like a best-of the twenty-two episodes.

JOEL: Yeah exactly. There's also some press we got locally in Minneapolis, and some messages people left on our answering machine. We knew who we were a little bit better once we did this. [video plays]

JOEL: I'm blown away by Josh Weinstein, I mean he was 17 when we were doing that. And he is really talented, I mean the voices he could do. It kind of got lost, but Trace is making a joke saying "it's pretty skinny, I think it's a carpenter aunt."

TRACE: No, they heard it.

JOEL: They just thought it was in bad taste! But then, Josh says "it's ant-orexic" which is really clever. We weren't writing it, we were just sitting there riffing on it as it went live. We didn't write the show back then.

TRACE: We hadn't seen the movie until we saw the movie and riffed on it. There was no prep, there was no writing.

JOEL: So when we, you know, got paid to do it for the first time, which was Comedy Channel, that was the first thing that I wanted to do: start writing them. Because I saw that clip and I thought "wow it should all be like that."

TRACE: And funny!

JOEL: Well prior to that there would be a lot of long spaces. Josh called it "first-thought theater" because we would just yell out what we thought.

TRACE: That's all we had, because these things were spooling by so fast, we had to say something. By the time you thought of something the moment would be gone; we never got those moments back.

JASON: So I think that clip really begs the question: how did you arrive at Dr. Forrester's character, how did that evolve, like with the costume and so on.

TRACE: Well once we got money for costumes, that helped a lot because I could hide behind something. I was doing a character that was kind of in that vein on stage in clubs in Minneapolis. I took some of that, and it really came together when we started writing those sketches and developing those characters. We talked a lot about what these guys are doing and why they're doing it, which helped a lot. It was also kind of based on some guys we knew in town.

JOEL: The piece I saw Trace do was what blew me away about him. I never really got who he was or what he was doing, and I saw him just do this piece which was amazing, and that became Forrester. Of course it's a reference to *War of the Worlds*— Dr. Clayton Forrester — Gene Roddenberry's character. Is that right?

TRACE: Yeah.

JOEL: No wait! Gene Roddenberry's the ... [to the audience] help?

UNIDENTIFIED AUDIENCE MEMBER: Gene Berry!

JOEL: Gene Berry. The — rodden part...

TRACE: Yeah get that — rodden out of there.

JOEL: So doing these shows locally we just took a day to make each show. We'd start in the morning, and just kind of figured out what the sketches would be. I'd bring props from home from my stand-up act. think I got fifty bucks extra for doing that at KTMA.

GENEROSO: So then you go to Comedy Central, you have more time, you're getting paid for it now, you have more money for props and for setup. The process essentially becomes a little bit more labored. Is it easier at that point to make better episodes? How different was the process once you got to Comedy Central?

TRACE: Well you know we had more writers that we pulled in. We did have more money to build standing sets, so the Mad Scientists had a real set and not, I don't know if you could tell, that was the television control room thinly disguised. That was a real luxury to have the standing set for the satellite interior, and the standing set for the Mad Scientists.

JOEL: Also the sets were for puppets. We built them on scaffolding and that was one of the things we were really interested in, was being able to invest in a set that could stay up. Because if we were in a normal situation it would have to be in a set that folded up, and that just doesn't lend itself to what we wanted to do. So we moved out to this industrial park in Eden Prairie, and had a big warehouse space. Kevin hung the light grid, that was one of my favorite memories: walking in there and Kevin's hanging up there, hanging the poles in the room to make the light grid. Trace designed the set, and it was what the inside of that spaceship might look like.

Wasn't it like a kit you could get? For a geodesic house, actually?

TRACE: No, that was just all two-by-fours and plywood.

JOEL: Oh wow. So that was Trace doing that. I never gave you much credit for that, I'm sorry.

TRACE: If I made it look easy, then that's my art.

JOEL: And I took the surface action from that original set...

TRACE: We have a picture from when we thought we had no money. Remember that one? Want to look at that one?

JOEL: Yeah sure. [about the projected picture] That was just bare-bones, what we could do like overnight where we made a stencil..

TRACE: Ask Josh about painting this sometime, he really enjoyed it...

JOEL: Yeah he's still mad about that. That was later, [another picture] that was what we got to...

TRACE: that's not fully detailed or lit...

JOEL: That's Jim Mallon and I think he's doing the wiring on those lights that went up. You can see there's blue screen back there. The doors open, and the premise was that those were ports for Gypsy, that she was like a vacuum cleaner in a house that has those ports to plug in all over the house. So the idea is that's where she's plugged in, and she might attach all over the ship.

The other thing about the table, that Trace designed, was it went completely down. We had some pretty ambitious ideas that we threw out but that thing completely goes down to the floor.

TRACE: There was an early episode where the table is down and Joel's in this elaborate drum kit walker thing. So we had envisioned doing more big, room-sized props in this space. But it became too costly and difficult to do.

JOEL: Also kind of dangerous.

TRACE: Not just kind of!

JOEL: Trace and Josh and later Kevin were back there, and if that thing dropped it would just crush...

TRACE: Yeah ... we had worked on this system that cabled it down gently and all this stuff. But then finally we just got the wood screws out and fixed it.

JOEL: So anyway, that's it. Good night! What were we talking about, it seemed kind of interesting...

TRACE: *Mystery Science Theater*...

GENEROSO: Then you went to Comedy Central and they gave you all kinds of money...

JOEL: Oh yeah! I think right away, we were able to start writing it and it just changed everything. I felt a lot more comfortable with that because I just don't do improv. I think Josh and Trace were really the ones who brought the game up so much.

TRACE: Yes. You are correct.

JOEL: I felt like those guys, being more improvisational, really helped in that KTMA thing. And I was always thinking, "boy I'd really like to write these so I could get more into it." So that's when everything got better, because we were able to use the time code of the movie and just write down where our line was and I think right away we went to three hundred lines per show. That gradually grew until, by the end of the first season we were around four or five hundred lines, which is the *Mystery Science Theater* we know now. Cinematic Titanic is at six hundred, roughly, so now we're better.

TRACE: Yes, we're better! But that kind of first-time-seeing-the-movie riffing spirit came through in the writing. How we wrote was we'd all throw out our riffs, and it all went into a big massive script. So it was a very free way to write at the time. Nobody was saying "no you can't do that, you can't do that."

JOEL: Yeah, instead of a traditional writing room where you have a big table and you would face each other and read your scripts, it really was anonymous: you're all looking at the TV and yelling out stuff. So people would come in, Jef Maynard would come in, Jim Mallon would come in, and yell and say stuff. We really encouraged it; the door was always open and we could always use somebody to say stuff. You'd get lots and lots of ideas, so it was this big mass of information, and Mike's job was to assemble it and ask "what's the funniest joke here?" and "where do we put this?" Then he and later Mary Jo, Frank, Paul Schersten, would do line-assign, which is finding a place where those lines go, where you can fit them between the dialogue so it makes sense. And who gets the line.

It's kind of deceptive, people always think we write our jokes and it's just not like that, everybody writes the jokes. If you notice, every third joke I get. Obviously I didn't write every third joke.

JASON: So when you were writing, then, did you go through the movie once or did you watch it a couple times to assemble the lines?

TRACE: We'd go through it multiple times, probably once as a big group.

JOEL: There was a three-day cycle. We went through the movie the first day and threw ideas out, figure out which riffs that people really sparked too, and we'd also have a lot of ideas that became a sketch. So we'd put the sketches up on a dry mark board with a heading, and then the second day we'd write the sketches. In the morning we'd look at the headings and look at the ideas and just brainstorm more ideas. So it's just a big mass of ideas, and then each writer got to pick which sketch they wanted to write. We were especially proud that the young writers got to go first and take the best sketches. Then if you were an older wiser, writer you could take the less funny sketch and make it funnier.

On the third day we'd do it again, and go through the movie again. It was a three-day writing cycle, then we needed time to do line assign and put it altogether. It was basically an eight-day cycle to produce a show.

TRACE: Once the writers got all the stuff, then in those first shows you and I would go off and make the props and sets and stuff, then we'd all come back. The day we shot we'd rehearse it twice and then shoot it in the afternoon. We must have all seen it about six times by the time we were done.

JOEL: The other cool thing was that because we were in silhouette you could drop in a line, if you had flubbed a line. That was another thing Mike did, he would go "ok you guys dropped a line here, dropped a line there" so we'd go back and just do those wild, record them and drop them in. Kevin was editing the show so he would be in charge of assembling it.

GENEROSO: Something I've always been curious about: by the time you get to Comedy Central, outside of KTMA, again you have the backing of a cable network and can probably get the films you wanted, but early on where there ever any films that you really wanted to do that they just absolutely positively could not get? I'm setting this up for this reason: I've heard this rumor about a John Travolta film, one he did after *Saturday Night Fever* called *Moment by Moment*.

TRACE: We looked at that movie, but I think it was out of our price range. Do you remember looking at that one?

JOEL: Yeah, it gets kind of frustrating. I just feel like behind the curtain of the show, so much screening goes on. Frank was the guy who screened all the movies, and he'd get a huge box of VHS tapes that he would just go home and watch. And he would come back with five or so, and we would all get copies and we would all take them home and watch them and sign off on them.

So you don't really have that, "I want that one!" like you're in a video store, "that's the one for me!" It doesn't really work that way, it's a screening process that we all went through and then we would zero in on the ones that we thought were ok. So it didn't really work like "wish fulfillment," it was more like, "can we afford it? Ok."

TRACE: There was one other one, that Elvis cowboy movie that we got excited about...

JOEL: Was that public domain?

TRACE: No, it wound up being Disney.

JOEL: Too rich for my blood.

JASON: To shift gears a little bit, can you guys talk about when you were on *Freaks and Geeks*, and what that was like?

JOEL: It was awesome.

TRACE: It was a great show, it was a real family atmosphere on the set. I was often mistaking these "high school students" for high school students because they were directed so correctly. I would talk to them like they were real kids, "so what are you doing after high school?" and they would say, "well I got a commercial, and then I have another movie," and I would go, "oh, you're not real kids." But it was a great show to work on.

GENEROSO: How did you get on the show? I'm just curious because with the both of you, it just seems like someone's plotting.

TRACE: I had met Paul Feig through Joel, and Paul called me up.

JOEL: Paul was part of the gang of people we knew in L.A., like the Higgins boys and Gruber, after they did their show in New York they went back to L.A. and I think we met a lot of people through them. Judd was a part of that, but I had met Judd Apatow when he was in high school. I was doing standup in New York and I was working this club called Caroline's, which I think is still around, and he was very plugged in even then. He was a kid in high school in Long Island who would come into the city and meet comics to interview us for his radio show at his high school. That's how I met Judd when he was a junior or senior in high school. So those guys knew us and they just used a lot of our friends, and also Josh Weinstein was a producer on the show so I think he had a lot to do with using his buddies.

GENEROSO: The part that Trace plays on the show makes sense — you were the chemistry teacher if I'm not mistaken.

TRACE: Yes.

JOEL: I was a disco clothing salesman.

GENEROSO: Why did they make you do that?

JOEL: I don't know, they just called and said "we have a part we really think you should play." I don't know why.

JASON: On a completely different note, coming from a Media Studies background, we were really interested in your take on intellectual property. Specifically, back in the day on Comedy Central you would always have that message, "keep circulating the tapes." I was wondering, now that you're doing Cinematic Titanic and we have technologies like Bit Torrent, how have your opinions changed and been informed by the technology?

TRACE: Stop circulating the tapes. Actually keep circulating the *Mystery Science Theater* tapes.

JOEL: Well, when we said "keep circulating the tapes" we were on a channel that was not seen all across the country, maybe half the country saw what we were doing. We found out people were making VHS tapes and sending them to their friends. We seized that and said "oh we should promote that." Because we were already paid, you know it was just a way of distributing the show. We had already been paid for making the show, so it didn't really hurt us to get as many people to watch it as possible. To us it was the same as if they were watching it on TV. I'm sure the channel didn't care because they were watching our ads, so it was working for them too. But it was really like our "I want my MTV," just a way to say that if you're really into the show you can make copies and send them to your friends. It really worked for us and we think it's likely that act is what made the show the peculiar success that it is. Twenty years later people still care about it and are interested in it. It's just so loaded, but I dunno, what do you think?

GENEROSO: I think that thirty or forty years ago The Grateful Dead encouraged bootlegging of their live concerts and that's how they got huge. But that was forty years ago and things have changed, now you can get almost the exact same thing you saw on television downloaded in about fifteen minutes. Given the fact that you folks are doing independent distribution I think it's a fairly rotten thing for people to do. You are putting stuff out, you distribute all your own stuff now.

TRACE: Right. Now we are putting out our own DVDs, there's nobody else behind us. In fact, if you watch the DVD, instead of the FBI warning it's one of us writing a suggestion that you don't necessarily want to copy it. There's no criminal penalty involved, but the guilt … I wouldn't wish that on anyone. But it really is the five of us who are Cinematic Titanic and making this show and distributing it personally.

JOEL: We put our own money together, and we've made enough to keep making new shows and keep it going and stuff like that. So it's good, but yeah, sometimes you encounter people who feel like it's their right to make a copy of it. I think one of the messages I'm going to write is, "if you didn't buy this we really hope you don't enjoy it."

TRACE: I don't think they will!

JOEL: Just to set that forward, that personally we don't really want you to because it's kind of a gesture that says if you bought it, we encourage it, but if you didn't buy it or you haven't bought a lot of them you're making things harder for us. We really are dependent on money coming in to keep doing it. We're not a corporation; we don't have endless amounts of money to take hits like that. So we don't really accept it. But it's still being figured out. But you know, it's analogous to when in the 60's people said, "hey if we just have lots of sex, all the time, all of our problems are going to go away!" It's kind of like that.

TRACE: And that worked great!

JOEL: "If everything's free, it will all work out!"

GENEROSO: I was born in 1968 so yeah, I totally understand. You're doing Cinematic Titanic right now, and if I'm not mistaken, you never did *Mystery Science Theater* live.

TRACE: No, we did once at the Uptown Theater, and then once later again in the series we did it when we were writing *This Island Earth* for the movie we did a live version to get the jokes timed up. So we did it twice.

GENEROSO: But now you're doing it as a tour and you're going to be coming here at the end of February, I'm just curious what…

JOEL: Yeah, we should announce that…

TRACE: Yeah…

GENEROSO: It will be at the Somerville Theater, and we only handed-out six hundred pieces of paper tonight…

JOEL: February 20, and 21.

GENEROSO: At the Somerville Theater. Did I mention it's at the Somerville Theater?

TRACE: Which is really easy to get to I hear, from here.

JASON: Yeah.

GENEROSO: Just a few stops on the Red Line. It should be a fantastic event. But your process, when you're doing it live, how does that essentially work? Now that you're doing it live, how does that change the dynamic of what you used to do as *MST3K*?

TRACE: Well the live shows are a completely different animal, really. I mean, it's in this form and you're laughing for a good two hours. Where else do you get that? In a standup act, at a standup club, a play, or a movie?

JOEL: And our movies are only ninety minutes so there's an extra half-hour of just laughing. We've been done for half an hour and there's still laughing.

TRACE: We're sleeping in the hotel room.

JOEL: Well we all met doing standup, and that's how it worked. For instance I met Trace and Josh through standup, and we did *Mystery Science Theater* at KTMA. When we finally got more money we could hire another writer and I said to Josh, "you're still doing the clubs, who do you like?" One day he said "I found a guy, let's go look at him." And it was Mike Nelson. We came in and sat down, and Mike's standup was really unique in that he was really trying to please himself. He was just kind of making himself laugh, and that's what I really liked about him. I mean he was amusing and really funny, but if anything you felt like he was doing it for himself. I liked that and I just said to Josh, "I really like him, let's put him in."

Obviously he became really, a real big part of our writing staff and obviously became really talented taking my place too. Then Mike found the next person, so whoever the newest person was would find the next person. We would call it trolling, going to a comedy club to find the next person. I don't know, did he find Bridget, and Bridget found Mary Jo?

TRACE: Somewhere, someone begot Frank.

JOEL: Oh yeah, I think Mike found Frank, he came next. But then each person would just bring in the next person, that's how we got our writing staff.

But anyway I was talking about standup, and the thing is that when you do Cinematic Titanic or *Mystery Science Theater* you're collaborating with the original work and kind of working with it. You really have to live with these movies and kind of make them make sense. Then when you add the audience there's this third element, and I think that's what makes it different. We're kind of between the audience and the movie in the room so it's going both ways: the audience is reacting to us and they're reacting to the movie and we're also reacting to the audience. So there's a lot more going on in the room than normal.

TRACE: When we were in Chicago we did three movies and we would do the same movie twice a night. The first show and second show would always be a little bit different because that audience mix would change the dynamic, and a laugh would be stronger on one joke and less on another. It would always change. The DVD is another experience because that's a joke in every moment where a joke could go, and in the live show you get a joke and a laugh, and that will blow out for or five jokes.

JOEL: We're editing live. If Trace lands a really good joke and I have my setup on the screen I just have to lay out; I'll think "oh my jokes not going to make any sense because they're not hearing what the guy's saying." Actually the audience is working with us, and the two shows are completely different because of the way they're reacting. We also learned that when a joke, like that joke in Frankenstein about the dwarf, do you want to repeat that...?

TRACE: There's a scene where Michael Dunn, actor, is going through a gate. And it's just a real kind of innocuous scene: the actor walks up to a gate and goes through it — and I don't know who wrote this joke; do you know who wrote this joke?

JOEL: [shakes head]

TRACE: We all wrote this joke. The line is, "that's the least you can expect from a gate:

is to keep a dwarf out." I see it on the page and I go, "wow, that's not going to go anywhere."

JOEL: But it killed! It was the biggest laugh of the show and I think you just can't know, you never know what people are going to laugh at. The other thing that comes into play is you learn to lean on jokes. You think, "wow they laughed at that, if I put more confidence into my read, if I say it like I know they're going to laugh, it's completely different again." So that's what we're learning. When we do live shows we're working that stuff out and that's going to go on a DVD. So we're working the material out with an audience and then going into the studio instead of the other way around. Hopefully we're making a better product that way because we'll find out what people think.

TRACE: If you steal these, you're stealing from yourselves.

JASON: Speaking of Cinematic Titanic, how did that come about? I think for a lot of fans there was this sense of "finally, this is resuming." So what was the catalyst?

JOEL: Well more than anything it's just so much fun. Doing *Mystery Science Theater* was my favorite experience in show business and I think the rest of us felt that way. We wanted to come back together and do it again. We're all still friends after twenty years and we wanted to take a run at it.

This is a really big year for us because we went from zero to sixty, from people going "can they really do it?" to demonstrating to people that we can still do it and bring new things to the lexicon. And also critics and fans have said it's as funny as it used to be so that's kind of the big challenge. Now Trace and I and the rest of the group are working on filling in the rest of the world of Cinematic Titanic. For instance, "why are they there? Why do they have to watch these bad movies?" The stuff we answered over time with *Mystery Science Theater.*

GENEROSO: There's one question I have left. My favorite episode that you ever did was *Catalina Caper,* and something really unique popped out about that. It is the only "comedy" that you ever went after. Why?

TRACE: Well, comedy-on-comedy doesn't layer properly. We also found puppet-on-puppet crime doesn't work.

JOEL: We found out through trial and error that if people are winking at the camera like they're saying "we know we're in a bad movie so we're being silly" it didn't work for what we were trying to do. Trace has this great analogy of how Margaret Dumont was such a good actress that you didn't really understand she was part of this ensemble, you thought she was really a stuffy society lady and the Marx brothers are just being hilarious. The illusion was there. We found that that had to be that way with the movie too, you had to feel like the movie was genuinely trying to move the audience. If it looked that way then we could do what we did. And I think that's interesting, I never thought of that, that *Catalina Caper* was a comedy. I think we just had so much contempt for it and that carried us through.

But those are just some of the things we learned. Same with narration. If there's a lot of narration forget it, if there's puppets it won't work. There are just things like that that along the way that we realized make it much harder to do what we do.

TRACE: Super violent movies, murders and that sort of thing, we'd cut scenes out.

GENEROSO: Can you think of anything else, Jason?

JASON: Nope!

JOEL: Great last question! Look at them, they're rocking! They're going out of their minds over that answer!

21

"Cambot Eye": The Synthesis of Man, Machine and Spectatorship

by Danielle Reay

The television show *Mystery Science Theater 3000*, featuring the character/creator Joel Robinson/Hodgson and his robot friends Crow T. Robot, Tom Servo, Gypsy and Cambot has become not only a cult classic, recontextualizing and satirizing movies from the past, but also smartly demonstrates some theoretical issues about the relationship between man and machine. This chapter chooses to take an equally playful tone in its analysis, mirroring the efforts and spirit of *MST3K*. It is my cinematic experiment. The essay re-imagines *MST3K* as not only as an inventive comedy series but explores its unintentional theoretical savvy. I do no want to suggest that *MST3K* is exclusively bound by the narrative and structural conditions later explained within this essay, but I would hope that the show's wit and humor lie not only in a cultural context but could also benefit from a formal analysis.

This analysis relies primarily on Cambot, the camera robot filming *MST3K*. It also focuses on the systems of technology present within the show. Cambot enables a system of control which aligns the spectator's vision with that of the camera. This pairing of perspectives also points to the permeability of various screens. These screens then become agents of torture and influence, allotting power to the camera and the images which it produces. Both man and machine experience this visual impact. In turn, Cambot, Joel, and the robots provide various examples of the demonstrations and complications of this relationship between camera, image and spectatorship.

For this essay I will focus on the episodes in which Joel Hodgson was host. These episodes will include selections from the early KTMA programs to the later Comedy Channel and Comedy Central shows. I feel that these episodes are most useful to the themes of this study because they offer more salient demonstrations of the show's mechanics as well as featuring a more self-reflective and explanatory tone due to the show's initial efforts to convey its premise and dynamics.

The premise of *MST3K* is described concisely in the theme song played at the beginning of the show. Joel has been sent into space against his will to live on the Satellite of Love by the mad scientists who work in Deep 13. The "mads" Dr. Clayton Forrester, Dr. Lawrence "Larry" Erhardt and TV's Frank subject him to horrible experiments where Joel is forced to watch bad movies. To keep him company, Joel has created robot friends using the parts which control the starting and stopping of the films. While most of the robots participate in the show by watching the films (Crow and Tom Servo) or running the higher functions of the ship (Gypsy), Cambot has the responsibility of filming the show. *MST3K* explores the theoretical potential of Cambot, the robot camera, while addressing important issues of consciousness tethered to machines. Through Cambot the audience first approaches the possibilities and complexities of artificial intelligence within the show. From this premise there develops many examples of Cambot's power to connect the viewer with the screen as the rest of the robots connect ideas of technology with humanity.

Cambot's purpose on the show is both stylistic and functional. *The Amazing Colossal Episode Guide* describes Cambot's role as both invisible yet essential. The guide explains, "the elusive Cambot is almost never seen, because Cambot is shooting the show" (1996: xxvii). Not only does Cambot shoot *MST3K* but he also seems to provide the visual link between the Satellite of Love and Deep 13, the mad scientists' subterranean secret location. During the screening of the movie, Cambot also seems to take the position of projector as well, simultaneously providing the movie and filming the show. This is confirmed early in the first Comedy Channel season during the episode *Robot Holocaust* when during a Commander Cody short the screen goes blank and a still image of the mad scientists appears with speech bubbles reading "Oops, the film broke." Joel then leaves his seat in the theater and walks towards us and Cambot. Tom Servo asks, "Is it Cambot, Joel?" Joel replies "I don't know. I can't tell," as he walks closer and closer until the silhouette of his head eventually fills the screen and presumably covers Cambot's lens, blocking both our view and preventing the image from being projected on to the theater screen (Mallon 1990, Episode 110). Both the characters in the show and the TV audience are simultaneously deprived of the ability to see the film or show respectively. Cambot as projector and film camera is both a technical reality and an inference created by the viewer's imagination. But this assumption is important to understanding the possibilities of Cambot within the context of *MST3K*. This dual responsibility puts emphasis on Cambot as a controller and enabler of the image and our ability to view the film and show. This ability transitions to other characteristics of both Cambot and the show as the relationship between vision, man and machine becomes more complicated within the dynamics of *MST3K*.

The audience only sees Cambot in the opening sequence. When the theme song announces the robot roll call Cambot can be seen only because he films his image in a mirror. (This is consistent throughout the show with the exception of early KTMA episodes and Mike's subsequent seasons when Cambot is shown without the use of the mirror). Joel holds the mirror across from Cambot and gestures towards Cambot's reflection. We see his camera body and name reversed in the mirror. Through this shot the viewer is made more aware of Cambot's responsibility as robot camera and sole filmic creator of the show because he is the only camera on board as made evident by the use of the mirror.

Cambot also demonstrates features of artificial intelligence which becomes evident through his response to Joel's verbal cues. Many times during the show Joel will give Cambot a command which Cambot will follow. Cambot can also control the lighting, audio or zoom to a still screen. This ability is featured most prominently in the end sequences where he freezes on an enlarged image of a piece of fan mail. Cambot is responsible for various special effects as well. In the last KTMA episode *Legend of the Dinosaur* Joel in partnership with Cambot constructs a special effects sequence which makes the robots and Joel appear small. Joel directly thanks Cambot for the special effects and the collaboration. This illusion/effect is achieved by Cambot projecting a portion of a film in the background. This projection, which is made extremely large, depicts a child reaching for something. Joel is then grabbed by a large inflatable hand and pulled back into the hallway (Mallon 1989, Episode K21).

The hallway door sequences are also an important stylistic feature of the show. They highlight some of the technological and theoretical features Cambot reinforces. The movement between the main area where Joel and the robots meet and the theater where they watch the movies is mediated by the space of the hallway. It is a connective portal from the main area to the theater and back. This connection is further mediated by a series of doors which open and close as the viewer moves to and back from the theater respectively. At times, the doors almost seem to represent a kind of lens, an opening and closing, letting in and out light and image. This is also reinforced by Cambot's movement through the hallway, guiding our vision and perspective as his lens moves to project the movie and film the show. This connection between Cambot's technical abilities and robotic consciousness begins to point to the theoretical literature regarding the power of the camera. Malcolm Turvey in his essay on Jean Epstein cites Richard Abel writing that "'for French writing on the cinema, this cognitive power was located in the new apparatus of the camera and, by extension, the projector and screen'"(Turvey, 1998: 29). This extension connects cognition, vision and technology through a pattern similar to Cambot's role and responsibilities on *MST3K*.

The audience's vision becomes so strongly dependant on and trained to rely upon Cambot that the viewer's perception becomes tethered to the camera. This is also reinforced by Joel's interaction with Cambot and the audience. Joel speaks to the audience because he directly addresses Cambot which in turn becomes the viewer. In many episodes the first segment is specifically explanatory towards the audience. Cambot becomes a vehicle for Joel's message or appeal to the viewer. Though Joel is addressing the audience he is also broadcasting through Cambot who in turn becomes the viewer's representative aboard the Satellite of Love. We relate to Cambot because he is our connection to the experience on the ship.

For the most part Cambot remains in a fixed position. When the movie sign appears Cambot visually ushers the audience through the opening and closing doorways that separate the main area from the Satellite of Love's theater. From there Cambot remains fixed until intermission where he retracts from the theater through the same doors and meets Joel and the other robots back at the main area. The only separation the viewer has from Cambot's perspective are the cuts to the scientists and breaks to commercials. These instances also reaffirm the link between Cambot's vision and the viewer's vision, but also reinstate the possibility that Cambot serves as not only a camera, but an intercessor between filmed space and viewer space, (this is complicated because Joel is presumably in outer space). Cambot also becomes a link between the Satellite of Love and Deep 13, two places completely separated, one subterranean, the other, in outer space. This relationship makes more plausible the possibility of Cambot uniting us, the TV audience, with the Satellite of Love, both in perspective and as a visual link between vast distances.

These links between the audience, Joel and the robots, and Cambot create ties not only between space and perspective but highlight the dynamics between the characters on the *MST3K*. With regards to vision and perception, Cambot provides an example of camera consciousness in a more literal way then previously realized in film theory. Cambot demonstrates his cognitive abilities by responding to Joel. At the end of the episode *Space Travelers* Joel reads a letter from a fan which begins, "my friend and I would like to see more of Cambot on the show." Cambot then nods the camera/himself up and down in agreement, the view of the show moving up and down in accordance with Cambot's actions. Joel responds, "that's impossible!" and moves on. This is impossible because as previously discussed Cambot is filming the show. (Mallon 1992, Episode 401). Yet Cambot's ability to respond and understand indicates an artificial intelligence or even camera consciousness which is important to his function on the ship and show.

In conjunction with his consciousness, Cambot's technological gifts are continually showcased and highlighted throughout *MST3K*. In the episode *Bride of the Monster* more of Cambot's special abilities are demonstrated on Crow. At the beginning of the episode the audience sees Crow deep asleep. Joel then announces that "through the magic of Cambot we will be able to see what he's dreaming." Joel attaches cables from Cambot to Crow's head. An image appears on screen which is presumably Crow's dream. The image is placed in the middle of a black and white grid, pairing the naturalistic image with a technological construction. Crow's dream consists of playing with Gypsy until Tom Servo appears in a candy striping costume. Crow and Tom then begin to snuggle and the real Tom begins to yell "turn it off, turn it off!" Joel then disconnects the cables and Crow wakes up (Mallon 1993, Episode 423). Two important points are demonstrated in this skit. First, the robots demonstrate some of their inherent humanity with their ability to dream, suggesting some sort of robot subconscious and a stronger demonstration of the link between man and machine. Second, the "magic of Cambot" highlights some of the special abilities allotted to the camera. Not only can Cambot observe, respond, film and project, but his lens can penetrate the mind. Though it is a robotic mind imbued with other extraordinary human characteristics, the mind, machine, perception connection becomes evident. Since dreams serve as a fertile ground for the exploration of the psychological, their presence within the robots points to a more profound and evolved artificial intelligence. Cambot's projection of Crow's dream brings the intangible psychological processes into a visual reality. The mind becomes viewable on a screen. Now the screen is not only the connection between the audience and camera. The screen also becomes the mediation between in the interior and exterior; a connection between mind and sight produced by Cambot.

The psychological elements of intelligence or personality are more immediately displayed through the robots Gypsy, Tom Servo and Crow T. Robot. As the theme song explains, Joel used "special parts to make his robot friends." Each of these robots has a specific personality even though they are mechanical in origin. Gypsy is described as "guileless, motherly, and quite independent," Tom Servo as "intellectual and a bit inflated," and Crow as "rambunctious and acerbic"(*MST3K ACEG* 1996, xxvii).

Along with personality and a vast knowledge of culture, history, and film, Joel has also programmed the robots with a certain degree of free will. In an early episode from season one, *The Crawling Hand*, Joel explains the premise of the show and his relationship with the different robots. He states, "(Cambot you don't have to put in applause).... I'm part of a bizarre movie watching experiment and now I guess so are you." This again demonstrates some of Cambot's abilities of mimetically simulating an inherently human sound with technology. This introduction also highlights the interaction between screen and audience by including the viewer in the experiment as well. The segment during the second intermission addresses the issues of the robots' free will and nicely illustrates some of the differences between or physical limitations of the robots. Joel wants to play rock paper scissors with the bots, (an occurrence that happens again on other episodes). Since Tom Servo can't move his arms and Crow's hands are permanently shaped like scissors, Joel always wins. In turn the robots decide that Joel wins everything and resolve to leave him alone. Joel then feels that the 'bots are ungrateful stating, "No, 'Thanks for making us intrinsically human.' Next time I make a robot no more free will" (Mallon 1989, Episode 106). This admission makes the robot's physical and mental composition more apparent. Joel has endowed them with free minds but inflexible and limited mechanical bodies.

Though Joel acknowledges that he has given the robots free will, many segments of the show are devoted to analyzing the inherent differences between man and machine. During a segment in *Black Scorpion*, Tom Servo and Crow try to understand Joel's natural biological processes by equating them with machine functions. They explain, Joel's sleeping like a "shutdown." Joel is also "programmed to grow hair." The robots eventually conclude that "human nature is a hard thing to figure" (Mallon 1990, Episode 113). This equation will later be made between the camera lens and the human eye as applied to Cambot. Certain artifacts from popular culture, such as magazines, are also transformed to accommodate the robots. Tom and Crow are at times seen reading *Tiger Bot* and *Robot Nation*.

Joel also explains that his ability to withstand the horrendous films the mad scientists send him is because he is human. In the introduction to the episode *Robot Holocaust*, Joel announces, "I can handle it because I'm a hu-man!" The robots then break into a harmonica blues number to which Joel sings, "Hey you, you people in front of your TVs, sittin' along that line, I'll be back from the commercial, in a few minutes time, ain't that a hu-man. H, U, M, A, N, a human, a human" (Mallon 1990, Episode 110). Here again Joel references both the existence of an implied audience and the specific screen through which we view the show. In the KTMA episode, *Superdome*, Joel also tries to convey some of the sensations of human pain to the robots through a device that he has invented to simulate different levels of physical pain. The machine uses an electrical impulse that allows the robots to understand the intensity of physical human pain. The settings on the machine range from stubbing one's toe to watching an hour of *Arsenio*. While Servo feels nothing on the stubbed toe setting, he writhes in pain at the *Arsenio* setting (Mallon 1989, Episode K15). This reveals that the robot's nature is not physical, but relies more on their mental capabilities. Their minds are tethered primarily to their ability to see and understand. *Arsenio* is visual torture, worse and more intensely felt than any sort of physical pain. The robots demonstrate that this is the sort of torture and agony they respond to. From the very early stages of *MST3K* this premise is realized and reinforced for both Joel and the robots.

The robots also have a distinct sense of self. In the episode *The Human Duplicators* Crow and Tom want to tell Joel that they are robots. They begin nervously after the end of the film. Crow starts, "Joel, Tom and I have something to tell you. I know we've alluded to it, never have we...." Tom then interjects, "Joel, Crow and I are robots and we want the world to know!" Joel replies, "Tom it's more than a little obvious." Tom and Crow then seemed shocked that Joel knew they were robots all along (Mallon 1992, Episode 420). This conversation, while mocking the undertones of the film which conveniently deals with the differences between original and copy with respect to man and android, also demonstrates certain features of the robot's psyche such as self awareness. Their acknowledgement of their own existence is remarkably certain. The robots' self awareness is a distinctly human feature, yet conversely, their admission is pointedly un-human. Their mock assumption that Joel was not aware of their mechanical composition alludes to their cognitive characteristics. Tom and Crow's ability to interact in a human way seemed to indicate to them that they were in some ways creating the illusion of humanity. Though the segment is a parody of the film and usually Tom and Crow recognize that they are robots, the discrepancy highlights complications in distinguishing man from machine. This mirrors some of the ambiguity inherent in the discussions of man and machine with consideration given to the difficult and flexible boundaries placed on determining and recognizing each entity.

There are also competing references to the existence of the robot's souls. In an intermission segment during the episode *Gunslinger* Joel and the 'bots lay in caskets contemplating death. When Tom asks Joel why they are doing this Joel answers, "Well aren't you curious?" Crow replies, "About being dead? We're robots Joel. We're not the ones who have to worry about it. You understand my point?" Joel then retorts "Well at least I have a soul" (Mallon 1993, Episode 511). Yet in response to a particularly painful scene in *The Black Scorpion* Tom Servo declares, "I feel very filthy, my very soul is defiled" (Mallon 1990, Episode 113). A soul within the machine seems to take on more spiritual and philosophical connotations than necessary within the context of the show. The existence of a soul may imply a kind of mock creationism placing Joel in a God-like position. The absence of a soul may point to the limitations of intrinsic authenticity within a robotic and mechanically constructed mind. Or the concern of souls may highlight a transition from a concern regarding the camera's ability to reveal of the soul of cinema, to the cinematically provoked soul of the viewer through spectatorship (Epstein, 1993: 315). Watching the bad film invokes a specific soul within the spectator, only apparent in moments of visual duress.

The robots also demonstrate the features of affection. These relationships between man and machine transcend to some of Tom Servo's romances on the show. Throughout *MST3K* the robots demonstrate their superficial attraction to both women and appliances. Inspired by their instructional short "What to Do on a Date" Tom asks Gypsy out to dinner with disastrous consequences (Mallon 1993, Episode 503). In the episode *Mad Monster* Tom sings "Macho Bot" as he makes failed advances on a blender (Mallon 1989, Episode 103). When the bots are attracted to human women they are women on the screen. In some ways these women are artificial, their images produced and constructed through the agents of technology. Poignantly, when Tom Servo sings his epic lament "Creepy Girl" to one of the heroines in *Catalina Caper*, he croons to her still image on a television set, the time code still visible in the corner. Tom Servo swoons to the TV, "could you find it in your heart to love a 'bot like me?" (Mallon 1990, Episode 204). He falls in love with the image mediated through technology rather than the reality of an actual woman. The presence of the TV and the time code make the image appear more mechanical. These features also make the viewer aware of its status as an image produced by technology.

The episode *The Hellcats* makes the viewer aware of how the framed image effects action. During a flashback intermission segment Joel recollects the time he tried different scopes out on Cambot's lens. Crow and Tom offer to participate in Joel's "visual joke" which involves placing different scope cutouts over Cambot's lens. When Joel changes each scope or frame, the robots' actions change accordingly with respect to the shape of the space they are seen through. For the "keyhole scope" Crow and Tom act out a secret affair, Crow stating, "You know you're the only man for me Servo." Other examples are the "Scope Scope" in which the robots act out a prime minister's assassination, the "Micro Scope" in which Crow pretends to be an amoeba, and the "Small Intestine Scope" where Tom feigns indigestion. The robots eventually get frustrated as the scopes become more absurd such as the "Scope's Monkey Trial Scope" a.k.a. "Inherit the Wind-O-Rama" (Mallon 1990, Episode 209). This segment demonstrates the lens's and the frame's power over the contextualization of the image. In certain ways, Cambot's frame, power and control dictate the kind of actions produced by those being filmed. This contextualization affects also the action and how the audience interprets what they see.

The permeability of screens or the breaching of screen space and audience space is mirrored in the way Joel interacts with the screen in the theater. During the movies Joel will often get out of his seat to poke a character on the screen or interact with the filmed scenery. These examples are just a few of the variety of ways Joel participates in the film with his actions. In the episode *Sidehackers* Joel and the robots demonstrate how the action of the film itself can affect the audience. During a chase sequence Joel and the robots shift and jolt from side to side in their seats reflecting the momentum of the motorcycles in the film (Mallon 1990, Episode 202). Joel and the robots also add audio information based on actions or events on the screen. In the episode, *Teenagers from Outerspace* Joel and the robots continually make muffled screams whenever a trunk of a car appears on screen (Mallon 1992, Episode 404). These visual cues incite participation between audience and screen which erases some of the imaginary and physical boundaries between the film and the spectator. This inclusion and participation may extend to the way in which we, the viewer of the show, relate to or align with Cambot's perspective. The viewer may seek to assign their vision to Cambot's both because of the technical construction of the show and the aforementioned examples of how Joel and the robots seek to participate with the action of the film. There is a permeability created and demonstrated that allows us to transcend our TV screens and enter into the show through not only our vision but our actions as well.

The show also affects Joel and the robot's actions in the intermission segments. Often Joel and the robots perform skits inspired by the film. After watching a cocktail singer segment in the episode *I Accuse My Parents* Joel and the robots perform a reenactment of the sequence. Gypsy stars as Kitty Reed wearing a blonde wig and a black sequined hat. Joel becomes a sophisticated diner, changing positions and costumes as Cambot pans across the stage. Crow and Tom Servo become waiters ushering champagne and drinks to the patrons. Gypsy proceeds to lip synch along with the song performed earlier in the film, "Are You Happy in Your Work." Eventually Crow and Tom collide knocking over their drink trays. The music becomes warped and stops. Tom exclaims, "I think we spilled some champagne cocktail into Cambot's sequencer!" (Mallon 1992, Episode 507). These skits become another demonstration of how what is on screen transcends into the actions of its audience. Within the microcosm of the Satellite of Love, Joel and the robots often reenact portions of the movie, or use themes from the film to inspire various arts and crafts projects, discussions, or skits. This impulse seems almost masochistic considering the implied torture in watching the bad movies. Yet many times they even become the characters features in the films. In the episode, *Manos: The Hands of Fate* Joel dresses up as "The Master" with and elaborate cape and fake facial hair. He attempts to intimidate and scare the robots but despite his costume and menacing demeanor, Crow informs Joel that he's just not scary (Mallon 1993, Episode 424).

Often the reenactments are as unsuccessful as the films they watch, failing in some way, whether foiled by champagne cocktail or a bad impersonation. This seems to mirror the way in which audiences in general take away certain habits, quotes, or information from what they watch, transforming them with adaptations from reel life to real life. Jokes and skits like these also allow the viewer to feel included. Many of the quips and allusions in the show are obscure and difficult to understand. Rather than alienate the spectator, these skits in some ways serve as a common place where the viewer is completely in on the joke on the simple condition that they have been watching the show. They engage the mind as Cambot controls the eye, allowing for further influence over the audience.

Other allusions point to an important knowledge of film history. In the episode *City*

Limits Tom Servo raps about the movies he'd rather be watching. He begins, "I wish I could see *Citizen Kane*. I wish I could see *The Rules of the Game*. I wish I could view *Seven Samurai*. But every film I see makes me want to die" (Mallon 1992, Episode 403). At the end of the episode, *King Dinosaur* Crow complains about having to watch four Robert Lippert movies for the mad scientists' experiment. He says, "I've never even seen a Kurosawa film. The works of Francoise Truffaut? Not familiar with them, sorry. Odessa step sequence? I don't think I know that one, no" (Mallon 1990, Episode 210). These examples demonstrate that the robots have been programmed to understand the differences in quality between the movies they watch in the experiment and the revered films of directors such as Kurosawa, Truffaut and Eisenstein. Joel and the robots continually reference a variety of notable films throughout the duration of the show, implying a comprehensive understanding of past cinematic achievements.

This heavy use of allusionism throughout the show references a certain "film consciousness" described by Noel Carroll in his essay "The Future of Allusion: Hollywood in the Seventies (And Beyond)." Carroll writes that allusions are "self-conscious gestures" that are directed toward an "informed viewer"(Carroll, 1982: 52, 56). He continues, "The game of allusion could begin; the senders and receivers were in place; the necessary conditions for allusionistic interplay were satisfied"(55).

This film consciousness and use of allusions also transfers to *MST3K* in more theoretical ways. Through Cambot's abilities, his responses, and purpose within the show, Cambot seems to transform Dziga Vertov's "kino-eye" theory into "Cambot-eye," providing an example of the eye/machine synthesis. An allusion to "kino" occurs on an early KTMA episode *Superdome* in which Tom is typing a letter chronicling a memory he has of one of Joel's attitude talks. As the light blinks and the buzzer goes off Tom Servo yells "Kino sign!" in place of the traditional "movie sign" (Mallon 1989, Episode K15). This reference seems to be more than a translation and may instead be an allusion to a technological tradition infused within film. Cambot's actions demonstrate many important principles of kino-eye theory in regards to power, perception and spectatorship. The superiority of the camera or the mechanical eye as initially theorized by Vertov seems realized and satirized through Cambot. Cambot and the robots become tangible examples of the synthesis between man and machine. Vertov exclaims in his *Variant on a Manifesto* that, "I am kino-eye, I am a mechanical eye. I, a machine, show you the world as only I can see it"(Vertov, 1984: 17). Again, this mechanical perspective has an intended or implied audience, remaking their perceptions and eventually their actions.

Ultimately Vertov believed that man should seek to become more machine-like. Vertov wrote, "Our paths lead through the poetry of machines, from bungling citizen to the perfect electric man"(Vertov, 1984:8). This "perfect electric man" had larger social implications for Vertov which do not transcend in the same way to *MST3K*. Yet the show does address certain social issues which John King discusses in his essay, "*Mystery Science Theater 3000*, Media Consciousness, and the Postmodern Allegory of the Captive Audience." For King *MST3K* highlights certain complicating and contradictory issues of isolation fostered by television. The inescapable inundation of popular culture present in the allusions on *MST3K* according to King represents "an allegory for the denatured postmodern American family held captive by television"(King, 2007: 45). According to King the spaceship also serves as a metaphor which reflects the kind of isolation created by TV. TV turns the viewers into a passive audience anxious to fit in with the popular culture. King continues, "psychologically, across American culture, what television promises is the allure of fitting in, of belonging;

ironically, what it asks them to do is to stay passively isolated at home. This in turn generates more anxiety about fitting in anxiety that can be conveniently assuaged by more ultimately unsatisfying television"(45). King also highlights the self-reflexive awareness of advertising and commercials. This impulse towards consumerism is frequently satirized on the show through the skits and intermissions (43–4). This social commentary discussed by King also connects man with machine (the TV). Yet it does not make man more like a machine per se. The process only strengthens man's dependency on and relationship with machine especially in regards to vision.

Cambot demonstrates a kind of dependency because he is mostly fixed and completely confined to the Satellite of Love. He is limited not in his ability to perceive or see better, but only by his immobility. According to Vertov, one of the important powers of the camera was its mobility, to move and be places no human could be. On the ship Cambot remains in the same position. Montage is also largely absent. The lack of editing agency allotted to Cambot reinforces the cadence of the show and also solidifies the viewer's perspective with Cambot's. Cambot is seeing not as a machine would see, but as a human would. Cambot's editing choices, or lack thereof, reflect how a person would see and watch if they were trapped on the Satellite of Love, reflecting real time on reel time. Though he is a camera with artificial intelligence, he uses very few of the special abilities allotted to him by the theories of Vertov with respect to mobility. Instead, he reflects certain limiting features of human vision.

Film theorist Jean Epstein would argue that "the cinema creates a particular system of consciousness limited to a single sense"(Epstein, 1993: 240). This sense, vision, insists that "only mobile and personal aspects of things, beings, and souls may be photogenic; that is, acquire a higher moral value through filmic reproduction ... mechanically speaking, the lens can alone sometimes succeed in revealing the inner nature of things"(Epstein, 1993: 317). Though Cambot is stationary it doesn't discount the accuracy of the images he produces nor his ability to "reveal the nature of things"(317). It both reasserts the validity of human perception but also recognizes the limitations. What Cambot is filming is not only the TV show but he is also filming a film. The implications of a camera re-filming the work of another camera may imply that the clarity with which the original is viewed is somewhat changed. The filmed film becomes a copy, and may be seen as somewhat removed from the intent of the original. But through the refilming and the recontextualizing, the original becomes understood in a new and at times more contemporary way.

With respect to *MST3K,* the films become understood and enjoyed for the humor inherent in their badness. Though taste is largely subjective, the Camp elements of the films become evident and corrective. As Susan Sontag acknowledges in her essay, "Notes on Camp" films such as these are "a good taste of bad taste"(Sontag, 1996: 291). This transformative ability within the observations of the show's characters also conforms with certain aesthetics and appreciation of Camp. Sontag also writes, "not only is there a Camp vision, a Camp way of looking at things. Camp is as well a quality discoverable in objects and the behavior of persons.... This distinction is important. True, the Camp eye has the power to transform experience"(283). This clarification seems to then turn Cambot into "Camp"bot. Cambot, with along with the quips and comments of Joel and the other robots transform the movies into distinctly Camp features. Cambot's perspective and filmed observations do discover the Camp quality in the film object. This rescues the artifact and allows it the ability to be transformed and observed in new and entertaining ways.

These observations, according to Jessica Royer, who makes a feminist reading of

MST3K, are a product of the male gaze. Royer argues that Joel, Mike (the head writer and second host) and the robots' observations simultaneously critique and reinforce certain stereotypes about women visible in many of the movies they watch. Royer states, "the humor of the observers' comments is at times productive and empowering but is still used to bond the male critics and exclude the women"(Royer, 2000: 131). Though the composition of the robots is gender neutral their opinions and personality are coded as masculine with the exception of Gypsy. Though Cambot is not gendered as distinctly as Tom and Crow he does serve as an extension or agent of their gazes. Yet Cambot is also an extension of the audience's gaze and perhaps serves as a reflection of its attitudes and perceptions rather than a distinctly male gaze.

Donna Haraway's essay "A Cyborg Manifesto: Science, Technology, and Social-Feminism in the Late Twentieth Century" argues that in some ways we, the audience, are all cyborgs, a "hybrid of machine and organism" (Haraway, 1991: 149). Haraway notes, "Contemporary science fiction is full of cyborgs-creatures simultaneously animal and machine, who populate worlds ambiguously natural and crafted" (149). She continues, "Machines were not self-moving, self-designing, autonomous. They could not achieve man's dream, only mock it" (152). Though Haraway stresses a socialist-feminist interpretation of the cyborg metaphor in which "consciousness" takes on Marxist connotations rather than sentient machine implications, her essay is valuable to understanding our relationship to machines. Haraway argues that "the new communications technologies are fundamental to the eradication of 'public life' for everyone ... televisions seem crucial to production of modern forms of 'private life'" (168). The implication of communications in conjunction with the largely private screen of the television reinforces the audience's reliance and even more so, dependence on their connection to the TV screen. Haraway addresses this general dependence stating, "there is no fundamental, ontological separation in our formal knowledge of machine and organism.... One consequence is that our sense of connection to our tools is heightened" (178). With *MST3K* Cambot is the ultimate tool, our connection to him is important and necessary. For the robots, it is not critical to have the "formal knowledge of machine and organism" (178). Their position and purpose within the show does not falter whether or not we consider them man, machine or a combination of both. The act and experience of spectatorship is universal and equal. The way in which we watch is mechanical, based on certain conditioned responses, our spectatorship enabled by machines and screens.

What *Mystery Science Theater 3000* constructs is a system. This system of screens, lenses and relays unite our minds through allusion and our eyes through Cambot's control. These mechanical partnerships themselves make evident a kind of technological pattern when we become spectators, inserting ourselves into the necessary place as viewer. In Antonin Artaud's text on cruelty and theater, *Theater and Its Double*, Artaud writes that, "there is no cruelty without consciousness and without the application of consciousness"(Artaud, 1958: 102). As an audience we participate in different demonstrations of consciousness; personal, filmic, and social. *MST3K* capitalizes on these variations of consciousness, providing a situation where man, machine, and everything in between are subjected to the same cruelty and included within the experiment. These tortures are ultimately redeemed for the audience, themselves susceptible due to the porous nature of the various screens and the influence they exude over and through us. Through the transformative abilities and powers of Cambot, the self-conscious and reflexive relationship between man and machine, and the awareness of an implied audience, *MST3K* becomes much more than hilarious, it becomes a pertinent demonstration and at times offers many examples of our real and theoretical connections to machines as an audience and as an individual. Perhaps this circuitry eventually becomes more than a connection, but instead, an ever increasing dependence and necessity.

MYSTERY SCIENCE THEATER 3000 EPISODES CITED

Mallon, Jim (producer), Trace Beaulieu (writer), Joe Hodgson (writer), et al. Episode 113 *The Black Scorpion* 1990.

Mallon, Jim (producer), Michael J. Nelson (writer), Trace Beaulieu (writer), et al. Episode 423 *Bride of the Monster* 1993.

Mallon, Jim (producer), Michael J. Nelson (writer), Trace Beaulieu (writer), et al. Episode 204 *Catalina Caper* 1990.

Mallon, Jim (producer), Michael J. Nelson (writer), Trace Beaulieu (writer), et al. Episode 403 *City Limits* 1992.

Mallon, Jim (producer), Trace Beaulieu (writer), Joel Hodgson (writer), et al. Episode 106 *The Crawling Hand* 1989.

Mallon, Jim (producer), Michael J. Nelson (writer), Trace Beaulieu (writer), et al. Episode 511 *Gunslinger* 1993.

Mallon, Jim (producer), Michael J. Nelson (writer), Trace Beaulieu (writer), et al. Episode 209 *The Hellcats* 1990.

Mallon, Jim (producer), Michael J, Nelson (writer), Trace Beaulieu (writer), et al. Episode 420 *The Human Duplicators* 1992.

Mallon, Jim (producer), Michael J. Nelson (writer), Trace Beaulieu (writer), et al. Episode 507 *I Accuse My Parents* 1992.

Mallon, Jim (producer), Michael J. Nelson (writer), Trace Beaulieu (writer), et al. Episode 311 *It Conquered the World* 1991.

Mallon, Jim (producer), Michael J. Nelson (writer), Trace Beaulieu (writer), et al. Episode 210 *King Dinosaur* 1990.

Mallon, Jim (producer), Joel Hodgson (writer), Trace Beaulieu (writer), et al. Episode K21 *Legend of the Dinosaur* 1989.

Mallon, Jim (producer), Trace Beaulieu (writer), Joel Hodgson (writer), et al. Episode 103 *Mad Monster* 1989.

Mallon, Jim (producer), Michael J. Nelson (writer), Trace Beaulieu (writer), et al. Episode 424 *Manos: The Hands of Fate* 1993.

Mallon, Jim (producer), Trace Beaulieu (writer), Joel Hodgson (writer), et al. Episode 110 *Robot Holocaust* 1990.

Mallon, Jim (producer), Michael J. Nelson (writer), Trace Beaulieu (writer), et al. Episode 202 *Sidehackers* 1990.

Mallon, Jim (producer), Michael J. Nelson (writer), Trace Beaulieu (writer), et al. Episode 401 *Space Travelers* 1992.

Mallon, Jim (producer), Joel Hodgson (writer), Trace Beaulieu (writer), et al. Episode K15 *Superdome* 1989.

Mallon, Jim (producer), Michael J. Nelson (writer), Trace Beaulieu (writer), et al. Episode 503 *Swamp Diamonds* 1993.

Mallon, Jim (producer), Michael J, Nelson (writer), Trace Beaulieu (writer), et al. Episode 404 *Teenagers from Outerspace* 1992.

REFERENCES

Artaud, Antonin. *Theater and Its Double.* Trans. Mary Caroline Richards. New York: Grove Press, 1958.

Carroll, Noel. "The Future of Allusion: Hollywood in the Seventies (And beyond)." *October.* 20 (Spring 1982): 51–81.

Epstein, Jean. "Magnification." In Richard Abel, ed. *French Film Theory and Criticism: A History/Anthology 1907–1939.* Princeton: Princeton University Press, 1993: 235–40.

_____. "On Certain Characteristics of Photogenie." In Richard Abel, ed. *French Film Theory and Criticism: A History/Anthology 1907–1939.* Princeton: Princeton University Press, 1993: 314–318.

Haraway, Donna. "A Cyborg Manifesto: Science Technology, and Socialist-Feminism in the Late Twentieth Century," *Simians, Cyborgs and Women: The Reinvention of Nature.* New York: Routledge, 1991: 149–181.

King, John. "*Mystery Science Theater 3000*, Media Consciousness, and the Postmodern Allegory of the Captive Audience." *Journal of Film and Media*: 59: 4 (Winter 2007): 37–53.

Mallon, Jim, Michael J. Nelson, Mary Jo Pehl, et al. *The Mystery Science Theater 3000 Amazing Colossal Episode Guide*. New York: Bantam, 1996.

Royer, Jessica A. "What's Happening on Earth? *Mystery Science Theater 3000* as Reflection of Gender Roles and Attitudes Towards Women." In Elyce Rae Helford, ed. *Fantasy Girls: Gender in the New Universe of Science Fiction and Fantasy Television*. Lanham, MD: Rowman, 2000: 115–33.

Sontag, Susan. "Notes on Camp." *Against Interpretation*. New York: Picador, 1996. 275–92.

Turvey, Malcolm. "Jean Epstein's Cinema of Immanence: The Rehabilitation of the Corporeal Eye." *October*. 83 (Winter 1998): 25–50.

Vertov, Dziga. "Variant on a Manifesto." In Annette Michelson, ed. *Kino Eye: The Writings of Dziga Vertov*. Berkley: University of California Press, 1984: 5–21; 35–50.

22

MSTies and Mastery:
Circulating the Tapes in a Digital Age

by Joseph S. Walker

While it may or may not be true, as asserted in Lawrence Kasdan's 1991 *Grand Canyon*, that "all of life's riddles are answered in the movies," the fervent fans of *Mystery Science Theater 3000* might well assert the alternate theory that we can learn much of what we need to know about life from the show's brand of movie mockery. In pondering the meaning and purpose of collecting, for example, we can turn to the host segments from the *MST* skewering of *The Giant Spider Invasion* (Murphy 1997, episode 810). While the actual film Mike and the 'bots are subjected to in this episode concerns huge arachnids invading central Wisconsin, the host segments are a parody of the science fiction classic *Invasion of the Body Snatchers*, with various cast members having their bodies and identities stolen by pod-borne invaders. When a pod version of Tom Servo turns up alongside the real Servo, Mike and Crow are initially baffled as to which is which until Mike asks a question "only the real Servo would know": "What do you have in your underwear collection?"

The pod Servo dismisses the question in a flat monotone: "Oh please, you would have to be a total pathetic loser of the lowest quality to have an underwear collection." At this, the real Servo chuckles confidently, then unleashes his broadside: "Three hundred and forty two pairs of cotton boxers no duplicates, seventy eight pairs of silk boxers, seven hundred and two pairs of high-cut briefs, fifty five pairs of low-cut briefs, seven banana warmers, one pair of 'Home of the Whopper' brief, one vintage pair of Joe Namath netted slingshot brief prototype! Loser, loser! I won!"

There is the collector's obsessive knowledge of and pride in his prizes; there is the arrangement of items in a series or context made possible only by the act of collecting itself (only through comparison with another pair of underwear could a pair be said to be high or low cut, let alone "vintage"); there is the misunderstanding and derision of the noncollector; there is the devotion to commercial objects which characterize a consumer mindset ("one pair of 'Home of the Whopper' brief"); there is the fetishism of objects which have been detached from their original purpose or use (as a nonhumanoid robot, after all, Servo doesn't need one pair of underwear, let alone 1,186 of them); there is the special attention to the unique item which grants the collection special distinction (surely not every underwear collector has a prototype!). Finally and most crucially, there is the vital connection between collecting and identity, a connection which is so strong that the two become virtually indistinguishable; Servo himself is confused as to whether he is "real" before being asked about his collection, at which point he regains a sure and victorious knowledge of himself. The collection *is* his identity.

Although studies have indicated that "one of every three Americans has at least one active collection" (Belk, 1995: 55), and collecting has even been described as "the chief mode of our culture" (Sarat Maharaj, qtd. in Windsor, 1964: 50), the academic or socio-logical consideration of collecting as a distinct cultural activity remains somewhat sparse compared to discussions of other human occupations. One concept that consistently runs through those texts which do exist, however, is that there is indeed a vital connection between collecting and identity, a connection which the *MST* segment, farcical though it is, in many ways embodies perfectly. For Paul van der Grijp, collecting "is a matter of authenticity, of creating new identities, both of the object collected and, by extension, of the collector" (2006: 12). Thus, for example, stamp collectors give the small pieces of gummed paper they obsessively pursue new identities, converting them from a purely prac-tical function within a specific exchange system to independent objects of desire and admi-ration in their own right. At the same time the collector himself gains a new identity, one which redefines the way in which he sees and relates to the world: "To collect is to launch individual desire across the intertext of environment and history" (Cardinal, 1994: 68). The collector himself is aware of this connection and the degree to which his identity is increas-ingly determined by his collection, for "Identity-creating through collecting has become a self-conscious game" (Windsor, 1994: 64).

The extent to which this game is a positive or productive one, however, remains open to debate, and certainly many writers who have discussed collecting echo, if in more elevated language, pod Servo's evaluation of the collector as "a total pathetic loser of the lowest qual-ity." Collecting is often seen dismissively as the most extreme expression of the mindless materialism of contemporary consumer societies. Many commentators in this vein approv-ingly quote the journalist Martin Kelner, who in a 1993 piece for London's *The Independent* newspaper wrote that "life is all about acquiring STUFF, then acquiring more STUFF. [...] Then you die" (qtd. in Windsor, 1994:50). Jean Baudrillard, perhaps rather predictably, suggests that the collecting impulse is a "mechanism of compensation during critical phases in a person's sexual development" which "runs counter to active genital sexuality" and is essentially "a regression to the anal stage" (1994: 9). For Baudrillard and other writers making similar arguments, collecting is essentially a mild form of perversion in which any genuine interest in the objects being assembled is secondary to the obsessive and somewhat pathetic needs of a narcissistic, regressive psyche.

Other writers, however, have recognized this as a rather extreme and reductive view and have been more likely to see collecting, and even the collecting of seemingly banal con-sumer objects, as productive in both narrative and social senses. Van der Grijp harshly cri-tiques the element of reductive belittling in arguments such as Baudrillard's, which seek a single, universal motivation for collectors; for him, it is vital to recognize that collecting is social rather than narcissistic, and inherently involves communication with others rather than a complete turning inward (2006: 18). Cardinal suggests that collecting is essentially the construction of "an intimate narrative ... through which selfhood is sewn into the unfolding fabric of a lifetime's experience" (1994: 68). For Belk, collecting is a natural response to consumer culture (1995: 139) which enables us to exercise "creative control in an otherwise alienated marketplace" (1995: 151) and therefore may, simply put, "be good for us as individuals" (1995:141). These more sympathetic critics retain a focus on the symbiotic relationship between selfhood and collecting, but discover in the art of collecting a means of creatively and deliberately constructing a healthy and mature identity, not a regressive return to infantile self-absorption. Seen in its most positive light, collecting is a means of both experiencing and exhibiting mastery over a capitalist environment which is more often understood as mastering us.

Discussions of collecting, of course, tend to assume that what is being "collected" is some kind of material object (or rather, some series of material objects, whether the parameters of the series are defined by the individual collector or by some collective consensus). What does it mean, however, to "collect" (or master) something like *Mystery Science Theater 3000*, a media text which, in its essence, consists not of objects but of experiences? The same question might be asked of any television series. To collect music by the Beatles, for example, means to collect albums and singles (and later, CDs) containing their recordings — that is to say, physical items — but for most of the history of television, programs have consisted of episodes which are watched at the moment of broadcast, and then accessible only through memory. Such memory could, especially in the case of those programs which attracted devoted cult audiences, be supplemented by sources such as episode guides or even "novelizations" of the scripts (as occurred with, for example, the original *Star Trek*), but the actual episode, in the days before the VCR, could only be seen again if it was rerun. Today, of course, technological advances exploited by consumer society have provided a new solution to this problem, in the form of the DVD (or, now, Blu-Ray) disk, usually sold in the form of box sets containing entire seasons of popular (or not-so-popular) series. The appeal of such box sets rests largely in their ability to immediately (and, some would say, artificially) gratify the collector's impulse to completion and mastery. A collector can spend decades hunting for every possible variation, edition, revision and format of all the music issued by the Beatles; with a single purchase, however, he can obtain the satisfaction of looking at his shelf and seeing *The Sopranos* or *The X-Files*, complete from beginning to end.

As MSTies are all too painfully aware such mastery is not so easily achieved with our favorite "cowtown puppet show," a situation made particularly painful because the show can be seen as one of the first to actively encourage its fans to aspire to such a collection. Early episodes of *Mystery Science Theater* famously included the phrase "Keep circulating the tapes" as part of the end credits, often juxtaposed with an expression of gratitude to "MSTies everywhere." Taping television shows on home VCRs had already become a common practice by the time *MST* became a nationally broadcast series in late 1989, although it was still somewhat controversial. Media companies had only reluctantly accepted the idea that home viewers had the right to "time-shift" their viewing experience through taping, and still insisted that such tapes were for private use only. Indeed, it was occasionally argued that viewers should erase their tapes once they were viewed in order to avoid violating copyright law in its strictest interpretations. In stark contrast to this general policy of suspicion and restrictions, the idea of urging viewers to "keep circulating the tapes" not only acknowledged that viewers were taping the series, but actually encouraged them to share their tapes with others.

What's particularly brilliant and effective about this move is using the phrase "*keep* circulating the tapes" as opposed to, say, the simpler "tell your friends" or even "circulate the tapes." The "keep" here hints of the existence of a group of fans already busily passing tapes from hand to hand, a group which the individual viewer is thus encouraged to seek out and join — or, if necessary, create. The phrase has an air of conspiracy and secrecy, too, with "tapes" speaking to a decidedly consumer-centered mode of interaction and recalling the activities of, for example, traders in music bootlegs. "Keep circulating the tapes" positions both *MST* and its fans as outside the mainstream, something rebellious and personal rather than conformist and commercial. Suggesting that fans constituted their own underground society also neatly aligns them with the aesthetic and tone of the actual program, which from the beginning represented itself as a mocking voice from outside the entertainment establishment rather than part of the Hollywood "machine." Inevitably, the phrase's invocation of a group of tape-trading fans became a self-fulfilling prophesy, and such groups did indeed form quickly, with the sharing of episodes becoming the basis of a fan community which would become highly vocal, organized and visible as the series continued, and which continues to exist today, more than a decade after the program left the air. In later interviews, members of Best Brains Inc. (BBI)— the production company behind *MST*— would indicate that they saw "keep circulating the tapes" simply as a necessary part of promoting an offbeat show airing on an obscure cable network, but in retrospect it can be seen as an early example of a kind of innovative, ground-level marketing in which fan activity and enthusiasm largely takes the place of "official," producer-driven promotion.

"Circulating" suggests a group of tapes in constant movement, but of course many early fans of *MST* kept their first-generation copies of all the episodes they taped, even if they then made dubs to be distributed by various means to other fans (including many who could not otherwise watch the show, which did not air on a network that reached all American homes). These fans in turn would often keep their second-generation tapes and distribute additional copies, and so on. Circulating thus shades into collecting which, as we have seen, shades into mastery. Certainly since the penetration of the VCR into the American home there had been fans who taped, labeled and catalogued their own collections of their favorite series, but *MST* may have been the first show to make this activity the basis of much of its interaction with the fan base. To a degree which was essentially unprecedented, MSTies also defined themselves as *collectors* of *MST*.

Several factors, beyond the "tapes" phrase which was actually part of the show, greatly encouraged this form of "collecting" the show. First, as already mentioned, *MST* aired on an obscure cable network (later merged with The Comedy Channel to form Comedy Central, a network which did and does reach most American homes) which was not available everywhere, thus increasing the demand for tapes among fans who moved or heard about the show from friends (for its final three seasons the series aired on the Sci-Fi Channel, which also did not reach all American homes). Even for those who received the right channel, some episodes were elusive; a few aired rarely due to complicated rights issues involving the movie being riffed, and BBI itself eventually requested that episodes from the first season, which were notably different in tone and pacing than later efforts, be held back from further broadcasts. Some episodes were thus "rarer" than others, allowing for collectors to seek and acquire the equivalent of "one pair of 'Home of the Whopper' briefs." Even once an episode was acquired, it was possible to continue seeking a copy that was of an earlier generation. Moreover, the fact that an episode of *MST* is two hours long, as opposed to the hour or half hour standard for most American programs, coincided neatly with the capacity of most commercially available VHS tapes when set to record at the slowest speed (and thus highest quality). A single tape thus held a single show, and while this might be expected to reduce the appeal of *taping* (since it would be more cost effective to fit two or four episodes on a tape), it actually increases the appeal of *collecting*, since each tape/episode therefore becomes a unique item in the series rather than a hybrid of several. Similarly, the fact that episodes could easily and accurately be referred to by the title of the movies being riffed made labeling the tapes both easier and more interesting.

Perhaps most crucially, it was difficult — actually, impossible — for even the most dedicated fans of the show with the best connections to other collectors to acquire a truly complete set of episodes. While it might initially seem odd that this would fuel collecting, anyone who has ever thought of themselves as a collector can understand how the existence of seemingly unattainable prizes can both ignite interest in a collection and keep it burning. The reason for the compelling gap in every known *MST* collection, of course, is the existence of the KTMA episodes, which remain to this day one of the touchstones of *MST* fandom.

The history of *MST*, including its origins and primitive first season on the Minneapolis public access station KTMA, has been well established and documented elsewhere. For our purposes, what is important is that the existence and pursuit of those early episodes, broadcast only to a small local market with little advertising or viewer awareness, quickly became central to the *MST* fan community. Because BBI regarded the largely ad-libbed KTMA episodes as being of poor quality and not representative of their work — and, even more to the point, because they hadn't even bothered to acquire the rights to the films riffed in those episodes — they were never broadcast nationally and, in fact, most appear to have been shown only once in the Minneapolis market. Residents of Minneapolis who had become fans of the show during its local run had tapes of many of the episodes, and through the process of "circulating" these quickly became available to the fan community at large. However, to this day the first three of the twenty-one known KTMA episodes have never surfaced in any form available to the fan community. This is despite energetic efforts on the part of various fans who have run ads in Minneapolis papers for years, petitioned to raid the archives of the station, and so on. Today, the discovery of the "missing" episodes remains a common fantasy of MSTies, and it must be acknowledged that it is not entirely impossible that this could happen. Hope is fueled by the story of the fifteenth KTMA episode, riffing the movie *Superdome*. This episode was broadcast in March of 1989, and for fifteen years every fan copy derived from a single original, which was missing the final host segment. In 2004, however, a copy was unearthed which had the complete episode and quickly made its way through the fan community. If this prize can turn up after fifteen years, reason fans, who's to say that tapes of the fabled first three episodes aren't waiting to be discovered in some Minneapolis attic?

These factors — the show's own promotion of taping, the difficulty of completing a set, the attraction of the format — combined to make possible the fetishistic object which was the original defining center of MSTie identity: the shelf of neatly labeled, carefully ordered VHS tapes containing the series. There have, of course, been other things for MSTies to collect. BBI and the official fan club have released a good deal of merchandise over the years, ranging from mugs to bumper stickers to t-shirts — and, of course, an episode guide, albeit one covering only the first six seasons. There have also been tapes (and later DVDs) which supplement the aired episodes: compilations of host segments, documentaries about the making of the show, and so on. Some actual props have been sold over the years, although there are a very limited number of these. Many fans have made their own versions of the 'bots, especially Tom Servo and Crow, aided by plans sold by BBI which reveal the mundane origins of their various parts (Crow's beak, for example, is a toy bowling pin split in two). "'Bot building" remains a popular activity among a subset of fans today, with the necessary parts turning up regularly on sites such as eBay. Nonetheless, there can be no doubt that for most fans the center of any *MST* collection must be the episodes.

Given this, it might seem to be a simple thing to calculate exactly how many episodes there are, but complications quickly arise. In fan parlance episodes are numbered from K01 (the first episode broadcast on KTMA) to 1013 (the thirteenth episode of the tenth nationally broadcast season) and constitute eleven seasons made up of one hundred and ninety-seven episodes. However, this number is immediately open to contestation and adjustment. Should the first three episodes be included in this tally? What about the theatrically released *Mystery Science Theater 3000: The Movie*, released between seasons six and seven; is this an "episode"? The first episode of the seventh season, *Night of the Blood Beast*, was broadcast with two entirely different sets of host segments; does this constitute two different episodes? What about episodes of *The Mystery Science Theater Hour*, which was a syndicated version of the show which split certain original episodes into two one-hour episodes and added new host segments? What about the various specials, such as those mocking clips from summer releases or Oscar nominated films? The fact that different fans could answer each of these questions differently meant that, despite their shared origin in a common body of televised texts, each MSTies collection was subtly different, thus allowing for both participation in the collective social activity of fandom and the construction of a particular and individual identity within that context.

Such distinctions would be, at least to a large extent, erased if there were to be a commercial release of the complete set of *MST* episodes, as there has been for virtually every other significant television series of its era (and, it could be argued, a large number of insignificant ones). In such a case, individual and idiosyncratic collections assembled through patient efforts would be largely displaced by identical boxes, and the "circulation" which remains a central part of *MST* fandom (though, as we will see, in altered forms) would essentially cease. This has not happened, however, and it remains highly unlikely that it will happen because any official release of an episode requires acquiring the rights to the film riffed in that episode. Though some of the movies are in the public domain and can thus be released without additional expense, the rights to other films are difficult, prohibitively expensive, or simply impossible to obtain. On fan discussion boards, it is received knowledge that some rights holders are offended at the *MST* treatment to the degree that they will refuse to ever surrender their rights.

Despite these difficulties some episode have received official releases, with interesting implications for the continuing circulation of episodes by fans. The media company Rhino began releasing individual VHS tapes of some episodes while the series was still on the air; these were eventually supplanted by box sets containing DVDs of (usually) four episodes, with Shout! Factory eventually acquiring the license for the series. The existence of these official releases constitutes a challenge to fan circulation of episodes because it confronts fans with the knowledge that such circulation is, technically, illegal. On the discussion boards and fan sites which today constitute the activity centers of *MST* fandom, the consensus response to this dilemma is to immediately suspend the "trading" of any episode once it has been announced that there will be an official release of it. Instead MSTies are encouraged to buy the licensed releases, even if they already have satisfactory copies of the episodes. This is assumed to provide additional income for the producers of the show, to encourage additional releases (which are often made attractive through the addition of interviews, trailers, and so on), and to reduce the likelihood of any serious attempt to stop or slow fan circulation, since it does not directly compete with the official releases. "Traders" (more often, as we will see, sellers) found to be in violation of this policy are subject to being shunned by the fan community at large, with their names and internet identities distributed and added to lists of the undesirable. As might be expected, this consensus breaks down to a certain extent when specific official releases go out of print or are withdrawn; should they then be returned to the list of episodes approved for circulating? How soon? Can the official release supplant tapes of broadcasts as a source of fan copies?

Dealing with the existence of official releases has been one of the major shifts in the nature and methods of "circulating the tapes" since the activity began. Another has been the shift away from tapes, as recordable DVDs have become the media of choice, making the concern over the decline of quality from generation to generation largely irrelevant. Far and away the most fundamental change, however, has been the inevitable professionalization of the activity. As originally conceived and practiced by the fan community, "circulating the tapes" was to take the form of trading, with each party in a transaction getting copies of episodes he didn't previously have. In this way, a complete collection (whatever that might constitute for an individual fan) could be gradually assembled, transaction by transaction. There was an idealistic, communal atmosphere to this form of circulation as it was talked about and, much of the time, actually practiced. Fans just starting their collections, for example, who would have little to offer more established traders who already had most or all episodes, could often arrange to trade blank tapes or other goods to get started; only rarely would cash be involved in a transaction.

It was probably inevitable that such idyllic circumstances would not endure, but the cancellation of *Mystery Science Theater* in 1999 assured that this initial stage of circulation was also at its end. New fans now had no way to obtain episodes to trade, and established fans satisfied with their own collections no longer had any motivation to trade. Today, the circulation of *MST* episodes which have not been officially released is dominated by a handful of individuals who maintain websites where, with varying degrees of openness, DVDs of the episodes are simply sold (because this activity is, despite its visibility, illegal, I will not identify these individuals or their websites here). Interestingly, many of these sites maintain a pretense of continuing the old trading ethos by including lists of items the proprietor is willing to trade episodes for, but these are usually so difficult to obtain or prohibitively expensive that it is unlikely many trades are conducted. These "traders," for the most part, subscribe to the guiding principle of not dealing in commercially available episodes, or at least not those currently in print; the few who do not do so are spoken of with derision in fan discussions. There can be little doubt that most of the dealers are themselves sincere MSTies motivated, at least in part, by the desire to help new fans discover and learn about the show, but the sites are also openly competitive with each other, sometimes holding special sales on themed groups of episodes, highlighting their reasonable prices, asserting that they have the highest-quality master tapes (particularly of the KTMA episodes), and so on.

"Circulating the tapes" thus continues to be a central activity, but one which has entered a kind of "second stage" on the borderline between underground commercial activity and open commercialization. While the source through which episodes have been obtained has changed its nature, however, the crucial point here is that the individual collector of *MST* still has the opportunity to craft a collection around his own interests and desires; individual collections can still vary in several respects. While the core group of episodes is stable, the differences in quality, packaging and appearance among the discs offered by the various web vendors (some, for example, have created art and logos to be printed on their discs) mean that no two collections will be precisely alike. The real variations, however, come with the "extras" each collector chooses to include or exclude from his collection. Each of the major

MST vendors offers, in addition to the episodes themselves, a wide selection of "extras," discs containing materials related in various ways to the series itself. While the available extras differ from site to site, among them are, for example, other television appearances by various members of the cast; compilations of ads for or news stories about the series; "unmstied" original versions of the films riffed on the series, particularly those which have never been officially released; production materials such as writers' run-throughs of specific episodes; compilations of the Saturday-morning serial shorts riffed on the show; "fan mstings," some surprisingly sophisticated, in which fans produce their own "episodes" of *MST*; and so on. By choosing which of these extras "really" belong in his collection, each individual MSTie defines for himself what "his" *MST*, and thus his identity as an *MST* collector, is.

The productivity of ventures such as these means that, although *Mystery Science Theater 3000* went off the air more than ten years ago, many collections continue to grow and change in very dynamic ways today as fans make their selections from the wide variety of new "riffs" available, all of which derive from and owe their existence to the original show. Perhaps more importantly, the success of the RiffTrax format points to a coming shift in the way such collections will be conceived of—a "third stage" which will, inevitably, supplant the "second stage" dominated by a handful of web vendors. For many fans who are accustomed to thinking of their collection in physical terms — the shelf filled with neatly labeled and ordered episodes — RiffTrax are challenging because they do not have a physical form; they are simply digital files, intended to be played while the riffed film is watched. Such fans have solved this problem by making their own physical copies; using a home computer and a variety of media manipulation programs, they "rip" the film from its original DVD, add the RiffTrax as a new audio track, and then burn the resulting file onto a new DVD. This DVD can then be placed in a case with a customized cover, one which is designed to closely resemble a commercial release (such covers have long been popular with fans seeking to attractively house their *MST* collections, and most "second stage" vendors offer their own versions. Most of these are designed to mimic the covers of the official Rhino releases, although many fans are fond of the work of Josh Way, a fan who has designed, and made available on the web, a highly attractive cover for every single episode of the series. His work is good enough that my entire collection, including episodes released commercially, is housed in Josh Way covers). The official RiffTrax fan forum regularly features discussions by fans who make their own physical RiffTrax collection in this way, in which they post their cover designs, tips for producing the highest quality products, and even pictures of their collections.

For such fans, "collecting" continues to be a matter of assembling and arranging physical objects. For a large and growing body of *RiffTrax/MST* collectors, however — "third stage" collectors — these physical manifestations seem both unwieldy and unnecessary; their "collections" consist simply of digital files stored on their computer or other device. Increasingly this is true not only of the new productions by RiffTrax (and Cinematic Titanic, whose "episodes" can be purchased through their website either as disks which are mailed to the buyer or downloads which are received instantly), but also of the original *MST* episodes. While I have said that the "circulation" of *MST* episodes is today dominated by the "second stage" web vendors, it might already be more accurate to say that most new fans actually obtain their episodes through the Digital Archive Project (DAP), a fan collective which aims to make all *MST* episodes available at all times through bitTorrent, a hugely popular program which allows users to share files with, essentially, anyone online. Although DAP nominally follows the standard practice of not dealing in commercially available episodes, it is notoriously difficult to remove a file once it has been released onto the net. Even for fans who lack the technical expertise to handle DAP files, most episodes can be viewed in their entirety — albeit ten minutes at a time — on YouTube.

The dawning "third stage" of *MST* collecting, then, will more properly be the end of collecting, at least as it is commonly understood. Instead of the carefully assembled, individual shelves of episodes which have defined each collector's identity, we are clearly headed for a time when all *MST* episodes (save the legendary K01 through K03) and offshoots will be available at any time to anyone with a sufficiently fast connection to the web. The individual collection is giving way to the collective storehouse — a shift which is, of course, occurring in various ways for all media texts, but which might be of special concern to the *MST* fan. For more than twenty years, *MST* fandom and MSTie identity has been founded on the simultaneous desire for and obstacles to completing a collection. Part of what has distinguished *MST* from other shows is the dedication and effort required to assemble such a collection, and fans have justifiably taken pride in their efforts to do so. What happens when this is no longer the case — when the immediate and casual access to any episode makes the very notion of the individual collection obsolete, when *MST*, like any other media text, is simply another file in the endless, roiling system? Given the symbiotic relationship between collecting and identity, will rendering collecting meaningless do the same to identity, even if only our identity as MSTies?

REFERENCES

Baudrillard, Jean. "The System of Collecting." In John Elsner and Roger Cardinal, eds. *The Cultures of Collecting*. Cambridge: Harvard University Press, 1994.
Belk, Russell W. *Collecting in a Consumer Society*. London: Routledge, 1995.
Cardinal, Roger. "Collecting and Collage-Making: The Case of Kurt Schwitters." In John Elsner and Roger Cardinal, eds. *The Cultures of Collecting*. Cambridge: Harvard University Press, 1994.
Van der Grijp, Paul. *Passion and Profit: Towards and Anthropology of Collecting*. Berlin: Lit Verlag, 2006.
Windsor, John. "Identity Parades." In John Elsner and Roger Cardinal, eds. *The Cultures of Collecting*. Cambridge: Harvard University Press, 1994.

PART EIGHT

History and Pre-History

23

"Hamlet will return in *Thunderball*": Historical Precedents of Riffing

by Mark McDermott

The ability to superimpose critical or humorous comments on an existing performance seems to be a recent development made possible by modern technology. Certainly the casual observer of *Mystery Science Theater 3000* and its spin-offs would see a similarity to earlier TV entertainments like the old horror movies presented on local TV by acerbic hosts in campy horror settings. But it is possible to dig a bit deeper and find occasional comedic presentations that wouldn't sound out of place being enacted by Joel or Mike, and the 'Bots.

This chapter will attempt to define the elements of riffing that set it apart from other types of literary or dramatic lampoons. Then, some examples of performance that fall under this definition will be offered for consideration. Though examples from the years before recorded performance, I hope to be able to make it possible to bring up more obscure, but no less enlightening examples.

A Riff by Any Other Name

Mystery Science Theater 3000 has named and codified the form of entertainment known as "riffing." Following are the elements that transform mere rudeness in movie theaters into riffing:

1. A riff is humorous commentary being made about a work not produced by the riffers. There are plenty of movies and plays where an actor breaks that "fourth wall" to address the audience about the play itself, and even gets heckled by audience members or the unseen narrator. These have been a part of the original script, not imposed from without by a third party without the cooperation of the producers.
2. It is also expected, though not mandatory, that the riffs be performed by characters with their own back-story and ongoing plot. This creates continuity between episodes of a series in which the presentations being riffed on are totally unrelated. *Beavis and Butt-Head* (1993–1997) built on this premise by focusing equally on the title characters' dunderheaded conversations on music videos and on their crude antics away from the TV.
3. The riffing is also effective if the characters of the original production remain ignorant

220

of the fact that their performance is being critically hammered. This tends to leave off many presentations based on vaudeville, in which veteran performers are used to dealing with hecklers in the audience. When Fozzie Bear reacts to being razzed by balcony-dwellers Statler and Waldorf, it merely shows that the apparent "riffing" is a part of *The Muppet Show*'s meta-textual script.

While they lay outside the scope of the above definitions, we will examine some of the more influential "Comedy Dubs" or "Gag Dubs." This is the term used by TVTropes.com (2010) and others to describe films created by dubbing comedic dialog or narration over older movies, or those originally shot in another language. This subset includes favorites like the Jay Ward–produced *Fractured Flickers* and Woody Allen's *What's Up, Tiger Lily?*

Euripides? Eumenides! or The Greeks Had an App for That!

It is not surprising that the earliest accessible ancestor of riffing can be found during the first literary movement of Western civilization, the Greek theatre. Aristophanes was one of the first to "riff" on the work of an equally famous competitor. Aristophanes was active at a plateau in popular culture similar to our own: A body of literature or drama that was popular with the public, and an audience familiar enough with many contemporary plays to recognize the tropes and clichés of another dramatist's work when they were being parodied.

The theatre of Aristophanes' time was presented during the festivals of Dionysus (Bacchus), first at the established City Dionysia, and then expanded to the Lenaia (dedicated to the female worshippers of Dionysus). Though the festivals were religious in nature, they celebrated Dionysus' status as the god of the man's darker nature: drunkenness and bawdy behavior (Theodoridis, 2010).

Several plays would be presented during the nearly week-long festivals, with first and second prizes awarded by a panel of judges. Performers and writers at the Dionysia had license to offer opinions that might be considered treasonous beyond the safety of the stage. Aristophanes' *Peace* (422 BCE) was one of his plays known to have won the festival prize, even though it criticized the Peloponnesian War, then in its tenth year. Many of Athens' prominent citizens were mocked throughout Aristophanes' plays, including Cleon, Plato and Sophocles, but Aristophanes twice drew his blade on the tragedian Euripides (c. 480 BCE–406 BCE). In *The Thesmophoriazusae* (412 BCE) Aristophanes called Euripides to task for the women characters in his plays. After Euripides' death, *The Frogs* (405 BCE) presented Dionysus himself as being so moved by Euripides' tragedy *Andromeda*, he descends to Hades to bring the poet back to Earth. Dionysus finds Euripides arguing with Aeschylus over who was the greater dramatist, for the chance to sit at Hades' side. Dionysus judges a competition in which each critiques the work of the other. Aeschylus' critique involves letting Euripides recite the expository openings of his plays before inserting "and he lost his prick!" After several other rounds of competition, Dionysus decides to take back Aeschylus instead (2010).

Although Aristophanes often quoted scraps of dialog from the writers he was satirizing, in *The Thesmophoriazusae (Women at the Festival)*, he presents a caricature of Euripides himself enacting scenes from his plays, while being heckled by other characters. The play's title refers to the Thesmophoria, an Athenian women's festival in honor of the goddesses Demeter and Persephone. A women's council has summoned Euripides to answer before them for his portrayal of women characters in his plays. Fearing for his life, Euripides convinces his father-in-law Mnesilochus to disguise himself as a woman and infiltrate the festival to plead his case. Once there, though, Mnesilochus delivers a rant against the other sex himself. The women penetrate Mnesilochus' disguise, forcing him to seek sanctuary in the festival's temple. Mnesilochus gets an urgent rescue plea out to Euripides, who arrives as characters from his plays, repeating lines obviously familiar to contemporary Athenians, while the women of the festival offer comments. Here Mnesilochus begins to quote the opening lines of Euripides' *Helen* (412 BCE). The role of "Seventh Woman" is so-called as she was the seventh unnamed woman to speak:

> MNESILOCHUS: I have contracted quite a squint by looking round for him, and yet Euripides does not come. Who is keeping him? No doubt he is ashamed of his cold Palamedes. What will attract him? Let us see! By which of his pieces does he set most store? Ah! I'll imitate his Helen, his lastborn. I just happen to have a complete woman's outfit.
>
> SEVENTH WOMAN: What are you ruminating over now again? Why are you rolling up your eyes? You'll have no reason to be proud of your Helen, if you don't keep quiet until one of the Prytanes arrives.
>
> MNESILOCHUS (as Helen): "These shores are those of the Nile with the beautiful nymphs, these waters take the place of heaven's rain and fertilize the white earth, that produces the black syrmea."
>
> SEVENTH WOMAN: By bright Hecaté, you're a cunning varlet.
>
> MNESILOCHUS: "Glorious Sparta is my country and Tyndareus is my father."
>
> SEVENTH WOMAN: He your father, you rascal! Why, 'tis Phrynondas.
>
> MNESILOCHUS: "I was given the name of Helen."
>
> SEVENTH WOMAN: What! you are again becoming a woman, before we have punished you for having pretended it a first time!
>
> MNESILOCHUS: "A thousand warriors have died on my account on the banks of the Scamander."
>
> SEVENTH WOMAN: Why have you not done the same?
>
> MNESILOCHUS: "And here I am upon these shores; Menelaus, my unhappy husband, does not yet come. Ah! how life weighs upon me! Oh! ye cruel crows, who have not devoured my body! But what sweet hope is this that sets my heart a-throb? Oh, Zeus! grant it may not prove a lying one!"
>
> EURIPIDES (as Menelaus): "To what master does this splendid palace belong? Will he welcome strangers who have been tried on the billows of the sea by storm and shipwreck?"
>
> MNESILOCHUS: "This is the palace of Proteus."
>
> EURIPIDES: "Of what Proteus?"
>
> SEVENTH WOMAN: Oh! the thrice cursed rascal! how he lies! By the goddesses, 'tis ten years since Proteus died.

This dialogue continues with the woman answering back to the parroted dialogue, until a magistrate (the aforementioned Prytane) arrives, and Euripides beats a retreat. The magistrate orders Mnesilochus bound to a post and prepared for a public lashing. His guard, a Scythian archer, binds Mnesilochus, then sits nearby. Euripides reappears disguised as Perseus, signaling Mnesilochus to act the title role of Andromeda.

Between lines from *Andromeda*, the in-laws inform each other of the need to buy off the guard to effect an escape. Euripides suddenly assumes the role of Echo from the same play and gives us several pages of the "Repeat after me" bit (which means that gag is over 2,400 years old). Euripides departs again, returning with a dancing girl and a flute player. He promises the women he will not write another word against them if they drop the charges. They agree, but refuse to intervene in Mnesilochus' case. For the Scythian, Euripides has the girl practice her nude dancing, then give him what we now call a "lap dance." The two head offstage to follow their instincts, giving Euripides time to free Mnesilochus and hurry off, leaving the chorus to misdirect the derelict guard with a "they went thataway!"[1]

"What's worse than clowns? Danish clowns!"

A Mɪᴅsᴜᴍᴍᴇʀ Nɪɢʜᴛ's ʀɪꜰꜰɪɴɢ

One of the more unusual episodes of *MST3K* was the Season 10 riff on *Hamlet*. This *Hamlet* was a 1961 German TV production, acted in German, with Maximilian Schell as the moody prince, then overdubbed back into English (2003). However, William Shakespeare (1564–1616) himself offered his own play-within-a-play featuring some definite riffs in *A Midsummer Night's Dream* (c. 1594–1596).

As in the Greek classical period, the Elizabethan theatre scene offered an ideal situation to allow one writer to riff upon another's work. English theatre saw a flowering of straightforward drama, as opposed to stylized mystery and morality plays. A burgeoning theatre scene gave the public many chances to attend and become familiar with theatre, and what separates good drama from bad. Developments in printing meant societies could preserve more plays for posterity, study, and revival.

It's certain the theatre-going audience was well familiar with the tragedy *Pyramis and Thisby*. Shakespeare himself pinched the plot for his own *Romeo and Juliet*, probably written around the same time as *Midsummer Night's Dream*. The original story of doomed lovers dates back to Roman mythology, first preserved in Ovid's *Metamorphoses* (c. 8 ᴄᴇ) and has been constantly modernized all the way to *The Fantasticks* (1960). In the final act of *Midsummer Night's Dream*, after all the tangled romantic and magical plot threads have been unraveled, Duke Theseus of Athens and his wedding party: Demetrius, Lysander, and Hippolyta, watch an amateur presentation of *Pyramis and Thisby*, and their high spirits overtake the production. No doubt audiences at the Globe has already endured performances of the story by local "rude mechanicals."

BOTTOM [as Pyramus]: … Thanks, courteous wall: Jove shield thee well for this!
 But what see I? No Thisby do I see.
 O wicked wall, through whom I see no bliss!
 Cursed be thy stones for thus deceiving me!
THESEUS: The wall, methinks, being sensible, should curse again.
BOTTOM: No, in truth, sir, he should not. "Deceiving me" is Thisby's cue: she is to enter now, and I am to spy her through the wall. You shall see, it will fall pat as I told you. Yonder she comes.

The players offer the setup scenes between Thisby and Pyramus; and Wall. Following this, the piece's Lion introduces himself, then a player disguised as the Moon, whom the Duke's friend Demetrius suggests is known in the neighborhood as a cuckold:

STARVELING [as Moonshine]: This lanthorn doth the horned moon present;—
DEMETRIUS: He should have worn the horns on his head.
THESEUS: He is no crescent, and his horns are invisible within the circumference.
STARVELING: This lanthorn doth the horned moon present;
 Myself the man i' the moon do seem to be.
THESEUS: This is the greatest error of all the rest: the man should be put into the lanthorn. How is it else the man i' the moon?
DEMETRIUS: He dares not come there for the candle; for, you see, it is already in snuff.

HIPPOLYTA: I am aweary of this moon: would he would change!
THESEUS: It appears, by his small light of discretion, that he is in the wane; but yet, in cour-
    tesy, in all reason, we must stay the time.
LYSANDER: Proceed, Moon.
STARVELING: All that I have to say, is, to tell you that the lanthorn is the moon; I, the man in
    the moon; this thorn-bush, my thorn-bush; and this dog, my dog.
DEMETRIUS: Why, all these should be in the lanthorn; for all these are in the moon. But,
    silence! here comes Thisbe.

The play within the play lurches to its conclusion, with the wedding party offering their
commentary as first Pyramus then Thisby commit prolonged suicide scenes.

Is it possible there were other plays out there mocking Shakespeare's work in the same way?
The Elizabethan theatre world had a lot of axes to grind, not the least against this rube who
came to London from the sticks to write plays set in locations he couldn't possibly have visited.

Precedents for Riffing in the Cinema and the Fourth Wall

The elements that *MST3K* would draw on to build their brand of comedy were present
in some form from the very start of motion pictures over 120 years ago. The earliest films
were "actualities," short clips of everyday surroundings or exotic places. Other early films
recorded vaudeville artists doing their acts, and as the movie industry discovered the narrative
form, many of these vaudeville performers became the first movie actors. These stage performers knew a thing or two about dealing with unruly live theatre patrons, and could
sometimes carry that interaction over to an imagined movie theatre audience.

Additionally, the growth of the movie industry offered opportunities to create many
tropes of the medium that could be seen as ancestors to riffing. Whether it was newsreel
actualities and "B-roll" footage in the studio library, or entire features slipping into public
domain due to bankruptcy or even secretarial error, there would arise a library of films free
to be re-presented in a format that mocked the originals.

Interacting with uncooperative audiences, re-connecting to crowd reactions lost in the
movies, began nearly with the start of projected movies. One of Edison's earliest narrative
films, *The Great Train Robbery* (Porter, 1903), ended with an outlaw drawing a bead on the
camera to "shoot" the audience. The visceral action placed the audience in the place of the
bandit's robbery victims, drawing them across the screen into the story.

Movie performers sought to keep their viewers in on the gag ever since. Warner Brothers
cartoon director Fred "Tex" Avery made the theater audience part of several shorts. Daffy
Duck's second appearance, in *Daffy Duck and Egghead* (1937), opened with Egghead, a prototype of Elmer Fudd, becoming so annoyed at the rotoscoped silhouette of a movie patron
who won't sit down, that he shoots him dead. Avery's gangster movie parody, *Thugs with
Dirty Mugs* (1939), shows its Edward G. Robinson inspired gangster, "Killer Diller," discussing his next caper, but getting distracted by a patron leaving his seat:

"Hey, bud! You in the audience! Where do you think you're going?"
"Well, Mr. Killer, this is where I came in."
"Well, you sit right back down there 'til this thing's over, see!"
(To his gang:) "That mug's trying to get out of the theater to squeal to the cops!"

The shadow gets up again in the next scene to inform policeman "Flat-Foot Flanigan
(with a Floy-Floy)" of Killer's plans, since he'd already seen the picture. These examples of

audience interaction seem to be major influences on the visual representation of *MST3K*'s riffers as audience shadows on the screen.

Many other vaudeville-based comedians built their awareness of the film audience into their movies, and even stepped outside the frame to comment on goings-on. *Hellzapoppin'* (Potter 1941), based on the 1938 musical revue by comedians Ole Olsen and Chic Johnson, demolished barriers between the movie, the studio, its audience, and even the film's projectionist, played by Shemp Howard ("Fifteen years I've been runnin' these pictures. Now, all of a sudden, I gotta be an actor!"). Olsen and Johnson demanded the projectionist reverse the film to review a missed plot point: "What'sa matter with you guys? Don't cha know you can't talk to me *and* the audience?" "Well, we're doin' it, aren't we?"

Comedy Dubs

Given the chaotic nature of the early movie distribution system, it seems impossible to imagine that some enterprising or bored editor in some rural theater at the end of the distribution chain didn't at some time take scraps of worn-out movies and paste clips together with new, humorous title cards. But we can say with a certainty that at least by the 1930's Hollywood was recycling its older films to humorous effect.

The most accessible example is the cartoon *Daffy Duck in Hollywood* (Avery, 1938). After wreaking havoc on a movie set, Daffy finds the studio's film library, and pastes together several live action clips into an early "Comedy Dub": a roaring lion appears to say "Motion pictures are your best entertainment," while footage of a beauty pageant segues to the announcement of its winner, a circus fat lady. Studio shorts departments sometimes offered similar fare, even some newsreels and travelogues could be considered comedy dubs, since most of the footage was shot silent and depended on a narrator to explain the action. Pete Smith produced some 200 one-reel "Specialties" shorts for MGM, featuring his sardonic narration over footage of the subject at hand.

By the 1960's, large film libraries could be purchased or accessed, as older studios went out of business and their films fell into public domain, or established studios sold their libraries to TV. Features and cartoons were immediately profitable, but newsreels and actualities of limited interest could be had cheaply. The growth of foreign film markets, whether art-house affectations or Japanese monster movies, opened an avenue for lesser-known features to enter the hungry American television market. Some of this more esoteric material would become the basis of what is now called the "comedy dub" or "dub parody" program.

Supplying new dialog or narration to old film footage is also an extension of adding comedic captions to photographs, a staple of late night talk shows, paperbacks, and mail-in contests. *The New Yorker* offers a weekly online caption contest and invites readers to submit new punch line for one of its cartoons.

The first American production to make this diversion the basis of a regular series was *Fractured Flickers*, a 1963 syndicated half-hour TV show created by *Rocky & Bullwinkle* writer Chris Hayward and produced by Jay Ward. Its onscreen narrator Hans Conried would introduce a short film like "Dinky Dunston, USC Boy Cheerleader," composed of clips from Lon Chaney's *The Hunchback of Notre Dame* (1923), with dialogue dubbed by Jay Ward's repertoire players: Bill Scott, Paul Frees and June Foray. Conried also read fake commercials, say, for a cheap real estate development, over footage of buildings being smashed by a cyclone from *Steamboat Bill, Jr.* (1928); and conducted interview segments with entertainers of the day: Fabian, Rod Serling, Bob Newhart, even Bullwinkle J. Moose as a hand puppet.

What's Up Tiger Lily? (1966) took the comedy dub to the big screen. Its genesis was with Henry G. Saperstein, owner of the UPA animation studio (*Mr. Magoo*). Seeing American International Pictures turning a profit by redubbing foreign films, inserting new scenes with American actors, Saperstein purchased rights to a 1965 Toho spy movie that AIP had found too convoluted to redub: *Kokusai himitsu keisatsu: Kagi no kagi (International Secret Police: Key of Keys)*. He engaged Woody Allen, fresh from his screenplay for the hit comedy *What's New Pussycat?* (1965), offering him $66,000 to dub over comic dialogue and make the movie into a TV special, with a new title reminding viewers of that earlier hit (Nesteroff 2010). Allen changed the plot's MacGuffin from missing microfilm to a stolen egg salad recipe. Allen also appeared behind the end credits as the film's projectionist while Mort Sahl's wife — *Playboy*'s August 1964 Playmate of the Month China Lee — disrobed, and the credit scroll read "if you have been reading this instead of looking at the girl, then see your psychiatrist, or go to a good eye doctor." Saperstein decided the movie could earn more money as a theatrical feature, so he expanded its running time by splicing in footage from other Japanese films, dubbed by an Allen impersonator, and adding musical numbers by The Lovin' Spoonful.

Further comedy dub projects appeared over the next decades. Philip Proctor and Peter Bergman of The Firesign Theatre produced *J-Men Forever* (1979), in which they appeared in black and white to frame a story constructed from Republic serials like *Spy Smasher, Captain Marvel*, and *Captain America*, with new dialog in which federal agents fight the Lightning Bug, a villain planning to conquer the world with rock 'n' roll. The movie was a favorite on USA Network's video variety bloc *Night Flight* (1981–1988). A California-based comedy group, the L.A. Connection, had been presenting re-dubbed movie theatrically, starting with *Attack of the Fifty Foot Woman* in 1982, then began performing live movie dubs and producing dubbed clips for the talk show *Thicke of the Night*. Starting in 1984, they produced 26 syndicated episodes of *Mad Movies with the L.A. Connection,* an expansion of the *Fractured Flickers* concept in which entire features were condensed into half-hour episodes, redubbed to produce a totally different story. Their version of *Nothing Sacred* (1937) re-wrote Carole Lombard into an older Dorothy trying to get back to Oz. The troupe also got out a theatrical release for *Blobermouth* (1990), re-presenting *The Blob* (1958) with an animated mouth telling Henny Youngman style jokes as it devours Steve McQueen's hometown.

Self-made Riffing

> STATLER: I like that last number.
> WALDORF: What did you like about it?
> STATLER: It was the *last* number!

Implicit in all of these idioms previously discussed is the willingness to make fun of the very presentation in which someone is appearing. The "Road" pictures of Bob Hope and Bing Crosby featured the pair's metatextual ad-libbing about their radio personas, personal relationship, and Paramount Pictures. *Road to Utopia* (1946) included humorist Robert Benchley as its narrator, sniping at the entire proceeds like he was narrating a *Mad* lampoon of the movie instead. By my narrow definition, *Mad*, while highly influential, offered little that could fit these definitions of proto-riffing, since their parodies involved caricatures of a show's actors commenting on the show itself, rather than specific plot points. One example that came much closer to the *MST3K* mode was a series of parodies of the VH-1 *Pop-Up Video* series (1996–2002), since they secured the right to print actual stills from music videos, overlaid with their "Pop-Off" jabs.

The influence of *Mad* on self-referential humor, though, is rather easily seen on other programs. *The Muppet Show*, somewhat like *Rowan & Martin's Laugh-In* ten years before, owed a debt to the *Hellzapoppin'* type of variety show where "anything could happen, and probably will." *The Muppet Show* added extra layers of meta-text by featuring Kermit the Frog's backstage travails in keeping the stage show together. A further layer of self-reference was added in the form of Statler and Waldorf, the geezers in the loge box who offered insults after nearly every segment.

"Unpleasant Dreams, Darlings!"

THE HOSTED MOVIE SHOW

An influence on the show's structure often cited by Joel Hodgson has been the *CBS Children's Film Festival*, a Saturday morning program featuring children's films from around the world, hosted by Kukla, Fran and Ollie (*Satellite News*, 2010).

Hodgson only noted the fact that he had watched the show, in which Fran Allison and her puppet friends Ollie Dragon and Kukla (puppeteered by Burr Tillstrom) discussed the featured films during the commercial breaks, sometimes explaining cultural differences in the international movies. On some episodes they would do short skits to fill time. The show had appeared occasionally on Saturdays and on summer weekday afternoons since 1967. It was given a permanent Saturday morning slot from 1971 until Fran and the Kuklapolitans were dropped in 1977, with abbreviated specials appearing until 1984.

The Best Brains' show was the latest in a line of local TV shows presenting genre movies, introduced by a themed host. The most popular of these shows ran horror movies starting in the 1950s, with a ghoulishly attired host who, during the low-budget days of early local TV, was also that station's weatherman, cartoon host, sportscaster or booth announcer. The host from which it might be said all others spawned was actress Maila Nurmi's Vampira. Nurmi hosted *The Vampira Show* on KABC-TV, Los Angeles, in 1954 dressed as a wasp-waisted version of the then-unnamed mother in Charles Addams cartoons (Greene 1994). In 1957, Universal offered "Shock!," a library of its horror and science fiction films to local stations, including suggestions for "host" characters and appropriate promotional gimmicks. Each host, be they named Zacherley the Cool Ghoul, Ghoulardi or Morgus the Magnificent, mocked the films and offered sick humor around the commercial breaks, and would directly address the viewers through the camera, or by reading their fan mail.

The use of themed hosts for genre narratives went back to the early days of radio drama. Alonzo Dean Cole wrote and directed possibly the first of these, *The Witch's Tale* (1931–1938) for the Mutual network. The pulp magazine hero The Shadow first appeared on radio in 1931 as narrator *of Detective Story Hour*, an anthology dramatizing stories from Street & Smith's *Detective Story Magazine*. He began fighting crime himself on radio in 1937 (Dunning, 1998). *Inner Sanctum Mysteries* (1941–1952) was hosted by Raymond Johnson — with the notorious squeaking door — the first narrator to inject morbid humor in his shows. His style was picked up by "Mr. Crime," the narrator of the comic book series *Crime Does Not Pay* (1942–1955), and in turn informed the "GhouLunatics" of EC Comics' horror titles *Tales from the Crypt, The Vault of Horror* and *The Haunt of Fear* (1950–1955). All these hosts spoke to the reader or listener, offering grisly puns and sick humor to lighten the grim tone of the stories. Their style was seen in all the horror hosts of the 1950's, as well as in some of the narrators of network television's dramatic anthologies. The opening of *Alfred Hitchcock Presents* (1955–1965), in particular, featured its host, making droll remarks about the upcoming story or his sponsors, sometimes while in some staged peril like standing in quicksand or wearing a hangman's noose.

It is worth noting that a virtually unknown hosted movie show appeared just one season before *MST3K*'s initial run. *The Canned Film Festival* (1986), was packaged by Dr. Pepper, and featured Laraine Newman as the manager-usherette of a run-down theater showing classics like *Robot Monster* and *Eegah!* to a regular cast of "locals." The discussions of the movie between commercials tended to be more factual than humorous, and the "leave me alone" attitude of Newman's character was much less engaging than Joel and the 'Bots' horseplay. The syndicated 90-minute program ran only 13 episodes.

AUDIENCE PARTICIPATION

"Say good-bye to all this..." *Good-bye, all this!*
"And hello to oblivion!" *Hi, Oblivion! How are the wife and kids?*

The most recent precursor to the riffing style of comedy has been the "cult" or "midnight movie" film that is experienced as part of an audience participation ritual. The best-known of this kind of film has been *The Rocky Horror Picture Show* (1975). Less than a year after its mainstream release, the adaptation of a campy musical spoof on Hammer horror films moved onto the midnight film circuit and almost immediately served as the nucleus of a film cult. Its adherents interact with the movie on many levels: shouting out in unison rude comments, or questions that are answered by the next line of screen dialogue; throwing objects — toast, rice, frankfurters, etc.— at proper cues; or dancing in the aisles and in front of the screen during "*Rocky Ho's*" musical numbers. Some showings involve "shadow casts" wearing costume reproductions and enacting the entire movie as it plays behind them on the screen. *RHPS*, in fan shorthand, has set a world record by remaining in continuous release for 35 years.

During the 1960's, theaters in cities and college towns often programmed midnight movies that greater audience involvement: old serials found patrons cheering the heroes and booing the villains. The rediscovery in 1971 of the exploitation classic *Reefer Madness* (1936) became a touchstone for the stoner culture; and profits for its distributor helped fund what is now New Line Cinema. Other films that have briefly inspired camped audience participation include *Mommie Dearest* (1981). Generally, there have not been many more pictures that have inspired as much communal activity. Possibly, once the *Rocky Horror* phenomenon was known, it become too difficult to create a movie that could recreate its cultural growth organically. There was also the decline of the midnight movie circuit in the face of home entertainment. However, some form of group interaction still lives on with camp and drag elements such as with the *Sing-a-Long Sound of Music*, complete with costume contests, recommended props and audience interactions. A British company, Sing-A-Long-A, now packages and tours "Sing-Along" showings for *Rocky Horror* and movies like *The Wizard of Oz, Mary Poppins, Hairspray* and *High School Musical 3*. On 8 July, 2010, Paramount released

Grease: Sing-A-Long, with subtitles for the musical numbers, some of which had lyrics cleaned up for younger audiences (Barnes).

Five Premises in Search of a Conclusion

The interaction between the prisoners of the Satellite of Love and the movies they are forced to watch is only the latest twist in a long history of interaction between the storyteller and his audience. Considering that the brightest lights in early drama engaged in a little sniping at works they didn't care for, it's surprising that so few other examples come to mind. At the end of the 19th Century, commercialization of the phonograph and motion picture enabled performers to produce recorded works for audiences anywhere in the world, and far into the future. This, in effect, shut off the give and take the performer had with their audience in the millennia before. Almost immediately, producers looked for ways to draw the audience into the artificial world of motion pictures. However, the effect can instead further insulate the fictional world from our own by creating another reality, with a fictional audience reacting as events on the screen spill out into their world, but not ours.

The screwball comedies of the 1930s were a milieu for stage comics to mediate a new form of movie reality. The Marxes, Olsen & Johnson, Bob Hope and others were at once characters in a movie, their onstage personae commenting on their screen characters, and the comedian pausing after each gag line so as not to step on the imagined audience laughter.

Radio was negotiating its own relationship with the audience by using regular narrators to introduce stories and fill in visual details missed by radio's aural dialogue. In radio horror series, the narrator could change from a neutral interlocutor to an active participant, interceding between the fantastic characters of the story and the mundane world of the listener.

This mediation of movie reality carried over to the wisecracking midnight movie hosts, letting frightened children know in certain ways that what they were watching was only a movie, and often not a very good one. The Satellite of Love crew, like the movie hosts preceding them, created new, derivative works that incorporated the old movies and their mockery of them. Shakespeare and Aristophanes may have made their riffing of another author's work a small part of their own work, but they were clearly prescient in the rise of this genre.

Note

1. George Theodoridis, a retired Australian teacher, has undertaken new translations of the Greek plays and poems at his web site, Bacchicstage.com. He most notably seeks to restore the bawdier humor of the comedies. Theodorisis told me in an e-mail (5 May, 2010), "I believe, since competition was the name of the game with the stage, Aristophanes and other writers would bring on the live prostitutes to 'work' on the judges so as to ascertain the laurels of the first prize ... but that sounds like 'corruption' and, of course, Greeks would never, ever stoop so low!"

References

Aristophanes, c. 405 BCE. *Frogs.* Translation by G. Theodorisis. Accessed June 25, 2010, at http://bac chicstage.com/Frogs.htm.

_____. *The Thesmophoriazusae.* Anonymous translation. *Aristophanes: The Eleven Comedies.* London: The Athenian Society, 1922.

Avery, Fred (director), Ben Hardaway. *Daffy Duck and Egghead.* "Looney Tunes Golden Collection Vol. 3" Warner Home Video, 2003 (originally released 1937).

Avery, Fred (director), Dave Monahan, et al. *Daffy Duck in Hollywood.* "Looney Tunes Golden Collection Vol. 3" Warner Home Video, 2003 (originally released 1938).

Avery, Fred (director), Dave Monahan. *Thugs with Dirty Mugs.* "Looney Tunes Golden Collection Vol. 3" Warner Home Video, 2003 (originally released 1939).

Barnes, Brooks. "Forget Shhh! Theaters Want You to Sing Along" *New York Times.* July 11, 2010. Accessed July 13, 2010, at http://www.nytimes.com/2010/07/12/business/media/12movies.html?nl=business&emc=ata3.

Cartoon Caption Contest. *The New Yorker.* http://www.newyorker.com/humor/caption.

"CBS Children's Film Festival." *Wikipedia.* Accessed June 5, 2010, at http://en.wikipedia.org/wiki/CBS_Children%27s_Film_Festival.

Dunning, John. *The Encyclopedia of Old-Time Radio.* New York, NY: Oxford University Press, 1998.

"Gag Dub." *TVTropes.com.* Accessed March 18, 2010, at http://tvtropes.org/pmwiki/pmwiki.php/Main/GagDub.

Greene, Ray. "A Biography of Vampira (Maila Nurmi)" *Box Office* magazine (April 1994): reprinted in The Official Website of VAMPIRA! Accessed June 5, 2010, at http://unpleasantdreams.com/vampirahistory.

Hayward, Chris, Jay Ward, Bill Scott, Ponsonby Britt, et al. *Fractured Flickers.* VCI Video, 2004 (originally broadcast 1963).

Kenrick, John. "The Sing-Along Sound of Music, Ziegfeld Threatre" *Musicals 101.* September 2000. Accessed June, 3rd 2010 at http://www.musicals101.com/singsound.htm.

Murphy, Kevin, and Dan Studney (2005). "The History of *Reefer Madness.*" *Reefer-Madness-Movie.com.* 2005. Accessed May 28, 2010, at http://web.archive.org/web/20060328163318/http://www.reefer-madness-movie.com/history.html.

Murphy, Kevin (director), Michael J. Nelson (head writer), Paul Chaplin (writer), et al. *MST3K* episode 1009. *Hamlet.* Rhino, 2003.

Nesteroff, Kliph. "The Early Woody Allen 1952–1971." *WFMU's Beware of the Blog.* February 14, 2010. Accessed May 25, 2010. http://blog.wfmu.org/freeform/2010/02/the-early-woody-allen-.html.

Patterson, Richard (director), Phil Proctor, Peter Bergman. 2002. *J-Men Forever.* Eclectic DVD. Originally released 1979.

Porter, Edwin S. (director). "Broncho Billy" Anderson. *The Great Train Robbery.* http://www.archive.org/details/TheGreatTrainRobbery1903, accessed June 15, 2010. Originally released 1903.

Potter, H.C. (director), Ole Olsen, Chic Johnson, et al. *Hellzapoppin'* Amazon Video on Demand. originally released 1941.

Roberts, Brian K. (director), Christy Snell and Terry Mulroy (writers). "New York & Queens." *The Drew Carey Show,* ABC (May 14, 1997).

Theodoridis, George. Correspondence with the author, 6/14/10.

Timeline: LA Connection Comedy Club. Accessed 10 June, 2010 at http://www.laconnectioncomedy.com/history/timeline.html.

"Twenty questions only Joel Hodgson can answer about MST3K." *Satellite News.* Accessed June 4, 2010, at http://www.mst3kinfo.com/satnews/brains/20q.html.

"The Witch's Tale." (2007) *RadioHorrorHosts.com.* Accessed June 8, 2010, at http://www.radiohorrorhosts.com/witchtale.html.

24

From Techno-Isolation to Social Reconciliation

by E. Mitchell

In the beginning there was light. And a puppet show. From the first flickering images projected on primitive screens at vaudeville exhibitions during the late Victorian era, to the technologically sophisticated cinematic creations of the 21st century, the cinema is, as film historian David Robinson observed, "a complex evolution rather than an invention," and it involves four key elements: "aesthetics, technology, economy and audience" (1973:1). What role does *Mystery Science Theater 3000* play in this cinematic evolution? It is a notable one with regard to the relationship between technology and audience.

Mystery Science Theater 3000 is a pop culture phenomenon that deserves more than a footnote in film history as an evolving cinematic art form that has reconnected audiences with the social component of the film experience in the face of an increasingly isolating technological age. An analysis of the past — specifically the participatory aspect of the cinema, alongside the evolution of isolating film technologies will reveal the contribution of *MST3K* in bridging the gap between passivity and participation, social isolation and integration, and consequently restoring a return to the roots of cinema as a shared experience.

The history of movies with regard to their impact on social behavior in America reveals a significant shift from past to present. The ever-evolving cinematic viewing experience has involved such forms as vaudeville, nickelodeons, neighborhood theaters, movie palaces, wide-screen extravaganzas, drive-ins, television, and ultimately home theaters. A look back reveals a level of active participation in the movie-going experience that peaked early, gradually waned, and then nearly disappeared as a result of evolving technologies. From the vaudeville and nickelodeon eras when the context of film viewing was outward and social, through the enervating effects of television, and up to the current development of personal recording devices, the viewing experience has grown inward and isolating.

MST3K is significant for reconnecting audiences to the social elements of the earliest film experiences. With its futuristic sci-fi setting and alienated host, it is the ultimate metaphor for techno-isolation serving as an emblem for viewers alone and adrift in a technological age. Yet, via the "Satellite of Love," *MST3K* literally and figuratively offers a vehicle for reconnection by stylistically recreating the social ambience of the past and inviting viewers along for the ride.

Re-establishing Connections

Vaudeville

With regard to film presentation, the movement away from social participation to isolation evolved slowly over the course of the twentieth century. In the beginning, at the turn of the century, vaudeville theaters were the main venue for the exhibition of the newly invented phenomenon known as motion pictures (Allen 1980). At that time, films were seen as a novelty form of entertainment used merely to accompany live acts. Movies were considered "visual acts" and sometimes referred to as "dumb acts," a term reflecting lack of sound rather than content (DiMeglio 1973).

But the irony of the "dumb act" designation for films is not lost with regard to *MST3K* whose basic construct, whether intentional or not, is a vaudeville show built around "dumb" films. In essence, *MST3K* represents a return to the roots of the earliest vaudevillian cinematic experience. And therein lies not only its historical significance in the complex cinematic evolution, but its welcoming familiarity and fundamental appeal. *MST3K* represents a return to the roots of cinema where everything old is new again and past meets present "in the not too distant future."

A closer look at the format of early vaudeville film exhibitions reveals a framework that parallels the *MST3K* formula. Nineteenth century vaudeville "dumb act" films were accompanied by live performances including such things as magic, music, melodrama, singers, dancers, clowns, comedians and last but not least, puppetry (Allen 1980). On *MST3K*, the wrap-around "host segments" accompanying the dumb act films, (or in this case, films selected for dumbness) are filled with examples of the aforementioned vaudeville elements.

Puppetry, of course, is the cornerstone of the live-act contribution to the show. Robotic puppets including Tom Servo, Crow, Gypsy and Cambot, ameliorate the social anomie of the human hosts Joel and Mike, by accompanying them on their consecutive odysseys in space. Like futuristic, techno-incarnations of vaudeville comics "the bots" acting as foils to the human masters of ceremony, provide novelty acts and serve as ringleaders for home viewers invited into the theater and encouraged to participate along with the presentations. The crew's commentary aided by their silhouetted images project a sense of live entertainment. During the breaks, the audience is not abandoned, but rather treated to a floor show provide by Joel/Mike and the robots. Just as in vaudeville, music is a mainstay along with comedic sketches, and melodramatic humor. As evidenced onscreen and chronicled in *The Amazing Colossal Episode Guide*, examples of classic vaudeville entertainment on *MST3K* abound:

Magic—Episode 401: "The Great Crowdini" escapes from chains; 312: Crow saws himself in half; 601: Joel attempts to saw Crow in half; 213: in a Houdini-like demonstration, Joel exerts mind control over a guitar; 409: Joel and the robots perform "a mystifying knife illusion."

Dance—Episode 607: the gang has a hoedown, complete with Servo wearing a squaredancing dress; 407: Mike and Servo get up and dance in the theater; 813: Mike performs a "Lord of the Dance" parody.

Music—Episode 401: Joel & bots sing a tribute to pants; 403: Crow sings an ode to actress Kim Cattrall; 404: Snack theme sung by Joel and bots; 408: Gypsy sings while hitting her head on a lyre; 401: 411: Crow sings a love song to Estelle Winwood; 418: The

"Rip Taylor" trio sings; 423: Broadway parody, *Hired! The Musical!* 612 The Servo Men's Chorus performs; 624: Dr. Forrester sings a loving tribute to Frank's departure.

Slapstick Comedy— Episode 601: Pie in the face gag; 609: Dr. Forrester throws large rubber balls at Frank; 618: Forrester drops a chomping dinosaur into Franks pants; 403: Tom & Crow drop ping pong balls on Joel; 405: Forrester jams a Thighmaster into Frank's skull. 409: Gypsy's sneeze causes Tom's gas filled body to explode.

Clown Comedy— Episode:405: Gypsy and Joel's futuristic hologram clown sketch includes classic props like rubber snakes, giant mallets and balloons; 413: Frank & Forrester wear clownish beanbag pants; 414: Crow throws a rubber knife at Servo/Frank &Forrester are dressed in troll costumes with rubbery hands; 422: Crow & Servo develop a clown act.

Ventriloquism— Episode 311: Joel rehearses a ventriloquist act for *Star Search*; 404: Dr. Forrester prepares for the possibility of a ventriloquism resurgence and performs with Resusci-Annie doll; 409: The bots try to confuse Joel by switching voices; 818: The entire *Devil Doll* episode is a tribute to "ventiloquy."

Vaudeville homage— Episode 407: Fanny Brice sketch; 409: Joel does a Will Rogers routine; 409: Lon Chaney sketch; 422: Gypsy has a one-woman show called *Gypsy Rose Me!*

The *MST3K* use of a basic comic trio structure combined with pie-in-face slapstick is suggestive of classic vaudevillian comedy teams like The Three Stooges (in fact, in episode 624, Mike and the robots offer a tribute to the stooges), and The Marx Brothers, with Gypsy serving in the Margaret Dumont role.

Probably no clearer example of the vaudeville connection can be offered than the lampooning "Tubular Boobular Joy" song performed in Episode 519. A musical trio comprised of Mike, Tom and Crow wearing vintage vaudeville straw hats and barber-pole striped vests, bursts into song after Crow does an imitation of Jimmy Durante, and Mike mimics Stan Laurel.

ACTUALITY FILMS

Another component of the vaudeville era film presentation was the use of what were called "Actuality films," precursors to newsreels and documentaries (Library of Congress). These short fact-based films were curiosities to early movie audiences just as *MST3K*'s use of educational "shorts" serve as comic curiosities to contemporary audiences.

In 1902, the first movie theater in Los Angeles presented a film short entitled "Lost in a Blizzard" (history.com). A hundred years later, *MST3K* featured a short called "Snow Thrills," in episode 311, one of more than fifty shorts used throughout the run of the show, reminiscent of the vaudeville practice of using film acts to fill the bill with variety.

NICKELODEONS

Were it not for a vaudeville performer's strike in 1901, films might have remained a novelty much longer than they did. Up until 1901, their main function was to fill time or serve as "chasers" used to clear audiences out of the theater after live shows. But the 1901 vaudeville strike left a major gap that needed to be filled. Suddenly the status of movies was elevated from novelty act to featured entertainment for the first time (history.com).

Nickelodeon theaters — named for their five cent ticket price — began to spring up. They retained elements of the vaudevillian entertainment model, but with greater emphasis on the film. Social interaction and audience participation were still a big part of the format.

In the earliest days, nickelodeons cultivated group participation. Films were becoming more sophisticated but it was still the silent era, so piano players were employed to fill the void and interpret the action of silent movies with live music. Patrons were invited to sing-along to the bouncing ball in pre-movie group entertainment, and live acts rounded out the bill.

Parallels in the *MST3K* format are apparent. Joel/Mike and the 'bots fill the void and interpret the action of dull movies through the use of humor, accompanied by music and live acts in the host segments. A nickelodeon-esque atmosphere prevails. In episode 212, there's even a reference to sing-alongs of the past when Tom, before bursting into song, says "I'd tell you to sing along with the bouncing ball, but we don't have one."

SERIALS

During the silent era and into the new age of "talking pictures," movie serials were popular for engaging audiences in participation through the continuity of episodic "good versus evil" story lines and climactic cliffhanger predicaments. Movie patrons booed the villains, cheered for the heroes and gasped at the cliffhangers. Reviving this art form, *MST3K* included serials in their repertoire, resurrecting long lost one-reelers like *The Undersea Kingdom* and *The Phantom Creeps*, encouraging contemporary participation through comedic commentary and laughter.

TALKIES

With the advent of "talkies" and the development of sound technology, movies became a more voyeuristic experience but still predominantly social, drawing people out of their homes to a communal location with shared community responses including laughter, tears and occasional spontaneous outbursts of commentary, welcome or not. The early theater programs included more than one movie. Just as vaudeville had included a variety of live acts, early movie experiences included a variety of film acts. Saturday matinees found patrons spending all day at the theater watching cartoons, newsreels, B-pictures, features and double features all on the same bill. Similarly, *MST3K* revived the variety format by including serials, shorts, b-movies, and sketch comedy all in a cartoonlike atmosphere.

When movies suddenly found their voice, early forms of clever cinematic commentary or "riffing" began to appear. American humorist Robert Benchley acted in as well as narrated a series of comedic shorts with an early riffing format. Benchley was famous, both in writing and in film, for humorously mocking himself and his own ineffectual efforts to accomplish the most mundane tasks, while simultaneously lambasting social etiquette. Benchley's "How to Sleep," "How to Eat," and "How to Behave" poked fun at propriety. *MST3K*'s satirical skewering of educational shorts from the 1940s and '50s is reminiscent of Benchley's societal spoofs, with lampoon-worthy subjects like "Posture Pals" and "Using Your Voice."

Benchley extended his riffing to feature-length films. In *The Road to Utopia*, Benchley's live image is occasionally superimposed over the film, (similar to the silhouetted images of Joel/Mike and the bots in the corner of the screen) popping in and out to crack wise and comment on the action. In *Utopia*, the action involves the misadventures of Bob Hope and Bing Crosby, a pair of notorious riffers in their own right — known for "breaking the fourth wall" in the popular "Road Pictures" by talking directly to the audience. With such whimsical moments as Hope advising patrons to get popcorn while Crosby sings, or Crosby mocking

Hope's ski-nose, engagement of audience involvement is a key component just as with *MST3K*.

Similarly, in the 1940s and '50s, a series of one reel "shorts" entitled *Joe McDoakes Behind the Eight Ball*, featuring narrator Art Gilmore, humorously critiqued the bumbling efforts of the everyman portrayed by actor George O'Hanlon in dealing with ordinary challenges (Carlson 2009). Titles like "So You Want to be Popular," "So You Want to Hold Your Wife" and "So You Want to Keep Your Hair," parallel *MST3K* shorts like "Keeping Clean & Neat," "Are You Ready For Marriage?" and "What to Do on A Date," among others. Furthermore, O'Hanlon would occasionally shatter the cinematic illusion by looking to the audience for acknowledgment. Just as with Benchley, the concept of breaking cinematic boundaries foreshadows the *MST3K* method where audience identification and implied commiseration empower the humor.

The rise of talkies coincided with the decline of vaudeville, but the connection between film and stage presentation lingered a while longer. As a part of movie industry promotional tours- often kicked off at Radio City Music Hall in New York — actors were called upon to participate in live stage performances, usually musical excerpts, songs and dances or re-enactments, from their films. *MST3K* resurrected this tradition of the film/stage interactive approach by mirroring movie-time moments in stage-show renderings during the host segments. Probably the most illustrative example would be the hilarious re-staging of the musical number "Happy in Your Work" from episode 507, *I Accuse My Parents*. With the soundtrack from the film playing in the background, Gypsy as a bewigged chanteuse, lip-synchs to the music while Servo and Crow dressed as waiters, perform race-about choreography in service to a mustachioed Joel, sitting ringside lifting imaginary martinis in comical imitation of the film.

Beyond the frequent musical interludes in the host segments, *MST3K* also acknowledged the influential impact of films in altering social behavior. In light of oft-noted examples like a drop in undershirt sales when Clark Gable appeared bare-chested in *It Happened One Night*, or the spread of the peek-a-boo bang in imitation of Veronica Lake, *MST3K* utilized the host segments primarily to mimic (and mock) the cinematic behaviors just witnessed.

In episode 613, when villainous henchman, Frank threatens to blow up everyone after watching violent films inspired by the B-movie *The Sinister Urge*, mad scientist Dr. Forrester waxes philosophical and sums everything up with the relevant social observation: "Frank is so easily influenced by motion pictures." So like the population at large.

TELEVISION

The phenomenon of television and its expanding use in the 1950s not only had a major economic impact on the movie industry, it also had a major social impact on movie-goers. The outward movement in pursuit of entertainment was suddenly turned inward. Television fostered isolation by keeping people in their homes. And by the end of the decade another form of technology would add to the social disconnection when widespread use of air conditioning in private homes took hold (an ironic turn of events considering air-conditioning had once lured audiences out to "air cooled" theaters prior to the development of home units).

The repercussions of this one-two punch of isolating technology were summed up by David Shi of Furman University in his article "Air Conditioning — It's Made the South What It Is": "Even more significant has been the social impact of air conditioning. Along with the nearly universal ownership of televisions, the spreading availability of air conditioning has reduced social interaction and made us a more private society" (2007:1).

At the onset of competition for movie-going audiences, the aspects of isolation and voyeurism were explored by director Alfred Hitchcock in his 1954 film *Rear Window*. It is a prescient look at society just before it becomes shuttered in due to the looming impact of air conditioning and television. In addition to being representative of the times, it is notable here because it curiously prefigures and parallels the construct for the *Mystery Science Theater* formula.

Actor James Stewart, not unlike Joel or Mike, finds himself in the everyman role, imprisoned against his will (in this case as a result of an immobilizing accident) with no other outlet than voyeurism. As a passive bystander, his observations and running commentary on his neighbors' activities drive the plot. He has two unwitting accomplices drawn in by proximity. His girlfriend, played by Grace Kelly, fulfills the role of Tom Servo sophisticated, subtle, superior and cultured. His nurse, portrayed by Thelma Ritter, is a Crow substitute, more crass, bawdy and blatantly comic. The trio leads viewers on a guided tour of the events unfolding before their eyes, interpreting what they see, tossing bon-mots, and using the visual drama like a Rorschach to occasionally reflect back on their own flaws. Just as with *MST3K*, in *Rear Window*, we as viewers watch some of the action over the shoulders of the actors. There are even moments when Stewart, Kelly and Ritter appear in darkened silhouette. Stewart's failing relationship with Kelly is mocked and mirrored in the action not unlike the way Servo and Crow taunt Mike about the past inadequacies of his love life reflected on film with the repeated riff, "Look familiar, Mike?"

Just as Joel and Mike don't want to be trapped on the Satellite of Love watching bad movies, Jimmy Stewart doesn't want to be stuck in his apartment watching the neighbors. But in each case they're prisoners of circumstance and ultimately a captive audience. When not watching the action, they are reflecting back on it. On *MST3K*, the sketches in the host segments serve as a working through of the material just as Jimmy Stewart's summation of the day's observations supplement and support the action.

In the final ironic parallel, at the conclusion of *Rear Window* Stewart ends up back where he started and so does Mike! Stewart goes back to square one, physically immobilized in his wheelchair with his companion Grace Kelly by his side; Mike winds up mentally immobilized watching bad movies alongside the robots. (At least Jimmy Stewart got the girl!)

Rear Window and *MST3K* are strikingly similar in symbolizing a breaking of the bonds of voyeuristic passivity through action. Jimmy Stewart fights the crime of murder; *MST3K* fights the crime of bad movies.

Ironically, *MST3K* represents both product and protest of the TV techno-isolating age. It is produced through the medium of television, yet innovatively re-invents the wheel by mocking its own connection to the source and letting viewers in on the joke. Television references are a big part of the riffing arsenal and serve as a conduit to reconnect scattered viewers like hecklers in an old vaudevillian peanut gallery rallying to react against the passive, hypnotic acceptance of mainstream mediocrity. The rallying cry: wake up, talk back and join in the fun!

DRIVE-INS

The growing widespread use of television in the 1950s suddenly created competition for movie-going audiences resulting in a well documented, far-reaching negative impact on theater attendance. The movie industry responded by offering things that TV did not — at the high end,

Technicolor widescreen extravaganzas. At the low budget end, gimmicks like 3-D and schlock horror. It is this very drive-in schlock genre that *MST3K* exploits for comic effect, drawing in generations of viewers drifting away into the isolating abyss of TV couch potato-ism.

Examples such as *Teenagers from Outer Space* and *Horror Beach Party*, considered too provocative for TV fare at the time, were targeted at teens to entice them back to the theaters. The informal and jovial atmosphere of the drive-in experience is recreated on *MST3K*. The silhouettes of Joel/Mike Servo and Crow almost appear as if they're sitting in the front seat of a convertible car and we, the audience, are able to eavesdrop on their conversation from the backseat. Fulfilling the 1950s sci-fi formula of protagonists persecuted by mad scientists (via Forrester, Frank, and Pearl) punishing films are projected up on the screen and we're along for the ride to witness the horror and scream, but this time, with laughter.

MST3K not only has reconnected audiences with drive-in movies, it has satirized the era to great comic effect. Probably best illustrated in episode 904, with a special host segment featuring a "'50s girl group" performed by Mike, Tom and Crow in drag, with beehive hairdos and ponytails singing the song "Where Oh Werewolf," it is reminiscent of movies like *I Was a Teenage Werewolf,* and pop tunes like "Leader of the Pack." Today, as drive-ins continue to fade from the American landscape, *MST3K* has managed to preserve their essence in comic homage.

HOME ENTERTAINMENT

Just as television changed the direction of entertainment in the 1950's, the recent development of home recording devices has changed the film viewing experience forever. For Baby Boomers growing up in the '50s and '60s, the concept of watching a movie at home was merely a fantasy, something available only to archival academics, or a privilege of the rich and famous who held private screenings in their Hollywood mansions. With the invention of the VCR in the 1970s, fantasy became reality. For the first time in history, anyone could watch just about anything, anytime. From VCRs to DVDs, DVRs and the internet, home viewing is now the rule rather than exception.

The impact of changing entertainment technologies is reflected in a shift in statistics regarding movie theater attendance. In 1930, 65 percent of the U.S. population went out to the movies on a weekly basis. By the year 2000, weekly movie attendance was reported to be only 9.7 percent (Pautz 2002). A dramatic shift has taken place. One of the byproducts of this shift has been a loss of the social component of the film experience.

In a recent poll and study conducted on movie-going behavior entitled "Movie Attendance Linked to Theater Experience," Mike Hunter of the PA Consulting Groups Management Team reported:

> This research reveals that Hollywood should reconsider how the movie-going experience is sold to the consumer. We may be at a time when going out to the movies should be more than just buying a ticket and purchasing an item from concessions, watching a film and then going home. We may be entering an era where consumers want the movie-going experience to be more of an event than an occurrence [2007:1].

Reconnecting Communities

Mystery Science Theater 3000 was ahead of the curve in anticipating and meeting the needs of modern movie audiences. The show could accurately be described as "an event" in terms of structure and outreach. Viewers adrift in their own private home-viewing orbits gravitated together toward the communal film experience offered by the entertaining *MST3K* format, harkening back to the roots of cinema as a social event, yet one adapted to modern day sensibilities.

From the outset, *MST3K* was unique in its concept of working in partnership with its viewers. Innovative in the creation of its own fan club, establishing a fan data base, and an accompanying outreach newsletter to solicit the help of viewers, the unique partnership approach helped in promoting and advancing the show at every step of the way. A successful collaboration was launched aboard the Satellite of Love, one that has resulted in a complex social reconnection on many levels.

INTER-GENERATIONAL

The *MST3K* fan base has proven to be multigenerational. Baby Boomers drawn to the show for its connection to their past — the last gasp of the drive-in era/creature feature film phenomenon — have a forum for group appreciation that not only they can enjoy, but can be shared with a younger generation, including their children and grandchildren. Movies that once frightened and amazed the more naive Boomers, and might be dismissed out-of-hand by the new more savvy, techno-generation can now be appreciated through humor. The comedic kitsch value has universal appeal.

This multigenerational universal appeal of *MST3K* is summed up in the Epilogue to the show's history at *Satellite News*: "Toddlers are instinctively drawn to it and senior citizens smile knowingly — even if neither gets the Courtney Love jokes" (Cornell, Henry). In the words of the show's creator, Joel Hodgson, "It appeals to an innate human desire to unabashedly say what you think. And for young kids, that seems to be the principle draw: the whole notion of grown-ups in power being heckled and ridiculed for their obvious inadequacies is irresistible" (*Satellite News*, "Show History: 1994").

The family aspect has even further dimensions. Unlike network "family" entertainment in which "standards and practices" routinely gives the green light to coarse language and graphic sexual content, *MST3K* has their own set of guidelines as illustrated in episode 441 when the crew considers a list of words you can't say on TV and the worst they can come up with is "hinder."

The concept of *MST3K* as an arbiter of family values and good taste might appear laughable on the surface (considering they make cheap jokes about cheap movies), yet the humor is filtered through the lens of their own mocking disapproval. Children often navigate the murky waters of primetime TV with no moral compass — when they watch *MST3K* they are not alone, but rather guided by a literate crew who routinely vocalizes their disgust with sleaze and chauvinism. Of course *MST3K* indulges in its fair share of obligatory ogling and ribaldry, but usually accompanied by some crushing reproach.

In the words of Richard Corliss: "The writers displayed great comedy taste: the creator's sense of what's funny, the smart editor's sense of what isn't" (2001:2).

CULTURAL

It would not be over-judgmental to say that contemporary prime-time television programming has devolved into a predictable pattern of mediocrity, and worse yet, moronic vulgarity, with an obsessive fixation on sex, violence and bathroom humor. To illustrate the extent of the downward spiral, one need only look at an incident dating back to 1960 when *Tonight Show* host Jack Paar was censored and edited for making a reference to "W.C.," an abbreviation for an oblique British term "water closet" which is an oblique reference to a bathroom. Something so vague was deemed unacceptable even on late night TV. Flash forward 50 years later to a recent prime-time TV show, *Accidentally on Purpose,* a "family hour" sitcom with a premise of unplanned pregnancy as a result of a casual sex, in which the plotline of the show focused on one character going to the bathroom on top of another character while seated on a toilet. To paraphrase the *MST3K* crew, please pass the eye bleach! Mind bleach would be even better. Television has become a cultural abyss.

By comparison, *MST3K* seems like a cultural oasis. To say that *MST3K* offers highbrow entertainment might be going too far, the premise, after all, is making fun of moronic movies, but the point is, their mission is to mock substandard entertainment rather than peddle it to the public with misplaced praise. Their process for making the lemons more palatable employs a level of wit, inspiration and inventiveness that often far exceeds the efforts and offerings on network television which undoubtedly accounts for *MST3K*'s success in attracting intelligent viewers and inspiring their loyalty and support. To be in on the jokes one must have at least a cursory knowledge of the references being made, and the cultural references on *MST3K* have a wide range, everything from the arcane to the urbane.

For example, there's an entire episode dedicated to *Hamlet.* In addition to Shakespeare, other topics include parodies of Eugene O'Neill's *Long Day's Journey Into Night*; discussions of "European resistance to post-war conservatism and sexual repression;" "the struggle of progressive thinking throughout the ages;" the Cold War and HUAC hearings; readings from *A History of the Gods,* and Charles Dickens' *Bleak House;* original comic sonnets, operettas and odes, and a steady stream of eclectic references as disparate as Wilma Rudolph, Isaac Asimov, Linus Pauling, Cole Porter, Henry Miller, Gertrude Stein and Aeschylus, among others.

Consider the unlikelihood of even one of the aforementioned references on a contemporary prime-time network television show and it becomes apparent why *MST3K* was listed by James Poniewozik of *Time* magazine as one of the "100 Best TV Shows of All Time."

In addition to literature, there are also metaphysical references, both Biblical and philosophical, discussions on the fate of the soul, morality, original sin, and the mysterious forces that control the universe. In the psychological arena, there have been parodies of Jungian analysis and a reproduction of the famous Harlow rhesus monkey studies, particularly apropos for the focus on social isolation, the very predicament of the crew of the Satellite of Love and the viewers at home, reconciled at last through common sensibilities, an interdependant cooperation, and mutual admiration.

Above all, the power of the cultural connection hinges on humor. *MST3K* may not be the only show that makes references to Melville or Tolstoy, but their recitation of Melville is performed by a mad scientist playing the accordion with a parrot on his shoulder. *Anna Karenina* is demonstrated as a pop-up book for children, and literacy is promoted through the invention of novels for the backs of cereal boxes.

SOCIETAL

The societal connections achieved by the *MST3K* community owe their success to the unique and interactive format of the show, coupled with its outreach approach and symbiotic relationship with its audience. *MST3K* was one of the first online discussion topics to gain momentum in chat rooms at the onset of internet use in the early 1990's. It was successful in creating a sense of community among fans, "a community they felt was their home in the online world ... so many close friendships had evolved in the communities" (*Satellite News,* "Show History: 1993," part 2).

But the amazing thing is that social interaction didn't stop abstractly and passively in the cyberworld, but rather radiated out into the real world through active participation on the part of the fans in the promotion of the show and the active participation of the cast in returning the favor by bringing the show out into the community through tours and conventions. The lost art and abandoned cinematic tradition of live entertainment and audience participation was revived.

At every step of the way, audience input was solicited, and eventually instrumental in the advancement of the show. When in jeopardy of cancellation, it was rescued by fan mail. When a postcard campaign solicited support for an *MST3K* movie, the fans responded by the thousands. As Satellite News reports, executive producer Jim Mallon said, "Probably the first time in history the general public wrote to a Hollywood studio demanding that a movie be made" ("Show History: 1994," part 1).

When the *MST3K* crew connected with their fans at a convention in 1995 taking the film *Zombie Nightmare* to college campuses, Universal executives were in attendance and duly impressed by the groundswell of support. *MST3K* fans were no longer a faceless entity; they had forged an impressive identity and earned a name: MSTies.

As a result of a successful collaboration between crew and community, *Mystery Science Theater 3000: The Movie* was produced in 1996.

Stinger

At the conclusion of most *MST3K* episodes (starting with 201), there is a "stinger," a carefully selected quintessential moment of madness that summarizes the insanity of the episode. In episode 311, the oft-mocked and oft-repeated catchphrase, "He learned too late that man is a feeling creature..." might very well be the ultimate ironic stinger for the *MST3K* experience. The insanity of its success in going from a cheap comic puppet show on local cable TV station in Minnesota to award-winning recognition on the Comedy and Sci-Fi networks, and finally earning a place in cinematic posterity with a feature-length film, is due in great part to reaching out and meeting the needs of other "feeling creatures" with similar sensibilities whose needs were not being completely met in the traditional movie marketplace. In an age when viewers are locked away in isolation, hypnotized by TV and computer screens, the opportunity to re-connect with other film fans has been exhilarating, and met with an enthusiasm that endures and thrives to this day despite the fact that the show officially went off the air over a decade ago.

The fan base, commandeered by Christopher Cornell, Brian Henry and Steve Finley at *Satellite News: The Official Fan Site for Mystery Science Theater 3000,* continues their work online, archiving, researching, discussing, informing, and most importantly connecting fans with the *MST3K* source, and with each other.

Still influential 20 years after its inception, *Mystery Science Theater 3000* has been significant for transforming techno-isolation into an opportunity for social reconciliation. In the words of *Time* TV critic James Poniewozik, "this basic cable masterpiece raised talking back to the TV into an art form" (2007:1).

In the ever-changing world of film, posited by David Robinson, where cinema is an evolution rather than an invention, *MST3K* represents a notable milestone in the ongoing process: reviving the past, reconnecting with the public, and possibly re-shaping the future of the film experience.

In the immortal words of mad scientist Dr. Clayton Forrester: "As the world is enchanted with our whimsy, we'll slowly take over their minds!"

REFERENCES

Allen, Robert C. *Vaudeville and Film 1895–1915: A Study in Media Interaction.* New York: Arno Press, 1980.

"American Variety Stage — Motion Pictures: Content and Historical Context." Library of Congress. Accessed 12/12/09 http://memory.loc.gov/ammem/vshtml/vsfhcnt.html.

Beaulieu, Trace; Chaplin, Paul; Mallon, Jim; Murphy, Kevin; Nelson, Michael J.; Pehl, Mary Jo. *The Mystery Science Theater 3000 Amazing, Colossal, Episode Guide.* New York: Bantam, 1996.

Carlson, KC. "The Joe McDoakes Collection." *DVDs Worth Watching* 11/3/09. Accessed 1/30/10. http://comicsworthreading.com/2009/11/03/the-joe-mcdoakes-collection/.

Corliss, Richard. "That Old Feeling: MST2K +1." *TIME* June 15, 2001. Accessed 2/1/10. http://www.time.com/time/columnist/corliss/article/0,9565,130927,00.html.

Cornell, Christopher, and Brian Henry. "The Almost But Still Not Quite Complete History of *MST3K.*" *Satellite News.* Accessed 1/5/10. http://www.MST3Kinfo.com.

DiMiglio, John E. *Vaudeville U.S.A.* Bowling Green, OH: Bowling Green University Popular Press, 1973.

Hitchcock, Alfred (director), Hayes, John Michael (screenwriter). *Rear Window.* Universal Pictures, 1954. Starring James Stewart, Grace Kelly, Thelma Ritter.

Hunter, Mike. "Movie Attendance Linked to Theater Experience." *PR Newswire* 1/4/07. Accessed 1/28/10. http://www.prnewswire.com/news-releases/movie-attendance-linked-to-theater-experience-increased-competition-for-consumer-time-according-to-pa-consulting-group-survey-53299617.html.

Pautz, Michelle. "The Decline in Weekly Cinema Attendance: 1930–2000." *Issues in Political Economy 2002 Vol.11.* Accessed 1/30/10. http://org.elon.edu/ipe/pautz2.pdf.

Poniewozik, James. "The 100 Best TV Shows of All-TIME." *Time.com* 2007. Accessed 1/5/10. http://www.time.com/time/specials/2007/article/0,28804,1651341_1659192_1652619,00.html.

Robinson, David. *The History of World Cinema.* New York: Stein and Day Publishing, 1973.

Shi, David. "Air Conditioning — It's Made the South What It Is." *Independentmail.com.* 6/24/07. Accessed 12/20/09. http://www.independentmail.com/news/2007/jun/24/air-conditioning-its-made-south-what-it/.

"This Day in History June 19, 1905: First Nickelodeon Opens." *History.com.* Accessed 12/20/09. http://www.history.com/this-day-in-history/first-nickelodeon-opens.

25

Fishing with Cheese on a *Blood Hook*: *MST3K*'s Unlikely Origins on a Lake in the Woods of Wisconsin

by Robert G. Weiner

Fishing is rude, I mean you have to get your hands in all that snotty crap and scales.
— *Blood Hook* (1986)

Now then — Slasher genre — For me, horror is about the thrill balanced with the dread. The best slasher stories carry this through. It's why we love Jack the Ripper stories, the anticipation is as important as the act. It's why nothing has been as good as Carpenter's *Halloween* — nobody else has the touch. In a way, *Alien*, the original is a kind of Slasher film, and one of the best, because again, the focus is not on the gore but the thrill and dread of anticipation — Am I safe? Am I next? I also think a sense of humor has helped to save the genre and Horror in general. *Scream* was fun, right? And think of all those Bruce Campbell movies (I love *Bubba Ho-Tep* by the way) For my liking, horror should never take itself too seriously.
— Kevin Murphy (2010)

Blood Hook: An Introduction

The eighties were *the* decade of the slasher film, and in their heyday were one of the most critically reviled subgenres of film ever produced. Even though today there are some insightful academic histories and critical evaluations (Rockoff, 2002, Harper 2004, Armstrong, 2009), the slasher is still widely regarded as the bastard stepchild of horror — a titillating film formula for adolescents, but rarely worth the time of the serious scholar. Despite this, not all slasher movies are the same. Although certain structures **do** recur — we're talking about genre, after all — they do not all follow precisely the same plot points. Yes, people die in them, and it's usually a knife or other cutting instrument that's the murderer's tool of choice, but not always. Dismissive critics also often fail to take into consideration the varied motivations of the movie killers. Not all slashers have a mindless killing machine hacking away, like Jason (*Friday the 13th*) or Michael Myers (*Halloween*). At least initially, the killer is often an enigma whose reasons for action are mysterious to the audience, belying the notion that slasher films substitute gore for genuine suspense; part of the fun in watching these kinds of movies is discovering what that back story is.

One particular slasher, *Blood Hook* (made in 1986 but not released until 1987), has become legendary among fans of *MST3K* (MSTies) because of its connection to Jim Mallon and Kevin Murphy. With sufficient distance from the era of Tipper Gore–style media hysterics, slasher films like this little low-budget picture deserve a reevaluation.

Blood Hook and *Mystery Science Theater* director Jim Mallon with Tom Servo.

Blood Hook was producer/director Jim Mallon's first film. As MSTies know, he directed numerous episodes of *MST3K* and the feature film in 1996, voiced the Robot Gypsy, and remains the legal gatekeeper of the *MST3K* legacy. Mallon also co-authored the scenario for *Blood Hook*. Kevin Murphy (who was a writer, a director for *MST3K* and voiced the robot Tom Servo) was key grip, sang, and wrote some music for *Blood Hook*. This was Larry Edgerton's and John Galligan's only produced screenplay, and many of the rest of the cast and crew seem to have dropped out of the film industry after *Blood Hook*. The film was originally going to be called *Muskie Madness*, but when it was picked up for distribution by Michael Hertz and Lloyd Kaufman of Troma, it was changed to *Blood Hook,* as the Troma bosses felt no one would know what a muskie (a large carnivorous freshwater fish common in the northern Midwest and Canada) was (www.imdb.com). The film had a premier in Minneapolis, Minnesota — prime muskie territory — as Kevin Murphy (2010) remembers:

> Yeah, the *Blood Hook* premiere was goofy and as flashy as we could make it with essentially no money. KTMA-TV, where Jim and I worked, sponsored the thing along with a few of their advertisers, and the cast and crew showed up in limos and entered through a boat dock built for the occasion. We all wore a combination of formalwear and fishing stuff. There was a lot to drink.

Summary of *Blood Hook* (Warning: Spoilers)

Blood Hook begins with a young boy, Peter, and his grandfather at a lake in Wisconsin. We hear a Carpenter-style synth cue, courtesy of soundtrack composer Thomas A. Naunas. A forest surrounds the lake. Peter is talking to his grandfather while music is playing from an old reel-to-reel player. Granddad is explaining the music to his grandson, when all of sudden he starts convulsing with his hands over his face, falling and disappearing into the water.

Some 17 years later, Peter (played now by Mark Jacobs) comes back to the lakeside town with some friends, having inherited his grandfather's property. We meet Leroy Leudke (Don Winters) the owner of a local bait and tackle shop. A family on vacation with their two children has arrived in town for the muskie contest, and they meet Leudke in his shop while stocking up on fishing gear. Mr. Leudke gives them some free stuff, including their bait. He admonishes the family: "Fishing's ok, but remember the lake is not a playground, we all have to treat the water with respect." Even though he is kind, the bait shop owner gives off a creepy vibe that foreshadows future events (Mallon, 1986).

Peter and his friends find the community celebrating "Muskie Madness," the contest to catch the biggest fish. They meet the previous muskie champ, Denny (Dale Dunham), the contest hostess Bev (Sandy Meuwissen), and a man who used to work for Peter's granddad Wayne (Paul Drake) as he angrily tries to take a loud radio from one of the annoying kids. We are also introduced to another creepy fellow, Evelyn (Bill Lowrie), an army vet who appears to be a survivalist with a gun obsession and who yaps incoherently. Like typical cynical, hyper-mediated '80s teens, Peter and his friends are not amused by the communities' weirdos, and seem intent on carrying out low-level antagonization, rather than understanding the locals or the place where they live. Despite this, Peter is drawn to the lake, which sparks memories of his childhood trauma.

Next, the annoying family and their kids are at the local restaurant. The mother talks incessantly about the movie *On Golden Pond* and loons, the large local waterfowl. The mother leaves the restaurant after a disagreement with her husband and walks out onto the pier, where she tries to communicate with the birds. Of course, she is the first to get "hooked" and dragged into the water, never to be seen again.

Like many '80s slasher films, the young women in the movie are generically pretty, but they also exhibit unappealing personalities. Peter's girlfriend, Ann (Lisa Todd), tries to get him to open up about his past life. Peter's friend Finner (Christopher Whiting) catches a fish, and makes eyes with chipper Bev, who happens to come by.

One by one, the teens are caught by the "Blood Hook." Peter reports one of his friends missing after finding blood in the boat, but the sheriff is skeptical of Peter's complaints. Rodney gets killed. Kiersten also is taken while music is playing—a reoccurring trope. There are several false leads as to who the killer might be.

Wayne tells Peter about accidentally shooting his granddad and how after shooting him, Peter's granddad gave Wayne a job. The audience also learns that Leudke went to Korea in 1951. The annoying father and perky Bev get hooked. The annoying family's children talk to the police about the disappearance of their parents, telling the sheriff, "I think something's gone wrong around here, I think something's very fishy" (Mallon, 1986). As soon as he starts singing and playing music, Finner gets hooked, and his ear is severed in the process; Leudke had gone mad when he heard Finner's boom box. Leudke strings Finner on a line like a muskie, skins him, and grinds him into chum.

Peter pieces together a connection between the killings, the singing cicadas (a persistent sound in the film), and the music that precedes the murders. He muses that the "The Devil's Tri-Tone" makes someone go crazy. Luedke had a metal plate put into his head after an injury in the Korean War, and the vibrations from the cicada songs and the victims' music apparently activates his homicidal frequency. Peter convinces Wayne that Leudke is the killer.

With Wayne now in charge, they devise a plan to catch Leudke. Wayne attacks and almost kills Leudke at the contest, after he wins the muskie prize with a 50-pounder, but he is stopped by the police. The sheriff does not want to believe Wayne. Peter wants to beat Leroy at his own game by casting his own hook, and setting up a trap. When both get snared, Leroy manages to catch Peter, and takes him as his prisoner back at the bait shot where Ann is. Leudke is just about to stab them both when the police arrive, and Leudke escapes into the woods. With all their other friends dead, Peter, Kiersten, and Ann leave the town. The sheriff finally believes Wayne and asks for his help to track down the killer, but the last thing the audience sees is the lake and the sound of Leudke's blood-curdling screams.

Blood Hook: Critics' Views

When *Blood Hook* was released in the mid–1980s, it went very quickly from theaters to video. The eighties saw the rise of the direct-to-video phenomenon, when many films (especially slashers and other horror films) were released on video by the hundreds, bypassing the big screen. The prime decade of the slasher was also the golden age of VHS and the mom-and-pop video store. Given the low cost of production for these films, it was a lucrative business, but not one that assumed a long shelf life for its product.

However, rather than being relegated to the VHS graveyard, over the years *Blood Hook* has received its share of attention from fans and scholars. Steven West in his multivolume guide to the genre, *Slash Hits* (2008), writes that the film is "likeably eccentric with some enjoyably nutty characters ... [and] post–*Re-Animator* gore humor" (23). West praises the film for being the "only slasher movie ever made in which the hero fends off the killer by playing him loud muzak..." (22).

In *Slimetime* (2002), Steven Puchalski is a little more critical. He states that with *Blood Hook* Troma "barfs up another one!" and that the film is "a chunk of true drivel" (42), but then he goes on to say that, unlike most Troma products, *Blood Hook* has a "couple moments humorous enough to keep you from shoveling the video tape down the garbage disposal" (42). Puchalski then goes on to deride the film in detail by pointing out that the cast of *Blood Hook* make the "supporting cast of *Deliverance* look like Rhodes' scholars" (42). Ultimately, the critic concludes that "there's more fun in watching a bug zapper on a summer night" than in watching the film (42).

John Kenneth Muir, in his opus *Horror Films of the 1980s* (2007), continues along the same lines. Muir gives the film a one-and-a-half-star rating, but seethes hatred in his written comments. He argues that Jim Mallon "has a lot of nerve skewering other genre movies when he has a skeleton like the atrocious *Blood Hook* in his own closet. This is a dire, poorly conceived slasher" (560). Muir goes on to argue that the film is like "so many of the worst slasher films ... [and] ... a genuine bore ... [having a] ... lack of humor" (560). The critic does not see the film as having any redeeming value, nor does he see any humor in the execution of the film. Despite having an "absurd" premise and "over-the-top" murders clearly intended to be comical, it's "depicted in a gory, bloody way, which isn't particularly funny" (560). Although Muir is known as a horror film historian, critic, and expert (having written more than ten books on the genre), his comments on *Blood Hook* seem strangely at odds with a true understanding of the slasher subgenre.

One of the things that sets *Blood Hook* apart from other films is its creative use of fish hooks to kill victims. Even though the word blood is in the title, there is actually very little blood in the film. As Kevin Murphy confirmed in the interview included at the end of this chapter, *Muskie Madness* was the original title, and *Blood Hook* was chosen as a marketing strategy. One is struck, upon repeated viewings, just how funny and original Mallon's little slasher pic is. The slasher genre became so popular because those films are entertaining. It's fun for an audience to jump out of their seats and laugh nervously. Of course, people like to be scared, but critics write off the comical aspects of slasher films in favor of "serious"

Promotional poster for *Blood Hook* (1986).

horror, from *Les Vampires* to *Se7en*. Although there is much to be admired in those types of films, the audience for slashers tends to appreciate a bit of silliness to punctuate the macabre. The sense of humor at play mediates between the tension and its relief, something not offered in, say, *The Omen*. Films like *Blood Hook* take certain genre conventions and make them comedic, and characters like Robert Englund's Freddy Krueger emphasize the short distance between clown and killer.

Mallon's film works for what it is because it does not take itself seriously enough to be validly criticized against the canon of "great" horror films. Since logical gaps in the narrative are a stalwart of slasher films, one might ask whether such formal particulars are the faults of budgetary constrictions alone or also a kind of "cinema of attractions," a syncreticism of vaudeville pratfalls and Grand Guignol thrills. Of course, some slashers are cleverly and coherently structured mysteries, particularly the Italian *gialli* that predate the '80s American slasher craze by a good decade. However, films like *Blood Hook* throw those priorities out the window in favor of visceral satisfactions, even if they do possess some interesting concepts and points of audience identification.

However, not all printed criticism of *Blood Hook* is negative. Kent Byron Armstrong in his *Slasher Films* (2009) argues that one of the original plot points of the film is having an "elderly male murderer" (9). The murders committed by "utilizing a fishing line to hook … prey (and) simply reel(ing) them in" is clever in catching "people instead of fish" (8, 16). Armstrong goes onto to argue, "*Blood Hook* is a very enjoyable film with a nice amount of humor and an excellent choice weapon of choice from the killer" (45). Jim Harper, in *Legacy of Blood* (2004), takes a much more positive view than most reviewers:

> Unsurprisingly *Blood Hook* isn't a particularly serious film. There are a lot of good characters, including the killer, who is a battle scarred vet with a metal plate in the head, just like Chop Top from *Texas Chainsaw Massacre 2*. There is some gore, but even the unrated version is fairly tame. The theory behind the murders is pretty farcical, which is in keeping with the general tone. It's probably one of the best films Troma has released" [68].

Blood Hook: Internet Reviews

There are also a number of reviews on the internet which provide some further insight. A sampling of online reviews shows the same type of divided critical stance. The folks at *Horroraddiction.com* (2009) regard the film as a "A very low-budget, off-beat and funny slasher that's half-parody and a lot of fun" with "sound design as exceptional for a film this low budget." With (relatively) high praise, the reviewer goes onto to argue that *Blood Hook* is "not as funny as *Student Bodies*, but it's funnier than *Splatter University*, *Decampitated*, *Scream* or *Scary Movie*." The website *VideoVacuum* (*VV*) has a different view, more in line with the negative comments expressed by most of the print critics, calling the film "far worse than 95% of the films shown on *MST3K*" with "Mallon exhibit(ing) ZERO style behind the camera and all of the death scenes are thoroughly lame and interchangeable to boot" (2009). (Going further than Muir, who gave the film at least one star, *VV* gives the film half a star). *Cranked on Cinema* also echoes this opinion to "avoid this trash! Don't get hooked in" (2009).

Badmovies.org summed up the movie with this comment "Plot wise, we hit rock bottom early on and start rolling sideways, what is really great is seeing a friend watch this for the first time. All it needed was the silhouettes of a man and two robots in the bottom right corner, it is not as if the director couldn't make that happen" (2001).

Blood Hook: A Summation

Blood Hook is certainly in the same category as other horror comedies like *Cemetery Man*, *Dead Alive*, *Shaun of the Dead*, *Evil Dead*, and *From Dusk till Dawn*, but with nowhere near the polished look of those films. Part of the film's charm is its obvious low budget feel, coming from its friends-hanging-out-together-making-a-movie location shooting in Hayward, Wisconsin; viewers get a good sense of that lakeside-summer fishy, putrid air, especially in the scenes that take place in the bait shop. In addition, the cinematography from Marsha Kahm is excellent. *Cranked on Cinema*, which loathed the film, points out Kahm's work is "exquisite" (2009). *Blood Hook*, like many other slasher films, has annoying teenagers, creepy townsfolk, incoherent plot points, and false starts, but it is very clever in its use of the killer and method of executions: A Korean War vet who is mentally ill with urge to kill by hearing the cicadas and loud music featuring the "Devil's Tri-Tone." The film released on videotape and DVD by Troma features the tagline "From the creator of *Mystery Science Theater 3000*," probably to generate more interest in what might at first appear to be just another slasher pic. The DVD also features two other genre films, *Zombie Island Massacre* and *Blades*, as a Troma Triple B-Header. Troma head Lloyd Kaufman confusingly introduces all three films on the DVD at once. Despite the low budgets and amateur filmmaking style, *Blood Hook* remains a clever and fun film to watch. Like *MST3K*, some of the critics just don't "get" *Blood Hook* for whatever reason (too simple, strange, or quirky). Little did Jim Mallon or Kevin Murphy know that this "silly" little horror film would eventually help shape their future careers, which themselves changed the landscape of American popular culture, irrefutably changing the way we watch a movie, especially the cheesy ones.

Interviews: Thomas A. Naunas and Kevin Murphy

Both Kevin Murphy and Thomas A. Naunas were interviewed for this chapter. Originally, their comments were going to be incorporated into the article, but it became apparent that the unexpurgated versions of the transcripts were worthy reading themselves. Hopefully, these interviews shed some light on the people who made *Blood Hook* and the world from which it emerged.

THOMAS A. NAUNAS: INTERVIEW BY ROBERT G. WEINER

WEINER: Tom, please talk about your background a little and your relationship to Jim Mallon, Kevin Murphy and *MST3K*.

NAUNAS: I was in a Comm Arts 101 class with Jim Mallon. This was right before he became President of the WSA at the University of Wisconsin and did some of the notorious tricks with Leon Varijan. These included the Pink Flamingos of Bascom Hill and Lady Liberty in Lake Mendota.

I have been working at Wisconsin Public Television since 1976. I'm a sound designer and music composer, with the title Distinguished Television Artist. Jim Mallon and Kevin Murphy eventually worked there too. We went and did *Blood Hook* together. I was location sound, sound designer and music composer for that movie. Then Kevin and Jim headed up to Minneapolis to embark eventually onto *MST3K*. Although I was still in Madison, I did live sound for every live theater production they did in the Twin Cities, and I also did sound design and location recording for *MST3K: The Movie.*

WEINER: Tell me about your role as location sound, sound designer and music composer for Blood Hook. Please also talk about writing all the rock synth stuff for the movie.

NAUNAS: I first met Jim Mallon in a Communication Arts class at the University of Wisconsin-Madison. It was the television production course. We became fast friends, working together on a class assignment. The following year Jim became President of the Wisconsin Student Association. In the eighties Jim worked with me at Wisconsin Public Television as a sound recordist. When he started getting the crew together for *Muskie Madness*, he was picking people from WPT. He asked me if I was interested in doing the sound recording, design, and music. I thought it would be great fun working with Jim and many of the crew from WPT on a movie. I especially liked the fact that sound played a role in the script (devil's triad, cicadas). I was very proud that there was only one looped dialog piece in the whole movie. And that piece was recorded at the same location several times to give us the option of slipping it in sync (the shot was very wide so we couldn't get the boom mike in as close as we wanted). The rest of the dialog you hear in the movie was what was recorded at the time. Jeff Seitz was my boom operator and he would be hanging out on the ladder checking to see if we would be getting any shadows, and how close in we could get as Rob Reed was lighting the set. There were times while we'd be waiting for the lighting to get finalized and we'd play a game with the Nagra tape recorder. Taking the idea from the scene in *The Shining* where Murder is on the mirror and "redrum" is repeated over and over. We would record "muskie madness" on the tape recorder, flip the tape over and then play it backwards. We'd memorize "sandam icksum" then record it back onto the Nagra and play it backwards. We'd laugh and laugh how odd and weird each person's version would come out. We did it with other phrases, but "muskie madness" was the most memorable. There is a stairwell railing in Vilas Hall (where WPT is located) that if you hit it hard gives out a very loud low rumble which I used in the sound track: Particularly when the funicular is started to add additional tension. I got a recording of cicadas and manipulated them to give them a sense of the devil's triad, so that when the music hits its triad, the cicadas are doing the same.

I had my music studio in my motel room during the filming of the *Muskie Madness.* This gave me the opportunity to work out ideas based on what we had been filming previously. Peter Emch suggested that there should be a reggae tune in the movie. So I started composing "Muskie Reggae." Soon we were singing the chorus while setting up shots. We also thought Rodney should have a rap song, so I put together a track that Kevin Murphy wrote a rap to. My wife Victoria Harper penned the opening tune, "Fishin'" while she was up visiting one weekend watching us film one of the scenes. She actually penned the song while on the beltline in Madison on her commute home from work the day before she visited us on site. Then she sang the song for Jim on set. Jim loved it! "Things Aren't What They Seem" was the rock song by The Red Echoes. I pulled together some friends who I had played with in a rock band in the seventies. Charles Deming was kind enough to record us on his eight track (I only had four tracks back then). It was a lot of fun to pull this all together and make it work. The movie score was composed in my studio using a Sequential Circuits Max synth and a Yamaha DX7. It was recorded to four tracks and mastered to mono. I would give them to Brad Wray at WPT who was editing the sound tracks together on the Steenbeck. We'd see how things were working and I would make adjustments. Then Jim would come down from Minneapolis and see what he thought, and make more adjustments. When we showed up at DuArt Film in NYC to mix the soundtrack, Dominick Tavella, the sound mixer, put the reels up and started playing the tracks. One of his first comments was, "Oh, CSM" CSM we asked? "Yea, Cheap Synthesizer Music!" Which of course, is, what it was? He did seem to like it though.

WEINER: What was it like working with Jim Mallon (director) back then compared with your working with him on the *MST3K: The Movie?*

NAUNAS: Jim was always great fun working with. *Muskie Madness* had a lot of variables involved, which he always took in stride. *MST3K: The Movie* was in a much more controlled environment.

WEINER: Anything else you would like to add...?

NAUNAS: It was one of those memorable life experiences that I'm so happy to have been involved with. There were a lot of hardships but also a ton of fun. It also taught me how an artist's vision can be messed with by economic considerations. The film title should have never been changed. It was intended as a camp film, not a serious horror film. I think it would have done better with the original title.

KEVIN MURPHY: INTERVIEW BY ROBERT G. WEINER

WEINER: Did you ever want to riff *Blood Hook* yourself? Do you even think it is worthy of riffing?

MURPHY: Sure I thought about riffing *Blood Hook*, but I'd question the outcome. We'd be mitigated by the fact that so many friends worked together on the thing, and the outright cheekiness of it, sort of precluded it. *Manos* was simply a failure, whereas *Blood Hook* was a cheeky tribute to films like *Manos*.

Kevin Murphy (2010), key grip on *Blook Hook. Courtesy of Kevin Murphy.*

WEINER: Was working on the film fun? Are there any general memories of working on the film that you would care to share?

MURPHY: Working on the film took six of the most exhausting yet fun months I've spent professionally, ever. I was on the crew and had very little idea what I was doing. We were in the North Woods, all working sixteen hour days, crashing to sleep at night in a tiny wood-paneled motel. And when we'd cut loose, it was almost dangerous. Imagine summer camp for adults with liquor and marijuana. I formed friendships in those six weeks of shooting that I still treasure and maintain.

WEINER: How was Jim Mallon as a director at this time? Do you think Mallon and the screenwriters' original vision for the film come off?

MURPHY: Jim was a freshman director, of course, but he held it together and got through some terrifically challenging times. Getting a film done is hard enough, making it good is another thing entirely. There's a wonderful photo by Michael Kienitz of Jim in a boat with Marsh the DP and Joanne the First A.D., and they're in a misty rain, all looking in a different direction, Jim looks thoroughly spent. It's the image I bring home all the time. It was fun, but damn was it w-o-r-k.

WEINER: What do you think was Jim Mallon's inspiration?

MURPHY: Well, cheesy movies for one, but also the unique weirdness you experience growing up and spending your summers in the back woods of northern Wisconsin. I mean sometimes it makes *Deliverance* look tame.

WEINER: What kind of distribution did the film get?

MURPHY: I really have no idea. I know they changed the name, which I always hated. I loved *Muskie Madness.*

WEINER: The sets look pretty dirty and with all that fish, was it pretty smelly there? What were the filming conditions like?

MURPHY: Yeah, Leroy Luedke's bait shop set did get to be a bit rank at times. It was built out of a lot of found wood and there were those damned fish needed, some chilled, some frozen, but get those babies under the lights and damn.

But worse than that were the endless days of exterior shots, often boat-to-boat, often in the rain, sometimes at night. I remember stepping over a pile of lighting cables and feeling the soft thrum of current escaping.

WEINER: At first glance, the film seems a lot like the "slasher genre" of *Friday the 13th* ilk (annoying teenagers, 1980s bad hair and creepy townsfolk), yet the film is quite different in many ways. Beyond that, I could not decide if the film is funny or a serious horror movie. Any comments?

MURPHY: Please. It's about a crazed bait-shop owner. The serious scenes are melodramatic to absurd points. The lead character is what we'd call these days a douchebag. The victims are kept on a fish stringer under the dock. The final battle is done with fishing tackle. It's anything but serious.

WEINER: How would you rank *Blood Hook*'s place alongside all those 1980s slasher films?

MURPHY: Indeed *Blood Hook* was a rare bird. Again, *Muskie Madness* being the original title, there was no blood implied. I think this was more about having fun with the tropes of horror with a winking eye.

WEINER: Unstable veterans are not new in films, but to have a Korean War survivor (it is usually Vietnam) was quite original and combining musical vibration as a motive for killing? Any comments?

MURPHY: Well think of it this way—doesn't everybody have a song that drives them toward a murderous rage? This is just taken one level further.

WEINER: Kevin, please tell me about your role as key grip.

MURPHY: I was made Key Grip after the DP was fired for being, I believe, an incompetent jerk, so everybody moved up the ladder one rung. Essentially I was rigging lights, setting up the dolly, building camera platforms and risking my life stringing high-powered lights over water onto floating rafts: doing all this in the rain.

WEINER: What was it like working with Jim Mallon (director) back then?

MURPHY: Oh, Jim was a young man full of piss and vinegar. He was a lot of fun, tried not ever to take it too seriously, I think even though the weight of the enterprise pressed down on him, he found a way to have fun nearly every day.

WEINER: Kevin, you wrote some lyrics and even sang on one track, "Rodney's Theme." Did working on *Blood Hook* music help prepare for the musical adventures of *MST3K* and RiffTrax? Any comments about the music you would care to make.

MURPHY: Tommy Naunas was the real musical mastermind behind the thing, so it's best to ask him. He wrote the "Muskie Reggae" with some of his musical pals, and I hastily threw together a very white rap lyric about Rodney, one of the victims, and how he'd die, which nastily enough plays on the jukebox in a restaurant while Rodney's eating. What it taught me is that I will probably never ever write a serious song, and that's fine by me.

WEINER: Despite the overacting and really annoying teens, the movie today is still kinda enjoyable, it's fun.

MURPHY: Yeah, I think the story is delightfully ridiculous. And there are moments that still make me laugh out loud.

WEINER: On the Troma DVD it says "*Blood Hook* from the creator of *MST3K*." Would you care to comment on that since Joel Hodgson is usually viewed as the creator of the show? I know Troma is trying to milk it, but is that really an accurate statement?

MURPHY: Well, here: Joel certainly conceived *MST*, and brought his considerably Joelian sensibility to it, but many people, primarily Trace Beaulieu, Josh Weinstein and Jim Mallon brought the thing to life. Not to credit them in helping to create the show is just plain inaccurate.

WEINER: What is your view of Troma in general?

MURPHY: The term "unapologetic schlockmeisters" springs to mind.

Thanks to Shelley E. Barba for help finessing the interview questions. Thanks to Mr. Kevin Murphy and Mr. Thomas A. Naunas for answering questions about the film. You both are a CLASS act. Special thanks to John Cline for previewing the work and making excellent suggestions and for the title.— R.G.W.

REFERENCES

Armstrong, Kent Byron. *Slasher Films: An International Filmography 1960 Through 2001*. Jefferson, NC: McFarland & Company, Inc., Publishers, 2009.

Borntreger, Andrew. "*Blood Hook*." *www.badmovies.org*. January 21, 2001. Accessed 6/27/2010. http://www.badmovies.org/movies/bloodhook/.

Harper, Jim. *Legacy of Blood: A Comprehensive Guide to Slasher Movies*. Manchester, GB: Critical Vision, 2004.

Lisk, Jamie. "*Blood Hook*" *Crankedoncinema.com*. July 12, 2009. Accessed 6/27/2010. http://www.crankedoncinema.com/reviews/1986/blood-hook.

Lovell, Mitch. "*Blood Hook*." *Videovacuum.livejournal.com*. March 19, 2009. Accessed 6/26/2010. http://thevideovacuum.livejournal.com/687738.html.

Mallon, Jim (director), Larry Edgerton, John Galligan, et al. *Blood Hook* DVD released on *Troma Triple B-Header: Blades/Blood Hook/Zombie Island Massacre*. Troma, 2004 (originally released in 1987 by Prism on VHS).

Moncrieff, Andrew F. "*Blood Hook*" *thehorroraddictionblogspot.com*. October 22, 2009. Accessed 6/26/2010. http://thehorroraddiction.blogspot.com/2009/10/blood-hook-1986.html.

Muir, John Kenneth. *Horror Films of the 1980s*. Jefferson, NC: McFarland & Company, Inc., Publishers, 2007.

Murphy, Kevin. Email to author (6/26/2010).

Murphy, Kevin. Email to author (5/27/2010).

Murphy, Kevin. Interview via email with author (5/27/2010).

Naunas, Thomas A. Interview via email with author (6/7/2010).

Naunas, Thomas A. Interview via email with author (2/18/2010).

Puchalski, Steven. *Slimetime: A Guide to Sleazy Mindless Movies*. Manchester, GB: Critical Vision, 2002.

Rockoff, Adam. *Going to Pieces: The Rise and Fall of the Slasher Film 1878–1986*. Jefferson, NC: McFarland & Company, Inc., Publishers, 2002.

"Trivia for *Blood Hook*." *International Movie Database*. 2010 accessed 6/25/2010 http://www.imdb.com/title/tt0090750/trivia.

West, Steven. *Slash Hits Volume Three: Mullet Massacre*. Northants, England: Midnight Media, 2008.

Afterword

by Mary Jo Pehl

Late one afternoon in the early 2000s, I was sitting in a movie theater in New York, waiting for the feature to begin. It was a "twilight" show, and I'd dashed from my job down the street to make sure I didn't miss the trailers. In the mostly empty theater, I sat a few rows behind a couple. In front of them were a few other folks. The lights went down, the movie started (I forget what it was) and as it played, the people in front of me kept up a running commentary. Unable to bear it any longer, a woman they were behind turned around and hissed, "Shut up! This isn't *Mystery Science Theater*, ya know!"

At that point, *Mystery Science Theater 3000* had been off the air more than two years. During its run on a local television station, then subsequent cable networks, it had acquired a fervent cult following. It had also been nominated for two Emmy awards, it won a Peabody award, and it was named one of *Time* magazine's 100 Best TV Shows of All-Time. But it wasn't until that rather surreal moment in the movie theater that its impact began to dawn on me.

Before I joined the show as a writer and actor, I was only vaguely aware of its existence. I spent seven years with *Mystery Science Theater 3000* (the longest continuous employment I've ever had) and all I knew is that I got to have a job writing comedy for a television show in my own hometown of Minneapolis. I got to watch bad movies on a big screen television all day, ensconced on nicely upholstered couches with some of the funniest, smartest people in the world. *And* there was free pop in the company refrigerator (that's "soda" to you non–Midwesterners; "coke" to you Southerners)!

I'd always been a movie fan but all this was my introduction to the likes of Ed Wood, Bill Rebane and Roger Corman. And I loved it. There may have been movies that brought us to tears (speaking for myself; I have a very delicate constitution) or drove us to drink (so I'm told, one afternoon trying to write *Robot Monster*, before I joined the crew), but on the whole, we have great affection for these awful, wonderful movies. More often than not, there is a lot of heart, sincerity and earnestness on the part of the director and the cast and crew. Believe it or not, none of the filmmakers set out to make a bad movie: it is just very difficult to make a movie, good or bad! Sure, the monster suit has a zipper in it; sure, Griffith Park has to pass for the deepest, darkest Africa; and, sure, the getaway car is a Ford sedan in one shot and a Chevy pickup in the next, but for me, it was always a thing of beauty to see how filmmakers worked with what they had, such as it was.

We writers would spend days with each movie, writing the hundreds of jokes that ended up in the final script. At any given time, there were 4 to 10 writers, each with his or her own background, life experience and regional influences. Each episode reflects that. Virtually ignored by the "suits" on either Coast, whether Comedy Central or Sci-Fi, we wrote to make each other laugh, and invariably each joke, no matter how obscure, would strike a chord with someone somewhere. We'd get fan letters (yes, in the days of actual "letters") from people who would write, "I thought I was the only one... (fill in obscure hobby or knowledge). The movies provided a springboard to create something new, unwilling or unwitting collaborators though they may have been.

And now, some 20 years after *Mystery Science Theater 3000* launched on a small UHF station in the Twin Cities, it seems to have spawned a genre unto itself. Sui generis at the time, movie mocking groups in the style and spirit of *Mystery Science Theater 3000* have sprung up across the land. We of Cinematic Titanic, a live theatrical version of *MST3K*, meet people who started watching the show in the late 80s/early 90s as kids or young adults and have introduced their children to the boxed DVD sets or the VHS tapes they've saved. As my friend and colleague J. Elvis Weinstein so aptly puts it, "*MST3K* fans have really long attention spans."

And now, apparently, there's a book about the whole *Mystery Science Theater 3000* phenomenon. To be honest I still don't get it. I was just really lucky to experience it myself. Excuse me — I shall now go read this book to gain some insight.

Mary Jo Pehl is a former cast member and writer of *MST3K*. She now works with Cinematic Titanic, a live show based on the same concept of riffing movies.

About the Contributors

Shelley E. Barba is a metadata librarian at Texas Tech University. She spends her days trying to figure out how to describe others' works. She often gives presentations at library conferences on the many uses of metadata in libraries and research ventures. Her work has appeared in the *Texas Library Journal* and the forthcoming *Obama-Mania*. She lives in Lubbock.

Jason Begy is currently a research associate in the Singapore–MIT GAMBIT Game Lab. His research topics include the functions of metaphor in game design and game criticism, the audiences of and design methods for casual games, and game history.

Michele Brittany, a recent graduate of the University of Washington–Tacoma, explored the concept of cinematic sight in her master's thesis, "The Cinematic Eye: Modern Ways of Seeing Urban Life Through City Symphony Films of the 1920s."

David Ray Carter is a film critic for *Film Fanaddict* Magazine, *NotComing.com*, and *PopMatters. com*. His areas of study are horror, exploitation, and "fringe" cinemas and he lectures on these topics in the U.S. and the U.K. The first episode of *MST3K* he saw is still his favorite: #107, *Robot Monster*.

Megan Condis is a doctoral candidate at the University of Illinois at Urbana-Champaign. Her dissertation is about drawn women in comics, animation, and video games. She would like to remind everyone to please watch out for snakes.

Michael Dean is the managing editor of *The Comics Journal* and holds a doctorate in modern studies from the University of Wisconsin–Milwaukee.

Michael David Elam is a Ph.D. candidate at Saint Louis University, where he studies medieval English and Norse language and literature. His interests are in the philosophy of beauty, the rhetorical qualities and authoritative value of literary aesthetics, and how aesthetics influence and interact with readers.

Generoso Fierro is the outreach coordinator for the Singapore–MIT GAMBIT Game Lab. He is the longtime DJ of the program "Generoso's Bovine Ska and Rocksteady" on WMBR and has directed and produced two feature documentaries, *Lynn Taitt: Rocksteady* and *I Am the Ruler*.

Erin Giannini is a Ph.D. student at University of East Anglia. Her work focuses on product placement, the effect of new technology on broadcast television, and the shifts in the broadcast model in the past 10 years.

Zachary Grimm spends a majority of his time working on two novels-in-progress, while also finding other writing adventures. Whenever possible he spends his time outside, whether hiking, fishing, or just sitting by the lake and writing.

Jeremy Groskopf is a doctoral student in media studies at Georgia State University, where he specializes in the industrial history of silent era film, as well as children's cultural history. He has been an avid *MST3K* viewer since he saw his first episode, *First Spaceship on Venus*, in 1991.

Alana Hatley is a student at Northeastern State University, in Oklahoma, where she also teaches composition courses. Her studies focus on 20th and 21st century American fiction and theory, with particular emphasis on postmodernism. She serves as the Satire Area chair for the Southwest/Texas Popular and American Culture Association's annual conference, and helps edit the book review journal *Southwest Journal of Cultures* http://southwestjournalofcultures.blogspot.com/.

Kaleb Havens is an Indiana University undergraduate majoring in English literature, telecommunications, and communications and culture. His short film *The Bike Thief* won honorable mention at the IU Multivisions award showcase. He is involved in post production on *Tycoons*, a five episode web series, which will premier on popefriction.com. He is writing a novel titled *Sprites*, under the sponsorship of a Hutton Honors Creative Activity Grant.

Sebastian Heiduschke is an assistant professor in the School of Languages, Cultures and Societies at Oregon State University, where he teaches courses in German studies and film. His research predominantly looks at intersections of East Germany's DEFA cinema with other areas, disciplines, and cultures.

Matthew H. Hersch received his Ph.D. in the history and sociology of science from the University of Pennsylvania, where he was the 2009-2010 HSS-NASA Fellow in the History of Space Science. He has also held a Guggenheim Fellowship at the Smithsonian Institution's National Air and Space Museum.

Cheryl Hicks is a graduate of California State University–Chico, receiving her degree in communication design and art. Her main research interests are horror and cult films of the '60s, '70s, and '80s. She is writing a study of feminine images in Japanese violent pink cinema of the 1970s.

Amanda R. Keeler is a Ph.D. candidate at Indiana University in the Department of Communication and Culture. Her dissertation, "Sugar-Coat the Educational Pill: Using Film, Radio and Television for Education," explores the emergence of educational uses of media technologies.

Kris M. Markman is an assistant professor in the Department of Communication at the University of Memphis. She holds a Ph.D. in communication studies from the University of Texas at Austin.

Mark McDermott's first *MST3K* was a repeat of episode 204, *Catalina Caper*, in a TV lounge at Morningside College (Sioux City, Iowa) during the 1995 Great Plains Popular Culture Association meeting. He has written articles and given presentations on numerous pop culture–related subjects, and lives in Downers Grove, Illinois, with his wife and two children. He also homebrews and writes about Chicago's craft beer scene, and hopes to turn that experience into a book on modern beer culture.

Ora McWilliams is a Ph.D. student in American studies at the University of Kansas. He is former managing editor of *The American Studies Journal*. He hopes to finish building an interocitor in the near future.

Cynthia J. Miller is a cultural anthropologist specializing in popular culture and visual media. She is currently scholar-in-residence at Emerson College, in Boston, and is an associate editor of *Film & History: An Interdisciplinary Journal of Film and Television Studies*. Her writing and photography have appeared in a wide range of journals, encyclopedias, and edited volumes. She serves on the editorial advisory boards of the *Southwest Journal of Cultures* and the *Encyclopedia of Women and Popular Culture*, and is editing a work on mockumentaries and an encyclopedia of B westerns.

E. Mitchell is the award-winning author of *The Amazing, Incredible, Shrinking, Colossal, Bikini-Crazed* CREATURE FROM THE PUBLIC DOMAIN, and currently writes the *Film Hound* blog for the *Seattle Post-Intelligencer*.

Kevin Murphy is a founding member of *MST3K* and voiced the robot Tom Servo for nine seasons. He published his account of the moviegoing experience, *A Year at the Movies*, in 2002, in which he watched a movie a day for a year. He also co-authored *The Mystery Science Theater Colossal Episode Guide*. He reunited with Bill Corbett and Michael J. Nelson, releasing four *Film Crew* DVDs and numerous *RiffTrax* DVDs, and provides Hollywood commentaries at RiffTrax.com. He is working on his next book and lives with his wife, Jane, in Minnesota. His website is www.kevinwmurphy.com/.

John Overholt is the assistant curator of the Donald and Mary Hyde Collection of Dr. Samuel Johnson and Early Modern Books and Manuscripts at Houghton Library, Harvard University.

Robert Moses Peaslee is professor of electronic media and communications in the College of Mass Communications at Texas Tech University, Lubbock. He teaches courses on blockbuster cinema, screenwriting, and electronic media in popular culture. Dr. Peaslee is particularly interested in the way new media formats such as youTube change the landscape of culture. He is currently working on a project looking at the culture and management of film festivals.

Mary Jo Pehl is a former writer and actor for *Mystery Science Theater 3000*, and currently tours as writer/producer/performer with *Cinematic Titanic*, a live show based on the same concept of mocking old, bad movies. She's contributed to magazines, newspapers, blogs, podcasts and radio, including NPR. She is writing a book of essays and a comic book.

Danielle Reay received her M.A. in cinema studies from New York University and works as a film writer and library services assistant. Her research interests include Russian and German film.

Joshua Richardson is a film student at the University of Kansas. His primary scholastic interests are fan culture and "trash" cinema. His favorite episodes of *Mystery Science Theater 3000* are the *Fugitive Alien* films. He watches the place while the master is away.

Rick Sloane is a writer, producer and director. At age 21 he directed his first feature film, *Blood Theater,* using free film school equipment and a fake ten-page script. *Hobgoblins* was his third feature, made when he was 25. He followed it with *Vice Academy,* which aired on USA Network and earned five sequels. *MST3K* rediscovered *Hobgoblins* ten years later and it became one of their highest rated episodes. He embraced the *MST3K* riffing and credits them for improving his movie.

Miranda Tedholm is a Ph.D. student at Indiana University–Bloomington's Department of Communication and Culture. She holds an M.A. in cinema studies from New York University as well as what has been described as an eerily encyclopedic knowledge of *The Onion.*

Joseph S. Walker was born in Peoria, Illinois, and is a freelance writer and educator living in Bloomington. He received his doctorate in American literature from Purdue University and devotes much of his time to online education. He has previously published a number of essays on contemporary literature and culture.

Robert G. Weiner is an associate humanities librarian for Texas Tech University and librarian for film studies. He has written numerous books and articles on topics including music, film, libraries and sequential art. He is the author of *Marvel Graphic Novels and Related Publications: An Annotated Guide,* co-author of *The Grateful Dead and the Deadheads: An Annotated Bibliography,* and editor or co-editor of books on topics ranging from Captain America to James Bond. He has been published in *Journal of Popular Culture, Texas Library Journal, West Texas Historical Association Journal* and the *International Journal of Comic Art.* He lives in Lubbock with an assortment of prairie dogs that bring joy to his life and safety to theirs.

Index